Modern
Managerial Finance

J. R. Franks

and

J. E. Broyles

London Business School

A Wiley—Interscience Publication

JOHN WILEY & SONS
Chichester · New York · Brisbane · Toronto

Library of Congress catalog card number
79–83955

ISBN 0 471 99751 X (cloth)

ISBN 0 471 27563 8 (paper)

Typeset in Great Britain by Preface Ltd., Salisbury and
printed at Unwin Brothers Ltd., The Gresham Press, Old Woking.

PREFACE

This finance text is intended for both the student and the executive. On the one hand the book is conceptually advanced and up-to-date, and on the other it is readable and non-mathematical. The above statements would appear at first to be inconsistent. A book which can challenge the student is usually too theoretical and mathematical for the executive. We set out to write a book which would be one of the first of a new generation of finance texts comprehensively based upon the results of modern research. This was done with the conviction that modern concepts could be reduced to common-sense statements unencumbered by mathematics. We were also intent on emphasizing those concepts which we knew from our executive teaching and consulting experience would have practical application.

Few books attain such diverse objectives, not because such objectives are impossible, but because they are extremely time-consuming. Earlier drafts of chapters have been used for several years on all major post graduate and executive programmes at the London Business School and in approximately 70 in-company training courses by us and by colleagues. The end result reflects this cumulative experience.

This book is intended for postgraduate students, business executives, and second-course undergraduates. We list undergraduates last only because some undergraduate teachers in Britain prefer a more mathematical treatment of finance. We think that those teachers who require a text which is conceptually up-to-date and which emphasizes those methods which are relevant and useful in industry will find that our book is useful reading for their students. Our brief introduction to the use of linear programming in finance in Chapter 4, for example, provides motivation for the student to pursue more mathematical treatments. Teachers using our text can introduce their own mathematically based materials in parallel with topics in this book, with a greater assurance that students will have a well-grounded understanding of finance before being absorbed in mathematical exposition.

Our book covers all essential elements of managerial finance exclusive of financial accounting and management accounting. However, a knowledge of accounting is not required for the reader to be able to understand the book. Part I provides a brief but comprehensive introduction to the sources of the modern financial concepts and to the organization and purpose of financial management in companies. Part II introduces capital project appraisal and many of the financial concepts that will be used throughout the book. Part III, on profitability and risk, concentrates on the insights which are to be gained from a study of capital markets and their implications for investment decisions within the firm. In Part IV we build on concepts introduced earlier to discuss dividend policy and the valuation of the firm, the usefulness of the stock market in valuing quoted companies, and acquisitions and mergers. In Part V, we discuss financial planning, bank borrowing, and working capital management. Finally, in Part VI, we cover the important issues in evaluating alternative sources of financing. We have covered financing, financial planning, and working capital management near the end of the book so that we can build on the framework provided by earlier chapters and thereby include a more consistent treatment. Review questions and selected exercises are provided at the end of each chapter to assist students in clarifying essential issues.

The book includes many chapters which contain material not found in other texts. The more unusual chapters include Chapters 5, 6, 8, 9, 12, 15, 19, and 20. Chapter 5 includes probably the most comprehensive treatment of the problem of inflation for capital investment decisions within the U.K. tax environment. Chapter 6 tackles a set of problems not usually dealt with adequately in other finance texts: how actually to define a capital project and its net incremental cash flows. Chapter 8 addresses the problem of selecting discount rates for individual capital projects. Chapter 9 applies related concepts to the problem of setting target required rates of return for divisions within a group. Chapter 12 contains useful new evidence concerning the profitability of acquisitions and mergers. Chapter 15 analyses debtors and creditors within the context of the modern financial concepts developed earlier in the book. Chapter 19 clearly resolves some important issues concerning the weighted average cost of capital and the tax advantages of debt financing for capital projects. Finally, Chapter 20 presents new material on leasing analysis not found in other books. In general, this text relates to the U.K. tax environment in a way that alternative American textbooks do not attempt.

The book stresses the contrast between competitive advantage in product markets and the relative competitiveness of capital markets. We argue that businessmen can increase the value of their companies by obtaining funds at relatively fair prices in a competitive capital market in order to finance activities in less competitive product markets. We show that competitive advantage is the source of the Net Present Value rules used in finance.

As already implied, we owe thanks to a large number of people. Countless suggestions from members of the Masters Programme, London Executive Programme, Senior Executive Programme, Sloan Programme, and the Corporate Finance Programme at the London Business School were invaluable and essential. The book also benefited enormously from comments by participants on short courses both within and outside the School, including executives on programmes at Plessey, I.T.T., Shell International Petroleum Company, Citibank, Bankers Trust Company, and Bank of America.

Drafts of chapters have been widely used by our colleagues, whose criticism has been essential. Among these critics are Professor R. A. Brealey, Dr Paul Marsh, Elroy Dimson, Dr Stewart Hodges, Dr Alan Budd, Raymond Ashton, Colin New, Dr Ian Cooper at the London Business School. Peter Zinkin and Swee Ung made detailed comments on the entire final draft. Joint research and teaching with Dr S. Hodges was largely responsible for the ideas in Chapters 14 and 20. Tony Mason at the Polytechnic of the South Bank commented on several drafts and supplied some exercises. Publishers' referees, including F. M. Wilkes, A. Prindl (Morgan Guaranty Trust), Paul Korsvold, and other, anonymous referees, made extremely useful comments which helped to give the final shape to the book. Thanks for typing assistance are due mainly to Rita Tricot and Marilyn Hendleman.

Finally, we would like to give special thanks to our wives, Claudia Franks and Anthea Broyles, whose own interests in scholarly activities made them more than usually tolerant.

CONTENTS

Preface   v

PART I   INTRODUCTION

Introduction   3
  Early development of the subject   3
  Sources of the modern theory of finance   4
  The transfer of knowledge   5
  A brief synopsis of the modern theory and its application   5
  Conclusions   7
  References and bibliography   7
1   Financial Management: Organization and Purpose   8
  Organizing the finance function   8
  The Finance Director   8
  The Controller 10
  Functions of the Treasurer 10
  How the Treasurer raises finance 11
  Financial objectives 13
  Conclusions 15
  References and bibliography 16
  Review questions 16

PART II   APPRAISING INVESTMENT OPPORTUNITIES

2   Opportunity Costs and Discounted Cash Flow 19
  Capital market opportunity cost 19
  Profitability 20
  Compound factors 22
  Discounted Cash Flow 25
  Annuities 26
  Perpetuities 28
  Conclusions 28
  References and bibliography 29
  Review questions 29
  Exercises 29
3   Comparison of Capital Investment Appraisal Methods 31
  Investment in the U.K.: an example 31
  The Payback Period 36

Problems and advantages in using the Payback Period 36
The Accounting Rate of Return 37
The Internal Rate of Return 39
Conclusions 42
References and bibliography 42
Appendix 3.1. Refinements to Corporation Tax adjustments . . 43
Review questions 44
Exercises 45
4 Rates of Return: The Pitfalls 47
The rate-of-return maximization fallacy 47
Internal Rates of Return: further problems 50
The significance of Net Present Value 52
Alternative measures: the Profitability Index 53
Capital rationing 54
Mathematical programming 56
Conclusions 58
References and bibliography 59
Review questions 60
Exercises 60
5 Inflation and the Investment Decision 62
Risk, required rates of return, and inflation 62
Inflation and capital allowances 64
Inflation and investment in stock 67
Inflation and residual values 70
Income and wealth effects 71
Money terms or real terms 71
Inflation and the risk premium 72
Inflation and borrowing 73
Conclusions 75
References and bibliography 75
Review questions 76
Appendix 5.1. Tax effect of Stock Relief 77
Exercises 78
6 Cash Flow Analysis: Defining a Project and its Benefits . . . 79
The investment decision-making process 79
Defining the project 81
Defining project costs and benefits 82
Contingent projects 84
Cost reduction projects 84
Determining the economic life of the project 85
The optimal replacement period 86
Comparing projects 88
The abandonment decision 89
Conclusions 90

References and bibliography 90
Appendix 6.1. Equivalent annual cash flow of a replacement chain   91
Review   questions   92
Exercises   92

PART III   PROFITABILITY AND RISK

7   Shareholders' Risk and the Required Rates of Return 95
Returns to equity shareholders 95
Measure of risk   96
Portfolios   98
The market model and systematic risk   102
The trade-off between risk and return in the capital market . . 105
Conclusion 109
References and bibliography 110
Appendix 7.1. Utility theory and risk   110
Appendix 7.2. Computing the variance of a portfolio's returns . 112
Review   questions   113
Exercises   113
8   Capital Project Risk and the Discount Rate 115
Why required rates of return must be related to risk   115
Traditional   risk   classification   methods   117
Risk premiums   119
Estimating the risk of companies and divisions   120
Estimating non-diversifiable risk of a capital project   122
The project risk factor 123
The revenue sensitivity factor   123
The operational gearing factor   125
Risk   classification   126
Meaning of systematic risk   126
Incorporating the term structure of interest rates   127
Implementation   128
Summary and conclusions 129
References and bibliography 130
Appendix 8.1. Ungearing β 130
Appendix 8.2. Example: Project β values and required rates of
    return   131
Appendix 8.3. Operational   gearing   132
Review   questions   133
Exercises   133
9   Divisional Forecasts and Performance Measurement 135
Role of forecasting 135
Monitoring of divisional performance 136
Measuring cash flow or reported earnings 136

Measuring asset values 139
Accounting return on historic book value of assets 140
Accounting return on written-down replacement value of assets 141
True Return on Investment 142
Diagnosing performance variances 144
Conclusions 146
References and bibliography 146
Review questions 147
Exercises 147

PART IV   VALUATION AND MERGERS

10 Dividend Policy and Valuation of the Firm 151
Debt and equity: the total value of the firm 152
Valuation of equity 152
The cash flows of the firm 152
The Discounted Free Cash Flow Model 154
Cash flow versus accounting earnings in valuation 155
The Discounted Dividends Model 157
Growth and the Discounted Dividends Model 157
The price-to-earnings ratio 159
Growth to horizon models 159
Free cash flow to the horizon 160
An alternative view of growth opportunities 161
Dividend policy 162
Conclusions 165
References and bibliography 166
Appendix 10.1. Dividend policy and valuation 167
Review questions 168
Exercises 168
11 Efficiency of the Stock Market 170
Purchase and sale of securities 171
Primary and secondary securities markets 172
Conditions conducive to efficiency in the capital market 173
Weak-form tests of market efficiency 175
Semi-strong-form tests of market efficiency 177
Strong-form tests of market efficiency 179
Conclusions 181
References and bibliography 182
Review questions 183
12 Acquisitions and Mergers 184
Profitability of past mergers 185
Sources of merger benefits 186
Mergers and financial synergy 187

Valuation of a quoted acquisition 189
The financing of mergers 190
Traditional methods of acquisition valuation 191
Valuation of unquoted companies 194
Pre-merger purchase of the acquiree's shares 195
The City Panel on Takeovers and Mergers 195
The Monopolies Commission 197
Conclusions 197
References and bibliography 198
Review questions 199
Exercises 199

PART V   FINANCIAL PLANNING
13 Financial Planning and Forecasting 203
Importance of financial planning 203
The cash budget and the bank overdraft 204
The funds flow statement and long-term financing 208
Cash flow and break-even points 210
Problems of financial forecasting 212
The tree diagram 213
Dependent forecasts 214
Cash flow implications 215
Scenarios of the future 216
Scenario building versus sensitivity analysis 217
Planning for contingencies 218
Conclusions 219
References and bibliography 220
Review questions 220
14 Bank Lending and Borrowing Decision 221
Sources of fixed-interest finance 221
Factors a borrower should consider 223
General criteria for loan decisions 223
Role of tangible assets in the lending decision 225
Data required for lending 225
Control of outstanding loans 226
Traditional debt ratios 227
Financial ratios and prediction of failure 230
The determination of loan interest rates 233
Conclusions 236
References and bibliography 237
Review questions 237
15 Working Capital Management: Debtors 238
Trade credit and total assets 238
Credit terms 239

A lending or an investment decision 240
Trade credit as a lending decision 241
Trade credit as an investment decision 244
The control of trade credit 247
Conclusions 250
References and bibliography 250
Appendix 15.1. Monthly discount rates 250
Review questions 250
Exercises 251

16 Working Capital Management: Stock 253
Planning and monitoring stock levels 254
Cost of carrying stocks 256
Designing the stock control system 256
Elements of a stock control system 257
Operating the inventory control system 261
Responsibility for the investment in inventory 261
Summary and conclusions 262
References and bibliography 263
Appendix 16.1. Economic order quantities 263
Review questions 264
Exercises 265

PART VI   FINANCING

17 Long-term Financing 269
Types of Securities 269
Sources of finance for companies 276
Methods of raising new finance 279
Importance of the stock market 282
Conclusions 284
References and bibliography 284
Appendix 17.1. Black and Scholes' option valuation model . . 285
Review questions 286
Exercises 287

18 Cost of Debt and Capital Structure 288
The risk of debt finance—pre-tax 288
Net Operating Income approach 290
The Net Income approach 292
Traditional approach 293
Modigliani and Miller 294
The effect of taxes 296
Interest rates, taxes, and asset prices 299
Borrowing without tax benefits 300
Gearing and the company's required rate of return 301

Inflation and borrowing 302
Conclusion 302
References and bibliography 303
Appendix 18.1. Modigliani and Miller: arbitrage proof 303
Appendix 18.2. Present Value of tax savings 304
Review questions 304
Exercises 305
19 Debt Financing and Project Valuation 306
Tax benefits and the project appraisal decision 306
The Weighted Average Cost of Capital 307
Adjusted Present Value method 308
Comparison between the two methods 311
Adjusted Present Value and bank lending 313
Interest charges and project valuation 313
Leasing and the investment decision 314
Conclusions 314
References and bibliography 315
Appendix 19.1. Geared-up cost of equity 315
Review questions 316
Exercises 316
20 Leasing 318
Issues in leasing 318
Analysis of the leasing decision: importance of the discount rate 320
The Myers, Dill, and Bautista method 322
Differences in taxes 322
Lessee in a temporary non-tax-paying position 323
Residual values 326
Choice of lease payments' schedule 327
Basis of the Myers, Dill, and Bautista method 328
Leasing and the investment decision 328
Conclusions 330
References and bibliography 330
Appendix 20.1. The effect of lags in tax payments on after-tax
  discount rates 331
Appendix 20.2. Determination of the value of tax benefits *TI* . 332
Appendix 20.3. Borrowing Opportunity Rate method (Vancil) . 333
Review questions 337
Exercises 338

Appendix A. Future Value Tables 339

Appendix B. Present Value Tables 351

Appendix C. Annuity Tables 361

Index 370

PART I

INTRODUCTION

INTRODUCTION

Managerial Finance has become a modern professional discipline with a coherent philosophy and a growing body of statistical research in support of the conceptual framework. Finance faculties in leading academic institutions around the world are now actively engaged in making the framework accessible to executives as well as to postgraduates and undergraduates. What makes the modern concept of finance exciting is the simplicity and the authority with which issues of concern to management can be resolved today. While modern financial concepts have now been thoroughly elucidated and researched in the learned academic journals, adequate interpretation for the layman and the student has been notably incomplete in recent editions of existing textbooks. For this reason, the authors have found it useful for their own teaching purposes to write a series of interpretive papers which have been used as handouts on executive programmes, postgraduate programmes, and in-company training activities. We have incorporated these materials into the body of this book.

EARLY DEVELOPMENT OF THE SUBJECT

Originally, finance was considered primarily as a part of economics. Subsequently, during the 1920's, with the emerging new technologies and new industries, the need for financing industry brought the subject into its own with an emphasis on methods of external financing. In the late 1920's, interest in various securities, notably equities, became particularly intense and extends to some extent to the present day. However, in the depression of the 1930's, attention turned naturally towards the problems of sound capital structure, liquidity, and bankruptcy. Various abuses which came to light during the period led to greater financial disclosure and the emergence of financial analysis as a discipline in finance. During the 1940's and in the first half of the 1950's, one finds a developing awareness of cash flow and of the methods of cash flow planning and control, but on the whole the approach was from the point of view of the external analyst. It

3

was not until the middle of the 1950's that the methodology of capital budgeting came to the forefront, with a greater recognition of the responsibility of financial management for optimal allocation of financial resources and for the financial management of corporate assets.

How each financial decision affects the value of the firm became the major preoccupation in asset management down to the present day. Linear and integer programming models intended to aid managers to maximize the value of the firm subject to various constraints attracted considerable interest. The effects of capital structure and dividend policy on the value of the firm became interesting and contentious issues.

Another trend in the teaching of financial management may be traced to the over-riding economic problems of our time. As in the 1930's, attention has again turned to the problems of cash flow, capital structure, and solvency. Working capital management and cash budgeting have received fresh impetus. Financial planning and forecasting in the face of uncertain future events has been a concern of participants in executive programmes. One such uncertainty which has assumed great importance in the U.K. concerns inflation, and much effort within Finance and Accounting faculties has concerned inflation accounting and the impact of unanticipated changes in the rate of inflation on the profitability of capital investment.

SOURCES OF THE MODERN THEORY OF FINANCE

In the early 1960's, however, a sequence of new issues emerged which are the source of the great changes in the subject which we see today. These issues were originally debated outside the discipline of financial management in such publications as the *Journal of the Royal Statistical Society* and *Econometrica*, and concerned the nature of capital markets. In 1964, Paul Cootner collected together the various learned articles published at that time in his book, *The Random Character of Stock Market Prices*, which concerned the so-called 'random walk hypothesis'.

From these early publications and their 'descendents' emerged the concept of the 'efficient market'. An efficient market is a market in which transaction prices fully reflect all information known to investors. The results of scores of statistical studies have shown that major capital markets evidence many of the characteristics of efficient markets. Thus it has been verified that, in most circumstances likely to be encountered by managers (in the absence of special, insider information), the expected value of an actively traded firm at any particular time is its market value at that time. This conclusion had immediate implications for portfolio management and for the philosophy of takeovers and mergers, for example.

A second strand of thought which has been of immense importance began when the theory of portfolio selection was first published in the *Journal of Finance* by Harry Markowitz in 1952. This work later led to a theory of how assets were priced in a competitive market. This latter theory, now known as the 'Capital Asset Pricing Model', aroused a great deal of controversy because of certain simplifying assumptions. Nevertheless, proponents of the model have shown that it provides useful insights for managers making investment decisions and that it is an efficient method for dealing with the problem of risk.

THE TRANSFER OF KNOWLEDGE

Although these two related strands of thought—efficient capital markets and the Capital Asset Pricing Model—came to be treated as mainstays in a new, more scientific discipline of investment management, they received relatively little emphasis in the various textbooks on managerial finance. In 1973, Mark Rubinstein published an article which provided a synthesis of the theory of corporate finance with the theory of portfolio management and with the Capital Asset Pricing Model. The article was an early example of the new insights now being brought to bear on the problems and methods of managerial finance. A more coherent framework has emerged tying together what had been an *ad hoc* collection of analytical methods into a more uniform whole having significant implications for the financial policy of the firm.

The importance of this framework lay not only in its evident consistency and simplicity, but more importantly in the wealth of empirical evidence which has appeared in the literature. This evidence substantiates sufficient of the major propositions to justify their use in financial practice.

A BRIEF SYNOPSIS OF THE MODERN THEORY AND ITS APPLICATION

In this brief introduction, we must be content with trying to convey only a flavour of recent developments and refer the reader to subsequent chapters for a more detailed treatment. The modern theory of finance is based upon the objective of maximizing the market value of the firm. Although the worker participation movement represents another claim on the value of the firm apart from that of the shareholders, the objective of value maximization will remain in the foreseeable future.

The financial aspect of the management function may be viewed in terms of an arbitrage process between imperfectly competitive product markets and an efficient or more perfectly competitive capital market. The very evident competition between investors in the capital market helps to ensure that no monopoly profits can be made there. Thus firms can be relatively assured of obtaining finance at a fair price on the one hand for the purpose of exploiting temporary competitive advantages in an imperfect product market on the other. The net gains obtainable through this process provide the means by which managers can increase the value of the firm.

Value maximization requires an appreciation of the meaning of capital market opportunity costs. Should management wish to undertake activities on behalf of shareholders which are less profitable than investments available to shareholders in the capital market at equivalent risk, management runs the risk of reducing the market value of the firm. In such circumstances, investors are unlikely to find the company's securities attractive.

Knowledge now exists—based on scores of statistical studies in the USA, in Europe, and now increasingly in the U.K. with the development of the London Business School data base of U.K. share prices—concerning the way in which security prices behave. Equities are now believed to be priced in such a way that if, for example, the current rate of interest on 30-day Treasury Bills is 10 per cent, then there can be little demand for riskier securities unless they are priced so as to promise a return higher than 10 per cent. The greater the risk, the greater the premium required. An implication for financial managers who wish to maximize the value of the firm is that they must choose capital investments with expected rates of return commensurate with their risk if the firm's share price is not to be influenced unfavourably by such decisions. In practice, this means cut-off rates for capital projects which vary according to the projects' risk classes.

Application of different required rates of return for each level of risk requires a theory of risk measurement. Until recently, the subject of financial management has been concerned with the 'total risk' of a capital project. However, the portfolio theory of Markowitz (1952) and Sharpe (1964) emphasized the relevance of covariation between the returns of projects within the company's portfolio of assets and the returns of all risky assets in the economy. Diversification could eliminate much of the total risk, but the risk resulting from such covariation (i.e. the common effects of broad economic factors) remains.

Since the shareholder himself can diversify, it follows that when the capital markets value the firm, a premium is required primarily for that 'non-diversifiable' risk which the investor cannot readily diversify away for himself. Company diversification becomes virtually irrelevant to the risk premium when shareholders are already sufficiently diversified. This is not to say that company diversification *per se* is not an important consideration to managers and employees who naturally wish to ensure the survival of the firm.

The measurement of non-diversifiable risk for capital projects is currently a subject of great interest. It has been found that non-diversifiable risk of a project should depend, among other things, upon the ability of management to match changes in project operating expenses to changes in project revenues and upon the sensitivity of the revenues to changes in revenues of the economy. In practice, however, an exact measure of project risk is not required. Projects can be put into several risk classifications based upon non-diversifiable risk criteria. Required rates of return are then based on these risk classifications. In this way the modern theory of finance provides improved insights regarding marketable securities, takeovers and mergers, and capital investments.

The question of financing is an aspect of managerial finance most closely related to the new developments in portfolio management, which has important implications for all financing instruments from equity to debt of various maturities. Thus the influence of portfolio research was first felt in the advanced courses in financial management in which the problems of financing were mainly considered. Now, with more recent pedagogical developments, it is feasible to introduce the implications of the modern conceptual framework from the first day of an introductory course in managerial finance.

CONCLUSIONS

In conclusion, we have seen that the subject of financial management has been in a state of development and change since its inception. However, current changes in the teaching of the subject seem to us to be particularly swift; we have not found any textbooks which adequately treat the application of the modern theory of finance to the practice of financial management. Although several recent American texts have been written in an attempt to redress this problem, this text may be unique in elucidating the modern concepts within the context of the U.K. taxation system.

REFERENCES AND BIBLIOGRAPHY

Cootner, P. H. (ed.), *Random Character of Stock Market Prices*, M.I.T. Press, Cambridge, Mass., 1964.
Lintner, J., 'The Valuation of Risk Assets and the Selection of Risky Investments in Stock Portfolios and Capital Budgets', *Review of Economics and Statistics*, **47**, 13–37, Feb. 1965.
Markowitz, H., 'Portfolio Selection', *Journal of Finance*, **7**, 77–91, Mar. 1952.
Modigliani, F. and Pogue, G. A., 'An Introduction to Risk and Return: Concepts and Evidence', *Financial Analysts Journal*, **30** (May–Jun), 68–80, and **30** (Mar.–Apr.), 69–86, 1974.
Rubinstein, M., 'Mean Variance Synthesis of Corporate Financial Theory', *Journal of Finance*, **28**, 167–181, Mar. 1973.
Sharpe, W. F., 'Capital Asset Prices: A Theory of Market Equilibrium under Conditions of Risk', *Journal of Finance*, **19**, 425–442, Sep. 1964.

1

FINANCIAL MANAGEMENT: ORGANIZATION AND PURPOSE

This book is about the philosophy of financial management and the techniques of financial analysis which should be applied to specific investment and financing proposals. Before we launch into a discussion of principles and techniques, it will be useful and necessary to examine the functions of financial management in an organizational context and the links between the organization and the external financial markets. In this initial chapter, we will sketch a broad picture of the responsibilities of financial managers and how they relate to one another in the organization and with the outside world. The reader may then better appreciate the context within which the philosophies and analytical methods are described in this book.

ORGANIZING THE FINANCE FUNCTION

The senior financial officer of the firm is the Finance Director, who sits on the Board of Directors and is responsible for all activities of the financial department. He may delegate responsibility for many of these activities to one or more Controllers and a Treasurer. The controllers tend to concentrate on those activities requiring accountants, whereas the Treasurer, who is responsible for the provision of finance, specializes in maintaining active relationships with banks and other providers of funds in the capital market. Often some or all of the Treasurer's functions are exercised by the Finance Director himself or they may be delegated to a Controller.

Figure 1.1 shows the organization of the Finance Department of a U.K. company. We shall now consider the responsibilities of the Finance Director, Controller, and Treasurer in turn.

THE FINANCE DIRECTOR

A seat on the Board requires of the Finance Director an active involvement in broad strategic and policy-making activity involving

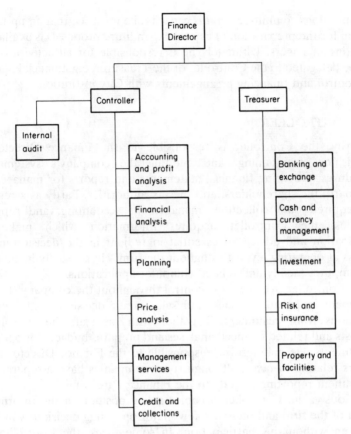

Figure 1.1. Organization of the finance function

financial considerations. Since most board members lack financial expertise, the Finance Director often occupies a strong position of influence.

The Board relies on the Finance Director for advice concerning dividend policy, major capital expenditures, acquisitions, and divestments. They also rely on him and his departmental staff for financial analysis and interpretations of economic developments, including the implications of Budget statements by the Chancellor of the Exchequer and financial aspects of current legislation.

These Board responsibilities require that the Finance Director participate in long-range planning and the preparation of long-term budgets linking capital expenditure allocations (on fixed assets) and financing requirements to strategic planning. Advising the Board on capital expenditure allocations may involve him in chairing a capital appropriations committee. In this capacity, he must see that an up-to-date manual for the preparation of capital expenditure proposals is available to operating managers. Ultimately he is responsible for all activities which may be delegated to the Controller or the Treasurer, e.g. financial planning and control and financing arrangements with City institutions.

THE CONTROLLER

Primarily, the Controller is responsible to the Finance Director for establishing, maintaining, and auditing the company's systems and procedures, preparing financial statements and reports for management, the Board, the shareholders, and the tax authorities. Partly as a result of the required data collection, management accounting, and reporting activities, the Controller acquires information which makes his participation and advice an essential ingredient in the decision-making process at operating levels throughout the firm. He is usually in charge of the computer facility and related computer applications.

The Controller oversees cost control throughout the company. He may participate in product pricing and sales credit decisions and supervise collections from customers. Together with his staff, he consolidates forecasts and related financial analyses and prepares budgets for operating departments. He may also be responsible to the Finance Director for all matters relating to taxes, although some companies have a separate Tax Department reporting directly to the Finance Director.

Obviously, the Controller occupies a key position in the information system of the firm and there are few major operating decisions which can be taken without his participation. In some firms, the Controller also exercises many of the functions attributed to the Treasurer (described below).

FUNCTIONS OF THE TREASURER

The main functions of the Treasurer concern managing the company's funds and keeping the company solvent by providing sufficient sources of finance to meet all likely contingencies. Thus the Treasurer and the departments under him are found to be involved in forecasting the financial needs and requirements of the firm and managing its cash flow. The Treasurer must maintain effective business and personal relationships with the firm's bankers because he is charged with procuring short-term and long-term requirements for funds based upon financial forecasts. He is also responsible for issuing and handling the firm's corporate securities, including shareholder registration, and managing the corporate debt.

The Treasurer is the custodian of company funds and oversees all cashier and payroll activities. He is thus in charge of corporate holdings in the securities of other firms, in Government securities and money market instruments. The Treasurer also arranges with Trustees for the management of employee pension funds. He manages the firm's foreign currency assets and liabilities, taking such measures as may be required to hedge against the possibility of losses due to changes in exchange rates.

The Treasurer's Department may also manage the company's real property portfolio and insurance. Treasury staff may advise on customer credit through contact with banks and credit agencies. Finally, the Treasurer's Department is often the centre for expertise in financial analysis in the firm and thus Treasury staff may be called upon to engage in special projects analysing proposed major capital expenditures, takeovers and mergers, and lease finance. Financial analysts in the Treasurer's Department are often called upon to participate in training programmes designed to make methods of financial analysis more widely known to operating managers.

In summary, the Treasurer is the company's main contact with the financial community. He plans long-term financing and manages short-term borrowing and foreign exchange exposure. His prime responsibility is to make certain that there are sufficient funds available to meet all likely needs of the company.

HOW THE TREASURER RAISES FINANCE

Most funds used by companies are generated internally from existing operations. Frequently, however, internal sources of funds are inadequate for short-term contingencies or to meet fully the needs for further expansion of activities. The largest source of external funding in the U.K. has been bank borrowing, followed in importance by the issue of ordinary share capital, *equity*. We shall now discuss briefly the differences between debt and equity financing, which will be enlarged upon in later chapters.

The owners' stake in the company is called the *equity* or *net worth*. The value of the equity depends upon the value of the firm minus any liabilities incurred by management in the course of business. The liabilities will normally include money owed for goods purchased, wages, and taxes. Another important liability is *debt*, money borrowed from banks or by issuing debt securities in the capital market.

The equity ownership of the company is divided among the shareholders according to the number of *ordinary shares* held. An ordinary share is a piece of paper or *security* signifying that the registered shareholder has a claim on the assets of the firm (net of liabilities). The shareholders' claim is proportional to the fraction of the total shares in issue registered in the name of that shareholder.

When a private company becomes a public company, ordinary shares or *equities* are sold to the public with the help of underwriters. An underwriter is usually a merchant bank who may buy the entire issue at a discount for resale to pension funds, insurance companies, or other financial institutions, or to the general public through stockbrokers.

Once there are shares already issued, the company may raise further equity capital through *rights issues*. A rights issue is an offer to existing shareholders to allow them to buy more shares in proportion to the number already held. These additional shares are offered at a sufficient discount on the current price to make the issue attractive. Shareholders who do not wish to take up the offer may sell the rights to other investors. Eventually, by a specified date, the rights will be exercised by an investor and the firm will obtain the required capital, unless of course, the market price for the company's ordinary shares falls below the offer price of the rights. In this case, if the rights issue has been underwritten by an institution, the rights will be taken up by the underwriter.

With sufficient equity capital, the firm will be in a position to borrow. Debt, however, is ordinarily a small proportion of the total financing employed by the firm. Borrowing is attractive since loans can usually be arranged more easily and with lower transactions costs than the issue of equity capital. Also, interest paid is tax deductible, which is not the case for dividends on ordinary shares. However, lenders wish to be relatively certain of getting their money back and so they limit the amount of borrowing which the firm can undertake.

Borrowing takes place mostly in three forms: bank overdrafts, term loans, and the issue of loan stock. In the U.K., companies may write cheques for sums greater than the cash they have in the bank. There are limits to such overdrafts of course, and these limits are agreed beforehand between financial management and the bank managers of the company's banks. Overdrafts are theoretically repayable on demand by the bank, but may continue for long periods at an interest rate which varies with short-term interest rates.

For long-term borrowing, the company may negotiate a term loan with a bank. A term loan is a loan repayable at the end of a fixed term of years. Term loans up to 10 years are currently obtainable at variable rates of interest.

Less frequently, companies sell debt securities in the capital market. These are issued and underwritten by a financial institution in a similar manner to equities. As with equities, flotation costs can be high. Such loan stock is repayable after a specified term of years, and a fixed rate of interest is payable each year. Interest payment and repayment of principal are mandatory. Default on these payments can result in the liquidation of the firm in order to enable the creditors to realize sums due to them.

Borrowing obviously entails some extra hazards when business conditions turn down and limit the firm's ability to meet obligations to creditors. U.K. companies therefore tend to use debt capital sparingly, preferring instead to make maximum use of internally generated funds and rights issues, supplemented by bank overdrafts

FINANCIAL OBJECTIVES

Having examined the organization of the financial function in detail, we should now consider how certain objectives of the firm dictate the need for financial management.

There are two principal ways in which the financial objectives of the firm have been viewed. The traditional view is that the objective of management is to maximize profits. Such an objective immediately raises questions as to how profits are to be measured and how they should be reported to the shareholders (owners). For this purpose, the accounting profession has, over a long period of time, developed conventions for measuring and reporting profits which have become the basis of much legislation, especially relating to taxation and dividend payment. As a result, financial reporting is an important aspect of the financial function in all public companies; and the qualified financial accountant is numbered prominently among the top ranks of financial management and staff. A need was also perceived to monitor and control costs in order to help ensure that profit objectives were being met by operating managers. Specialists in this field have formed themselves into various professional bodies of management accountants, who have also found a prominent role in business organizations, especially with regard to the development and operation of financial control systems.

In recent years, however, the advent of high rates of inflation has brought to the surface many long-standing reservations concerning the adequacy of existing accounting conventions to describe the value and performance of business enterprises. Attempts to introduce a generally acceptable system of 'inflation accounting' have underlined the importance of the concept of *Economic Value*.

Whereas historic accounting depreciates the historic costs of an asset by some arbitrary formula representing 'value used up in the business', Economic Value reflects the Present Worth of the asset in terms of the expectations of cash flow that the asset can generate in the future. One asks, in effect, how much should the owners be willing to pay to have such an asset as a part of the business from now on? The concept of Economic or Present Value gives rise to the second principal way of viewing the financial objective of the firm: that the object of management is to maximize Economic Value, i.e. to maximize the wealth of those who have an ownership stake in the firm.

Thus we find, in addition to the activities of financial reporting and financial control, a third stream of activity within the financial management function, that of financial analysis. The purpose of financial analysis is to determine whether investments to be undertaken by management on behalf of shareholders serve to maximize the wealth of shareholders; and to inform management of the financial implications of specific decisions. Financial analysis has now become an important if subsidiary part of the formal education of accountants.

Is there any inconsistency between accounting profit maximization and Economic Value maximization? In principle, it could be argued that there should be no difference in the long run. However, in practice, we find that these two views of the world lead to somewhat divergent behaviour. Profit maximization is usually practised in terms of accounting profits as conventionally defined. The resulting difference is often biased towards the short-term annual accounting profits and pays too little regard to longer-term benefits for which the shareholder and the stock market gladly pay.

The wealth maximization approach encourages the assessment of all future benefits that are expected to arise from an investment and provides a means of giving appropriate weights to future benefits depending upon when they are expected to occur. These weights are derived from rates of return prevailing in the capital markets, so that the analyst's assessment of the worth of an investment will correspond as closely as possible to the values set by the capital market. In this way, the analyst can estimate whether a particular undertaking is likely to increase the net wealth of the shareholder in terms of stock market values.

Virtually every undertaking by the firm is designed to generate future cash flow benefits. These benefits, as we have said, can add to the capital market valuation of the firm. But each such undertaking requires investment expenditures. The required cash derives ultimately from the owners' claim on assets. Consequently, unless the owners' (the stock market's) assessment of the Economic Value of the benefits exceeds the investment required for the undertaking, no *net* positive benefit will be generated. Such a project may be described as unprofitable in the sense that it will not result in any net increase in the market value of the firm.

We will devote considerable attention to methods of estimating the net economic value to shareholders from business activities. However, transcending all techniques are certain economic principles which underlie all profitable activities. We will emphasize in various ways throughout this book that, in a world of perfect competition, management could not expect business activities to do any better than to cover the costs of finance of each activity. Thus management should not expect to find profitable ventures in areas where they do not expect to enjoy some advantage over competitors. Such an advantage may derive from exclusive patents, technological advantage arising from consistently superior research and development, natural cost advantages, customer loyalty, advantages in distribution, location, or scale. Unless competitive advantage forms the basis for profitability assessment, no amount of skill in financial analysis will prove that an investment project can be expected to be profitable.

Thus, we shall find that financial analysts are likely to become less preoccupied with techniques and increasingly more involved with assessment of comparative competitive advantage in the decades ahead. Increasingly, we shall find the financial manager not only involved with the financial aspects of every facet of the business but also with economic assessment of worldwide industrial developments and the strategic positioning of the firm within this larger context.

So far we have discussed financial analysis and profit maximization in terms of the capital market. We do so because the firm, public or private, small or large, is always a participant in the capital markets, either directly or indirectly. A large firm may borrow or raise new equity either directly from the stock market or from institutions such as Clearing or Merchant Banks. Small firms usually raise money directly from Clearing Banks. However, banks raise their capital from shareholders and from the money market. In addition, the owner of the small company is able to invest surplus funds directly in the capital market via the quoted shares of other companies. He must also compete with larger companies that have access to the capital markets.

In summary, we are suggesting that the manager in the large company must be encouraged to understand that funds generated by the business have a cost that is related to the opportunity cost of the funds were they to be put into the hands of shareholders and lenders. A failure to appreciate the financial implications of decision making in these terms must impair the growth of the business. The owner of the small firm is only too well aware of the cost of finance because he is usually both the shareholder and borrower. However, some financial decisions require a little more than a mere appreciation. The decision to lease or buy, the pricing of contracts, and an understanding of how to charge for risk or how to hedge (purchase insurance) all require a framework of financial analysis that can incorporate the opportunity costs of finance.

CONCLUSIONS

Financial management is organized to assist operating managers to attain the financial objectives of the firm and to report financial results to the owners, creditors, and employees. For this purpose, the Controller's Department operates the financial reporting and control system and the Treasurer's Department raises and manages funds and maintains active relationships with institutions in the financial community which are potential sources of capital for the company. The Finance Director draws upon the information, analysis, and advice of both financial departments in advising the other members of the Board of Directors concerning financial planning and policy and major capital investments.

Most funds used by companies are generated internally. After allowing for repayment of the firm's debts, these internally generated funds belong to the owners or shareholders and are thus part of the firm's equity. The Treasurer can also arrange with underwriters for the sale of new ordinary shares. The funds raised in this manner further increase the shareholders' stake in the firm. The Treasurer can also borrow money from suppliers and banks or by selling corporate bonds. The funds raised from borrowing do not, however, increase the owners' equity. Borrowing increases the scale of the company's resources and activities without increasing the equity (other than certain tax effects). It also increases the owners risk. For this reason, most U.K. companies limit the borrowing which they undertake, preferring to employ internally generated funds and occasional issues of ordinary shares.

Because all surplus funds belong to the legal owners of the company, management should try to tailor the financial objectives of the company to suit the interests of shareholders. Some companies measure financial objectives in accounting rather than in economic terms. Increasingly, however, companies are recognizing that shareholders' interests are best served by policies which increase dividends and capital gains on equity capital. Modern financial analysis is directed towards measuring management decisions in terms of the way in which they affect shareholder wealth. There are, of course, other considerations affecting many decisions today. However, it falls to financial management to keep operating managers informed of the implications of their decisions on the value of the firm.

In the following chapters, we will enlarge upon many of these points. The reader will learn how to analyse the financial implications of decisions and how to relate management decisions to the value of the firm in the capital market.

REFERENCES AND BIBLIOGRAPHY

Ratzer, P., 'Organisation of the Treasury Function', transcript of talk given at the London Business School, 1976.

REVIEW QUESTIONS

1. What are the major responsibilities of the chief financial officers of the firm?

2. Describe the different methods of financing the firm and the characteristics of the financial instruments employed.

3. What are the two principal ways in which the financial objectives of the firm have been viewed? Describe advantages and disadvantages of each.

4. What are the conditions in the market place for the firm's products which are most likely to provide the potential for a net economic value to shareholders?

PART II

APPRAISING INVESTMENT OPPORTUNITIES

2

OPPORTUNITY COSTS AND DISCOUNTED CASH FLOW

Management is constantly faced with the choice between two alternatives: investment in business activities or investment in the capital market. The capital market includes the banking system, the money market, and the stock market. Funds not invested in the business may also be returned to the owners or shareholders in the form of dividends. The shareholders would then be faced with the choice of reinvestment or consumption, at their discretion. Ultimately, the choice to be made by management may be regarded in terms of a comparison between direct investment in economic activities or investment in capital market securities.

This comparison may be viewed in two interrelated ways. First, rationality demands that investment in economic activities available to management must be expected to be at least as profitable as investment in capital market securities of equivalent risk. Second, the opportunity that the capital market affords of reinvesting future cash flows generated by an investment activity demands that consideration be given to the timing of these cash flows. Since returns received from reinvestment of cash flows can contribute importantly to the relative profitability of an investment project, a consistent method of comparing projects with different cash flow patterns over time is required.

In this chapter, we discuss ways in which capital investment projects are compared to the capital market. In particular, we examine the relationship between Discounted Cash Flow and compounded returns from alternative investment in the capital market.

CAPITAL MARKET OPPORTUNITY COST

Let us see how returns available in the market relate to an investment in physical assets. To take a simplistic example, why would you prefer an investment promising a certain return of £1000 in one year's time over another promising the same certain return in 5 years' time, when both require the same initial investment of £500? Why should it be obvious that it would be better to receive the £1000 earlier than later?

Phrases such as 'the time value of money' indicate the correct preference but are too imprecise to support the fine distinctions that often have to be made. However, reinvestment considerations tell us that the £1000 received in year 1 can be reinvested in years, 2, 3, 4, and 5 and will be worth more than the £1000 in year 5 which is offered by the alternative investment. If the reinvestment rate can be estimated, then the expected worth of the investment at the end of 5 years can be computed.

Continuing with our example, we know which investment is preferable, but how do we decide whether to invest in both? The first investment returns £1000 in 1 year for an investment of only £500 and the investment is risk-free. 'That has to be profitable', you say, 'because a return of 100 per cent per annum is offered, and where else could we find such an attractive risk-free return'? In reaching such a conclusion, one relies on the capital market as an alternative investment opportunity. The expected return from the capital market represents an *Opportunity Cost*. If the best return which one can obtain in risk-free securities is, say, 10 per cent, then your £500 would be worth only £550 in one year. Against this opportunity, one can measure the returns from an investment proposition of similar risk.

The second investment proposal returned £1000 at the end of 5 years in exchange for the initial investment of £500. This investment, though less attractive than the first, might still provide useful employment for funds which otherwise would reside in the capital market. At the end of the first year, the £500 becomes £550 at the current market rate of 10 per cent and would be worth £55 more, i.e. £605, at the end of the second year if the interest received in the first year is reinvested. At the end of 5 years, the initial investment of £500 at 10 per cent will have compounded to the sum of £805 approximately. Thus, the second investment proposal, though less attractive than the first, is profitable in its own right since it returns £1000 at the end of 5 years.

PROFITABILITY

The Opportunity Cost concept provides the definition of profitability for capital investment by companies. Since, incrementally, companies can employ their funds in the capital market, that market provides the appropriate reference point against which to measure profitability. Put another way, a profitable investment project is one which provides a return sufficient to attract capital from the capital market. If the company finds that it cannot raise funds for a favoured project, the project is usually not sufficiently profitable: there are higher returns currently available elsewhere in the market at that level of risk.

Figure 2.1 illustrates the capital market investment opportunities available to management and shareholders as alternatives to investment in the assets of the firm. Risk is measured along the horizontal axis and

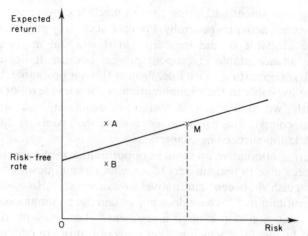

Figure 2.1. Alternative investment opportunities available to management and to the shareholders in the capital market

expected return is measured along the vertical axis. At zero risk, we find such securities as 30-day Treasury Bills providing a known and secure rate of interest, which we shall describe as the *risk-free rate*. At a higher risk, at point M, we find the average portfolio of risky securities, mostly ordinary shares in a variety of companies.

Because the returns on risky securites are very volatile, it is difficult to judge expected future returns on the basis of a limited sample of recent history. A better guide perhaps would be the average returns on ordinary shares over the past 50 years, which have exceeded the risk-free rate by roughly 7^1/$_2$ per cent (after adjustment for tax). As discussed in greater detail in a subsequent chapter, in a competitive market we would expect that risky securities would sell for less than risk-free securities promising equivalent dividends and that, therefore, their returns per unit of investment may be expected to be higher.

For these reasons, we plot the return on the average portfolio of risky securities above the risk-free rate of interest. Management and shareholders have the alternatives of investing at the risk-free rate or in risky securities promising higher returns—or they can invest in linear combinations of the two. Thus we have joined the two points by a straight line representing the variety of investment opportunities available in combinations of risk-free securities and risky securities. Furthermore, by borrowing and buying risky securities, management and shareholders can extend their opportunities along a similar line to the right, taking higher risks in the hope of obtaining still higher returns.

Thus Figure 2.1 represents the capital market opportunities at each level of risk, which offer a basis for comparison when decisions are being made concerning investment within the firm in machines, processes, buildings, and in economic activities generally. For each such risky project, there is an alternative available of the same risk in the capital market. Point A represents an acceptable investment project because it lies above the capital market opportunity cost line. Project B is not profitable since better returns are available in the capital market at the same level of risk.

Obviously, we shall require a method of estimating risks and returns before such comparisons can be made; and we shall consider this problem in more detail in succeeding chapters.

Considering alternative investment opportunities in the capital market, we have been able to find answers to some important questions: 'How can one distinguish between alternative investments?' 'How should one measure profitability?' 'Where does one obtain the minimum required rate of return criterion for capital investment?' Let us now discuss the techniques by means of which market rates of return are employed in the analysis of investment projects.

COMPOUND FACTORS

Table 2.1 represents the investment of a sum of £1000 in a risk-free deposit earning 10 per cent per annum. The second column shows the way in which 10 per cent is added to the sum accrued in each year. At the end of the first year, the £1000 has £100 added to it at 10 per cent, making the principal amount £1100. At the end of the second year, 10 per cent of the principal of £1100 is added, assuming reinvestment of interest received. Thus, interest of £110 accrues, bringing the total to £1210 at the end of the second year. The process continues, shall we say, for 5 years. At the end of 5 years, the wealth of the investor has increased by £610.50, resulting from the alternative of investing £1000 risk-free at 10 per cent in the Capital Market. The third column illustrates the computation of compound factors and the fourth shows the compound factors at the reinvestment rate of 10 per cent.

The computation of compound factors involves raising the sum of 1 plus the reinvestment rate to various powers. Thus if R is the reinvestment rate expressed as a fraction (e.g. 10 per cent expressed as 0.10), the compound factor F is

$$F = (1 + R)^t$$

where t is the number of periods for which interest is received to date. Thus at the end of the third year, the compound factor for our example in Table 2.1 is

$$F = (1 + R)^3$$
$$= (1.10)^3$$
$$= 1.331.$$

Table 2.1. Illustration of terminal wealth resulting from the investment of £1000 invested at 10 per cent for 5 years

End of year	Capital and interest		Compound formula	$S \times$ Compound factor
0		1000	S^*	S
1	+10 per cent	100		
		1100	$S(1 + 0.1)$	$S(1.1)$
2	+10 per cent	110		
		1210	$S(1 + 0.1)^2$	$S(1.21)$
3	+10 per cent	121		
		1331	$S(1 + 0.1)^3$	$S(1.331)$
4	+10 per cent	133.1		
		1464.1	$S(1 + 0.1)^4$	$S(1.464)$
5	+10 per cent	146.4		
		1610.5	$S(1 + 0.1)^5$	$S(1.6105)$

$^*S$ = sum originally invested.

If we multiply the compound factor F by the initial sum invested, we obtain the sum that will accrue at the end of the third year:

$$1000 \times F = 1000 \times 1.331$$
$$= 1331,$$

as indicated in Table 2.1. Compound factors for each year for a variety of reinvestment rates are given in Future Values in tables in Appendix A (see pp. 339–350).

Table 2.1 represents the capital market investment opportunity for the sum of £1000 to be invested for 5 years when the going rate is 10 per cent. Let us compare a risk-free investment project to this capital market opportunity. Table 2.2 represents a project requiring an initial investment

Table 2.2. An example of a capital investment project

End of year	Cash flows (£)
0	−1000
1	+ 300
2	+ 300
3	+ 300
4	+ 300
5	+ 300

Table 2.3. Illustration of the computation of Net Terminal Value for a capital project

End of year	Cash flows (£)	Compound factor	Compounded cash flows (£)	(£)
0	−1000	$(1.10)^5$		−1610.51
1	300	$(1.10)^4$	439.23	
2	300	$(1.10)^3$	399.30	
3	300	$(1.10)^2$	363.00	
4	300	$(1.10)^1$	330.00	
5	300	$(1.10)^0$	300.00	
		Total Terminal Value	1831.53	1831.53
		Net Terminal Value		221.02

of £1000 and generating returns of £300 per year for 5 years. Is the project profitable? The cash flows of £300 per year add up to £1500, which is £500 more than the initial investment of £1000. This return is less than the £611 expected from the capital market in the same period in Table 2.1. However, we must not forget that cash flows generated by the project can be reinvested. Table 2.3 illustrates this process. The £300 received at the end of year 1 is reinvested in the capital market at 10 per cent for 4 years to the end of the project. The £300 received at the end of year 2 is reinvested for only 3 years and so on. There is no opportunity remaining for reinvestment of the £300 received at the end of year 5 at the end of the project.

Thus a 4-year compound factor is applied to the first £300, a 3-year compound factor is applied to the second £300 and so on to obtain the total funds received from the project—including returns from reinvestment by the end of the project's life. In a similar way, a 5-year compound factor is applied to the initial investment to obtain the compounded wealth obtainable from alternative investment in the capital market.

Consequently, in Table 2.3 we see that the total wealth of £1831.53 generated by the project exceeds by £221.02 the wealth generated by the alternative investment given a market rate of return of 10 per cent. Thus the Net Terminal Wealth generated by the project is positive, and the project is profitable in relation to the standard set by the capital market. If the Net Terminal Value had been negative, the project would be deemed unprofitable in the sense that the alternative investment in the Capital Market at the same level of risk is more profitable.

We now have a Net Terminal Value Rule for investment which is easily understood since it derives directly from alternative investment and reinvestment opportunities available in the capital market. We will now consider the Net Present Value Rule, which derives from the same considerations.

DISCOUNTED CASH FLOW

Reinvestment opportunities are employed in an equivalent but less obvious form in Discounted Cash Flow analysis. Discounted Cash Flow methods usually take one of two forms, either to compute a *Net Present Value* (NPV) for an investment proposal or to compute an *Internal Rate of Return*. Both methods employ a *discount rate*, defined below. Many who use these methods do not know how to relate the discount rate to alternative opportunities in the capital market. This confusion has frequently led to investment in unprofitable projects and in the rejection of profitable ones.

The Net Terminal Value of the project in Table 2.3 was £221.02. We might pose the question, 'How much money invested today would generate the same Net Terminal Value at the end of the 5-year life of the project'? The sum invested today which could be made equal to the Net Terminal Value of the project through reinvestment is called the 'Net Present Value'. When the project has a positive Net Terminal Value and is therefore profitable, it will also have a positive Net Present Value. The Net Present Value has the advantage of measuring profitability in terms of today's money.

Let us examine an example familiar to the reader. An individual invests £100 at 10 per cent for 2 years, and receives the total sum of £121 at the end of the second year. Note that we have merely compounded the original sum invested by the factor $(1 + 0.1)^2$, which is of course equal to £121. Now, if we want to know the present (today's) value of £121 to be received at the end of 2 years, we reverse the above process by dividing the terminal sum by 1.21, bringing us back to £100.

The more usual way to compute present value is to multiply the future value (£121) by the discount factor (1/1.21). The discount factor for year 2, discounting at 10 per cent, is

$$\frac{1}{(1 + 0.1)^2} = \frac{1}{1.21} = 0.826\ 45.$$

One can understand that this discount factor is nothing else but the sum invested now at 10 per cent compound which would be worth £1 in 2 years' time. We could have obtained this discount factor by merely turning to the Present Value tables in Appendix B (see pp. 351–359) and looking up the discount factor for year 2 at a discount rate of 10 per cent.

Table 2.4 illustrates the use of discount or Present Value factors applied to the cash flows of the project which was discussed earlier. In the second

Table 2.4. Illustration of the computation of Net Present Value for a capital project

End of year	Net cash flows (£)	Discount factor at 10 per cent	Present Values (£)	(£)
0	−1000	1.000 00		−1000.00
1	300	0.909 09	272.73	
2	300	0.826 44	247.93	
3	300	0.751 31	225.39	
4	300	0.683 01	204.90	
5	300	0.620 92	186.28	
		Total Present Value	1137.23	1137.23
		Net Present Value		137.23

column are listed the net cash flows for the project. In column 3 are listed the discount factors taken directly from the tables in Appendix B. The Present Value of each cash flow is derived in the fourth column of Table 2.4. This Present Value is obtained by multiplying the net cash flow by the corresponding Present Value factor for each period. Some of the net cash flows for a project will be negative and thus their Present Values will also be negative. Adding up the Present Values of all the positive and negative net cash flows yields the Net Present Value at the bottom of the final column in Table 2.4. The reader should verify that discounting the Net Terminal Value of £221.02 in Table 2.3 at 10 per cent yields the same Net Present Value of £137.23 as was obtained in Table 2.4 by discounting each cash flow separately.

The Net Present Value of the project is positive and therefore the project is profitable. Why is it profitable? To answer this question one must always recall the underlying basis of Discounted Cash Flow methods. The project is profitable because a positive Net Present Value indicates that the project can generate more wealth in imperfect product markets than an equal sum of money invested in the capital market at the same risk. However, the NPV for the project will not measure profitability if the discount rate does not equal the expected rate of return in the capital market for investments in the same risk class. The choice of discount rate and the measurement of risk is the subject of Chapter 8.

ANNUITIES

Frequently, one finds that the cash flows are identical in every period, and in this case annuity tables offer a short-cut means of discounting these equal cash flows to present value. An *annuity* is defined as an equal sum to be received in each of *n* successive periods.

The way in which this short cut operates may be seen easily in the following example, in which we must find the Present Value at 10 per cent of an annuity of £100 to be received for 5 years. Annuity factors for a variety of required rates of return and numbers of periods are given in Appendix C (see pp. 361–369). In order to compute the Present Value of an annuity, one merely multiplies the cash flow to be received (equally in each period) by the appropriate annuity factor defined by the required rate of return and the number of periods.

For example, the project in Table 2.4 was actually an annuity. The Total Present Value could have been found in one step. In Appendix 3 we find the five-year Annuity Factor at 10 per cent is equal to 3.7908 which, when multiplied by 300, yields 300 × 3.7908 = 1137.24.

Often, cash flows may change in such a way that they can be treated as a combination of annuities. Table 2.5 is an illustration of such cash flows. An annuity of £100 is to be received for 3 years. Subsequently, an annuity of £200 is to be received for the following 2 years. What is the Present Value of these two annuities?

The annuities in Table 2.5 can be viewed in several ways. One way is to note that annuity factors are cumulative Present Value factors. The reader can verify that the annuity factors in Appendix C are cumulative sums of the Present Value factors given in Appendix B. Thus the annuity factor for the £200 to be received at the end of years 4 and 5 can be obtained by subtracting the annuity factor for three periods from the annuity factor for five periods. The £100 annuity for the first three periods can be calculated in the usual way with the three-period annuity factor.

Another way is to treat the £200 annuity for years 4 and 5 in two stages. First, one can discount the £200 annuity to its Present Value as at the end

Table 2.5. Illustration of cash flows which can be treated as combinations of annuities in Present Value calculations

End of year	Net cash flows (£)	Annuity factor at 10 per cent	Present Values (£)
0	0		
1	100		
2	100		
3	100	2.486 85	248.68
4	200		
5	200	1.303 94*	260.79
			509.47

*Five-year annuity (3.790 79) minus three-year annuity (2.486 85) equals 1.303 94.

of year 3. Second, this Present Value as at the end of year 3 may then be discounted to Present Value as at the end of year 0. Thus,

$$200 \left(\frac{1}{(1.1)^1} + \frac{1}{(1.1)^2} \right) \left(\frac{1}{(1.1)^3} \right) = 200 \ (1.735 \ 54)(0.751 \ 315)$$

$$= 200 \times 1.303 \ 94.$$

The figures in the brackets are available directly from Appendix C and Appendix B, respectively.

Since project cash flows are often expressed partially as annuities, the annuity tables are found to be very useful in practice.

PERPETUITIES

Let us consider the special case of an annuity with an infinite life. An equal sum of money to be paid in each period forever is called a *perpetuity*. Examples of perpetuities are Government securities called Consols which pay a fixed payment of interest every year but which are never repaid.

Perpetuities are easy to value. To see why this is so, consider the answer to the following question. For an interest rate of 10 per cent, how much income would I receive every year from an investment of £1000? The answer is obviously £100:

£100 = 0.10 × £1000.

Now suppose we turn the question round the other way. What is the value today of £100 to be received every year in perpetuity if the relevant interest rate is 10 per cent? The answer is, of course, £1000:

£1000 = £100/0.10.

In general, the Present Value of a perpetuity is given by the sum which is to be received (for one period) divided by the interest rate. Only one simple calculation is required, making the use of tables unnecessary for perpetuities.

CONCLUSIONS

We have shown how Net Present Value relates to the expected Net Terminal Wealth to be generated by a capital investment and we have illustrated the way in which compound tables, Present Value tables and annuity tables can be used to facilitate the required computations for these investment criteria. A project with a positive Net Present Value is profitable because the return is greater than that which could be obtained from equivalent investment in the capital market.

REFERENCES AND BIBLIOGRAPHY

Baumol, W. J., *Business Behaviour, Value and Growth*, The Macmillan Company, New York, 1959.

Bierman, H., Jr and Schmidt, S., 'Capital Budgeting and the Problem of Reinvesting Cash Proceeds', *Journal of Business*, **30**, 276–279, Oct. 1957.

Capital Investment Decisions, Harvard University Press, Cambridge, Mass., 1964. (15 articles reprinted from *Harvard Business Review*, 1954 to 1964.)

Carsberg, B., *Analysis for Investment Decisions*, Haymarket Press, London, 1974.

Dean, J., 'Measuring the Productivity of Capital', *Harvard Business Review*, **32**, 120–130, Jan.–Feb. 1954.

Fama, E. F. and Miller, H., *The Theory of Finance*, Holt, Reinhart, and Winston, New York, 1972, Chaps. 1 and 2.

Fisher, I., *The Theory of Investment*, Augustus M. Kelley, Publishers, New York, 1965.

Hirshleifer, J., *Investment, Interest and Capital*, Prentice Hall, Englewood Cliffs, N.J., 1969.

Jean, W. H., 'Terminal Value or Present Value in Capital Budgeting Programmes', *Journal of Financial and Quantitative Analysis*, **6**, 649–652, Jan. 1971.

Kuh, E., 'Capital Theory and Capital Budgeting', *Metroeconomica*, **12**, 64–80, Aug.–Dec. 1960.

Osborn, R. *The Mathematics of Investment*, Harper and Row, New York, 1957.

Renshaw, E. F. 'A Note on the Arithmetic of Capital Budgeting Decisions', *Journal of Business*, **30**, 193–201, Jul. 1957.

Samuelson, P. A., 'Some Aspects of the Pure Theory of Capital', *Quarterly Journal of Economics*, **51**, 469–496, 1937.

Solomon, E., 'The Arithmetic of Capital Budgeting Decisions', *Journal of Business*, **29**, 124–129, Apr. 1956.

Wright, J. F., 'The Marginal Efficiency of Capital', *Economic Journal*, **69**, 813–816, Dec. 1959.

REVIEW QUESTIONS

1. How can one obtain the cost of capital for an individual project?

2. What is the rationale for the Net Terminal Value Rule?

3. What is the rationale for the Net Present Value Rule?

4. How can Present Value tables and annuity tables be obtained from Future Value tables?

5. What is the Net Present Value of a security traded in a competitive capital market?

EXERCISES

1. What would be the Present Value of a sum of £100 to be received every year forever when the interest rate is 12 per cent on Consols (Government securities which pay interest but are never redeemed)?

2. A Government bond pays £9.25 every year for 4 years. At the end of the fifth year it repays its principal value of £100 in addition to making the final coupon payment of £9.25. What would be the current price of the bond when interest rates on 5-year bonds are 11 per cent?

3. A mortgage for £10 000 is to be repayed in five equal annual instalments, including interest payments on the declining balance at 8 per cent. Calculate the amount of the annual instalment and then split each instalment into an interest payment and a repayment of principal.

4. Company XYZ is considering the purchase of a machine which would result in the following net incremental cash inflows:

End of year	1	2	3	4	5
Net incremental cash flows	£5000	£4000	£3000	£2000	£1000

The appropriate required rate of return for a project of this type is estimated to be 15 per cent. What is the maximum amount the company could pay for the machine and still be financially no worse off than if it did not buy the machine?

5. A company is contemplating a project which involves an initial expenditure of £600 and thereafter yields an annuity of £100 per annum. The riskiness of the project implies a required rate of return of 14 per cent. Use the appropriate table to determine what the life of the project would have to be in order to make the project profitable.

6. A firm has two investment opportunities open to it, only one of which the firm can accept. The cash outlays required by the two projects and their resulting net incremental cash returns are shown below:

End of year	0	1	2	3	4	5
Project A	−£1000	£200	£400	£300	£500	£700
Project B	−£1000	£250	£250	£250	£700	£700

Assuming that the riskiness of these projects implies a required rate of return of 15 per cent, show a method by which Present Value tables and annuity tables can be used in calculating the Net Present Values of the two projects. Are either of the projects financially acceptable or should management reject both?

3

COMPARISON OF CAPITAL INVESTMENT APPRAISAL METHODS

What are the major methods of capital project appraisal currently being used by companies? What are the strengths and weaknesses of these methods? How do corporation taxes and investment incentives affect the capital investment decision? In a survey of 103 large British companies carried out in 1973, Carsberg and Hope (1976) found that while 26 per cent of the firms gave qualitative considerations primary importance in investment decisions, 76 per cent regarded numerical calculations normally to be of fundamental importance. The numerical methods used in descending order of importance were the Internal Rate of Return, Payback Period. Accounting Rate of Return, and Net Present Value. In this chapter we will evaluate a project using all four methods.

INVESTMENT IN THE U.K.: AN EXAMPLE

We will take as our example a proposed investment in plant and machinery in a regional development area of the United Kingdom. The project involves an investment in plant and machinery totalling £900 000 and £100 000 Working Capital (required increases in Working Capital should always be included even though they do not represent investment in Fixed Capital). Table 3.1 summarizes the expected cash flows before tax.

The project has a 5-year life and over that period a total of only £900 000 incremental cash flow is generated from operations compared with the total initial investment of £1 million. As a compensating factor, however, management believes that the machinery will realize £200 000 at the end of year 5 and that the investment in Working Capital will be realized through the sale of stock and the collection of accounts receivable as the project is 'wound down' at the end of its life. Thus the project generates £200 000 over 5 years net of its initial investment.

Would *you* invest in this project? Let us remember that we have not yet considered Corporation Tax and Regional Development Grants and their impact on cash flows. How would you anticipate the result: will the project be more profitable before or after Corporation Tax and grants?

Table 3.1. Pre-tax net incremental cash flows for an investment in plant and machinery

| | End of year | | | | | | |
| | 0 | 1 | 2 | 3 | 4 | 5 | 6 |
				(£'000)			
Plant	−300						
Machinery	−600					+200	
Working capital	−100					+100	
Net revenue		+100	+200	+300	+200	+100	
	−1000	+100	+200	+300	+200	+400	0

In Table 3.2 we have filled in the missing sums, which will require some explanation. First, there is the question of the Regional Development Grant for capital investment. The United Kingdom has been divided up for this purpose into four classes of development area: Special Development Area, Development Area, Intermediate Area, and Northern Ireland. Cash grants are available for new machinery, plant, mining and other works, and buildings. Grants range from nil to as high as 40 per cent in Northern Ireland and are now free of all Corporation Tax. Available U.K. grants are summarized in Table 3.3. Similar incentives are available elsewhere in the European Economic Community.

Table 3.2. Post-tax net incremental cash flows for an investment in plant and machinery in a United Kingdom development area

| | End of year | | | | | | |
| | 0 | 1 | 2 | 3 | 4 | 5 | 6 |
				(£'000)			
Plant	− 300						
Machinery	− 600					+200	
Working capital	− 100					+100	
Grant (20 per cent)		+180					
Effect of 100 per cent initial allowance on Corporation Tax payments		+450					−100
Net revenue		+100	+200	+300	+200	+100	
Corporation Tax at 50 per cent			− 50	−100	−150	−100	− 50
	−1000	+730	+150	+200	+ 50	+300	−150

Taxable earnings elsewhere in the company are sufficient to absorb capital allowances. Stock relief offers an additional incentive which is discussed in Chapter 5

Table 3.3. Summary of incentives for industry in the areas for expansion

Incentive	Special Development Areas	Development Areas	Intermediate Areas	Northern Ireland
Regional Development Grants				Capital and Industrial Development Grants
New machinery, plant, and mining works	22 per cent	20 per cent	Nil	30–40 per cent*
Building and works (other than mining works)	22 per cent	20 per cent	20 per cent	
Tax allowances				
(A) Machinery and plant	100 per cent first-year allowance on capital expenditure incurred on machinery and plant (other than private passenger cars)			
(B) Industrial buildings	54 per cent of the construction costs can be written off in the first year and subsequently 4 per cent per year			

Note that Regional Development Grants in Great Britain for machinery and plant and buildings are not treated as reducing the capital expenditure in computing tax allowances; neither are capital grants in Northern Ireland.
A booklet describing these and other incentives is available from the Department of Industry.
Incentives marked* are subject to the provision of sufficient additional employment to justify the assistance sought.

The project in our example is an investment in new machinery and plant in a Development Area and therefore qualifies for a 20 per cent grant of £180 000. The funds are usually received within twelve months of purchase of the equipment.

The other set of Government incentives which we should consider and which applies currently in 1978 to all areas of the U.K. is the 100 per cent first-year tax allowance available on expenditures of machinery and plant (other than private passenger cars). This allowance permits a company to reduce its taxable profits when purchasing specific items of capital equipment up to the full amount of the capital expenditure. For industrial buildings the allowance is less—currently on 54 per cent in the first year and 4 per cent per year thereafter on the original expenditure until the building is written off (for Corporation Tax purposes).

The new machinery and plant for our project qualify for a 100 per cent allowance of £900 000 against profits from this and other activities within the company. Below, we show the effect on a company's tax liability of a purchase of £900 000 of plant and machinery. We have assumed that the Government permits the company to write off (that is, depreciate) for tax purposes the whole of the cost of the equipment in the first year:

Computation of company's tax liability (*in* £'000)

Earnings before capital allowances and tax	1000
Capital allowances	900
Taxable profits	100
Corporation Tax payable (at 50 per cent)	50

The reader can see that, without the capital allowance, the tax payable would total £500 000. Thus the 100 per cent capital allowance on purchases totalling £900 000 results in a reduction in tax of £450 000. Clearly, this answer could have been arrived at by simply multiplying the total capital allowances (£900 000) by the tax rate (50 per cent). It is interesting to note that the higher the tax rate, the more valuable are the capital allowances.

If insufficient profits are available to absorb all the allowances, the capital allowances create 'losses' which may be carried forward and set against taxable profits in future years. Assuming a notional 50 per cent rate of Corporation Tax, £450 000 in Corporation Tax is saved by taking a first-year capital allowance on the £900 000 investment in new machinery and plant. (Although investment in Working Capital does not qualify for capital allowances, investment in stock now qualifies for 'stock relief' as explained in Chapter 5.) In the example, we have assumed that the tax saving arising from the 100 per cent first-year allowance is not realized until the tax on the period's profit becomes due approximately 1 year later.

The exact timing of tax payments in the U.K. depends upon the accounting year end and the dividend distribution, as discussed in more detail in Appendix 3.1.

Have we now finished with the effects of Corporation Tax? Well, we have taken all the allowances in the initial year, but we must pay Corporation Tax on the full amount of the incremental cash flows in each of the 5 years of the project's operation. Thus the cash flow of £100 000 in year 1 incurs a £50 000 Corporation Tax liability to be paid in year 2 and so on.

There is one final step in Corporation Tax adjustments to these cash flows which we must not forget. Note the tax payment of £150 000 in year 6. Of this £150 000, £50 000 is clearly a payment of tax on the earnings in year 5. What of the remainder? Recall that the plant and machinery were written off for tax purposes in the first year using the 100 per cent initial allowance. Thus the plant and machinery are carried on the books at zero cost for the computation of tax when the asset is realized. The £200 000 expected to be realized on the sale of the machinery will be treated as a gain (balancing charge) for tax purposes and will be subject to a Corporation Tax balancing charge of £100 000 (at 50 per cent) in year 6.

We have now completed all the Corporation Tax and Development Grant adjustments to the cash flows for this project. Compare the bottom line of Table 3.2 with Table 3.1. Would you say that the effect of Corporation Tax and Development Grant has been favourable or unfavourable to the profitability of the project? Would you say that the impact has been modest—or large? You will have seen in Table 3.2 that, although an investment of £1 million is required in year 0, there is now an inflow of £730 000 in year 1, making the effective net investment over the first 2 years relatively small—only £270 000. This increase in cash flow in year 1 from only £100 000 is entirely due to the effect of Corporation Tax savings and the Regional Development Grant. The effect of these two incentives is favourable and substantial.

Because the firm is able to defer payment of some of its Corporation Tax liabilities by means of the 100 per cent initial allowance on capital investment, additional capital projects become more profitable in relation to other activities which do not have such favourable tax side effects. However, the benefit of the initial allowance is reduced if there are no taxable profits immediately available against which the allowance may be taken. Of course, the cash grant *per se* is always favourable, but one should bear in mind the reasons such grants were deemed necessary by the authorities and whether there are related geographical implications which would be unfavourable to the project.

How profitable is the project now in the light of these incentives? Is the project sufficiently profitable to be attractive? By what criteria should the profitability of projects be judged? The first criterion used by most analysts is the Payback Period.

36

THE PAYBACK PERIOD

The Payback Period is defined as the length of time expected for the project to generate sufficient cumulative cash flows to repay the initial investment. What is the Payback Period for our project example and how does one compute it? Looking at the bottom line of Table 3.2, we merely add the cash flows starting from year 0 until the cumulative sum becomes positive. Our project recovers its initial investment in 2.6 years. Normally such a short Payback Period would be considered attractive, provided there are sufficient positive cash flows after the payback period to make the project profitable. Of course, a rapid return of capital does not of itself ensure profitability. Thus, the Payback Period cannot properly be described as a measure of profitability. Payback is clearly a measure of 'liquidity', although a short Payback Period may be a favourable omen of profitability.

PROBLEMS AND ADVANTAGES IN USING THE PAYBACK PERIOD

The Payback measure has a number of limitations. The measure ignores cash flows after the Payback Period, which are necessary for the project to be profitable. A lesser criticism is that the timing of cash flows during the Payback Period are also ignored. As a result, there is no objective maximum Payback criterion. In a sense, projects with longer lives can justify a longer Payback Period, but there is no precise relationship which relates cash flow patterns for a project to a specified life, or to a specific risk. After all, two projects may have the same cash flows but may have entirely different risk. There should be different minimum Payback standards, but how can we sensibly adjust the measure for risk?

Nevertheless, the Payback Period criterion has sufficient advantages to make it one of the most commonly used measures—usually employed in conjunction with other criteria more closely identified with profitability. The Payback Period is easy to understand and to interpret: its liquidity implications are clear. Lenders use the Payback Period as an indicator of when a project loan can be repaid. Multinational companies use the Payback Period as a measure of length of exposure to political risks in foreign countries. Some companies sharpen the measure by using the Discounted Payback. They discount cash flows to present value before cumulating them to obtain the 'Discounted Payback Period'.

Perhaps the most important feature of the Payback Period is that it is less sensitive to biased or exaggerated forecasts than other investment criteria in use. If forecasted cash flows are excessively optimistic, the resulting bias is most likely to be concentrated in the years beyond the Payback Period. Simulation studies by Marsh and Brealey (1974) have indicated that, when forecasting is sufficiently biased, the use of Payback can result in better decisions compared with other methods.

The popularity of the Payback Period measure has rested somewhat on two favourable conditions: a large number of repetitive projects and stable interest rates and risk premiums. The 1970's have seen sharp changes in risk and interest rates, making it difficult to adapt the established Payback rules to the new circumstances. For these reasons, we consider that the Payback Period should not be considered a measure of profitability, but rather as an extra safeguard against biased forecasting. Let us now examine our project in terms of what may be the most commonly employed measure of profitability, the Accounting Rate of Return.

THE ACCOUNTING RATE OF RETURN

Since the Payback Period does not measure profitability, we must consider other measures in order to more fully gauge the financial viability of the project. Another such measure, and one most commonly in use, is the Accounting Rate of Return, often called 'Return on Investment' or the 'Return on Capital Employed'. There are as many ways of computing the Accounting Rate of Return as there are accounting conventions for the calculation of earnings and of capital employed. A typical calculation would follow the conventions which we use below.

The rate of return may be approximated by a fraction. The bottom line should represent the average amount of capital employed and the top line would represent an average of accounting earnings from the project. What is the average amount of capital employed in the previous example? Initially, there is the £1 million initial investment, which most accountants would adjust for the cash grant. Depreciating straight line to zero, the *average* capital employed over the life of the project would be half the initial amount.

$$\text{Average capital employed} = 0.5 \times (1\,000\,000 - 180\,000)$$
$$= £410\,000$$

In the numerator, we require accounting earnings after tax, which we may compute by taking the average incremental cash flows over the life of the asset, subtracting average depreciation, and adjusting for Corporation Tax. Referring to our example in Table 3.1.

$$\text{Average incremental cash flows} = (100 + 200 + 300 + 200 + 100)/5$$
$$= 180$$

(where all values are in £'000). From the average earnings totalling £180 000, we subtract depreciation, which, to choose a particular convention, we take to be straight-line. We can depreciate the cost of the machinery and plant totalling £900 000 (not the Working Capital) over the projected 5-year life:

Annual straight-line depreciation = 900 000/5
= £180 000.

The Accounting Rate of Return may now be computed:

APR =

$$\frac{\text{(Average incremental cash flow} - \text{Depreciation)}(1 - \text{Corporation Tax rate})}{0.5 \times \text{(Capital investment} - \text{Cash grant)}}$$

$$= \frac{(180\ 000 - 180\ 000)(1 - 0.5)}{410\ 000}$$

$$= 0.$$

Although the project has a relatively attractive Payback Period of 2.6 years and also generates positive cash flows after the Payback Period, the Accounting Rate of Return is zero. An unattractive project, you might say—but is it? A close examination of the cash flows in Table 3.2 reveals a project which does not appear unattractive. Zero profitability certainly is not what was expected. Something is wrong. Could it be the arbitrary choice of accounting conventions that has affected the rate which was obtained? For example, if the machinery is expected to be sold for £200 000 at the end of 5 years, the annual depreciation might have been calculated, (900 000 − 200 000)/5, to be £140 000 per year instead of £180 000, thus raising the Accounting Rate of Return to (only) 4.8 per cent. Is this all the explanation we require? Apparently not.

For U.K. investments, one difficulty with the Accounting Rate of Return is the use of accounting depreciation rules in the place of capital allowances. The reader should understand the difference between accounting depreciation and capital allowances. In appraising an investment, management's primary interest is the cash flow earnings generated by the project. Accounting depreciation is merely a book entry which does not alter cash flows. Now, when the accountant comes to report profits at the end of the year, he deducts an amount called depreciation to reflect approximately the amount of capital used up in production for the year. However, the depreciation charge does not represent any movement of cash and, consequently, should be omitted from the appraisal of a project. If a large capital allowance can be taken initially, then any method such as accounting depreciation which effectively spreads the tax savings due to the capital allowance over a longer period ignores the importance of the timing of the investment incentive. Furthermore, the observance of the accounting convention which treats a grant as a reduction in capital employed in the donominator of the Accounting Rate of Return, rather than as an economic benefit to the firm in the numerator, can underestimate the profitability of investment projects (as the reader may verify in our example above) in some cases and overestimate it in others.

In general, the main disadvantages of the Accounting Rate of Return are that it

(a) relies on accounting conventions;
(b) ignores the timing of cash flows and thus is appropriate only when cash flows are equal in every year;
(c) does not consistently account for differences in project lives;
(d) uses accounting depreciation rather than capital allowances and thus usually understates project profitability.

On the other hand, the advantages of the Accounting Rate of Return criterion appear to be that it:

(a) is understood by management;
(b) is consistent with the return-on-investment divisional performance measure used in many companies;
(c) provides a conservative measure of profitability

Thus the Accounting Rate of Return measure in the above example is likely to have understated the profitability of the project. It would be appropriate now to turn to what is considered by many to be a more reliable indicator of profitability, the Internal Rate of Return.

THE INTERNAL RATE OF RETURN

There are basically two Discounted Cash Flow (DCF) methods. The first is the Net Present Value (NPV) method, which we have discussed in Chapter 2 and will encounter again in Chapter 4. The NPV method measures a project's profitability in terms of its incremental effect on the market value of the firm. On the other hand, the Internal Rate of Return method seeks to establish a rate of return which reflects the timing of cash flows but does not, however, employ market discount rates.

The Internal Rate of Return is defined as that discount rate which would make the Net Present Value of the project equal to zero. The Internal Rate of Return cannot be solved for directly and must be obtained by a process of trial and error.

To illustrate, suppose that we think that the Internal Rate of Return falls between 10 per cent and 15 per cent. We could then compute the NPV at each of these rates. If the NPV computed at the 10 per cent discount rate proved to be positive and the NPV computed at the 15 per cent discount rate proved to be negative, then a discount rate which would result in a zero NPV (neither positive nor negative) is to be found between 10 per cent and 15 per cent. The two trial discount rates would then be said to 'bracket' an Internal Rate of Return, which could then be approximated more closely by successive trials, each narrowing the range between the brackets.

Let us compute the Internal Rate of Return for our example of Table 3.4, which lists in the second column the net incremental cash flows from the bottom line of Table 3.2. In the subsequent columns of Table 3.4 are the Present Value factors at 10 per cent and 15 per cent (from the table in Appendix B) and the corresponding Present Values of the cash flows from the second column. The total Net Present Value at the 10 per cent discount rate is seen to be +£73.6 and at the 15 per cent discount rate it is seen to be −£7.4. Thus our trial discount rates bracket the Internal Rate of Return for the project.

The Internal Rate of Return must be about $14^1/_2$ per cent since the zero NPV is about 'ten times closer' to the −£7.40 NPV at a 15 per cent discount rate than it is to the +£73.60 NPV at the 10 per cent discount rate.

This rough estimate can be determined more closely. The total absolute 'distance' between the two NPV's is approximately £81 $(73.60-(-7.40))$. This distance corresponds to a difference in discount rates of 5 per cent (15 per cent − 10 per cent). Thus the interpolated value k for the Internal Rate of Return is given by

$$k = 10 + \frac{73.6}{81} \times 5 = 14.5 \text{ per cent.}$$

Of course, this estimate is only a rough approximation produced by fitting a straight line to the NPV curve. The straight line approximates the curve adequately only when the trial discount rates are sufficiently close together. To be sure of our result, we should now use a trial discount rate of 14 per cent and then interpolate between 14 per cent and 15 per cent to see whether any significant change occurs in the resulting Internal Rate of Return. The reader might like to try this in order to test his understanding.

Let us summarize our results. Our proposed investment in new machinery and plant has a relatively attractive expected Payback Period of only 2.6 years. However, we needed a measure of the profitability of the project. The Accounting Rate of Return for the project was found to be very close to zero depending on the accounting conventions employed. However, we distrusted this measure mainly because it did not reflect the 100 per cent initial capital allowance incentive. Thus we turned to the Internal Rate of Return as a measure of profitability which reflects the timing of all expected cash flows including the investment incentives. The Internal Rate of Return of approximately 14.5 per cent suggests that the project would be profitable if the returns from investing in the market in equivalent investments is less than 14.5 per cent.

The relative effects of Corporation Tax, capital allowances, and grants on the Internal Rate of Return for the project are summarized in Table

Table 3.4. Illustration of computation of Net Present Value for two trial values of the discount rate at 15 per cent and 10 per cent

Year	Net cash flows (£)	Discount factor at 15 per cent	Discount factor at 10 per cent	Present Value at 15 per cent (£)	Present Value at 10 per cent (£)
0	−1000	1.000 00	1.000 00	−1000.0000	−1000.0000
1	730	0.869 57	0.909 09	634.7861	663.6357
2	150	0.756 14	0.826 45	113.4210	123.9675
3	200	0.657 52	0.751 32	131.5040	150.2640
4	50	0.571 75	0.683 01	28.5875	34.1505
5	300	0.497 18	0.620 92	149.1540	186.2760
6	− 150	0.432 33	0.564 47	− 64.8495	− 84.6705
			Net Present Value	− 7.3969	+ 73.6232

Table 3.5. Effect of Corporation Tax, capital allowances, and Development Grant on the example of Table 3.2

	IRR (per cent)
Pre-tax	5.4
Post-tax (depreciation)	3.0
Post-tax (100 per cent capital allowances)	4.8
Post-tax (capital allowances and grant)	14.5

3.5. Pre-tax, the IRR is 5.4 per cent. Corporation Tax calculated on the basis of earnings after straight-line depreciation (no longer the practice in the U.K.) would have reduced this return to only 3 per cent. Replacing depreciation with 100 per cent capital allowances for tax purposes brings the return up to 4.8 per cent. However, the regional development grant increases the Internal Rate of Return by nearly 10 per cent to 14.5 per cent. Thus we see that grants are potentially the most effective form of investment incentive.

CONCLUSIONS

On the basis of an example, we have compared three of the most widely used capital investment criteria: Payback Period, Accounting Rate of Return, and the Internal Rate of Return. We found these criteria to provide somewhat inconsistent indications of the desirability of the project. This inconsistency arises because the three criteria do not measure the same thing. Payback Period is a measure of project liquidity and does not measure profitability. The Accounting Rate of Return seeks to measure return in terms of the incremental impact of a project on the Profit and Loss Account but does not measure the economic value of the project. The Internal Rate of Return criterion is intended as a measure of profitability in terms of the project's cash flow contribution to the firm. Of the three, the Internal Rate of Return appears to have the better conceptual basis.

In the next chapter we will discuss further the pitfalls in the use of rate-of-return criteria in capital project appraisal. In particular, we will focus on a comparison between the Internal Rate of Return and Net Present Value.

REFERENCES AND BIBLIOGRAPHY

Capital Investment Decisions, Harvard University Press, Cambridge, Mass., 1964. (15 articles reprinted from *Harvard Business Review*, 1954 to 1964.)
Carsberg, B. and Hope, A., *Business Investment Decisions Under Inflation: Theory and Practice*, The Institute of Chartered Accountants in England and Wales, 1976.

Dean, J., *Capital Budgeting: Top-Management Policy on Plant, Equipment and Product Development*, Columbia University Press, New York, 1951.

Istvan, D. F., *Capital-Expenditure Decisions: How They Are Made in Large Corporations*, Bureau of Business Research, Graduate School of Business, Indiana University, 1961.

Marsh, P. and Brealey, R., 'The Use of Imperfect Forecasts in Capital Budgeting', in *Proceedings of The European Finance Association*, North-Holland, Amsterdam, 1974.

Merrett, A. J. and Sykes, A., *The Finance and Analysis of Capital Projects* Longmans, London, 1963.

Merrett, A. J. and Sykes, A., *Capital Budgeting and Company Finance* Longman, London, 2nd edn., 1973.

Ravenscroft, E. A., 'Return on Investment: Fit the Method to your Need', *Harvard Business Review*, **38**, 97–109, Mar.–Apr. 1960.

Reform of Corporation Tax, Cmnd 4955, H.M.S.O., London, 1972.

Sarnat, M. and Levy, H., 'The Relationship of Rules of Thumb: Restatement and Generalisation', *Journal of Finance*, **24**, 479–490, Jun. 1969.

Scholefield, H., 'Taxation Commentary: What has Happened to Investment Incentives', *Journal of Business Finance*, **3** (4), 54–62, Winter 1971.

Scholefield, H. and Franks, J. R., 'Investment Incentives and Regional Policy', *National Westminster Bank Quarterly Review*, 34–40, Feb. 1972.

APPENDIX 3.1 REFINEMENTS TO CORPORATION TAX ADJUSTMENTS

Corporation Tax (currently 52 per cent) in the U.K. is paid in two instalments. If the firm pays a dividend to shareholders, it must pay Advanced Corporation Tax (ACT) equal to

$$\frac{34}{66} \times \text{Dividend},$$

where currently the standard rate of tax is 34 per cent. If the standard rate were to change to 33 per cent, the factor would be 33/67. ACT is payable within 14 days after the end of the calendar quarter during which the dividend is paid.

Subsequently, the company pays Mainstream Corporation Tax 9 months after the accounting year end. The amount of Mainstream Corporation Tax payable will depend on the amount of Advanced Corporation Tax already paid. The total of ACT and Mainstream Corporation Tax payable is equal to 52 per cent of trading profits net of capital allowances, stock relief, and interest payments.

For most companies, one can assume that project cash flows will have no short-term effects on dividend payments and ACT. Thus, all tax effects can be treated as Mainstream Corporation Tax effects.

Mainstream Corporation Tax is not paid until 9 months after the accounting year end. If an investment expenditure occurs at the end of an accounting year, the effect of the capital allowance in reducing tax will not be felt until 9 months later. On the other hand, if the investment expenditure occurs at the end of the first month of the accounting year, the tax effect is not felt until *twenty* months later.

In this chapter, tax payments were shown as paid with a 1-year lag. One way of adjusting for the precise tax payment is to multiply the tax figure by

$$(1 + R)^n,$$

where the power $n = (12 - \text{lag})/12$ and R is the risk-adjusted discount rate for the project. Thus, if the lag is 10 months, we multiply by

$$(1 + R)^{2/12} = (1 + R)^{0.167}.$$

If, on the other hand, the lag is 20 months, we have

$$(1 + R)^{-8/12} = 1/(1 + R)^{8/12}$$

as the factor applied to a tax payment or credit. These particular adjustments are appropriate only when the project end-of-year coincides with the accounting year end.

By applying the above factor first, one can then discount all tax payments or credits as though they occurred 1 year after the accounting year end (as in Table 3.2).

A more straightforward method is to use quarterly discounting. Tax payments can then be shown at the end of the quarter in which they actually occur in relation to each accounting year end.

Other project cash flows may also be entered in the nearest quarter in which they occur. The quarterly discount rate r is given by

$$r = (1 + R)^{1/4} - 1,$$

where R is the annual rate. If a cash flow is spread evenly throughout the year, it may suffice to enter the entire amount at the end of the second quarter, that is at mid-year for discounting purpose. This method will give a more accurate result than the end-of-year discounting employed in the chapter.

Companies with active investment programmes often accumulate sufficient capital allowances so that they pay no Mainstream Corporation Tax. Thus the project analysis excludes Corporation Tax payments or allowances until that period when the company is expected to begin paying Mainstream Corporation Tax. The tax deferral due to the capital allowances must be moved forward to the tax-paying commencement date. Similarly, all Corporation Tax payments must be cumulated and carried forward to the first tax-paying period.

REVIEW QUESTIONS

1. Define and explain the following terms: (a) Payback Period; (b) Net Present Value; (c) Internal Rate of Return.

2. Evidence shows that most firms use the payback period in conjunction with and, in some cases, in place of more sophisticated methods of project appraisal such as Discounted Cash Flow. What advantages and disadvantages do you see in using Payback?

3. Why should the minimum Payback criterion be different for different kinds of projects?

4. Give a critical appraisal of the Accounting Rate of Return method for evaluating investment opportunities.

5. More firms in the U.K. use the Internal Rate of Return criterion than use the Net Present Value. Why might this be the case? Are they right in doing so?

EXERCISES

1. A project requiring the following stream of investments yields the net incremental cash returns indicated below:

End of year	0	1	2	3	4
Net incremental cash flow	−£5000	−£4000	−£3000	+£7000	+£10 000

The cash flows shown include regional development grants and are net of taxes.

(a) What is the Payback Period for the project? Explain the basis of your calculation.
(b) Under what precise circumstances would you invest in the project?

2. An investment project would generate the following net incremental cash flows:

End of year	0	1	2	3
Net incremental cash flows	−£2400	−£500	+£2000	+£2000

The above cash flows include Regional Development Grants and are net of taxes.
If the required rate of return considering the project's risk is 15 per cent, would the project be financially attractive?

3. Whiz Kidd has £15 000 which he can commit to an investment at the present moment in time. He has an opportunity to sign a fixed-price contract to supply goods to a large industrial customer in equal fixed amounts over a period of 4 years. He also has an opportunity to secure all his raw material by means of fixed-price contracts. He intends to supply the labour himself, if necessary, which he is willing to commit at a constant wage; and he can obtain adequate health and life insurance. Thus the project is virtually risk-free.

However, Whiz Kidd is not certain whether he should sign the contract since he could more easily purchase Government bonds for £15 000 paying 14 per cent per annum (after tax) on face value and redeemable for £15 000 at the end of four years when the contract would also be completed.

The net incremental cash flows for the project (including Whiz Kidd's labour and extra insurance net of all taxes and including investment incentives) and for bonds are given below:

End of year	0	1	2	3	4
Project	−£15 000	£5000	£5000	£5000	£5000
Bonds	−£15 000	+£2100	+£2100	+£2100	+£1700

Employing payback and at least two other different investment criteria, indicate which course of action would be most financially attractive.

4. The X company is preparing to invest in a project which would generate the following net incremental cash flows:

End of year	0	1	2	3	4
Plant and machinery	−£4000	£900	£1300	£1500	£1500

The project consists of plant and machinery to be installed in an existing building near London. The company also has space in a building in a development area of the U.K. where the plant and machinery might be installed. However, due to increased installation and transportation costs, the net incremental cash flows would be changed to the following:

End of year	0	1	2	3	4
Plant and machinery	−£4500	£800	£1100	£1250	£1250

Both projects will attract a 100 per cent capital allowance in the first year. Corporation Tax is payable at 52 per cent. Depreciation is charged on a straight-line basis over 4 years. Scrap value included in the year 4 cash flow is £500.

(a) Which alternative is more attractive from the point of view of

   (i) Payback Period;
   (ii) Accounting Rate of Return;
   (iii) Internal Rate of Return;
   (iv) Net Present Value at 15 per cent?

(b) What decision would you make in view of your answers to part (a)?

4

RATES OF RETURN: THE PITFALLS

A recent survey has shown that 85 per cent of respondents in large U.K. companies use either or both of the Net Present Value and the Internal Rate of Return methods in capital project appraisal. Indeed, for these firms the Internal Rate of Return appears to have become the most widely used quantitative method, in preference to the Payback Period and the Accounting Rate of Return. But are the full implications and the limitations of decision making based on rate-of-return criteria really understood? Contacts with hundreds of financial managers have not revealed a clear awareness of the problems inherent in the use of rates of return. Given the general use of Internal Rate of Return and Accounting Rate of Return criteria, these problems may have critically influenced many major capital investment decisions in recent years. We shall now try to clarify some limitations of rate-of-return criteria.

THE RATE-OF-RETURN MAXIMIZATION FALLACY

Suppose we were to offer two risk-free investments which are mutually exclusive; that is, you may invest in one or the other but not in both. We impose a further stipulation that only one of each of the investments is available. Investment A has a rate of return of 100 per cent for 1 year and investment B offers a rate of return of 30 per cent for 1 year. The available return in the capital market for the risk class is, let us say, 15 per cent. Which is the preferable investment?

The rate of return maximizer will take investment A every time: 100 per cent is even better than 30 per cent, and only 15 per cent is required for this level of risk. However, the Net Present Value maximizer requires more information before he can make the choice. We now reveal that investment A requires an investment of only £1000 and investment B offers the opportunity of investing £1 million profitably. One does not require financial genius to detect that a 30 per cent return on £1 million is a very much better proposition than a 100 per cent return on £1000 even after deducting the 15 per cent cost of capital. Investment A benefits the rate-of-return maximizer by only £730 or $(-1000 + 2000/1.15)$ and the Net Present Value maximizer is enriched by £130 435 or $(-1\,000\,000 +$

Table 4.1. Example of two mutually exclusive projects with identical initial investments but where rate of return comparisons are misleading

| | End of period | | | | NPV |
	0 (£)	1 (£)	2 (£)	IRR (per cent)	10 per cent (£)
Project A	−10 000	+ 2000	+12 000	20	1736.
Project B	−10 000	+10 000	+ 3125	25	1674
A − B	0	− 8000	+ 8875	10.9	62

1 300 000/1.15). Clearly, the Net Present Value maximizer has reached the better decision.

'What an extreme example', you say. 'Surely rate-of-return comparisons will always be valid for projects requiring roughly the same initial investment'! Unfortunately, the nature of profitability comparisons is not so simple as that. To illustrate, let us take another example (Table 4.1) of two mutually exclusive projects A and B, both requiring the *same* initial investment. Both projects are in the same risk class, although project A's positive cash flows arrive mainly in period 2 whereas project B's positive cash flows arrive mainly in period 1. Project A's internal rate of return is only 20 per cent and project B's is 25 per cent. The required rate of return for this risk class is 10 per cent. Well, you may think that project B is clearly preferable to project A since the rate of return is higher and both require the same initial investment—but this is not the case. Using a discount rate of 10 per cent for this risk class, one finds that the Net Present Value is £1736 for Project A and for Project B the NPV is only £1674. Project A is the better project, even though its rate of return is lower and the initial investment is the same.

Why should the Internal Rate of Return comparison be so perverse? Remember that the IRR is the discount rate being used in the calculation. If the discount rate does not represent capital market reinvestment opportunities in securities of equivalent risk, then the resulting value of the Internal Rate of Return will exhibit a bias.

Since the cash inflows are received much earlier in project B than in project A, the reinvestment assumption is more critical for project B. The £10 000 received at the end of period 1 from project B is assumed to be reinvested at 25 per cent, whereas the £12 000 received from project A at the end of the project's life is not reinvested. For this reason, project B shows a higher Internal Rate of Return than project A, even though project A has the higher Net Present Value at 10 per cent.

For example, in Table 4.1 we have subtracted the cash flow stream of project B from that of project A. This comparison reveals that if one were to accept project A in preference to project B, one would forego additional available cash from project B in period 1 in order to obtain the additional £8875 available from project A in period 2. Is it worth it? Well, the internal rate of return on the A – B stream is 10.9 per cent, which is greater than the 10 per cent cut-off rate, so we might choose A in preference to B. Alternatively, we can obtain the New Present Value of the A – B stream. The NPV is +£62 (which we already knew by subtracting £1675 for B from £1737 for A). Thus project A is better than B because its Net Present Value is greater. Value is greater.

The greater opportunity for reinvestment inherent in the cash flow profile of project B gives it the edge when the assumed discount rate exceeds 10.9 per cent. However, the alternative market opportunities for the risk class of these projects offered is only 10 per cent. If market opportunity costs were to increase to over 10.9 per cent, project B would then be the more attractive investment.

Consider further the two projects, A and B, illustrated in the graph in Figure 4.1. For any given discount rate, a project will have a corresponding Net Present Value. In Figure 4.1, an NPV is plotted corresponding to each discount rate for each project. Along the horizontal axis, the NPV is equal to zero and thus the Internal Rate of Return for each project is found where the project's curve crosses the horizontal axis. As it happens, each

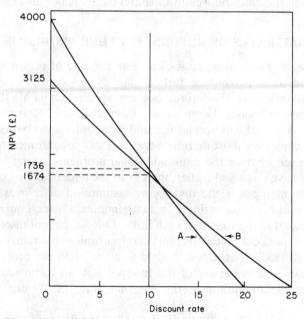

Figure 4.1. NPV's versus discount rates for projects A and B

project has only one Internal Rate of Return: for project A it is 20 per cent and for project B it is 25 per cent. Now, it would be tempting to believe that project B is 'better' than project A. If the object of financial policy were to maximize the rate of return on projects, then B might be preferable. However, the object of financial policy is to maximize the Net Present Value for the firm. What are the NPV's of the two projects? Well, if the market discount rate for project A and for project B is 10 per cent, then we see that the NPV at that discount rate is higher for A than for B, so that project A maximizes the Net Present Value of the firm rather than project B.

Clearly, Net Present Value based on available capital market opportunities *always* provides the correct financial criterion for selection between projects. Internal Rates of Return are correct only when, by chance, they are identical in value to capital market opportunities in the same risk class as the project.

We can conclude that capital projects should *not* be compared to one another on the basis of rates of return, even if the projects have identical initial investments. Such comparisons can result in the choice of projects with smaller Net Present Values. The contradictions inherent in the use of rate-of-return comparisons do not apply to a similar use of Net Present Value, which can be directly related to expected net increases in the value of the firm. The proposition that choosing projects with the largest rates of return will increase the wealth of shareholders is not always true.

INTERNAL RATES OF RETURN: FURTHER PROBLEMS

The foregoing should make it clear that any rate of return which can be expressed as a percentage rather than as an absolute value presents potential difficulties in interpretation and application within the context of sound financial policy. However, the Internal Rate of Return in particular has now achieved widespread use and will continue to be used for some years to come. We must therefore consider this popular measure in further depth to see whether there are additional problems arising from its use.

As we have discussed earlier, the key to the understanding of discounted cash flow methods is the underlying assumption of reinvestment in the capital market. Discounting is a mathematical device equivalent to the compounded reinvestment of cash flows. One should not discount at a rate of, say, 30 per cent unless the market opportunities for reinvestment at the equivalent risk are expected to yield a return of 30 per cent. Some of the pitfalls inherent in the use of the Internal Rate of Return arise from the fact that the definition of the Internal Rate of Return violates this principle.

The Internal Rate of Return is defined as the discount rate which makes the Net Present Value equal to zero—whatever rate that may be. Only in marginal cases will the discount rate obtained in this manner equal the equivalent market opportunities. At any given time the market has fixed its investment rate for each class of risk. This rate is reflected in expected returns on a wide variety of securities available in the capital market. Discounting should reflect the reinvestment of cash flows at the expected rates available in the market place. The NPV method does this automatically if the expected return on securities of equivalent risk in the capital market is used as the discount rate.

Another problem with choosing *ad hoc* discount rates independently of market rates is that there is often more than one such arbitrary discount rate which will make the NPV equal to zero, and thus more than one Internal Rate of Return for a project. It is a mathematical problem arising from the definition of the Internal Rate of Return. Remember that we are solving for an unknown discount rate which is raised to various powers in the discounting formula:

$$\text{NPV} = 0 = C_0 + \frac{C_1}{1 + k} + \frac{C_2}{(1 + k)^2} + \ldots + \frac{C_T}{(1 + k)^T}.$$

Thus the solution for the value of the unknown k can have more than one root. Fortunately, multiple positive real values for k arise only under particular conditions which depend on the number of changes of sign of the cash flows in the sequence. For example, if the initial cash flows are all negative and are followed by cash flows which are all positive, there will be only one value for k since there is only one change of sign in the cash flow sequence.

Suppose, however, that a major overhaul expense should occur at the middle of the project's life, interrupting the sequence of positive cash flows. There would then be three changes of sign: one after the period of initial investment, one moving from positive to negative entering the period when the overhaul takes place, and another change of sign back to positive in the subsequent period after the overhaul. In this example there could be as many as three different values for k.

While there may be several discount rates which make the NPV of the project equal to zero, none of these may be appropriate for the project given its opportunity cost of capital. Internal rates of return based upon reinvestment rates that do not reflect market opportunities may often make little economic sense.

The reason that many companies use a rate of return measure is to be able to compare the rate of return for an investment to the required rate of return, i.e. the return on alternative investments in the capital market for the same risk. One can adopt a rule that the Internal Rate of Return for the project must exceed the required rate of return. However, if there should be multiple Internal Rates of Return for the project and even if none are below the reinvestment opportunity rate or required rate of return, it can be shown that the investment may not be profitable since the Net Present Value can still be negative. Although multiple IRR's are encountered infrequently, suitable precautions are called for. Thus, some analysts plot NPV against discount rates as we did in Figure 4.1.

If all this seems a little frustrating, we can at least hold on to the fact that the Net Present Value method offers an alternative which is always correct providing the appropriate discount rate is employed. A project with a positive Net Present Value is always profitable and the Internal Rate of Return is thus not really necessary for project selection.

THE SIGNIFICANCE OF NET PRESENT VALUE

We have said that a project is profitable if there is a positive Net Present Value. But what does such a result mean in marketing or economic terms? In a competitive product market where there are no supply problems, you would expect producers to make an adequate return on the funds invested. What is an adequate return? Clearly, one which at least approximates the risk-adjusted required rate of return. Thus, one would not expect to see a large positive Net Present Value for a proposed project in a highly competitive market. A large NPV must derive from a comparative competitive advantage of a product in a market or from a supply shortage that cannot be easily remedied, for example, because of barriers to entry. Thus, the justification of a project does not depend merely upon forecasts of cash flows but rather upon the competitive environment of the product market. If a large NPV is not justified on such grounds it may merely reflect the results of biased cash flow forecasting.

A positive Net Present Value reflects a competitive advantage or scarcity value often termed an *economic rent*. It is important to ask how long such advantages will last. Barriers to entry, the time lags in introducing substitutes, cartels—such obstacles may preserve high prices for some time to come. However, in economies such as that of the U.K., competition from both internal and external sources will combine to reduce high prices; as a consequence, economic rents will disappear with the passage of time, i.e. cash flows can be expected to decline as competition intensifies until new investment by competitors is no longer profitable.

In 1974, the oil producing countries formed a cartel to increase the price of oil above the competitive price. If we had been advising an oil company with a field in the North Sea, what advice would we have given—to keep the oil in the ground or produce and sell it? One usually expects that economic rents will decline with time because of competitive forces. In 1974 the price of oil was higher than competitive forces would have permitted. One could have forecast that the cartel would weaken, demand for oil would fall, exploration activity would be stimulated and the search for substitutes would be increased. Furthermore, in many countries it would become attractive to insulate houses and factories rather than to burn oil, and to burn alternative fuels such as coal and natural gas. All such moves have taken place and have combined to lower the demand for oil, reducing the effectiveness of the cartel and greatly reducing the real price of oil in the subsequent period. Would *you* have kept the oil in the ground?

We have discussed this particular situation because it demonstrates the importance of knowing the origins of the economic rent reflected in the Net Present Value of a project. Furthermore, one must forecast when the high prices or comparatively low costs will end and incorporate the forecasts into the cash flows of a project. Somehow, to assume that economic rents are constant over the life of a project may simply not reflect the realities of the market place.

It may then be asked why profitability calculations are necessary at all? Perhaps all that is necessary is to show that the product has a comparative advantage. In some cases market information and analysis may be sufficient providing that the product's comparative advantage extends to costs. However, with other projects it is difficult to 'eyeball' the decision with only the facts of the market place. Such decisions as a decision to locate a factory in place A or B, or a decision to manufacture a product rather than to sub-contract, require estimates of costs and savings and, ultimately, Net Present Value calculations.

ALTERNATIVE MEASURES: THE PROFITABILITY INDEX

We have discussed the Accounting Rate of Return and the Internal Rate of Return. We have demonstrated how rate-of-return maximization can be inconsistent with maximization of the value of the firm, and we have shown that the peculiar definition of the Internal Rate of Return leads to further inconsistencies. Because of these problems, some alternative profitability measures have been suggested. The most prominent is the so-called Profitability Index.

Providing that the correct discount rate is used and that one has an unbiased forecast of net cash flows for the investment, a positive Net Present Value will always indicate whether the investment is profitable. However, management frequently wishes to have some measure of the return from a project in relation to the funds required. For this reason the Profitability Index was devised. The Profitability Index (PI) is defined as the Present Value of net cash returns (PV) divided by the Present Value of net cash investments (I):

$$PI = PV/I$$
$$= (NPV + I)/I$$

The Profitability Index for our project A in Table 4.1 is

$$PI = (11\ 736/(10\ 000)$$
$$= 1.1736.$$

What does this figure mean? The project generates 1.1736 units of Present Value for each unit of investment. This fact may be of interest since, if a project has a positive Net Present Value but a low Profitability Index, the net advantage to the firm may not be commensurate with the scale of resources required.

The Profitability Index has also been used as criterion for ranking projects under conditions where capital is scarce and is rationed. Projects with the largest Profitability Index are accepted first until the available funds are used up. The idea is to maximize the total Net Present Value for the limited funds available. Thus the value of I represents net funds required during a period of capital rationing. This problem is really a job for a computerized model, but the Profitability Index ranking procedure can lead to a reasonable approximation for allocating limited funds in single period.

CAPITAL RATIONING

If the capital available for projects is expected to be budgeted or rationed for more than one period, then the ranked Profitability Index will not always suffice as a means of selecting the most profitable combination of projects. Table 4.2 illustrates an example of such a choice. Four projects, A, B, C, and D, are in prospect, each commencing in a successively more distant period. Only £1000 is available for all four projects, but funds earned from one project may be reinvested in other projects. Idle funds may be reinvested in the money market at 10 per cent until required for investment in a project. What combinations of projects are feasible within the budget? What is the most profitable combination?

This financial planning problem can most easily be solved by the method demonstrated in Table 4.3 (which is derived from Table 4.2). All the

Table 4.2. Cash flows of four prospective capital investments and the capital budget

Period ending	A (£)	B (£)	C (£)	D (£)	Budget (£)
			Projects		
0	−1000				+1000
1	+ 200	−500			
2	+ 200	+100	−550		
3	+ 200	+100	+100	−660	
4	+ 200	+100	+100	+132	
⋮	⋮	⋮	⋮	⋮	

Table 4.3. Cumulative net funds requirements for four prospective capital investments and the cumulative capital budget

| Period ending | Projects | | | | Budget (£) |
	A (£)	B (£)	C (£)	D (£)	
0	−1000				1000
1	− 900	−500			1100
2	− 790	−450	−550		1210
3	− 669	−395	−555.5	−660	1331
4	− 534	−335	−501.05	−594	1464
⋮	⋮	⋮	⋮	⋮	⋮

All cumulative figures shown assume that idle cash is reinvested at 10 per cent after tax.

figures in Table 4.3 are cumulations of the earlier figures compounded at 10 per cent, the expected reinvestment rate. Take, for example, the figure shown for project A. The first figure is still −£1000. The second figure is −£900 = −£1000 × 1.1 + £200. The third figure is −£790 = − £900 × 1.1 + £200 and so on. The principle which can now be applied to the revised figures in selecting projects is that the cumulative net commitments to projects must not exceed the cumulative capital budget after allowing for opportunities for reinvestment of any idle cash.

This principle can be applied by comparing sums from left to right in Table 4.3 with the cumulative budget in the final column. By this means, all feasible combinations can be found. Let us apply the method. Project A can be undertaken since the £1000 required does not exceed the budget of £1000. Can any other project also be undertaken along with project A? Consider project B. Since the combined cumulative net requirements of £900 for A and £500 for B exceed the cumulative budget of £1100, the combination of A and B is infeasible. The same is true of A and C. Now let us consider A and D. The cumulative net requirement for A and D is £1329 = £669 + £660. Since £1329 does not exceed the cumulative budget of £1331 at that stage, both A and D are feasible within the budget. The profitability of such a combination of projects would be indicated by their combined Net Present Value, both discounted to a common date, period zero. However, there may be other feasible combinations of projects which could be more profitable.

Consider next combinations of project B with projects other than A (already considered). Project B can be combined with project C since the cumulative net requirement for funds, £1000 = £450 + £550, does not exceed the cumulative budget of £1210. Similarly, project B can also be combined with project D within the cumulative budget. By the same method, we find that projects C and D are also feasible together.

To summarize, projects are feasible in the following combinations within the cumulative budget:

A, D   B. C   B, D   C, D.

The immediate decision is whether to invest in project A since investment in A would pre-empt investment in any other project but D. If project combinations including B or C were more profitable, we would not invest in A. To make the choice, we simply add the Net Present Values as of period 0 within each feasible combination of projects. That feasible combination with the largest total Net Present Value provides the optimal selection of projects within the cumulative budget.

MATHEMATICAL PROGRAMMING

We have just demonstrated the manual solution of an integer programming problem. A more formal presentation of the problem is given in Table 4.4. The meaning of the terms in Table 4.4 is made clear by comparison with Table 4.3. All the comments we have made concerning Table 4.3 apply also to Table 4.4. However, we have now shown the *objective function*, which is simply the maximization of the total Net Present Value for the selected combination of projects:

$$\text{Maximize } P_1X_1 + P_2X_2 + P_3X_3 + P_4X_4$$

Table 4.4. Programming formulation for the example of Tables 4.2 and 4.3

| | Projects | | | | |
	A	B	C	D	Budget
Objective Maximize	P_1X_1	$+ P_2X_2$	$+ P_3X_3$	$+ P_4X_4$	
Subject to constraints					
	$1000X_1$	$+ 0X_2$	$+ 0X_3$	$+ 0X_4$	≤ 1000
	$900X_1$	$+ 500X_2$	$+ 0X_3$	$+ 0X_4$	≤ 1100
	$790X_1$	$+ 450X_2$	$+ 550X_3$	$+ 0X_4$	≤ 1210
	$669X_1$	$+ 395X_2$	$+ 555.5X_3$	$+ 660X_4$	≤ 1331
	$534X_1$	$+ 335X_2$	$+ 501.0X_3$	$+ 594X_4$	≤ 1464
and					
		$X_j = 0,1$	$j = 1,2,\ldots,N$		

where P_j represents the Net Present Value of project j and X_j is a variable signifying whether project j has been selected. With the integer programming method X_j can have only two values, 1 or 0, depending upon whether project j is or is not selected, respectively.

Also shown in Table 4.4 are the budget constraints, where we still observe the principle that the cumulative compound net cash requirements for projects must be less than or equal to the cumulative compound capital budgets available. Again the value of the X's signify whether or not the project is in the budget. We have also changed the signs of the cash flows for project cumulative compound net cash requirements in order to put them on the left-hand side of each of the inequality constraints.

The method is easily adapted to reflect constraints other than capital rationing. For example, we could add a row to Table 4.4 to reflect constraints on the availability of key management or technical personnel required in each period to implement projects successfully. The coefficient of X_j in a row of Table 4.4 could represent the number of man-years required to implement project j in a particular period, and in the final column of the same row we would have the total man-years available in that period.

If two of the projects are mutually exclusive, we can include the constraint:

$$1X_j + 1X_k \leq 1,$$

where projects j and k are the mutually exclusive projects. Thus, should X_j take the value 1 in the optimum solution, X_k would have to take the value 0 and vice versa. If, instead, project j were contingent on project k, i.e. if project j could not be undertaken unless project k were undertaken first, we would include the constraint

$$1X_j - 1X_k \leq 0.$$

Note that this constraint is equivalent to

$$X_j \leq X_k$$

and that therefore, if the value of X_k is zero, the value of X_j must also be zero. Only if the value of X_k is equal to one can the value of X_j be one. Thus with this constraint we have ensured that project j will be contingent on project k in the optimal solution.

The coefficients of the X's in Table 4.4 are arranged in the format usually required for input to computer programs designed to solve linear optimization problems. Broadly speaking, there are two methods which are used to solve such *mathematical programming* problems: *integer programming* and *linear programming*. If X is only allowed to have the values 0 or 1, the problem is defined as an integer programming problem. On the other hand, if X is allowed to have fractional values, we have a linear programming problem.

In our example there were only four variables, one for each project. Computer programs exist which can solve integer programmes for up to around 20 variables with reasonable efficiency. For much larger numbers of variables, the linear programming method of solution may be required. A linear programming solution will allow fractional values of X, indicating that only a fraction of a project is required in the optimal solution. Such a solution may not be technically feasible and the assumed costs and revenues may not apply to projects which are not implemented at full scale. Unfortunately, simply rounding fractions up or down will not, in general yield the optimum integer combination, even if the constraints were still satisfied. Nevertheless, linear programming solutions usually provide a useful starting point for management decisions and many linear programs provide facilities for sensitivity analyses, which can provide additional insights concerning the likely best choice of projects.

A problem with this type of financial planning analysis is that certainty is being assumed. One does not have full information at period 0 concerning future projects. Investment opportunities may subsequently be revealed which are not now known. Also, projects now anticipated may be made obsolete by competitive developments. Furthermore, capital budgets may be increased or reduced depending on the success of other parts of the business or of financing in the capital market. Finally, the concept of a budget may be too simple in cases where leasing, joint ventures, and mergers provide alternative methods of financing particular projects.

Nevertheless, the motivation to use mathematical programming methods arises from several real needs. Because of flotation costs, long-term financing tends to be raised in large 'lumps' and short-term bank overdrafts are used to fill in between flotations. When credit restrictions are in force, bank borrowing becomes more difficult and companies may experience capital rationing in the short term. Mathematical programming promises to help management to make the most of its scarce resources, which may at times include cash. Even when capital is readily available to the Group, management may wish to allocate capital budgets to divisions as though capital were a scarce resource. This practice forces divisional managers to set priorities in their investment programmes. Mathematical programming can play a useful role in the establishment of optimal capital budgets for this purpose.

CONCLUSIONS

The Net Present Value method is the most consistent and straightforward method of financial analysis when the correct capital market required rate of return is employed for discounting. The Internal Rate of Return often fails in its purpose because its definition prescribes the use of discount rates other than the correct one. Furthermore, no rate of return is useful for making comparisons unless the projects are in some sense identical in 'scale'—although the appropriate definition of scale for this purpose is not clear. To make life a little easier, however, positive NPV's always imply profitable expectations, and where projects are mutually exclusive, the one with the largest NPV is preferable. Thus the financial aspects of investment decisions can always be based on the Net Present Value method. Rates of return can be computed if necessary in order to satisfy the curiosity of senior management, but, if rates of return are not supplemented by other criteria, they can produce erroneous information for making choices or comparisons between projects.

Should there be limitations on cash or other resources available for capital investment, the NPV method should still be used. The objective becomes the maximization of total Net Present Value for the combination of projects selected, subject to constraints on the total required by the selected projects of each limited resource. For this purpose we described the Profitability Index and discussed briefly the use of both integer and linear programming methods.

REFERENCES AND BIBLIOGRAPHY

Anthony, R. N., 'Some Fallacies in Figuring Return on Investment', *NAA Bulletin*, **42**, 5–13, Dec. 1960.

Bierman, H., Jr and Smidt, S., 'Capital Budgeting and the Problem of Reinvesting Cash Proceeds', *Journal of Business*, **30**, 276–279, Oct. 1957.

Bierman, H., Jr and Smidt, S., *The Capital Budgeting Decision*, 3rd ed., Macmillan, New York, 1971.

Broyles, J. E., 'Compact Formulations of Mathematical Programmes for Financial Planning Problems', *Operational Research Quarterly*, **27** (4), 885–893, 1976.

Carsberg, B. and Hope, A., *Business Investment Decisions under Inflation*, The Institute of Chartered Accountants in England and Wales, London, 1976.

Chambers, D. J., 'An Approach to Capital Budgeting', *European Business Review*, 7–11, May 1967.

Charnes, A., Cooper, W. W., and Miller, M. H., 'Application of Linear Programming to Financial Budgeting and the Costing of Funds', *Journal of Political Economy*, **32** 20–46, Jan. 1959.

Dean, J., 'Measuring the Productivity of Capital', *Harvard Business Review*, **32**, 120–130, Jan.–Feb. 1954.

Hirshleifer, J., 'On the Theory of Optimal Investment Decisions', *Journal of Political Economy*, **66**, 329–352, Aug. 1958.

Kolb, B. A. 'Problems and pitfalls in Capital Budgeting', *Financial Analysts Journal*, **24**, 170–174, Nov.–Dec. 1968.

Merrett, A. J., and Sykes, A., *Capital Budgeting and Company Finance*, Longman, London, 1966.

Rockley, L. E., *Capital Investment Decisions: a Manual for Profit Planning*, Business Books, London, 1968.

Teichroew, D., Robichek, A. A., and Montalbano, M., 'An Analysis of Criteria for Investment and Financing Decisions Under Certainty', *Management Science*, **11**, 151–179, Nov. 1965.

Weingartner, H. M., *Mathematical Programming and the Analysis of Capital Budgeting Problems*, Prentice-Hall, Englewood Cliffs, N.J., 1963.

REVIEW QUESTIONS

1. What are the major pitfalls in the use of rate-of-return measures as investment criteria?

2. What is the 'rate-of-return maximization fallacy'? How would you explain this fallacy to a practising financial manager?

3. Under what conditions will the Net Present Value Rule always provide the right choice between mutually exclusive projects?

4. Comment on the following statement: 'Projects of the same size or scale of initial investment can be ranked according to their Internal Rates of Return'.

5. What is the cause of the multiple internal rate of return problem? Explain why the Net Present Value can be negative even if all values of the IRR are above the discount rate.

6. In economic terms, what is the significance of a positive NPV? What assumptions are implicit when one estimates that a project has a positive NPV?

7. Explain the uses of the Profitability Index and its drawbacks.

8. Discounted cash flow methods rest on an assumption of efficient capital markets. An efficient capital market, in turn, would imply that sufficient funds will always be available for profitable projects at or above the appropriate required rate of return for the project's risk. In reality many managers make their decisions within a context of assumed capital rationing. Discuss whether capital rationing is likely to be a reality for the decision maker or merely an administrative convenience.

9. Explain the principles underlying the integer programming method which was outlined in this chapter.

EXERCISES

1. You are offered the choice between a grant of £1000 and a subsidized loan of £5000 with interest at 1 per cent per year after tax and repayable at the end of 5 years. Plot the Net Present Value versus discount rates for this loan. Under what specific circumstances should you prefer the loan to the grant? Make any necessary assumptions.

2. Plot the Net Present Value versus discount rate for the following net incremental cash flows:

End of year	0	1	2	...	9	10
Project	−£178	£81	£81	...	£81	−£919

   (a) What is the NPV at 20 per cent and at 30 per cent?
   (b) What is the Internal Rate of Return for the project?
   (c) What is the NPV at the required rate of return of 15 per cent?
   (d) Explain how IRR's can exceed the required rate of return in some cases and yet the NPV can still be negative and the project unacceptable.

3. Given below are the net incremental cash flows for mutually exclusive capital projects

End of year	0	1	...	9	10
Project A	−£4750	£1000	...	£1000	£0
Project B	−£4572	£ 919	...	£ 919	£1000

(a) Plot the NPV versus discount rate for each project.
(b) Plot the NPV versus discount rate for the difference between the cash flows of A and B.
(c) Explain why obtaining the Internal Rate of Return for the difference between cash flows for two mutually exclusive projects will not always provide a rational criterion for choice between them.

4. Consider the mutually exclusive projects having the following net incremental cash flows:

End of year	0	1	2	3	4	5
Project A	−£900	£300	£300	£300	£300	£300
Project B	−£225	£ 85	£ 85	£ 85	£ 85	£ 85
Project C	−£350	£120	£120	£120	£120	£120
Project D	−£550	£165	£165	£165	£165	£165
Project E	−£400	£155	£155	£155	£155	£155

With the aid of annuity tables determine for each project:

(a) the Net Present Value if the required rate of return is 12 per cent;
(b) the value of the Internal Rate of Return;
(c) the value of the Profitability Index;
(d) which projects are acceptable if the capital budget available for these projects in year 0 is only £1000.

5. A division of a large firm is considering the four projects for which net incremental cash flows are given in the table below. Also shown in the table is the divisional budget for capital investments which has been approved by headquarters for the first three years. Cash flows generated by the projects may be applied to the budget, and budgeted funds not immediately invested in projects may be held in reserve for later use and invested in safe securities at 10 per cent after tax. If the required rate of return for each project is 15 per cent, which projects should be accepted? What is the maximum obtainable total Net Present Value?

Period ending	Project A	B	C	D	Budget
0	−£900				+£1000
1	£495	−£400	−£900		+£ 200
2	£495	£205	£495	−£1500	+£ 200
3	£495	£205	£495	£ 735	£ 0
4		£205	£495	£ 735	£ 0
5				£ 735	£ 0

5

INFLATION AND THE INVESTMENT DECISION

In this chapter we analyse some of the effects of changes in the rate of inflation on the profitability of capital investment. We discuss the effects of inflation on interest rates and on a project's risk and required rate of return. We show how the favourable impact of capital allowances on taxes is reduced with increasing rates of inflation. We examine the way in which taxes on stock appreciation are affected by the Government provision for Stock Relief. Finally, we show that changes in the rate of inflation can have selective effects on the demand for products and thus on the profitability of individual capital projects. As a result of all these effects we argue that profitability calculations should be made in nominal (money of the day) terms rather than in real (inflation adjusted) terms.

RISK, REQUIRED RATES OF RETURN, AND INFLATION

How are required rates of return for an investment affected by inflation? The required rate of return is usually expressed in *nominal* terms, i.e. in the money of the day regardless of the expected impact of inflation on purchasing power. The nominal required rate of return for a capital investment may be divided into two parts, the risk-free nominal rate of interest and a risk premium required as compensation for the project's risk. The nominal rate of interest may also be expressed as the sum of two parts, the *real* rate of interest and the expected rate of inflation for the period of the investment.

In competitive markets, changes in the expected rate of inflation should be reflected speedily in changes in the nominal rate of interest. Clearly, if interest rates do not reflect expected rates of inflation, markets in particular assets may not be competitive, and a trading profit may be obtainable. For example, suppose the anticipated price increase for wheat for a particular period is 15 per cent, the nominal interest is 10 per cent, and the real rate of interest is zero. How would consumers or wholesalers behave? Presumably some would buy and borrow until the rate of interest increases to 15 per cent. In a competitive market we would not expect opportunities for making profits in excess of that justified by risk to last very long. Net of transactions

Table 5.1. Initial investment and net revenues for project with zero inflation

Cash flow item	0	1	End of year 2 (£'000)	3	...
Net revenues		+600	+600	+600	...
Corporation Tax			−300	−300	...
Investment	−3000				
Total	−3000	+600	+300	+300	...

costs and storage costs, we would expect excess returns to be eliminated by market competitors. Thus competitive pressures would move current interest rates towards a point where interest rates reflect market expectations of inflation.

The proposition that interest rates fully reflect anticipated rates of inflation or price changes was offered by Irving Fisher (1930), and is known as the 'Fisher Effect'. Of course, this relationship between interest rates and inflation cannot always be perfect since there are storage costs for goods and other transaction costs, and for some assets the market may not be very competitive, even before Government intervention.

The Fisher Effect is often used as a basis for the assertion that a change in the anticipated rate of inflation should have no effect on the profitability of capital investment. For example, compare the situations in Table 5.1, a project in the absence of inflation, and Table 5.2, the same project with 10 per cent inflation. Is it true that the NPV is the same in both cases?

In Table 5.1 at zero inflation, the company assumes a *real* (inflation-free) rate of interest of 1 per cent plus a *real* risk premium of 7 per cent. The Net Present Value of the project at 8 per cent is thus equal to £1028.

In Table 5.2, on the other hand, the net revenues are inflated at a 10 per cent compound rate. Obviously, the NPV will increase unless the discount

Table 5.2. Initial investment and net revenues for project with 10 per cent inflation

Cash flow item	0	1	End of year 2 (£'000)	3	...
Net revenues		+660	+726	+798.6	...
Corporation Tax			−330	−363	...
Investment	−3000				...
Total	−3000	+660	+396	+436	

rate increases proportionately. According to Fisher, the new discount rate R would be determined by

$$1 + R = (1 + 0.08)(1 + 0.10),$$
$$R = 18.8 \text{ per cent.}$$

Discounting the figures in Table 5.2 at 18.8 per cent, one obtains exactly the same Net Present Value as in Table 5.1. However, analyses such as this are too simplistic. Important cash flow items which do *not* change with the rate of inflation have been omitted. Also we must ask whether the Fisher Effect is an accurate description of the relationship between changes in interest rates, inflation, and required rates of return.

In a recent paper, Fama (1974) tested whether the market for 1- to 6-month U.S. Treasury Bills, during the period 1953–71 correctly used all information about future rates of inflation. He concluded that

> there are definite relationships between nominal interest rates and the rates of inflation subsequently observed. Moreover, during this period, the bill market seems to be efficient in the sense that nominal interest rates summarise all the information about future inflation rates that is in . . . past inflation rates.

He also suggested that evidence implying contrary conclusions is based on earlier periods, when the market might have been less efficient, and when only poor data was available.

Many observers believe that recently the real rate of interest has been negative. Negative real rates of interest are not likely to persist unless there are low levels of investment. Negative real rates of interest imply that consumers are unwilling to bring forward consumption and capital investment even when a delay means losses in real terms. However, for purposes of our analysis we shall assume that the real rate of interest is positive and equal to 1 per cent. Historically, the real rate of interest in the U.K. has averaged about 0 per cent and in the U.S. about the same. In order to isolate the effect of other changes, we shall assume that the Fisher Effect is the best available approximation to the relationship between inflation and interest rates.

INFLATION AND CAPITAL ALLOWANCES

As mentioned earlier, our example in Table 5.2 was too simplistic. Important cash flow items were omitted which do not change proportionately with the rate of inflation. Table 5.3 illustrates the same project with some missing items supplied. Note that the £3 million investment is now divided between Building, Plant and Machinery, and Stock. Additional entries include adjustments to Corporation Tax due to capital allowances on the building and on the plant and machinery. Further

Table 5.3. Cash flow items including effects on Corporation Tax of capital allowances and stock

Cash flow item	0	1	End of year 2 (£'000)	3	...
Net revenues*		660	726	799	...
Corporation Tax			−330	−363	...
Building	−1000				
Effect of Capital allowances on Corporation Tax at 50 per cent		270	20	20	...
Plant and Machinery	−1000				
Effect of capital allowances on Corporation Tax at 50 per cent		500			
Stock*	−1000				
Corporation Tax on FIFO stock gains		0	−50	−55	...
Stock relief		615	1	0	...
Total	−3000	2045	367	401	...

*Increases in the money value of replaced stock are automatically included in inflated Net Revenues.

adjustments are also made for taxation of stock gains and for stock relief. We shall consider each of these items in turn. First, let us examine in more detail the effect of capital allowances under inflation.

In Table 5.4 we show the effect of the capital allowance for industrial

Table 5.4. Investment in industrial building and tax effect of capital allowances

Cash flow item	0	1	2	Year ending 3 (£'000)	...	12	13
Building	−1000						
Tax effect* of capital allowances at 50 per cent Corporation Tax		+270	+20	+20	...	+20	+10

*Capital allowances on industrial building currently are 54 per cent in the first year and 4 per cent thereafter cumulatively to 100 per cent. These allowances have been used to reduce Corporation Tax at 50 per cent.

buildings on Corporation Tax over a 13-year period. The capital allowance on an industrial building is 54 per cent of its cost in the first year and 4 per cent each year for the following 11 years and 2 per cent in the twelfth year. Thus the first-year allowance on a £1 million building is £540 000 and the second-year allowance is £40 000. Set against taxable profits in the company, the capital allowance of £540 000 will save £270 000 in taxes and the £40 000 allowance will save £20 000 (if we use 50 per cent as the rate of Corporation Tax).

Since capital allowances are based on initial costs, they do not change at all with changes in the expected rate of inflation. Thus if changes in the expected rate of inflation result in changes in interest rates and required rates of return, the Present Value of the tax effect of the capital allowance will change as a result. In Table 5.5 we show the effect of changes in the discount rate on the Present Value of the tax benefits on the capital allowance on an industrial building. As the discount rate is changed from 0 to 25 per cent, the Present Value of the tax benefit falls from £500 000 to £275 000. The Net Present Value cost of the building rises from £500 000 to £725 000. Obviously, if increases in the expected rate of inflation increase interest rates and discount rates, the Net Present Value of the project will fall in real terms. The reason is that capital allowances are not indexed with the inflation rate.

Now let us consider the 100 per cent initial allowance on the plant and machinery, which amounts to a tax saving of £500 000 occurring with a delay of between 9 and 21 months. Because of both this delay and the fact that the nominal value of the tax saving is also unaffected by inflation, the Present Value of the tax effect changes if the discount rate varies with the rate of inflation. The effect of inflation on the Present Value is less in this case than for an industrial building because of the smaller time lag. If, however, the company is not currently in a tax-paying position, the capital allowance will result in 'taxable losses' which can be carried forward. The tax

Table 5.5.

Discount rate (per cent)	Present Value of tax effect at 50 per cent Corporation Tax (£'000)	Net Present Value of cost of building (£'000)
0	+500.00	−500.00
1	+481.41	−518.59
5	+420.66	−579.34
10	+366.44	−633.56
15	+327.43	−672.57
20	+298.05	−701.95
25	+275.05	−724.95

effect of the capital allowance may be delayed for several years until the company is again in a tax-paying position. This added delay will reduce the Present Value of the tax benefit of capital allowances and will also make the Present Value more sensitive to changes in the discount rate which result from changes in the expected rate of inflation.

INFLATION AND INVESTMENT IN STOCK

U.K. taxation has been levied on profits based on the value of stock on a first-in first-out (FIFO) basis, as illustrated in Table 5.6. This method of taxation has the effect of taxing the increase in the value of stock due to inflation whether or not the stock has to be replaced at a correspondingly higher price. Clearly, if items of stock are bought in one period and then sold in a later period when prices are higher because of inflation, there is a taxable gain under FIFO. If the stock is not replaced, there is a strong argument in favour of taxing the gain. However, under FIFO, the tax must be paid even if the company must replace the stock at a much higher cost. Thus companies have found themselves paying taxes on stock gains which were not being realized in practice after allowing for reinvestment in stock.

In our example, the company has invested £1 million in stock. Inflation is forecast at 10 per cent (compound). In the first year the stock gain is £100 000 and in the second year the stock gain rises to £110 000 because the initial value of the stock changes with inflation. The resulting taxes, paid with a time lag, are shown in Table 5.6.

In Table 5.7 we treat the investment in stock as though it were an investment project. An investment in stock of £1 million results in tax

Table 5.6. Corporation Tax on stock gains under FIFO

| | End of year | | | | |
| | 0 | 1 | 2 | 3 | ... |
			(£'000)		
Value at end of period	1000	1100	1210	1331	...
Value at beginning of period		1000	1100	1210	...
FIFO stock gain		100	110	121	...
Corporation Tax* at 50 per cent			−50	−55	−60.5

A constant physical volume of stock is assumed.
*A one-year lag in payment of Corporation Tax is assumed.

Table 5.7. Cash flows associated with investment in stock with inflation at 10 per cent without stock relief

	End of year				
	0	1	2	3	...
				(£'000)	
Investment in stock	−1000				
Corporation Tax at 50 per cent on stock gain		0	−50	−55	−60.5 ...
Total	−1000	0	−50	−55	−60.5 ...

payments rising from £50 000 starting in the second year due to FIFO and inflation at 10 per cent. There are no positive cash flows since in our example the stock is being replaced as it is sold, in perpetuity.

How important is this 'tax leakage' due to FIFO under inflation? In Table 5.8 we compute the Present Value of the investment in stock at a variety of discount rates. If the discount rate does not exceed the rate of inflation, the Present Value cost of stock becomes infinite! However, if we accept the Fisher Effect, discount rates would exceed the rate of inflation at positive real rates of interest even for risk free projects. Still higher discount rates will prevail for risky projects. Nevertheless, at all discount rates considered, the Net Present Value of investment in stock is substantially above the original cost under FIFO taxation. For this reason, companies in the U.S.A. have increasingly elected to be taxed under the last-in-first-out (LIFO) stock valuation rule, a practice not now permitted in the U.K. Under LIFO, taxes on stock gains are paid in full but only when the stock is no longer being replaced.

It is evident that at high rates of inflation investment in stock-intensive projects will be discouraged. One should recognize that a minimum stock of raw materials and work in progress is required to keep most manufacturing processes going. For much of manufacturing industry, the level of stock becomes relatively insensitive to changes in the rate of inflation and interest rates for the life of the particular project or process. Although the adverse effect of taxation on stock gains may not be sufficient to justify abandonment of an existing project, project profitability will be affected adversely when the rate of inflation exceeds the rate which had been expected.

Because the tax effects of inflation under FIFO on stock gains were causing liquidity problems for many companies and discouraging investment, the Government introduced 'Stock Relief' in late 1974. The purpose of Stock Relief was to ease the burden of taxation of stock gains under FIFO without actually changing this method of taxation.

Table 5.8.

Discount rate (per cent)	Present Value of tax effect (£)	Net Present Value of investment in stock (£)
10	$-\infty$	$-\infty$
11	-4545	-5545
15	-909	-1909
20	-455	-1455
25	-303	-1303

Stock Relief provides an adjustment to Corporation Tax whenever the monetary value of the firm's total investment in stock changes. Thus, if the company increases the physical quantity of stock which it holds at the same cost or replaces stock at a higher cost, Corporation Taxes may be reduced. Stock Relief is equal to the change in the value of stock held *minus* 15 per cent of trading profits (net of capital allowances and interest payments). Because the incremental effect of a project on capital allowances and trading profits of a company can be extremely uneven, it is difficult to generalize whether Stock Relief fully offsets the adverse effect of FIFO taxation of stock gains under inflation in particular instances.

A calculation of Stock Relief for our example, together with assumptions, is given in Appendix 5.1. The results are entered in Table 5.9, which shows how Table 5.7 must be adjusted for Stock Relief. Because of the incremental effect of increased stock Relief on net trading profits in year 0, a very large reduction in Corporation Tax of £615 000 results in year 1. In this particular instance, Stock Relief is negligible after year 1 at 10 per cent inflation.

In Table 5.10 we have calculated the Net Present Value of investment in stock for our project under a variety of discount rates. At relatively high discount rates (above 20 per cent) the present value of the net tax effect of

Table 5.9. Stock: effect on Corporation Tax under FIFO with Stock Relief and inflation at 10 per cent

	\	\	End of year		
	0	1	2	3	...
			(£'000)		
Investment stock	-1000				
Corporation Tax under FIFO		0	-50.0	-55.0	60.5 ...
Stock Relief		615	1	0	0
Total	-1000	$+615$	-49	-55	-60.5 ...

Table 5.10.

Discount rate (per cent)	Present Value of tax effect (£)	Net Present Value of investment in stock (£)
10	$-\infty$	$-\infty$
11	-3990	-4990
15	$-\ 373$	-1373
20	$+\ \ 58$	$-\ 942$
25	$+\ 210$	$-\ 790$

stock appreciation and Stock Relief is seen to be positive with inflation at 10 per cent. However, for a less risky project with lower discount rates, the tax effect of stock appreciation is still unfavourable despite Stock Relief. Although Stock Relief measures obviously reduce the adverse tax effects of inflation on stock-intensive projects, the benefit appears greatest for high-risk (high-discount-rate) projects.

INFLATION AND RESIDUAL VALUES

Our example presented in Table 5.3 treats the investment as a perpetuity. Most projects have a finite economic life because of, for example, competition, deterioration, and obsolescence. Machinery must be replaced eventually and buildings may be sold for other uses. Inflation will affect the projected residual values of assets, including working capital, and any anticipated taxes resulting from eventual liquidation should be included in the cash flow forecast together with residual values.

If an asset is sold, Corporation Tax and in some cases Capital Gains Tax may be payable. If a 100 per cent initial allowance had been claimed on a £10 000 machine to reduce taxes and the machine is later sold for £2000, these proceeds are taxable at the prevailing rate of Corporation Tax. Note that if one expects to sell the machine in 5 years' time for £2000 at today's prices, the forecast price should be inflated for purposes of analysis.

To take a more complex example, consider the building initially worth £1 million. In 5 years' time, capital allowances worth 70 per cent of this figure will have been taken. Thus if the building is sold for more than 30 per cent of its original value, Corporation Tax is payable on the difference. Under conditions of inflation, one may expect the building to sell for more than its original value. In this case, one should forecast a payment of Corporation Tax on the full amount of the capital allowance already taken plus Capital Gains Tax on any gain in excess of the original cost of the assets after allowable transactions costs.

We have shown that, because of the methods of assessing Corporation Tax in the U.K., unexpected changes in the rate of inflation can change the profitability of capital projects. Less often considered is the fact that the structure of personal taxation can also affect the profitability of capital projects when there are unexpected changes in the rate of inflation. In the following section we will discuss this problem.

INCOME AND WEALTH EFFECTS

A change in the *general* level of prices due to inflation should not alter the balance of consumer expenditure between different goods and services. However, in a progressive income tax system, inflation will change the marginal rates of tax paid by individuals. If inflation were to affect pre-tax incomes and prices uniformly, some consumers would be worse off as they moved into higher tax brackets. They would, as a consequence, alter their consumption patterns. The resulting shifts in demand for different goods and services will have varying effects on project revenues depending on the responsiveness of prices and costs to these shifts in demand.

An income effect may also be present if some consumer groups such as pensioners live on fixed incomes that are unrelated, or react slowly, to changes in the rate of inflation. Such forms of income redistribution which take place as a consequence of a change in the rate of inflation will alter the demand pattern for goods and services and, therefore, have different effects on the revenues of specific capital investments in real terms.

Inflation may also change wealth levels and the distribution of wealth. For example, unexpectedly high inflation levels lead to unexpectedly high interest rates and to a fall in the value of bond prices. If you like, bond holders lose when inflation increases beyond that anticipated. In contrast, borrowers who have fixed-interest loans gain. Rising inflation may also induce Government controls on prices and profits, thereby affecting the value of risky assets (e.g. security prices). It is probable that significant shifts in wealth will occur and thus alter demand and consumption patterns. For some products, wealth effects may be an even more important influence on demand patterns than income effects.

MONEY TERMS OR REAL TERMS

It is often assumed that calculations performed in real terms avoid the necessity to project future costs and prices and therefore avoid forecasts of the rate of inflation. This view is mistaken since the real rate of return must be used in the discount rate, and to estimate the real rate requires a forecast of the expected rate of inflation. In addition; capital allowances, which are fixed in nominal terms, must be deflated by the expected rate of inflation. Thus, it is not possible to avoid the problem of forecasting general and specific price changes.

Inflation provides capital gains on fixed and current assets; in order to estimate the taxes payable, the computations must be made in the money of the day. In addition, particular components of the cash flow calculations, e.g. capital allowances, may be fixed in nominal terms, and therefore should be treated separately.

The forecast rate of inflation for the economy may have implications for the Gross Domestic Product and for industry growth in real terms. Thus an assumption about the future rate of inflation is an important input to the project cash flow forecast affecting not only prices, but volume as well. In an environment of Government controls over pricing and profitability, this warning is already self-evident.

Usually, one should use the forecast of inflation underlying interest rates when estimating expected future cash flows for a project.

Because of relatively high rates of savings or low rates of capital investment in the economy, or because of direct Government intervention in the bond market, interest rates may deviate temporarily from those which might be expected with the Fisher effect. Under such conditions it is more difficult to derive inflationary expectations from interest rates.

Let us suppose we were analysing a 15-year project and, given an expected rate of inflation, we find that there is a negative real rate of interest. It would be wise to assume that this real rate will not continue for long. In the past, in the U.K. and the U.S., real rates of interest have mostly been between 0 and 1 per cent. Presumably, interest rates will begin to reflect expected positive real interest rates eventually.

The relationship between interest rates and expected rates of inflation is important. The analyst must ensure that the inflation forecasts he uses in projecting each flow are consistent with those assumed by the market in setting interest rates. It would be inconsistent to use an inflation rate which is different from that expected by the market, and then to accept current interest rates when choosing a discount rate. For example, if one is forecasting a rate of inflation of 15 per cent when current interest rates imply a rate of inflation of only 10 per cent, then it may be necessary to add the 5 per cent (pre-tax) to the current capital market required rate of return when determining a suitable discount rate.

INFLATION AND THE RISK PREMIUM

The required rate of return or discount rate for a capital project can be estimated by adding a premium for project risk to the risk-free rate of interest as described in more detail in Chapter 8. We have already shown how interest rates are affected by changes in the rate of inflation. Uncertainty about future rates of inflation can affect not only interest rates but cash flows. Consequently, the riskiness of projects vulnerable to the

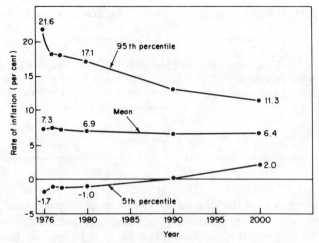

Figure 5.1. Inflation. Simulated distributions of the geometric annaul rates in the U.S.A. for the period
1976–2000. After Ibbotson and Sinquefield (1976)

effects of inflation will be determined in part by uncertainty about future
rates of inflation in the economy.

If inflation should turn out to be much higher than expected, then the
Gross Domestic Product may suffer in real terms, industrial growth may be
hit, and project profitability may fall below expectations. If inflation should
fall well below expectations, project profitability may be enhanced.

Ibbotson and Sinquefield (1976) demonstrated a method of establishing
a range of inflation forecasts implied by interest rates (Figure 5.1). They
forecast a mean annual rate of inflation for the U.S.A. of 7.3 per cent for
the period 1976–80, declining in 1980 to 6.9 per cent. In addition, they
estimated that there was a 5 per cent probability that annual inflation
during this period would be as low as −1 per cent or as high as 17.1 per
cent. They provided a probability distribution of inflation rates which can
be useful to the corporate planner and analyst.

For the analyst, the question arises as to the short- and long-term impact
of different inflation rates on the economy since under particular
circumstances one may assume that the Gross Domestic Product and
corporate profits will be affected by different inflation rates. In Table 5.11
we show an example of some scenarios relating inflation, growth, and
revenues for a project. Clearly, such estimates should be based on a detailed
economic and market analysis.

INFLATION AND BORROWING

One often hears from financial managers how cheap it is to borrow in an
inflationary period. What do such statements imply about the competitive

74

Table 5.11. Inflation rates, growth in the economy, and project profitability

Inflation rate (per cent)	Change in Gross Domestic Product (per cent)	Change in industry demand (per cent)	Net revenue of the project (£ million million)
10	4	8	1
15	2	4	0.2
20	0	−2	−0.6

state of the money market and the expectations of borrowers and lenders? If interest rates reflect inflationary expectations, then only unexpected changes in the inflation rate will benefit a borrower or lender. The borrower gains if inflation is greater than that expected when the loan was taken out. The lender will gain if the inflation rate is lower than expected. Thus one should understand the critical difference between expected and unexpected rates of inflation.

Of course, we are assuming in the above proposition that the loan is taken out at fixed rates of interest. If the loan were based on the current interest rates ruling (i.e. variable interest rate loan), the reduced risk to lenders from unanticipated changes in inflation would presumably be reflected in the loan interest rate. In addition, neither borrower nor lender would gain or lose from interest rate variations.

Suppose interest rates do not reflect inflationary expectations? Before we can answer this question we must ask why they would not do so. If lenders are simply slow-witted and cannot forecast inflation rates in an unbiased way, then borrowers may gain. However, it is unlikely that lenders are systematically less intelligent than borrowers. Another reason might be Government intervention in the market. However, it is difficult to see how the Government can impose biased interest rates for very long or by very large amounts. Any observer of interest rates during the period 1975–77 will have noticed that interest rates were consistently below the expected rate of inflation; that is, the real rate of interest was negative. Under these conditions, sensible consumers would tend to borrow more and bring forward consumption. Such borrowing and purchasing would go on until interest rates rise. Then why did real interest remain negative for so long? There are two possible explanations. The first is that the economic outlook was so uncertain that individuals and companies preferred to hold cash; that is, there was a strong desire for liquidity. The second possible reason was that with Government trying to hold the exchange rate below a competitive level, foreign money poured into the domestic money market and lowered and interest rate. (Domestic money was kept in the country by rigorous exchange controls.) How long such a state can last is difficult to say. However, in a reasonably competitive and 'open' economy it is unlikely to last very long.

What does such an analysis imply for the financial manager? It is not inflation that brings a gain to borrowers or lenders but *unexpected* changes in the rate. Second, the decision to take out a fixed interest loan exposes the borrower to a risk that inflation and interest rates will fall. Finally, since negative real interest rates should not persist too long in an open economy such as the U.K. it would be wise in a project appraisal to make this assumption.

CONCLUSIONS

Even when competitive markets are assumed, we have shown that a change in the expected rate of inflation can affect corporate profitability in real terms as a result of personal and corporate taxation being levied on a nominal basis. Management which ignores the income and wealth effects of inflation on consumer spending will make incorrect forecasts of product revenues for capital projects. Corporation Tax based on the FIFO stock valuation method will reduce profitability in real terms under inflation as a result of tax leakages unless off-setting Stock Relief provisions are granted. Without stock relief, management's ability to restore profitability through price increases would depend upon the elasticities of demand for its products. However, since prices on products requiring investment in stock have to increase at a greater rate than the prices of other goods (or services) requiring less stock, it would be surprising if real profitability were unaffected.

It should be clear that project cash flows must be estimated in nominal terms because the Corporation Tax system is not indexed. Also, estimates of the effects of differential rates of inflation and price controls on product inputs and outputs require forecasts in nominal terms. Even if it is thought desirable to deflate these forecasts into real terms, the problem of assessing the expected rates of inflation reflected by the market in interest rates cannot be avoided.

REFERENCES AND BIBLIOGRAPHY

Bromwich, M., 'Inflation and the Capital Budgeting Process', *Journal of Business Finance*, **1**, 39–46, Autumn, 1969.

Carsberg, B. and Hope, A., *Business Investment Decisions under Inflation*, The Institute of Chartered Accountants in England and Wales, London, 1976.

Fama, E. F., 'Short Term Interest Rates as Predictions of Inflation', unpublished working paper, Sep. 1974.

Fisher, I., *The Theory of Interest*, Macmillan, New York, 1930.

Franks, J. R. and Broyles, J. E., 'Inflation and the Investment Decision', in *Inflation: A Management Guide to Company Survival* (C. West, ed.), Associated Business Programmes, London, 1976, pp. 114–126.

Hicks, J. R., 'Inflation and Interest Rates', Banca Nazionale de Lavoro, 1974.

Ibbotson, R. G. and Sinquefield, R. A., 'Stocks, Bonds, Bills and Inflation', Special issue on Simulations of the Future (1976–2000) *Journal of Business*, **49**, 313–338, July 1976.

Mundell, R., 'Inflation and Real Interest', *Journal of Political Economy*, **71**, 280–283, June 1963.

Roll, R., 'Interest Rates on Monetary Assets and Commodity Price Index Changes', *Journal of Finance*, **27**, 251–278, May 1972.

Definitions

Net revenue	= Current sales – Current expenses – Costs of stock replaced
Stock gain on goods sold	= Difference between stock costs on FIFO basis and replacement basis
Trading income	= Current sales – Current expenses (excluding stock replacement) – FIFO cost of stock used
Therefore: trading income	= Net revenue + stock gain

Assumptions

This analysis looks at the incremental effect of the project assuming:

(a) the company is in a tax-paying position and can utilize all of its capital allowances and tax savings;

(b) the company is in a net stock profit relief position in all years of the project:

(c) the project is an incremental activity in an ongoing business. If this were not the case and, for example, a new subsidiary were set up to operate the project, the initial purchase of stock would be treated differently by the Inland Revenue.

REVIEW QUESTIONS

1. Describe the 'Fisher Effect'. What is the relevance of the Fisher Effect to Discounted Cash Flow methods?

2. Under what circumstances would you expect real rates of interest to be similar in different countries?

3. Why would you expect changing rates of inflation to affect project profitability? Why would the effects differ from one industry to another?

4. What is the impact of unexpected changes in the rate of inflation on:

   (a) fixed interest rate borrowing?
   (b) variable interest rate borrowing?

Appendix 5.1. Tax effect of Stock Relief as anticipated in April 1978

| | End of Year | | | | | |
| | (£'000) | | | | | |
	0	1	2	...	13	14
Net Revenues	0	660	726	...	2071.36	2278.50
Stock gain on goods sold		100	110	...	313.84	345.23
Trading income	0	760	836	...	2385.20	2623.73
Interest		− 66	− 66	...	− 66	− 66
Capital allowances	−1540	− 40	− 40	...	− 20	0
Taxable trading income	−1540	654	730	...	2299	2558
Closing stock less opening stock	1000	100	110	...	313.84	345.23
Less 15 per cent taxable trading income	+ 231	− 98.1	− 109.5	...	− 344.85	− 383.7
Stock Relief	+1231	+ 1.9	+ 0.5	...	− 31.01	− 38.47
Tax effect of Stock Relief at 50 per cent	+615.5	+ 0.95	+ 0.25	...	− 15.5	−19.2

78

5. If companies were given an option to choose LIFO or FIFO as a stock valuation rule for tax purposes, under what conditions would they choose one or the other? Which method has the most neutral effect with regard to changes in the profitability of investment in stock intensive industry when there are unanticipated changes in the rate of inflation?

EXERCISES

1. If the expected rate of inflation is 8 per cent, and the real rate of interest is 2 per cent, what is the nominal interest rate?

2. The rate of interest is 12 per cent, the expected rate of inflation is 15 per cent, and the real rate of interest is 1 per cent. Explain carefully why you would not expect such conditions to prevail? How would equilibrium be restored?

3. A company invested £500 in stock for 5 years. The expected rate of inflation is 10 per cent and the nominal discount rate is 19 per cent. Using the following valuation rules, calculate the Present Value of the investment in stock under (a) FIFO, (b) LIFO.

4. An asset costing £1000 today is estimated to be worth only £100 after 5 years if there is no inflation. However, the expected rate of inflation is 8 per cent and the nominal interest rate is 9 per cent. What is the Present Value of the asset's residual value after tax at the end of 5 years if capital allowances are 20 per cent of the initial value per annum and Corporation Tax is 52 per cent?

6

CASH FLOW ANALYSIS: DEFINING A PROJECT AND ITS BENEFITS

We have examined alternative methods of analysing the profitability of proposed investment projects using some specific examples based upon the U.K. tax environment. Financial analysis is an essential feature of the management decision-making process. We would now like to discuss the way in which financial analysis fits into the decision process and to show how the actual definition of investment alternatives is critical to the approach which must be taken by the financial analyst.

THE INVESTMENT DECISION-MAKING PROCESS

Up to this point we have treated capital investment proposals as a set of opportunities to be evaluated by rational economic analysis. However, such proposals do not materialize easily and are frequently the product of a complex and subtle organizational process. One writer (King, 1975) has identified various stages in this process:

Triggering	Evaluation
Screening	Transmission
Definition	Decision

The triggering stage is that part of the process in which investment opportunities are first perceived. Ideas for new projects are often not put forward sufficiently quickly, possibly because the preparation of project proposals requires costly management inputs and may also entail personal political risks for project sponsors. Often, an investment opportunity is ignored until the need becomes obvious and when competing companies may have already taken the first steps.

In the screening stage, important decisions usually have to be made using crude criteria with readily available but limited information. Because project studies are often expensive in terms of the executive and staff resources required, the decision must be made as to which are worth further study. The danger is, of course, that worthy projects are eliminated on the basis of scanty information.

If the project merits further investigation, the definition stage is reached, during which the technical and economic characteristics of the project are chosen. Because of the limitations of time, manpower, and human ability, the information obtained may be inadequate. The alternatives actually considered will be few, and the choice for evaluation will be critical.

In the subsequent evaluation stage, project proposers will prepare economic analyses to justify choices already made at the triggering, screening, and definition stages. The tools of financial analyses such as Net Present Value, Internal Rate of Return, Payback Period, and Return on Investment will be marshalled in order to justify a choice between the few alternatives actually considered in detail.

At each successive stage, increasing commitment by some individuals to the project may be observed and there are often status costs and benefits for individuals when the project study, once initiated, is dropped or is continued to fruition. Thus project proposals can develop an organizational momentum and commitment which may overide objective analysis. Intentional bias in forecasting can arise and financial analyses may be manipulated for political ends.

In an hierarchical organization, the case for investment, depending on size and strategic importance, has to be transmitted upwards through the organization. Transmission begins at an early stage when informal soundings in the hierarchy are taken to verify whether such a project is likely to be accepted and whether a full investigation is worth initiating. Sponsors are sought who are well placed in the power structure so that, when the formal proposal is ready for transmission upwards, a smooth passage has been prepared. Informal transmission serves the constructive end of acquainting the proposers of current trends in managerial policy and planning in relation to the kind of investment activity being considered. Project proposers should be working in harmony with the broad thrust of corporate planning and purpose if the efforts involved are to be found acceptable. Transmission of the formal proposal documents serves as a summation and confirmation of previous communications regarding the project.

The final decision stage has, in a sense, been pre-empted by the preceding stages, where the real choices have already been made. The formal proposal often does not even present alternatives. The decision is a 'go or no go' choice regarding a project. Top management are often loath to reject proposals prepared by qualified staff at this stage except on current planning, policy, and strategic grounds. The formal decision is not entirely a 'rubber stamp' operation, however, since changes in planning, policy, or strategy may have altered the acceptability of the project. The decision stage also serves to formalize the commitment of those individuals who must carry the project through to completion and make it a success.

Thus, capital investment results from a lengthy organizational process in which the triggering, screening, and definition stages may be where the critical decisions are made. The problem of bias arising from personal commitment at these early stages is countered in many large organizations by use of project teams. Once a project is triggered, a multi-disciplinary team is appointed to screen, define, and evaluate alternatives. The decision to continue or to drop a study then becomes a more impersonal decision.

Project definition often turns on technological, marketing, and strategic considerations. Technology is so specific that it must remain outside the scope of a finance text. However, we shall indicate some facets of the interface between financial analysis and corporate strategy in the definition of capital projects.

DEFINING THE PROJECT

Whether or not a project will turn out to have been profitable will usually depend on one of three crucial factors: scarcity, market position, and unforeseen developments.

If we were to live in a world of perfect markets for all goods, available supplies would be matched virtually instantaneously to needs, and competition would put all factors of production on an equal footing. In such a world, all Net Present Values would approach zero as competition would drive returns down to a level equalling the cost of captial.

In the real world product markets cannot adjust instantaneously to needs. Thus Net Present Values derive from supplying demands left unfulfilled by imperfect markets. If investments are well-placed in markets characterized by scarcities which cannot immediately be filled by competition, then conditions for charging *economic rents*, i.e. prices which more than cover the cost of capital, will exist. Similarly if there are barriers to entry (e.g. due to technology or scale) which enable the firm to maintain a competitive advantage, rates of return in excess of those obtainable in the more competitive capital markets will exist. Capital project proposals that show large Net Present Values which cannot be justified on the basis of anticipated scarcity or competitive advantage are likely to include mistaken if not biased forecasts. Thus a capital project proposal should include an analysis of the competitive advantages which make the project profitable.

On a more detailed level, a number of questions need to be answered before a project is sufficiently well-defined for an adequate financial analysis. The following are typical of the kinds of questions that need to be asked:

(a) In which market segments is the company likely to maintain substantial market strength in relation to competitors?

(b) Will the project entail a unique cost or quality advantage not easily duplicated by competitors?

(c) Will demand exceed likely supply from all sources including substitutes during the early years of the project?

(d) What is the *range* of demand being projected for the relevant market segment in each period?

(e) What market share is conservatively projected for each period?

(f) What alternative capacity levels should be considered to meet this uncertain demand?

(g) How low might prices have to be to fill each alternative capacity level?

(h) At worst, what will each alternative level of capacity cost, and how long is it likely to take to install?

(i) Should capacity be built up in stages as means of resolving uncertainty?

(j) What would be the initial and subsequent operating costs for each alternative level of capacity?

(k) Will advances in technology subsequently reduce costs to potential competitors?

(l) In the light of the answers to these questions, how profitable can the project be expected to be?

(m) Will sufficient management and technical staff resources be available to manage the project profitably at the installation and operating stages? Can the required scarce resources be employed more profitably elsewhere?

DEFINING PROJECT COSTS AND BENEFITS

Those project costs and benefits which can be assigned cash values are susceptible to financial analysis. Other factors which cannot easily be assigned a value can be weighed qualitatively in conjunction with the financial analysis. If the project's NPV is not negative and the qualitative considerations are favourable, then the project can go ahead. If the NPV is negative, on the other hand, one has a measure of how much any net favourable qualitative benefits would have to be worth before the project may proceed. Suppose, for example, that the NPV is equal to −£10 000. We might not be able to measure the net qualitative benefits in cash terms precisely, but may with some conviction believe that these benefits exceed

£10 000 in value to the firm. Examples of such benefits often fall into the categories of industrial relations, public relations, and environmental protection. Also involved are those commercial and strategic factors which are too subtle or complex to be analysed within the time available.

There are other factors which can easily be assigned a value but which are frequently omitted on the grounds that they are 'not cash flows'. An oil company proposed to build a refinery on land which it already owned but which had a market value of £10 million. The value of the land was omitted from the analysis on the grounds that the land was already owned, that it represented a 'sunk cost' and did not require an incremental investment. This approach is incorrect and has cost the company many millions of pounds over the years. No asset represents a sunk cost to the extent that it has a market value. The company is investing marketable land in the refinery project, and the land should be shown as an investment of £10 million in the analysis. If the market value of the land is too high for the refinery to be profitable, the company should consider selling the site and obtaining another site sufficiently low in cost to make refining profitable. The balance in cash can be invested in the capital market and in other projects. The alternative of being able to sell an asset and realize the cash and any tax benefits from the sale represents an *opportunity cost* which should be charged as one of the investment expenses associated with a project which pre-empts the sale of the asset.

Another item frequently omitted from the analysis is Working Capital, on the basis that it is not a fixed asset. Any new or enlarged activity which requires a net increase in Working Capital requires additional investment for this purpose. When the project is started up, the additional Working Capital required (including cash) should be shown as part of the initial investment. At the end of the project's economic life, when the Working Capital is expected to be realized, the resulting cash flow should be shown, taking into account the effect that inflation and taxes will have had on the net Working Capital investment.

The underlying principle involved in defining the cash flow benefits associated with a project is based on the concept of *net incremental cash flow*. In determining net incremental cash flow, one asks three questions:

(a) What would be the cash flows of the firm *with* the project?
(b) What would be the cash flows of the firm *without* the project?
(c) What is the net difference between the above two states of the world in each future period?

Often the term 'cash flow' is used loosely where 'net incremental cash flow' is intended. The net incremental approach implies that opportunity costs should be included as costs and that the cash value of marketable assets employed in the project should also be included.

CONTINGENT PROJECTS

Some projects cannot be undertaken independently of other assets. Such projects are called *contingent projects*. For example, investment in a new machine may be contingent on an annex being added to the factory. Investment in a contingent project should only take place if *both* of the following two questions can be answered affirmatively:

(a) Do the net incremental cash flows of the contingent project have a positive Net Present Value?
(b) Do the two projects, i.e. the contingent project and the project on which it depends, when taken together, have a positive Net Present Value?

Care must be exercised in the analysis of contingent projects, and it is important to realize that, except for completely new investments, most investment projects are contingent projects. If a project is contingent on other assets, then one must be satisfied that it would not be more profitable to abandon one or more of the other assets than to undertake the project. An example is the investment in conversion from steam to diesel engines on some railways, where a full analysis would have revealed that the most profitable action would have been to liquidate selected routes altogether. The net incremental cash flow concept does *not* imply that contingent projects can be analysed in isolation from any assets, activities, or other projects on which such projects depend.

COST REDUCTION PROJECTS

Once management has established that an activity is unlikely to be abandoned, they may wish to investigate projects intended to reduce operating expenses. Although such projects can be viewed in terms of minimizing the present value of costs, the analysis can be made more consistent if undertaken from the point of view of net incremental cash flow; that is, we ask what is the present prospect for cash flows throughout the firm and how these will change if the project is undertaken. For example, the introduction of new machinery may *bring forward* the sale of old machinery. Thus, under the continue-as-we-are scenario, the realization from the sale of existing machinery appears some years hence. Under the alternative accept-the-project scenario, the sale of the old machinery may appear earlier and perhaps at a higher value. In the net *incremental* cash flow, the sale of the existing machinery would appear twice, at different points in time and with opposite signs. Of course under both scenarios all tax effects, including the effects of balancing charges or allowances on the sale of machinery, should be included.

An example of such projects is the *make or buy decision*. Net incremental cash flows for the make or buy decision are based on a comparison of two states of the world:

(a) cash flows expected if we *buy*;
(b) cash flows expected if we *buy*;

In common with other cost-reducing projects, the decision to buy often implies bringing forward the sale of machinery. Consideration of other effects—such as provision of space and other costs of carrying additional stock—may be necessary. Make or buy decisions require careful consideration of the qualitative and strategic factors. How is it that the supplier can make the item more cheaply than we can? Would it be profitable for us to buy machinery like theirs? Will they want to renegotiate the price in the future? Are they the best suppliers? Will adequate quality be maintained? Might they let us down? Might we need to keep existing machinery in reserve?

Subcontracting offers an added flexibility during business downturns. The scale of one's own operations can more easily be reduced by simply reducing purchases. Obviously, the Present Value of net incremental cash flows for 'buy' versus 'make' must be compared to the net qualitative and strategic costs and benefits before a decision can be taken.

DETERMINING THE ECONOMIC LIFE OF THE PROJECT

An asset may be technically capable of carrying on its intended activity at a satisfactory standard for many years. This operational life is often mistakenly used as the life of the asset for purposes of financial analysis. Given the increasing costs over time of operating the asset, it would be better to ask what is the *profitable* operating life of the asset? At some point before the end of its operational life, it may be better to sell or scrap the asset. Thus the economic life will usually be shorter than the operational life of an asset.

If the asset is specific to a particular product or product group, then the product life may determine the economic life of the asset. As product volume declines towards the end of the product's life, fewer resources will be required and assets can be expected progressively to be sold or scrapped if not turned to other uses within the firm. Product life can often be expected to be shorter than the operational lives of the specialized assets required and may be the determining factor in the economic life of the asset.

Similarly, if a project is contingent on the continued operation of one or more other assets, the economic life of the project will be determined by them. The shortest economic life among these assets may place an upper limit on the economic life of the project.

If an asset is not specialized to one product and is not contingent on the continued operation of other assets or activities, then the economic life is more likely to be determined by the replacement decision. At what point in time do we expect to find it most profitable to replace the asset with something newer or better?

Thus the economic life of a project will be determined by the shortest of the following lives:

(a) profitable operating life;
(b) economic life of assets or activities on which the project is contingent;
(c) optimum replacement period.

Clearly, the estimation of the economic life of a project requires a great deal more care than has been commonly suggested.

THE OPTIMAL REPLACEMENT PERIOD

The economic life of an asset is often determined by the optimal replacement cycle. Replacement analysis is based upon a comparison between the rising maintenance costs of ageing capital equipment and the lower costs resulting from new technology built into new capital goods.

What will be the replacement period for a new machine, for example? If we ignore inflation and changes in technology, we can assume that old machines will be replaced by identical new machines in a perpetual chain. The replacement cycle may repeat every 1, 2, or more years. The optimum cycle determines the *maximum* expected economic life since new technology or other factors discussed earlier could make the cycle shorter. The optimum cycle is that which results in the lowest Present Value of costs for the perpetual chain.

In Table 6.1 we have an example of a machine being replaced by another like it after 2 years. In Table 6.2 the machine is replaced after 3 years and in Table 6.3 it is replaced after 4 years. Which replacement cycle is optimum? The Present Value of costs in each successive table is greater because the assumed life is longer and thus encompasses more periods in

Table 6.1. Net of tax costs and scrap value after 2 years

	0	1	2	3	4
Investment	£1000				
Operating costs		£200	£300		
Scrap value			(£200)		
Present Value at 10 per cent	£1264				

Table 6.2. Net of tax costs and scrap value after 3 years

	0	1	2	3	4
Investment	£1000				
Operating costs		£200	£300	£400	
Scrap value				(£100)	
Present Value at 10 per cent	£1655				

Table 6.3. Net of tax costs and scrap value after 4 years

	0	1	2	3	4
Investment	£1000				
Operating costs		£200	£300	£400	£ 650
Scrap value					(£ 50)
Present Value at 10 per cent	£2140				

which there are costs. Thus the tables are not comparable. The tables can be made comparable if they are each converted to an equivalent perpetuity. We can then compare the equivalent annual costs on this basis.

In Table 6.1, the Present Value of costs is £1264 and the life is 2 years. The equivalent annual cost is given by

$$C_2 = \frac{PV}{A_{2,R}} = \frac{1264}{1.736} = 728,$$

where $A_{2,R}$ is the two-year annuity factor at the required rate of return $R = 0.10$. The equivalent annual costs for Tables 6.2 and 6.3 are $C_3 = 666$ and $C_4 = 675$, respectively. Since C_3 is the lowest equivalent annual cost, we know that a 3-year replacement cycle is optimum (to the nearest year) for identical machinery. However, the above analysis assumes identical cash flows in each replacement period; that is, inflation and new technology have not been considered.

Suppose that costs are expected to be influenced by inflation at a compound rate g. However, let us also suppose that technological change will reduce costs at the rate k per year in real terms. These technological improvements are enjoyed only when the old machinery is replaced, while the effects of inflation are felt in every period. The equivalent annual costs adjusted for inflation and technological change can be compared on the basis of the following formula derived in Appendix 6.1:

$$C_T = \frac{PV_0}{A^*_{T,R}}$$

where C_T is the equivalent annual cost for replacement every T years, PV_0 is the Present Value of operating cost cash flow for the first T years, and the $A_{T,R}^*$ is the annuity factor for replacement period of T years adjusted for inflation and technological improvement, i.e.

$$A_{T,R}^* = (1 - f^T)/R,$$

where $f = (1 + g)(1 - k)/(1 + R)$, R is the required rate of return, g is the rate of inflation per year, and k is the rate of reduction of (real) operating costs per year due to technological change. That value of T which minimizes equivalent annual cost in this formula provides an estimate of the replacement period for the investment.

The above analysis concerns cost minimization. However, in similar manner, we can determine an equivalent annual net cash flow by dividing the *Net* Present Value for a capital project by the T period annuity factor. If replacement is certain, then the economic life will be that value of T which *maximizes* equivalent annual net cash flow.

COMPARING PROJECTS

Financial analysis of capital investments should always involve a comparison between an investment in the project and an investment in the capital market at the same risk. This comparison is implied by the choice of discount rate in the Net Present Value calculation. How does one compare mutually exclusive projects? The obvious answer is to compare their Net Present Values. The largest NPV is the most favourable to the shareholders and adds most to the value of the company. In other words, we answer the question, 'Which project makes the most favourable comparison with the capital market?' If we are comparing any number of alternatives, there is little difficulty because all can be compared to the same base case, the capital market.

In practice this means that all resources required for the project must be treated as investment expenditures to the extent that they could be used to raise cash. Otherwise the full comparison with alternative investment in the capital market would not be complete.

Some companies prefer to compare one project with another. In this way resources which are common to both alternatives can be ignored. There are a number of serious objections to this procedure. It is indeed possible to select the best of two alternatives in this manner if both involve the same risks and require the same discount rate. However, incremental comparisons of this nature will not reveal whether either is profitable since direct comparisons to the capital market are no longer being made. One may not be determining which project is most profitable, but merely which is least unprofitable. Also, if two or more alternatives involve different risks, they are not directly comparable since they require different discount rates. Each must first be compared to the capital market and the following questions answered: 'Are any of the alternatives profitable?' 'Which of the profitable alternatives has the largest Net Present Value?' Whether comparisons are between mutually exclusive choices or between projects which are independent of one another, the procedure always should be based on a comparison with the alternative for all projects, that is investment in the Capital Market.

THE ABANDONMENT DECISION

Knowing when to liquidate a project can be as important as knowing when to invest. A project may be undertaken in the light of expectations which do not fully materialize. Given subsequent developments and with the benefit of hindsight, management may wish that they had not decided to proceed with the investment. However, this will not usually mean that the time has come for abandonment. The resale or liquidation value of the typical project is so much less than the original investment that immediate abandonment may not be profitable. The analysis of abandonment follows the same principles as any other investment analysis. Two questions must be asked:

(a) What is the Present Value of after-tax cash value of benefits which will continue if we do not abandon?
(b) How do these compare with the cash that could be realized after tax from liquidation?

The realizable cash from disposal of the assets represents the effective investment in the proposal 'not to abandon'.

The abandonment decision is rather more important than is often supposed, since most capital investments which are made, unless they involve the start up of some entirely new activity, are contingent on the continuation of an existing activity of which the project is intended to be a part.

Production engineers in a company showed that large marginal benefits were obtainable by investment in specialized machinery. However, the product in question was no longer profitable and the proposed marginal improvements, though substantial in relation to the cost of machinery, were insufficient to make the product profitable. Furthermore, no cumulative set of further improvements were foreseen which could make the product profitable. Obviously, the real question at hand was not whether to invest in better machinery but when to abandon the product.

In principle, no further investments should be considered in existing activities until one has established that abandonment is unlikely in the foreseeable future. Abandonment of major activities often takes some years to accomplish. The problem for the financial analyst is to aid in determining how the various phases of abandonment can take place most profitably. If the assets are not readily saleable, then it may be prudent to 'milk' the operation for cash over some extended period. Thus revenues are maximized by whatever short-term marketing measures are appropriate while cash expenditures, for example on new machinery and maintenance, are strictly budgeted in accordance with the overall plan for phasing out the operation. In this way the Net Present Value of the phasing-out operation can often be made to exceed the Net Present Values of either continuing a normal operation or of immediate liquidation.

CONCLUSIONS

Capital investment is an important aspect of the activities of operational management. Financial managers have an important role to play in helping to define project alternatives and in estimating profitability in an objective manner. Projects emerge as a part of the organizational decision-making process and are subject to the same human influences as other management activities. Project analysis requires professional skills which tend to be concentrated in the financial departments of the company. These skills are most essential in defining alternatives, identifying relevant cash flows and opportunity costs, and in making the appropriate comparisons with the capital market. Thus organizational means are required to ensure that qualified staff make constructive contributions, particularly at the triggering, screening, and definition stages. Finally, it is a primary responsibility of financial managers to ensure that capital investment activities are objectively analysed in the light of shareholder interests as managers in other functional areas are often less sensitive to their obligations in this regard.

REFERENCES AND BIBLIOGRAPHY

Aiken, M. and Hage, J., 'The Organic Organisation and Innovation', *Sociology*, **5** (1), 63–82 Jan. 1971.

Bierman, H. and Smidt, S., *The Capital Budgeting Decision*, Collier–Macmillan, New York, 1975.

Bower, J. L., *Managing the Resource Allocation Process*, Harvard University Press, Cambridge, Mass., 1976.

Braybrooke, D. and Lindblom, C. E., *A Strategy of Decision*, The Free Press, New York, 1963.

Carter, E., 'Behavioural Theory of the Firm and Top-Level Corporate Decisions', *Administrative Science Quarterly*, **16**, 413–428, Dec. 1971.

Franks, J. R. and Scholefield, H., *Corporate Financial Management*, 2nd ed., Gower Press, London, 1977.

Haynes, W. W. and Solomon, M. B., Jr, 'A Misplaced Emphasis in Capital Budgeting', *Quarterly Review of Economics and Business*, 39–46, Feb. 1962.

Hertz, D. B. 'Investment Policies that Pay Off', *Harvard Business Review*, **46**, 96–108. Jan.–Feb. 1968.

Johnson, R. W. *Capital Budgeting*, Wadsworth, Belmont, Calif. 1970.
King, P. F., 'Is the Emphasis of Capital Budgeting Theory Misplaced?' *Journal of Business Finance and Accounting*, **2**(1), 69–82, Spring 1975.
March, J. and Simon, H. A., *Organisations*, John Wiley, New York, 1958.
Pettigrew, A. M., *The Politics of Organisational Decision-Making*, Tavistock Publications, London, 1973.
Shon, D. A., *Invention and the Evolution of Ideas*, Tavistock Publications, London, 1963.
Simon, H., 'Theories of Decision-making in Economics and Behavioral Science', *American Economic Review*, **49**, 253–283, 1959.

Appendix 6.1. Equivalent annual cash flow of a replacement chain

A project is replaced every T years. The Present Value of the project for the first T years is PV_0. The Present Value of the replacement project T years hence will be

$$PV_T = PV_0(1 + g)^T (1 - k)^T \tag{1}$$

where g is the annual rate of inflation and k is the annual rate of (real) cost reduction due to technological change. The Present Value of the replacement chain is given by

$$PV = PV_0 + \frac{PV_T}{(1 + R)^T} + \frac{PV_{2T}}{(1 + R)^{2T}} + \ldots \tag{2}$$

$$= PV_0 (1 + f^T + f^{2T} + \ldots)$$

where

$$f = (1 + g)(1 - k)/(1 + R)$$

and R is the required rate of return.

The sum of this infinite geometric series is given by

$$PV = PV_0/(1 - f^T). \tag{3}$$

The Equivalent Annual Cash Flow C for a perpetuity is given by

$$PV = C/R$$

$$C = R \times PV$$
$$= R \times PV_0/(1 - f^T) \tag{4}$$

Therefore, if we let,

$$A_{T,R}^* = (1 - f^T)/R,$$
$$f = (1 + g)(1 - k)/(1 + R),$$

solve for R in terms of $A_{T,R}^*$ and substitute in (4)
we have the result that,

$$C = PV_0/A_{T,R}^*.$$

92

REVIEW QUESTIONS

1. Describe the various stages in the capital investment decision-making process.

2. What are the three crucial factors upon which the profitability of a capital project will normally depend?

3. What questions would you require to be answered before considering investment in a new product?

4. Describe a simple way of weighing qualitative factors into the financial analysis of a project.

5. How would you treat fixed assets already owned by the company when analysing a project making use of those assets?

6. Provide a working definition, of 'net incremental cash flow'.

7. Define the 'economic life' of a capital project.

8. Describe the factors determining the optimal replacement period for machinery and equipment.

9. What is the distinction between mutually exclusive and contingent projects? How are each analysed?

10. What principles underlie the abandonment decision? When is it profitable to 'milk' an asset for cash?

EXERCISES

1. STU Ltd make 20 000 units per year of component A for use in their own manufacture. These cost the company £64 000 per year pre-tax to make. The components are used in a product with an expected product life (at this rate) of 5 years.
   One of STU Ltd's suppliers have offered to supply the component for only £3 each at an annual contract for 20 000 units. If STU Ltd buy the component outside, they must carry £10 000 additional stock. However, partially offsetting this fact is the possiblity of selling machinery which would be no longer required for £5000 pre-tax. The machinery had been purchased for £25 000 and a 100 per cent capital allowance had been taken. The machinery has a useful life of another 5 years. However, in 5 years' time the machinery will become worthless as scrap value will not exceed removal costs. The company's required rate of return for the product is 20 per cent. The company pays Corporation Tax at 50 per cent with a 1-year lag.
   Should STU Ltd buy Component A from this supplier? What are the financial and the strategic considerations?

2. An asset belonging to EZ Company has worn out. However, it can be completely overhauled at a cost of £100 and continue producing net cash flows of £20 per year. If sold as is, the asset would bring in cash of £100. A brand new replacement can be purchased for £200. The economic life is the same for overhaul as for puchase. Considering the risk, the required rate of return is 15 per cent. What should the management of EZ company do? (All above figures are net of taxes and investment incentives.)

PART III

PROFITABILITY AND RISK

7

SHAREHOLDERS' RISK AND REQUIRED RATES OF RETURN

We have suggested that the valuation placed on a company by the Stock Market is related to cash flows and to the risk associated with the firm's current and expected future investment activities. We wish now to explain the principles of risk relating to those cash flows and the implications of diversification for measuring the risk of an individual project. We will require a measurement tool for risk and we will find that an understanding of the way in which risk is measured in the Capital Market will be very useful. The behaviour of the Capital Market provides a basis for a procedure relating required returns to the riskiness of investment in capital projects.

RETURNS TO EQUITY SHAREHOLDERS

The definition of returns to shareholders plays a fundamental role in financial policy. If management wishes to increase the value of the firm it must understand how the firm is to be valued. One obvious basis for valuation of the firm is the expected returns to investors and associated risks. As risk has not been well understood, management has focused its attention on measures of return and framed its financial strategies accordingly. Unfortunately there are various measures of return available and each has its adherents.

What measure of return is most relevant to investors in the Capital Market? Is it earnings? Earnings per share? Price earnings ratio? . . . Or something else? A number of companies have treated this question in too little depth, often with unfortunate implications for their choice of investments. For example, the maximization of reported earnings would suggest cosmetic adjustment to accounts.

Such considerations are well known and have led many to use an Earnings per Share maximization strategy. This strategy accounted in part for the conglomerate takeover movement of the 1960's. Companies with a high Price-to-Earnings ratio found that they could increase their Earnings per Share simply by purchasing with shares companies with lower

95

Price-to-Earnings ratios. It was thought by some that the arithmetic of recomputing the Price-to-Earnings ratio of the resulting company would somehow make the aggregate worth more than the sum of the pre-merger parts. The resulting purchase of earnings of inferior quality and smaller growth prospects diverted management's attention from sources of genuine growth. The fallacy in this rationalization for takeovers has long since become evident.

Earnings per Share maximization has led to other strategies, some still being pursued. One such strategy involved the use of debt in the capital structure to increase Earnings per Share and to gain tax advantages. However, debt is a double-edged sword and will increase the risk of the firm while increasing the expected return. The increased risk is often not fully appreciated by management until the economy is in recession and earnings decline more rapidly than would have been the case if there had been less debt.

What returns in fact do investors receive: Earnings? Earnings per Share? Price to Earnings ratio? None of these? Investors can realize a return in but two forms—dividends and capital gains. Thus, returns to shareholders are defined as dividends received and capital gains experienced during a period, expressed as a fraction of the value of the investment at the beginning of the period:

$$\text{Returns} = \frac{\text{Dividends} + \text{Change in Market Value}}{\text{Initial Market Value}}.$$

This definition of returns to shareholders when adjusted for transactions costs and taxes is one which will stand up to rigorous examination. This definition suggests that if management wishes to benefit shareholders, it must try to maximize the Net Present Value of investments in order to increase dividends and capital gains to shareholders.

MEASURE OF RISK

Every private investor knows that expected dividends and capital gains are not the only factors to be considered: something called risk lurks in the background of every investment decision, whether the investment is being made by a private investor or is being made by management on his behalf. Virtually all decisions involve a large element of uncertainty about the future and are taken in the expectation of returns which might not fully materialize or could result in losses. Because the element of risk is so important in investment decisions, we must take at least as much care in the definition of risk as we must do in the definition of return.

What is risk? Mathematicians and statisticians measure risk in terms of variation from the mean or expected return, i.e. 'How wrong could our best estimate be?' Investors think of risk as the probability of having to take an

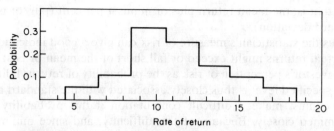

Figure 7.1. Histogram showing the probability distribution of ranges of rates of returns using the data from Table 7.1

unacceptable loss. These two aspects of risk are closely related. The second can be derived from the first. Let us begin with the statistician's measure.

The likelihood of a given outcome or return in the future is described by its probability. The most likely return on an investment, for example, may be thought to be in the range 9–10 per cent; the likelihood of realizing a figure in this range may be considered to be three chances out of ten of an 0.30 probability. As the 9–10 per cent range is thought to be the most likely return, the likelihood of other returns below 9 per cent and above 10 per cent tapers away according to some probability distribution (Figure 7.1 and Table 7.1). For one distribution of expected returns, the Normal Probability Distribution, 67 per cent of all expected outcomes would fall within a range given in terms of 'standard deviations'. If the mean were 11 per cent and one standard deviation were 4 per cent, there would be a 67 per cent probability that the actual return would fall in the range 7–15 per

Table 7.1. Probability distribution

Range of rate of return (per cent)	Likelihood (chances out of 20)	Probability*
5–6	1	0.05
7–8	2	0.10
9–10	6	0.30
11–12	5	0.25
13–14	3	0.15
15–16	2	0.10
17–18	1	0.05
	20	1.00

*The likelihood 2 chances out of 20 may be represented by the probability 2/20 or 0.1. The probability distribution can be viewed graphically in the form of a 'histogram', as shown in Figure 7.1.

cent; that is, the mean return plus or minus 4 per cent (plus or minus one standard deviation).

Thus the statistician's measure of risk can give a good indication of how far actual returns might exceed or fall short of the mean or best estimate. The investor's perception of risk as the probability of returns falling below some specified level is thus closely associated with the standard deviation, but we must make a difficult computation if this probability is to be determined closely. Because of this difficulty, and since minimizing the standard deviation minimizes the probability of loss, the standard deviation (or the standard deviation squared, termed the variance) has generally been regarded as a more useful measure of risk in financial investment.

The economist's view of risk aversion, framed in the context of utility theory, is closely identified with the standard deviation. The early development of the theory of investment portfolios was based on the assumption that investor behaviour can be characterized by those types of utility function for which the standard deviation provides a sufficient measure of risk. A brief account of the association between utility theory and risk is given in Appendix 7.1.

PORTFOLIOS

No discussion of risk in the field of finance is at all complete without consideration of risk reduction by means of diversified holdings of investments. Nearly all investments today—either by individuals or by companies—are undertaken within the context of a set of other investments, i.e. a portfolio. If risk can be reduced in some degree by appropriately diversified holdings, then the standard deviation or variability of returns of a single investment must be an overstatement of its actual risk. Diversification is undertaken in the expectation that the risk of the whole portfolio will be less than the weighted sum of its parts. Portfolio theory shows that such a rationale for diversification is correct.

Let us take a simple example. We shall assume that the world consists of only two companies, Imperial Chemical Industries (I.C.I.) and Shell. We have shown (hypothetical) expected returns and standard deviations for these two securities in Figure 7.2.

As we would expect, since Shell has a larger standard deviation, investors logically require greater returns compared with I.C.I. Now, a question that should interest us is, what would happen if we put half of our money into Shell and the other half into I.C.I.? What would be the expected return and risk of our portfolio? The expected return is easy to compute and must be 13 per cent. But what is the standard deviation or risk of the portfolio? The reader might be tempted to say 25 per cent, i.e. point A. That answer would be correct only under the condition that returns for the two companies are perfectly positively correlated, making efforts to diversify ineffective.

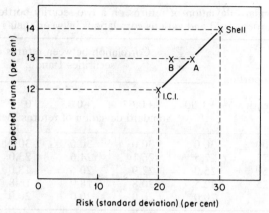

Figure 7.2. Risk and return for two securities

The returns on investment in the shares of I.C.I. and Shell would be perfectly positively correlated if deviations from the average returns on I.C.I. were to be accompanied always by corresponding deviations for Shell in the same direction and in a constant proportion. Thus, the behaviour of Shell could be predicted from the behaviour of I.C.I. and *vice versa*. If such were the case, no diversification would result from holding the shares of I.C.I. and Shell in any combination. In Figure 7.2, all combinations of I.C.I. and Shell would fall on a straight line between the values for Shell and I.C.I. alone; for example, at point A. However, although returns on investments in I.C.I. and Shell are positively correlated, they are not *perfectly* positively correlated. Unique factors affect the returns on I.C.I. or Shell which are not common to both companies. Thus the line in Figure 2 will bend through some point B to the left.

Table 7.2 illustrates the way in which the standard deviation of returns for a two-security portfolio changes with proportions (weighted by market value) held and with the degree of correlation between their returns. Columns 1 and 2 give the proportions held in securities 1 and 2, respectively. The standard deviation of returns for security 2 is assumed to be 30 per cent. Thus, in the first row, representing a portfolio in which only security 2 is held, we find that the standard deviation of the portfolio returns is 30 per cent in all columns. Similarly, in the bottom row, representing a portfolio in which only security 1 is held, the standard deviation of portfolio returns is identical to that of security 2, assumed to be 20 per cent. In the remaining portfolios, in rows 2, 3, and 4, the standard deviation of portfolio returns depends upon the degree of correlation of returns between securities, as may be seen by reading from left to right. In column 1, we have the case of perfect positive correlation and there are no gains from diversification. Thus, reading down column 3,

Table 7.2. Standard deviation of returns on a two-security portfolio for various proportions held and various correlations between their returns

Proportion in security 1	Proportion in security 2	Correlation between returns on securities 1 and 2				
		+1.00	+0.67	+0.33	0	−1.00
		Standard deviation of returns (per cent)				
0	1.00	30.0	30.0	30.0	30.0	30.0
0.25	0.75	27.5	26.1	24.6	23.0	17.5
0.50	0.50	25.0	22.9	20.6	18.0	5.0
0.75	0.25	22.5	20.8	18.9	16.8	7.5
1.00	0	20.0	20.0	20.0	20.0	20.0

It is assumed that the standard deviation of returns for security 1 is 20 per cent and that for security 2 the standard deviation is 30 per cent. Computation is illustrated in Appendix 7.2.

we see that the standard deviation for the portfolio is no less than the weighted combination of the standard deviations for the two securities. However, in columns 4, 5, and 6, one sees that the standard deviations of portfolio returns are progressively less as the correlation between the securities declines. The same principles hold for portfolios of three or more securities. (The calculations on which Table 7.2 is based are illustrated in Appendix 7.2) We may conclude that risk may be reduced through portfolio diversification without necessarily reducing the expected returns.

If assets were available which were perfectly *negatively* correlated, a combination (not shown in Table 7.2) between them could be found which would reduce risk to zero. An amusing example of negative correlation is returns from sales of umbrellas and ice cream at the seaside. Rain or shine, either one or the other of these activities generates income. Even here, the correlation would not be perfectly negative and a merger between umbrella and ice cream vendors could not be expected to yield a risk-free enterprise. In the Stock Market, one rarely finds negatively correlated securities. Consequently, although diversification of holdings of securities is worthwhile, the advantages are limited.

Unfortunately, elimination of all risk cannot be achieved even by means of the widest possible diversification. A holding in each of all the shares quoted on the London Stock Exchange would still leave one with a very considerable degree of risk–as typified by the fluctuations in The Financial Times Actuaries Index! The risk that cannot be diversified away is that in the economy at large. This remaining risk is variously called 'non-diversifiable' or 'systematic' risk, or 'market' risk.

Figure 7.3 illustrates the way in which risk has been found to vary with the number of securities in portfolios selected at random from the London Stock Exchange. On the vertical axis, 100 per cent represents the average

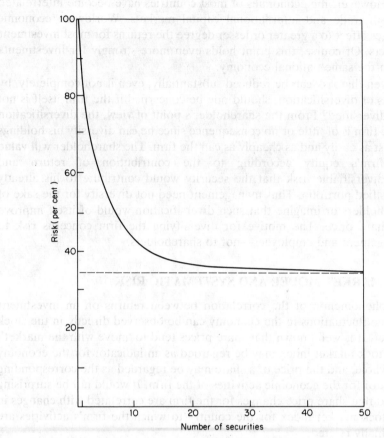

Figure 7.3. Average variation of risk with the number of randomly selected securities in a U.K. portfolio

risk on one security. Moving to the right, more securities are added to the portfolio as indicated on the horizontal axis. The curve shows the way in which risk diminishes rapidly at first as shares of different companies are added to the portfolio. However, as the number of companies in the portfolio are increased, the advantages of adding each additional company are reduced. In the U.K. market, for the period represented in Figure 7.3, risk could not be reduced on average by more than 65.5 per cent through diversification. The remaining 34.5 per cent represents 'non-diversifiable' risk reflecting uncertainties in the economy common to all shares in the portfolio.

Why couldn't risk be completely eliminated by means of *international* diversification? If each risk were undertaken in a different national economy and each national economy were wholly independent of the others, then after about twenty such investments, very little risk would be left. However, the economies of most countries have become interrelated through trade and international capital markets. Worldwide economic changes affect to a greater or lesser degree the returns for most investment projects. Of course, this point holds even more strongly for investments within the same national economy.

Given that risk can be reduced substantially, even if not completely, by means of diversification, should one be concerned if the firm itself is not well diversified? From the shareholder's point of view, the diversification of the firm is of little or no consequence since he can diversify his holdings at least as easily and as cheaply as can the firm. The shareholder will value the firm's equity according to the contribution of return and 'non-diversifiable' risk that the security would contribute to his already diversified portfolio. Thus management need not diversify for the sake of shareholders or imagine that such diversification would of itself improve the share price. The motive for diversifying the firm concerns risk to management and employees—not to shareholders.

THE MARKET MODEL AND SYSTEMATIC RISK

The phenomenon of the correlation between returns on an investment and the fluctuations in the economy can be observed directly in the stock market. It is well known that share prices tend to 'move with the market'. The stock market index may be regarded as an indicator for the economy as a whole, and the price of a share may be regarded as the corresponding indicator for the economic activities of the firm. It would not be surprising to find that share price changes for the firm are correlated with changes in the stock market index for the country to which the firm's activities are principally related.

Thus the returns on investment in a particular company may be expected to vary in some relation to the stock market index. The monthly return R for a share is measured as the price change during the month plus any dividends paid, all divided by the price at the beginning of the month (adjusted if necessary for any capitalization changes). For example,

Price at end of period   = 110,
Price at beginning of period = 100,
Dividend during period   = 5;

hence,

$$R = \frac{(110 - 100) + 5}{100} = 0.15.$$

The monthly return R_m on the market can be approximated by a similar computation using the Financial Times Actuaries Index as the price of a 'market portfolio'. The riskier the share the larger we can expect R to be in relation to R_m. For example, when R_m is negative, R will tend to be an even greater negative value if the share is of above-average risk.

The volatility of monthly returns R for the share in relation to corresponding monthly returns R_m for the market may be seen more readily if we plot them in a scatter diagram, as illustrated in Figure 7.4. The points tend to scatter upwards to the right. The line drawn through the points represents the average relationship between R and R_m revealed in the scatter. The steeper this line, the greater is the magnitude of R in comparison to R_m and thus the greater the volatility of the security in relation to that of the market.

For example, let us suppose that the slope of the line is greater than 45° to the horizontal axis and that, for the purpose of illustration, the line passes through the origin. In a period when the market rises and the return on the market is, say, plus 20 per cent, the resulting return on the security may be expected to be greater than 20 per cent. However, should the market fall, resulting in a return of minus 20 per cent, one can expect the negative return on the security to be even greater.

The line in Figure 7.4 should be drawn so that the sum of the squared deviations of the points from the line are minimized. The slope of this least

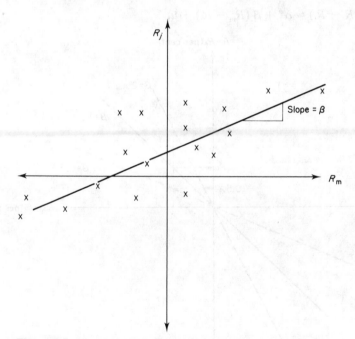

Figure 7.4. A scatter diagram of monthly returns on a security with corresponding monthly returns on the market index, together with a regression line relating the two. R_j is the monthly return on security j; R_m is the monthly return on the market index

squares line in the scatter diagram is called the 'beta coefficient' (β). This diagram has been called the 'Market Model' and is attributable to Sharpe (1963) and to Markowitz (1959).

In fact, if one constructed a portfolio that consisted of all risky assets in the securities market, the line in Figure 7.4. would pass through the origin and slope upwards at 45°. There would be no scatter. We can say this with certainty since both axes would then represent returns on the market represented by, for example, the Financial Times Index. The value of β in this case is equal to one.

Has risk been eliminated when the scatter about the line is eliminated and the value of β is equal to one? No. The risk of the portfolio would then be equal to the risk of the market as a whole, and the beta coefficient for the market as a whole is, by definition, equal to one. But this value of one does not represent a constant absolute level of risk. The variance of returns on the Market Portfolio will change with the level of uncertainty about the future of the economy. β, then, is only a measure of risk *relative* to the market as a whole.

In Figure 7.5, we can illustrate how securities are expected to behave as the market changes. The model is often put into the following form:

$$(R - R_f) = \alpha^* + \beta (R_m - R_f) + \tilde{u},$$

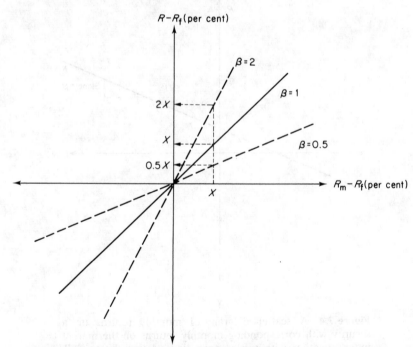

Figure 7.5. Graphs of $R - R_f$ versus $R_m - R_f$ for various values of the beta coefficient

where $\bar{u}$ is a random error term. This equation merely states that the return in excess of the risk-free rate of interest on a security is proportional to some coefficient (β) times the excess return on the market. The value of α^* is of no little research interest, but has been found to be quite close to zero on average except when the security's price changes are reflecting the benefits of abnormal economic gains or losses.

Let us assume that the market moves X per cent (after subtracting the risk-free rate of interest). If the security or portfolio had a beta coefficient of 0.5, we would expect the security to move $0.5X$ per cent. Similarly, if the security had a beta coefficient of 2.0, then we would expect its price to move up twice as fast as the market, i.e. $2X$ per cent.

We shall consider the systematic risk of capital projects in the next chapter. We shall need to know the way in which the capital market relates required rates of return to systematic risk in order to establish profitability criteria for capital projects. To this central problem we now turn our attention.

THE TRADE-OFF BETWEEN RISK AND RETURN IN THE CAPITAL MARKET

We wish to consider what might be the relationship of expected returns (dividends and capital gains) for investments in the capital markets to the associated risks. It is observable that investors hold portfolios, which is evidence that investors are 'risk averse'. To be risk averse means that one would not take increased risk without an expectation of higher return. Also, as the capital market behaviour reflects diversified investment, it would be non-diversifiable risk for which the market in aggregate would expect a higher return. Thus we have an hypothesis that the capital markets require higher returns for increasing levels of systematic (non-diversifiable) risk from investments. We could refine this hypothesis further by specifying, for example, a straight-line relationship between returns and risks, and look for evidence of such a relationship.

Why might the relationship between returns and systematic risk in the capital markets be straight-line? To take a simplified view of the world, let us suppose that investors had an opportunity to make only two kinds of investments: in riskless short-term Government securities and in the Market Portfolio of risky securities. For example, an investor could put all his funds into short-term Government securities and achieve a positive rate of interest with zero systematic risk. The β value of the 'portfolio' would be zero. Alternatively, he could put all his assets into the Market Portfolio and the β value of the portfolio would then be equal to exactly one, by definition. Suppose the investor's risk preferences were such that he

106

wanted a portfolio with a β value of exactly 0.5. How would he achieve such a portfolio with great precision?

By combining short-term Government securities and holdings in the Market Portfolio, an investor can build a portfolio displaying any desired β value between 0 and 1. For example, to build a portfolio with a β value precisely equal to 0.75, he would put three quarters of his assets into the Market Portfolio and only one quarter into a risk-free asset, for example, 30-day Government bonds. This is a practical procedure: anyone can do it if he has sufficient capital to make a portion of his portfolio representative of the market. The least expensive way of doing this is to buy a unit trust and adjust one's holdings of Government securities for the β value of the unit trust.

If the investor wishes to hold a high-risk portfolio, he can add to his Market Portfolio with borrowed money. For example, he can obtain a β value equal to 2.00 for his own stake in the portfolio by doubling the amount of his investable funds through borrowing and investing in the Market Portfolio.

We have described a situation which could apply more generally to the market as a whole. Investors can interpolate β values between 0 and 1 by lending to the Government. Investing a portion of assets in Government or other short-term money-market instruments is a standard method of controlling risk employed by institutions. Because this process of interpolation and extrapolation is essentially a linear or straight-line relationship, it has been hypothesized that the relationship between returns and systematic risk (β) in the capital market must be linear. Figure 7.6 summarizes this linear relationship. In the diagram, the horizontal axis measures the degree of systematic risk represented by the beta coefficient and the vertical axis measures the expected rate of return. The minimum

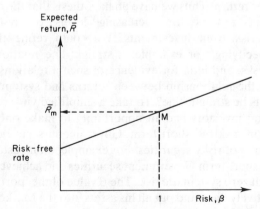

Figure 7.6. The trade-off between risk and
return in the capital market

required rate of return when β is zero is where the line cuts the vertical axis—at the value corresponding to the risk-free rate of interest. Thus we have one point on the line. To draw a line we require one more point. An obvious choice is the point corresponding to the Market Portfolio or the Financial Times Index (denoted by M in the diagram) since the value of β is known to be equal to one for the market. Measuring along the horizontal axis to the point where β equals one, we then plot the point M directly above it. The height of this point represents the expected rate of return on the Market Portfolio. The line extending through these two points is called the Market Line.

The intercept of this straight line is equal to the risk-free rate of interest. Thus the line may be written,

$$E(R) = R_f + (E(R_m) - R_f)\beta$$

where $E(R)$ is the expected value of the return R on an investment, $E(R_m)$ is the expected value of the return R_m on the Market Portfolio, R_f is the risk-free rate of interest, and β is the beta coefficient measuring systematic risk for the investment relative to the risk of the market. Thus, if interest rates R_f are currently 5 per cent and the expected excess return on the market over and above interest rates is 10 per cent and the β value for the investment is 1.10, the expected return on the investment is

$$E(R) = 0.05 + 0.10 \times 1.10$$
$$= 0.16.$$

This equation represents the well-known 'Capital Asset Pricing Model' attributable to Sharpe (1964), Lintner (1965), and Mossin (1966).

What reason is there to believe that individual investments within the Market Portfolio should be compared to this line at locations depending on their β values? Suppose an individual security having a β value of 0.5 were so over-priced that its rate of return (X in Figure 7.7) fell below the Market Line. How many would buy it? Any investor could create for himself a better investment by putting half his money into a risk-free asset and the other half into the Market Portfolio. He would then have an investment on the Market line at a β value to 0.5 (Point Y), which is superior to our hypothetical investment below the line. Clearly, the investment below the line is over-priced and would not be expected to attract much demand until the price fell sufficiently to put the security back on the line.

Similar arguments hold for *underpriced* securities above the line. Investors currently investing on the line would buy the security until it found its way back on to the line. Thus we would expect on logical grounds alone that the market line is straight and that securities would be expected to fall on such a line under equilibrium conditions in an efficient capital market.

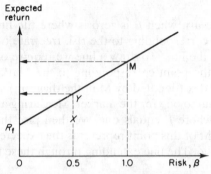

Figure 7.7. An over-valued security

There are two issues here which are often confused:

(a) Capital market opportunity cost;
(b) Capital market equilibrium.

The first concerns how rational investors, managers for example, should invest; the second concerns the way the market could be expected to behave providing that a sufficient number of market participants invested in this way.

Any investment, whether in securities or in real assets, can be compared to an alternative investment in the capital market at equivalent risk obtainable from linear combinations of government securities and the market portfolio. Rational investment requires that one must expect at least as much return as one can obtain easily in this way from the capital market before investing elsewhere. In this sense every investment in real assets has a *capital market opportunity cost.*

The second issue as to whether the capital market behaves as if investors are evaluating securities in this manner is not yet wholly resolved. Figure 7.8 presents the evidence of Black, Jensen, and Scholes (1972). They measured β values for each of 1200 shares traded on the New York Stock Exchange. They then created ten portfolios. The first portfolio contained the 10 per cent of securities with the highest β values. The second portfolio contained the 10 per cent with the next largest β values and so on. On the graph are plotted the excess of portfolio returns over the risk-free rate against the β value for each portfolio for the period 1935–65. Straight-line relationships were also observed during each of the years in this period. However, Richard Roll (1977) has revealed some methodological problems with such tests. Until these problems are better understood, we cannot say whether the market line describes the behaviour of *individual* securities within the market Portfolio.

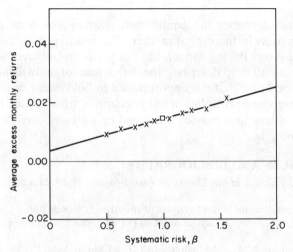

Figure 7.8. Historic relationship between risk and return based on ten portfolios traded on the New York Stock Exchange between 1935 and 1965 and including virtually all the New York Stock Exchange equities. (After Black *et al.*, 1972.)

We do know, however, that managers and shareholders can purchase portfolios of securities which approximate the behaviour of the Market Portfolio and that they can also buy risk-free Government securities. Furthermore, these two forms of assets, risky assets and risk-free assets, can be held in any linear combination. Thus Figure 7.7 does describe a set of capital market opportunity costs appropriate for use as a profitability criterion for rational investment policies.

CONCLUSION

Efficient capital markets are characterized by large numbers of shareholders who are owners of diversified portfolios. Many companies provide a large and varied number of projects that produce such a portfolio. However, since the shareholder can diversify as cheaply as can the firm, managers need not further reduce risk to shareholders by holding a more diverse set of projects. Since diversification will not eradicate those risks traceable to unexpected fluctuations in the general economy, rates of return required by shareholders are based on those risks which remain after allowing for diversification.

Because investors are able to purchase linear combinations of the Market Portfolio and risk-free securities, theory would suggest that this linearity also describes the equilibrium relationships between risk and expected returns in the capital market. The resulting equilibrium model, the Capital Asset Pricing Model, has not yet been sufficiently well tested for us to say that it describes the behaviour of individual securities. However, we know that the opportunities to hold linear combinations of risk-free assets and portfolios of risky securities are available to managers and shareholders, and provide a rational opportunity cost for alternative investments.

REFERENCES AND BIBLIOGRAPHY

Arrow, K. J., *Essays in the Theory of Risk-Bearing*, North-Holland, Amsterdam, 1971.

Black, F., 'Equilibrium in the Creation of Investment Goods under Uncertainty', in *Studies in the Theory of Capital Markets* (M. C. Jensen, ed.), Praeger, New York, 1972.

Black, F., Jensen, M. C., and Scholes, M., 'The Capital Asset Pricing Model: Some Empirical Tests', in *Studies in the Theory of Capital Markets* (M. C. Jensen, ed.), Praeger, New York, 1972.

Jensen, M. C. (ed.), *Studies in the Theory of Capital Markets*, Praeger, New York, 1972.

Lintner, J. 'Security Prices, Risk and Maximal Gains from Diversification', *Journal of Finance*, **20**, 587–615, Dec. 1965.

Lorie, J. H. and Brealey, R. A. (eds), *Modern Developments in Investment Management: A Book of Readings*, Praeger, New York, 1972.

Lorie, J. H. and Hamilton, M. T., *The Stock Market: Theories and Evidence*, Irwin, New York, 1973.

Markowitz, H. M., *Portfolio Selection: Efficient Diversification of Investments*, Wiley, New York, 1959.

Modigliani, F. and Pogue, G., 'An Introduction to Risk and Return: Concepts and Evidence', *Financial Analysts Journal*, **30** (Mar–Apr.), 68–80, and **30** (May–June), 69–86, 1974.

Mossin, J., 'Equilibrium in a Capital Asset Market', *Econometrica*, **34**, 768–783, Oct. 1966.

Roll, R., 'A Critique of the Asset Pricing Theory's Tests', *Journal of Financial Economics*, **4**, 129–176, 1977.

Sharpe, W. F., 'A Simplified Model for Portfolio Analysis', *Management Science*, **9**, 277–293, Jan. 1963.

Sharpe, W. F., 'Capital Asset Prices: A Theory of Market Equilibrium under Conditions of Risk'. *Journal of Finance*, **19**, 425–442, Sep. 1964.

Sharpe, W. F., *Portfolio Theory and Capital Markets*, McGraw-Hill, New York, 1971.

Sharpe, W. F. *Investments*, Prentice-Hall, Englewood Cliffs, N.J., 1977.

Sharpe, W. F. and Cooper, G. M., 'Risk-return Class of New York Stock Exchange Common Stocks, 1931–1967'. *Financial Analysts Journal*, **28**, 46–54, Mar.-Apr. 1972.

Solnik, B., 'The International Pricing of Risk: An Empirical Investigation of World Capital Market Structure', *Journal of Finance*, **39**(2), 365–378, May 1974.

APPENDIX 7.1. UTILITY THEORY AND RISK

An individual with wealth w expects some usefulness, satisfaction, or *utility* $U(w)$ from the consumption possibilities which wealth w affords. It is usually assumed that the individual always prefers more wealth to less (non-satiation) and that therefore $U(w)$ is an always-increasing function of w.

If this individual is an investor, he may anticipate that his wealth w will increase to an amount W with a degree of uncertainty depending upon the riskiness of the portfolio of investments that he chooses to hold.

Suppose that the investor was offered a choice between future wealth W made secure by a safe investment and an uncertain future wealth, which, for simplicity, we shall assume would be either $W-h$ or $W+h$ with equal probability of 0.5 for each.

If the investor is risk averse, he will prefer the certain outcome; that is, his utility from the consumption of a known future wealth W is greater than his expected utility from the same wealth (on average) which has been made uncertain:

$$U(W) > 0.5 \, U(W - h) + 0.5 \, U(W + h).$$

Multiplying the above relation by two and rearranging terms we find

$$U(W + h) - U(W) < U(W) - U(W - h);$$

that is, utility increases less rapidly at higher levels of wealth than at lower levels of wealth. Thus the risk-averse investor displays diminishing marginal utility for wealth. For the risk-averse investor, it is nice to win but it really hurts to lose. The gain in utility from an increase in wealth does not make up for the loss in utility from an equal loss of wealth, if the investor is risk averse.

The shape of a typical utility function is given in Figure 7.A1. Wealth W is measured along the horizontal axis and utility of W is measured along the

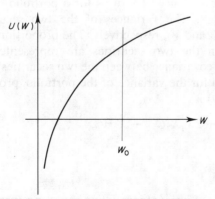

Figure 7.A1. A utility function displaying properties of non-satiation and diminishing marginal utility for wealth

vertical axis. The slope of the curve is always positive (the first derivative $U' > 0$) signifying that the investor always obtains increasing utility from increasing wealth. However, the slope of the curve becomes more horizontal or less positive (the second derivative $U'' < 0$) with increasing wealth; that is, absolute increases in wealth becomes less useful as the individual becomes more wealthy.

Note that, as a result of this shape, if we move to the left of wealth W_0 in Figure 7.A1 more utility is lost than is gained if we move a corresponding amount to the right. If, as a result of risky investments, W is allowed to deviate randomly around W_0, there will usually be a net loss of utility on average because of the steeper slope of the utility curve for negative deviations than for positive deviations.

If one thinks of the standard deviation as a measure closely associated with the range of possible outcomes h in the above expressions, one can begin to appreciate the connection between standard deviation and risk aversion in the theory of portfolio selection. Whether the standard deviation alone is adequate to describe risk for portfolio-building purposes depends upon the precise shape of the utility function $U(W)$ and the probability distribution of future returns. For log normally distributed returns (a reasonable approximation to capital market returns) and a number of utility functions commonly employed in economics, the standard deviation provides an adequate measure of risk for portfolio building purposes.

For a deeper discussion of risk, utility theory and risk aversion see Arrow (1971) and Markowitz (1959).

APPENDIX 7.2. COMPUTING THE VARIANCE OF A PORTFOLIO'S RETURNS

Consider first the variance of returns for a portfolio containing just two securities 1 and 2. The variances of the two securities' returns are represented by V_1 and V_2, respectively. The proportions of the portfolio's value invested in the two securities are represented by X_1 and X_2, respectively. The covariance between the two securities' returns is given by $C_{1,2}$. The formula for the variance of the portfolio, provided originally by Markowitz (1959) is

$$V_p = X_1^2 V_1 + 2X_1 X_2 C_{1,2} + X_2^2 V_2,$$

where

$$C_{1,2} = r_{1,2} s_1 s_2$$

in which $r_{1,2}$ is the coefficient of correlation between returns on securities 1 and 2, s_1 is the standard deviation of returns for security 1, and s_2 is the standard deviation of returns for security 2.

Returning to our example of Table 7.2 in the text, let us compute values for the situation in which

$$r_{1,2} = 0.33, \quad X_1 = 0.75, \quad X_2 = 0.25,$$
$$s_1 = 0.20, \quad V_1 = 0.04$$
$$s_2 = 0.30, \quad V_2 = 0.09$$
$$C_{1,2} = 0.33 \times 0.20 \times 0.30 = 0.0198.$$

Thus

$$V_p = (0.75)^2 \times 0.04 + 2 \times 0.75 \times 0.25 \times 0.0198 + (0.25)^2 \times 0.09$$
$$= 0.035\ 55,$$
$$s_p = \sqrt{V_p} = 18.9 \text{ per cent,}$$

which is the value found in the fourth row, third column in the body of Table 7.2.

The more general expression for the variance of portfolios of two or more securities is given by

$$V_p = \sum_{i=1}^{N} \sum_{j=1}^{N} X_i X_j C_{i,j},$$

where N is the number of securities.

REVIEW QUESTIONS

1. In what form do shareholders of a publicly quoted company receive their returns? Is this different from a privately held company?

2. How does the Net Present Value Rule improve shareholders' returns?

3. Why is diversification in shareholders' interests? Should the company diversify? (If so, under what circumstances?)

4. Describe how you would measure the beta coefficient of a company that was traded on the Stock Exchange. How would you convert this into a required rate of return on an investment in the company's shares.

5. How might an increasing level of debt affect the beta coefficient of a company.

6. If an investor held a diversified portfolio of shares valued at £1000, with a beta coefficient equal to 1.0, how could he most effectively change the risk of the portfolio to (a) a β value of 0.5; (b) a β value of 2.0.

EXERCISES

1. Three securities have beta coefficients of 1.0, 0.5, and 0.8, respectively. The investor puts his money into each of the securities in equal amounts. What is the beta coefficient of his portfolio?

2. Estimate the beta coefficient of any company quoted on the London Stock Exchange. Use monthly data for a period of at least 2 years.

114

3. What is the expected return and risk of the following two-security portfolio?

	Expected return (per cent)	Standard deviation (per cent)
Security A	10	30
Security B	12	40

The correlation coefficient (A, B) = 0.2 and you should assume that funds are invested equally in the two securities.

4. What is the expected return and risk if we invest equally in a further security to the two in Question 7.3 with the following characteristics?

	Expected return (per cent)	Standard deviation (per cent)	Correlation (C,A) (C, B)	
Security C	15	50	.15	.30

5. Given the following statistics, what is the required rate of return for Company X?

$$\beta \quad = \quad 1.5,$$
Return on the F.T.A. = 10 per cent,
Risk-free rate of interest = 6 per cent.

What use is this rate of return in valuing a project within the company?

8

CAPITAL PROJECT RISK AND THE DISCOUNT RATE

The principle objective of management in capital investment is to increase the value of the firm. The best measure of this value that we have is the market value of the firm's securities traded in a competitive capital market. A competitive capital market prices assets by implicitly discounting cash flow forecasts at rates of return that reflect the risk of the asset. In order to predict the likely effect of a proposed capital project on the value of the firm, management must discount expected cash flows at the rate which the market would require as if that project were quoted separately from the rest of the company. Correspondingly, management increases the value of the firm when investing in projects with higher returns than those offered by an alternative investment in the capital market at the same risk.

In the preceding chapter, we examined the way in which rates of return in the capital markets are related to that risk which cannot be eliminated by diversification. It follows that in order to set a discount rate for a proposed capital investment, we must know the risk class of the project. Thus the two principal questions which we wish to answer in this chapter are: 'What methods of estimating risk for capital projects are operational?' and 'How should discount rates be assigned to particular capital projects?'

WHY REQUIRED RATES OF RETURN MUST BE RELATED TO RISK

Figure 8.1 represents the way in which capital markets are understood to relate increasing expected rates of return to increasing risk. The upward sloping line is called the Capital Market Line and represents the trade-off between risk and return on all securities available to investors as represented by The Financial Times Actuaries Index (F.T.A.). If management is representing the interests of shareholders when appraising capital projects, they must require a rate of return no less than that which shareholders could obtain by investing the funds in securities of equivalent risk. Thus, they will wish to find projects that are above the Capital Market Line, for example projects B, C, and D. In contrast, project A is below the line and is therefore unacceptable.

115

116

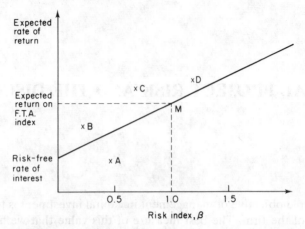

Figure 8.1. The trade-off between risk and return in
the capital markets

However, many companies do not systematically adjust project required
rates of return for risk. They employ the same *Test Discount Rate* (TDR)
for all projects regardless of differing individual risk characteristics. For
example, one method of selecting the TDR is to compute a *Weighted
Average Cost of Capital* (WACC) which will be discussed in detail in
Chapter 15. The WACC is intended to reflect that debt is a less costly
source of finance after tax than equity. The question is asked: 'Given the risk
of the company's existing assets, what is the "cost of equity" and the "cost of
debt" for the company?' If the company's capital structure is composed of,
for example, 80 per cent equity and 20 per cent debt, then the weights 0.80
and 0.20 are applied to the costs of equity and debt, respectively, to obtain a
weighted average cost. Providing that the principles discussed in Chapter 15
are applied, the WACC may be employed for those projects having identical
risk to the average of existing assets. However, there are large classes of
capital projects having a level of risk which differs significantly from the
average and thus would require a different return than a single Test
Discount Rate or Weighted Average Cost of Capital.

Nevertheless, there is a widespread belief that the use of a single cut-off
rate reflecting the average risk of the whole company will result in correct
capital investment decisions. In Figure 8.2 we have plotted the risk-return
line of Figure 8.1 and superimposed the horizontal line representing a
single Test Discount Rate (TDR), or single cut-off rate for capital projects
regardless of the projects' differing levels of risk. The point at which the
two lines cross represents the average risk and average return for the
company.

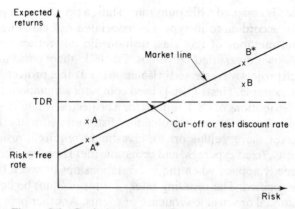

Figure 8.2. Capital market opportunities and the test discount rate

The risk-return characteristics of two capital projects, A and B, are also plotted in Figure 8.2. Project A is a profitable low-risk project which offers a rate of return exceeding alternative capital market returns (A*) on investments in the same risk class. However, project A would be rejected using the single Test Discount Rate as the decision criterion. The use of the single TDR does not take account of the project's attractive low risk in relation to its return. On the other hand, project B would be accepted even though its expected return is less than that available (B*) from alternative investment in the capital market at the same risk. Thus we find that the single average rate of return criterion does not produce correct decisions on average. It may be seen from the above example that the use of single Test Discount Rate as an investment criterion will bias investment towards high-risk, unprofitable projects and away from profitable, low-risk projects.

If the use of a single, average discount rate results in wrong decisions, then many companies who use such a criterion are unlikely to be allocating their resources in the most efficient manner. A better procedure would be to base a discount rate on the capital market's required rate of return for the risk class of the project.

TRADITIONAL RISK CLASSIFICATION METHODS

Assigning a different discount rate to each project according to its own risk presents some administrative difficulties. Those companies which employ risk-adjusted discount rates use a risk classification scheme. Various types of project are separated into risk classes according to their perceived risk, and each risk class is assigned a discount rate. Thus, a project has a preassigned discount rate according to its type and associated risk classification.

Traditional methods of risk classification did not reflect the fact that shareholders own diversified portfolios. Portfolio theory was unknown or ignored: each project was assessed in isolation from other projects or from the market. For example, Hertz (1964) used computer simulations to generate frequency distributions of DCF returns for a project. The analysis was based on random numbers drawn from probability distributions for: market size and growth, market share, selling prices, investment required, residual value, operating costs, fixed expenses, and economic life. However, the method is often incorrectly applied when the interrelationships between factors over time are unspecified. The resulting rates of return cannot be linked to any economic rational or sensible sequence of events. Another objection to the simulation method is that portfolio diversification is not considered, and thus the method does not directly measure systematic or non-diversifiable risk.

A second method, which is more widely used, is sensitivity analysis. The object of sensitivity analysis is to obtain an estimate of the possible range of Net Present Values for the project. A computer model of the project can be used for this purpose, which may be as elaborate as that used in simulation. The difference is that random numbers are not used. Instead, the analyst tries inputing numbers at each end of the plausible range of values for each variable to see the effect on the Net Present Value. Variables may be changed one at a time or in combination. Should the results be particularly sensitive to a variable, more information may be sought.

Sensitivity analysis has been thought to be inferior to simulation because probabilities are not used. However, sensitivity analysis, when properly implemented, can point up those features of a project which are most sensitive to uncertainty. For example, sensitivity analysis can indicate the sensitivity of the project's Present Value to changes in the economy. The fixed-variable expense structure of project costs (operational gearing) will then dictate the effect of the resulting range of sales volume on the range of Present Values. Projects with the greatest range of Present Values in proportion to the investment required will tend to belong to the highest risk class. However, the use of sensitivity analysis for risk classification requires a uniform and consistent procedure of analysis for all types of projects; otherwise project comparisons implicit in risk classification will not be valid. We shall suggest a risk classification framework later in the chapter.

Most companies, however, have not used computer models for risk classification. Usually, rough rules of thumb have been employed. For example, cost reduction projects are put into Class A (low risk), scale-expansion projects into Class B (average risk), new products into Class C (high risk) and Research and Development in Class D. For the average company this method may be all that is required: it is simple, direct and inexpensive to apply. In most cases, computer analysis would probably not result in different risk classifications than these. However, refinements to this method are possible.

RISK PREMIUMS

The discount rate for a project is determined by the risk-free rate of interest plus a risk premium for the project's risk. Let us examine a project which has risk equivalent to the average of industrial and service companies in the U.K. private sector. If the arithmetic average risk premium for the F.T. Actuaries Index is $7\frac{1}{2}$ per cent per annum and the risk-free rate of interest were 6 per cent (both after tax), we would expect a minimum return of $13\frac{1}{2}$ per cent on this type of project.

The premium of $7\frac{1}{2}$ percent has been estimated by comparing the difference between annual returns on a representative sample of companies traded on the stock market with annual returns on short-term Government fixed interest securities known as Treasury Bills. For example, if in a particular year dividends plus capital gains averaged 14 per cent on shares and Treasury Bills yielded 5 per cent, then one would find that the realized risk premium on the market was 9 per cent. The historical risk premium is obtained by taking an arithmetic average of annual risk premiums over a great many years, adjusted, when appropriate, for personal taxes.

The pre-personal tax risk premium in the U.S.A. since 1926 has averaged 8.8 per cent per annum (Ibbotson and Sinquefield, 1976). On the London Stock Exchange between 1919 and 1975, the risk premium for the average company averaged 9.1 per cent post-Corporation Tax and pre-personal taxes. Under the current imputation tax system in the U.K., post-tax returns to shareholders *include* the prepayment of personal taxes. Therefore it is now necessary to adjust historical post-Corporation Tax returns for the personal taxes which were paid in order to arrive at a shareholders equivalent required rate of return comparable to the current system.

Since 1919, many personal tax rates and many different methods of computing tax have prevailed, and precise tax adjustments to the historical market rates of return are not available. However, an estimate can be found by contrasting two extreme sets of assumptions. First, if no dividends had been paid and investors held their shares for capital gains in the very long term, taxes on annual returns would have been negligible. Under this assumption the after-tax risk premium would have been close to 9 per cent per annum. Taking the other extreme, assuming that all earnings were paid out as dividends and taxed at, say, 35 per cent, we would find the risk premium reduced to 6 per cent per annum. The truth lies somewhere between these two extremes; that is, close to $7\frac{1}{2}$ per cent per annum approximately.

The cash flows of a 1-year project which has a risk index equal to 1.0 (equivalent to the Financial Times Actuaries Index) would be estimated after Corporation Taxes and discounted at a rate that reflects the risk-free rate of interest after personal taxes of 34 per cent (at the standard rate) plus the risk premium of $7\frac{1}{2}$ per cent. Thus, for the average firm, the required rate of return is approximated by the risk-free rate after personal taxes, plus the historical $7\frac{1}{2}$ per cent risk premium.

The $7\frac{1}{2}$ per cent risk premium for projects of average risk was, of course, obtained from an *historical* average. Although the past can provide a useful guide to the future, one must be aware that traumatic economic changes such as an oil crisis introduce uncertainties which can alter risk premiums. While an average of 50 years' data contains many such crises, one must still judge whether the current outlook involves significantly more than, or less than, the average degree of uncertainty. In 1973 and 1974, at the height of several crises, the risk premium increased significantly in the view of many financial executives who were requiring much higher returns on new capital projects. By 1978 the risk premium appeared to have returned much closer to normal.

In the succeeding sections, we shall examine the risk index of a number of industries and companies in the U.K. and then explain how such data can be used to set discount rates for divisions of firms, risk classes, and individual projects.

ESTIMATING THE RISK OF COMPANIES AND DIVISIONS

Table 8.1 shows estimated β values for several industries, varying from $\beta = 0.69$ for Paper and Packaging to $\beta = 1.51$ for Miscellaneous Consumer Goods. Estimates of β values based on historical data can never be exact, and the standard error of estimate for each industry is given in the third column of the table. The probability is 0.67 that the true β value for the period lay between plus or minus one standard error (third column) of

Table 8.1. Estimated industry β values using F.T.A. industry indexes

Industry index	Estimated β values	Standard error
Paper and Packaging*	0.69	0.09
Chemicals*	1.02	0.09
Breweries*	0.82	0.10
Miscellaneous consumer goods (durable)	1.51	0.31

*Source: Hodges (1972).

the estimated β value in the second column. These β values must also be adjusted for differences in capital structure, as detailed in Appendix 8.1.

Companies within the same industry may vary in risk because of operational factors such as competitive structure, pricing arrangements, the level of fixed expenses, and financial gearing. However, measured differences in β values for companies in the same industry may reflect measurement error rather than any underlying or true differences. The measurement error for individual companies tends to be somewhat larger for individual companies than for industries.

Table 8.2 shows estimated β values for some companies in the U.K. Brewery and Distillery industry. Here we do find examples of β values which vary more widely than mere measurement error would suggest. This industry illustrates a good example of differences in competitive structures for different companies. Brewers tend to market their products regionally where market share can vary to a marked degree. Companies which are able to maintain a large market share because of various local barriers to entry can exhibit below-average systematic risk.

Current estimates of β for most quoted companies can be obtained from the London Business School and Data Stream in the U.K. and certain stockbrokers in France and the USA. If industry β values are not obtainable, β values of carefully selected companies representative of an industry can be averaged together for this purpose. If the variations are wide between the β values of companies within the industry, it may be more useful to rank the companies according to their β value. One can then estimate where one's own company might fall on the same scale.

When one knows the value of β for the company, one can then estimate the shareholders' required rate of return for the whole company. However, companies will often consist of many divisions, each operating in a different industry. One division will be involved in different business risks than another and will thus require a different value of β.

For example, the value of β for the Norcros Group has been estimated to be 1.04. Thus the shareholders would require a return of 13.8 per cent for the Group when the after-tax risk-free rate is 6 per cent:

$$R = 0.06 + 0.075 \times 1.04$$
$$= 0.138.$$

Table 8.2. Estimated company Betas in the Breweries and Distilleries industry

Company	Estimated β values	Standard error
X	0.45	0.23
Y	0.89	0.23

However, the Group consists of four divisions, each in a different industry. By looking at the β values of other companies in the same industry, we find that the consumer goods division would be associated with an average industry β value of less than one. In contrast, the construction activities of the Group would be associated with an industry β value averaging 1.33 but varying between 1.00 and 1.8 for individual companies. Clearly, the β values and required rates of return for different divisions of Norcros will not be the same. However, the β values of the individual divisions, weighted by their asset values, would equal the β value of Norcros.

We do not mean to imply that all projects within a division have the same required rate of return. Within one division, many projects will have differing risks and correspondingly different required rates of return. In the subsequent analysis, we provide a pragmatic approach for establishing risk classes for projects within a division of a company.

In this section, we have been using recent historical data to estimate the systematic risk of a company or an industry. However, allowance does have to be made when there are changes affecting the nature of underlying business activities. A company's risk can alter as a result of an acquisition, the sale of a subsidiary, or an internal diversification move. In such circumstances, historical data may become unreliable. As always we ask ourselves whether we have any strong reasons to believe that the value of β is significantly different from one.

ESTIMATING NON-DIVERSIFIABLE RISK OF A CAPITAL PROJECT

The determination of the appropriate discount rate for a project requires identification of the project's non-diversifiable risk. What aspects of a project's risk cannot be diversified away by shareholders? Diversification cannot alter the sensitivity of a project's revenues to changes in macroeconomic factors, for example, growth and consumption. Diversification cannot alter the relationship between fixed expense and variable expense (operational gearing) for the project. Thus we shall consider how these two factors affect the risk of capital projects.

Two alternative approaches to the task of project risk classification can be taken. The first would be to classify projects according to ranking based on *absolute* values of revenue sensitivity and operational gearing. A second approach would be to rank projects on the basis of these same factors measured *relative* to those of the division. The second approach is preferable since the industry β values are available and can be matched with the division's activities.

Implementation of the divisional approach involves risk assessment in three steps.

(a) Determine the value of β for the division (or that part of the industry relevant to the division).
(b) Measure the risk of the project relative to the risk of the division. This relative risk is reflected in the value of a factor F to be defined below.
(c) Obtain the value of β for the project by multiplying the divisional β by the value of F for the project.

We will now suggest some aids in the determination of the value of F.

THE PROJECT RISK FACTOR

The *project risk factor* may be expressed as the product of a number of factors contributing to non-diversifiable risk. Thus,

$$F = f_1 \times f_2 \times f_3 \times \ldots .$$

Several such factors may contribute to the non-diversifiable risk associated with a capital project. We will concentrate our discussion on the volatility of revenues and the operational gearing (change in profits induced by changes in volume) of the project. Thus, by estimating factors f_1 relating to revenue volatility and f_2 relating to operational gearing, we can obtain an approximate value for the project risk factor F in the risk estimation procedure. Any remaining factors we shall assume to be equal to one.

THE REVENUE SENSITIVITY FACTOR

If we have an estimate of a value of β for the division, we can estimate the β value for a project by measuring its systematic risk relative to that of the division. The sensitivity of sales revenue to economic change is a major contributor to the systematic risk of capital projects. Thus we wish to estimate the value of a factor of f_1 measuring how the revenue sensitivity of a project compares with that of the division. First, we must estimate the revenue sensitivity of the division. Then we estimate the revenue sensitivity of the project. Finally, we obtain the value of f_1 by dividing the former into the latter.

Table 8.3 indicates how the revenue sensitivity of a division can be estimated in relation to a change within the industry. Companies A, B, C, and others have divisions operating in the same industry with respective revenues as shown in the table. How sensitive would the revenues of Company B's division be to a 15 per cent decline in industry revenues? As may be seen, the effect of such a change depends upon the relative strength of the company and of other companies in the industry. The 12 per cent drop forecast for Company B's sales compares with a 10 per cent drop for Company A and a 15 per cent drop for Company C. The weighted average

Table 8.3. Determination of relative revenue sensitivities for the division of each company in an industry

Company and industry	Revenues	Possible variation from expected revenues (per cent)
A	100	−10
B	70	−12
C	50	−15
Others	80	−25
Industry	300	−15.3*

*Revenue-weighted average change of revenue for companies in the industry.

of changes for all companies in the industry must equal the assumed 15 per cent drop for the industry.

Now consider the project's revenue sensitivity on the same basis. Suppose that you estimate that a 15 per cent drop in industry revenues could be expected to produce a 20 per cent drop in project revenues. The project is atypical for the division in Company B since you will recall that under the same circumstances the division's revenues were expected to decline only 12 per cent. Now we can calculate the estimated value of f_1, the project's revenue sensitivity factor, relative to the division:

$$f_1 = 20/12 = 1.67.$$

From the revenue point of view, the project is a relatively risky one for the division, but whether this matters will depend upon whether the project's expenses are variable or whether they are relatively fixed in comparison to the division's other assets.

A more formal analysis of revenue sensitivity makes use of *ordinary least squares* regression. In the same way that we obtained values for the beta coefficient, relating the returns on a company's shares to returns on the market, we can obtain a corresponding f coefficient relating percentage changes in a division's sales to percentage changes in industry sales. Industry and trade associations are often good sources of data concerning industry sales, which may be used together with divisional data to analyse sales revenue volatility.

If little is known of the structure of the market in these terms, then one can do no better than to assume that market share will be constant with unexpected changes in industry revenues. Thus the value of f_1 is expected to be equal to 1 in the absence of further information.

If a project's revenues are generated solely from *savings* in fixed expenses, the resulting value of f_1 will be very low, if not zero, since fixed expenses will be relatively insensitive to industry sales.

For most projects, net cash flows are generated by revenues less fixed and variable expenses. The volatility of net cash flows results from the variation of revenues and from the degree to which expenses are fixed. Thus we now consider the effect of operational gearing.

THE OPERATIONAL GEARING FACTOR

If fixed expenses are relatively high in relation to mean industry fixed expenses, changes in revenue will result in relatively more volatile net cash flows. The relationship between changes in net cash flow to fixed expense is called *operational gearing*. In Present Value terms, operational gearing can be determined from the following equation derived in Appendix 8.3:

$$G = \frac{PV + FE}{PV},$$

where PV is the Present Value of project net cash flows excluding the initial investment, and FE is the Present Value of project fixed expenses excluding non-cash charges. The computation of these present values will require an initial assumption concerning the appropriate discount rate.

The operational gearing factor f_2 is the ratio between the operational gearing for the project (G) and the operational gearing of the division (G_D):

$$f_2 = G/G_D.$$

The division's operational gearing G_D may be estimated from the weighted average of typical projects in the division.

The product of the revenue sensitivity factor f_1 and the operational gearing factor f_2 determines the degree to which F $(F = f_1 f_2)$ adjusts the divisional value of β for these specific differences between the project and the division. The β value for the project is estimated to be the β value of the division multiplied by the value of F. The resulting value of β may then be used to obtain the project's required rate of return or discount rate.

The reader may enquire why F does not equal the sum $f_1 + f_2$ rather than the product $f_1 f_2$. The reason is best explained intuitively. A project will tend to be risk-free if the revenue sensitivity is zero, since fixed revenues will tend to fix variable costs and yield net cash flows with little or no systematic risk—even when operational gearing is high. One can readily see that when $F = f_1 f_2$ we have the desired result that zero revenue sensitivity implies $F = 0$ and $\beta = 0$ for the project. However, if F were the sum of f_1 and f_2 this would not be the case.

126

Table 8.4. Value of F for four risk classes
related to a division

Division-related risk class	Value of F	
	Range	Mean
A	0–0.67	0.33
B	0.67–1.33	1.00
C	1.33–2.00	1.67
D	2.00–2.67	2.33

RISK CLASSIFICATION

For most companies, the use of specific discount rates for each project according to its risk may be unfeasible for purely administrative reasons. As mentioned earlier, many companies have adopted a risk classification scheme instead. Typical projects may be divided into four classifications according to their risk. For this purpose, F values may be calculated for various types of projects as an aid to risk classification (as in Table 8.4). The range for each risk class can be set according to the results of our calculations of F factors in the previous section. For example, fixed expense reduction, scale expansion, new products, and research and development may typify four classes. A risk premium can be assigned to each risk class and added to the appropriate after-tax interest rates as in Figure 8.3. An example of the application of the above risk estimation and risk classification procedure is given in Appendix 8.2.

MEANING OF SYSTEMATIC RISK

It is important at this stage to remind the reader that systematic (or beta) risk reflects the sensitivity of a division's revenues and profits to changes in

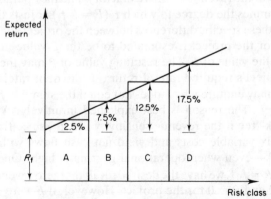

Figure 8.3. Required rates of return and risk classes

the economy and industry. Changes in income which are unrelated or uncorrelated with the economy do not affect a firm's systematic risk. Let us take an unusual example. The β values of many gold-mines are close to zero, implying that the shareholders' required rate of return is close to the risk-free rate of interest. The implication is that portfolio investments in gold-mines are not risky. This conclusion would seem counter-intuitive to a manager in the industry. He would claim that the gold price is volatile and so are gold mining profits; however, that is not the point. Changes in gold mining profits are relatively uncorrelated with changes in the U.K. economy. Thus much of the unique risk attached to a gold mine can be diversified away when held in combination with other securities.

One should be careful to discriminate between components of risk that are important to shareholders and components which are unique to the business and which shareholders can diversify away. Although unique risk is of great importance to employees, suppliers, and others, the possibility of diversification minimizes the importance of this type of risk to shareholders and thus has little effect on the shareholders' required rate of return or discount rate. Only those risks which the company has in common with all other companies have a material effect on the discount rate.

INCORPORATING THE TERM STRUCTURE OF INTEREST RATES

When discounting cash flows expected several years hence, what does one use for the risk-free rate? Clearly, the interest rate on 30-day Treasury Bills may not suffice.

Schaefer (1977) estimated the spot rates of interest prevailing as at August 1975 for 15 years into the future. The estimates are reproduced in Table 8.5.

If the project were risk-free, then the cash flow for each period would be discounted by the spot rate of interest for that period. Thus in August of 1975 the project analyst would discount the cash flow (in money terms) expected in year 10 by 8.0 per cent assuming zero risk.

Table 8.5. Estimated spot rates of interest for selected periods up to 15 years as of August 1975

Year	After-tax interest rate (per cent)
1	7.0
5	7.3
10	8.0
15	8.9

128

Table 8.6. Discount rates for selected periods up to 15 years as of August 1975

Year	After-tax spot rate (per cent)	After-tax risk premium for $\beta= 1$ (per cent)	After-tax required rate of return (per cent)		
			$\beta= 0.33$	$\beta= 1$	$\beta= 1.67$
1	7	7.5	9.5	14.5	19.5
5	7.3	7.5	9.8	14.8	19.8
10	8	7.5	10.5	15.5	20.5
15	8.9	7.5	11.4	16.4	21.4

What must we do if the project is risky? We have already stated that the post-tax risk premium for the average project is $7\frac{1}{2}$ per cent for one period. Research on estimating the changes in the risk premium over time is incomplete. Until further evidence is available, we recommend that one-period risk premiums be used. Thus in August 1975 we would have used the discount rates shown in Table 8.6.

Table 8.6 reveals that differences in the after-tax required rates of return due to differences in the spot rate of interest over time were not large in comparison to differences due to risk or β values. However, as term structure changes, the differences in spot rates can change and may at times become important.

IMPLEMENTATION

On the basis of the foregoing, we recommend that project discount rates should be established according to a procedure which includes the following steps:

(a) A common set of criteria should be developed for risk classification of capital projects. These criteria should relate to systematic risk, that portion of risk related to macroeconomic uncertainties which cannot be diversified by shareholders.

(b) In each line of business, a staff study should undertake to classify typical projects by risk classes according to the degree of perceived non-diversifiable risk. To the extent possible, the same set of criteria for risk classification should be used in all such studies.

(c) A central authority should establish the risk premium which is to be associated with each risk class for the purposes of computing a discount rate. These risk premiums may be revised from time to time based on changes perceived in the total risk for the economy as reflected in the capital markets. For example, a precipitous drop in the market index may result from an increase in the market's risk premium.

(d) The current discount rates for projects should normally be determined by adding the risk premium for the project's risk class to the risk-free rate corresponding to the life of the project. Risk-free rates should be based on prevailing spot interest rates and adjusted for tax.

(e) Interest rates reflect the market's expectation of inflation. Therefore, all computations should be based on projected cash flows stated in money (rather than 'real') terms reflecting expected differential rates of inflation for all costs and revenues after tax.

SUMMARY AND CONCLUSIONS

Risks related to unanticipated macroeconomic changes cannot be eliminated through diversification even by Government. Thus, although private and institutional investors tend to hold diversified portfolios, they are subject to risk. Because investors are risk averse, rates of return in the capital market have been found to reflect risk premiums. Investors can choose from a variety of investments from Government bonds paying risk-free rates of interest to equities promising higher expected rates of return but subject to non-diversifiable risk. The opportunity cost to the shareholder of investment in real assets is the rate of return obtainable from the same funds invested in the capital market in portfolios of equivalent risk. Managers entrusted with shareholders' funds should not invest in capital projects unless the expected returns exceed those available to shareholders in the capital markets.

Capital projects with high risk require high rates of return to be profitable in relation to capital market opportunities. It is not valid to assume that a single discount rate representing an *average* 'cost of capital' will lead to the right decisions on average. The use of a single Test Discount Rate regardless of risk will bias capital investment towards high-risk projects which are unprofitable.

Thus, the typical capital projects should be grouped into risk classes according to the exposure to broad economic risks that each represents. The discount rate for each risk class should reflect the appropriate capital market risk premium. The discount rate should equal the tax-adjusted risk-free rate of interest plus the risk premium for the project's risk class.

Practical criteria for the risk classification of capital projects can be used. Non-diversifiable risk is associated with the relative volatility of revenues and expenses, and an outline of a risk classification scheme has been suggested.

If the world economy should become significantly more or less risky, occasional adjustments to the risk premium for each risk class may be required. Such changes should normally follow large and abrupt changes in capital market prices.

130

Thus, as we have shown, modern financial methods provide a coherent framework for profitability assessment of capital projects. By using risk-adjusted discount rates based on current capitalization rates in the capital market, management can determine Net Present Values which predict the likely net effect of a project on the market value of the firm. This approach, when applied within the context of soundly based corporate planning and strategy, can be expected to help maximize the value of the firm.

REFERENCES AND BIBLIOGRAPHY

Brealey, R. A. and Dimson, E., 'The Excess Return on U.K. Equities: 1919–1975', unpublished manuscript, London Graduate School of Business Studies, 1976.
Broyles, J. E. and Franks, J. R., 'Capital Project Appraisal: A Modern Approach', *Managerial Finance*, **2**, 85–96, Mar. 1973.
Carlton, W. T. and Cooper, I. A. 'Estimation and Uses of the Term Structure of Interest Rates', *Journal of Finance*, **31**, 1067–1083, Sep. 1976.
Fama, E. F., 'Risk-adjusted Discount Rates and Capital Budgeting under Uncertainty', *Journal of Financial Economics*, **5**(1), 3–24, Aug. 1977.
Hertz, D. B., 'Risk Analysis in Capital Investment', *Harvard Business Review*, **42**(2), 95–106, Jan.–Feb. 1964.
Hodges, S. D., Unpublished Ph.D. thesis, London University, 1972.
Hodges, S. D. and Schaefer, S. M., 'A Model for Bond Portfolio Improvement', *Journal of Financial and Quantitative Analysis*, **12**, 243–260, Jun. 1977.
Ibbotson, R. G. and Sinquefield, R. A., 'Stocks, Bonds, Bills and Inflation: Year-by-Year Historical Returns (1926–1974)' *Journal of Business*, **49**, 11–47, Jan. 1976.
Myers, S. C. and Turnbull, S., 'Capital Budgeting and the Capital Asset Pricing Model: Good News and Bad News', *Journal of Finance* **32**, 321–336, May 1977.
Rubenstein, M., 'A Mean-Variance Synthesis of Corporate Financial Theory', *Journal of Finance* **28**, 167–181, Mar. 1973.
Schaefer, S. M., 'On Measuring the Term Structure of Interest Rates', Institute of Finance and Accounting Working Paper, London Business School, 1974.
Schaefer, S. M. 'The Problem with Redemption Yields', *Financial Analysts Journal*, **33**, 59–67, Jul.–Aug. 1977.
Sharpe, W. F., 'Capital Asset Prices: A Theory of Market Equilibrium Under Conditions of Risk', *Journal of Finance*, **19**, 425–442, Sep. 1964.
Stapleton, R. and Subrahmanyam, D., 'A Multiperiod Equilibrium Asset Pricing Model', unpublished manuscript, New York University, 1976.

APPENDIX 8.1 UNGEARING β

The values of β were obtained from an analysis of changes in Financial Times Actuaries Industry indices in relation to changes in the Financial Times Actuaries Index of 500 industrial companies. Strictly speaking, these values require adjustment for our purposes since the measured β values reflect the financial gearing of the constituent companies. For capital projects, we wish to estimate an ungeared value of β reflecting only the operational risk of assets, free of any financial risk superimposed by borrowing. The adjusted value of β (i.e. β^*) may be found by the following equation.

$$\beta^* = \beta/(1 + D(1 - T^*))$$

where β is the value of the beta coefficient measured from Stock Market data, D is the ratio of the market value of debt to the market value of outstanding equity for a company (or average for an industry), and T^* is the effective discounted tax rate advantage to corporate borrowing. $T^* = (0.52 - 0.34)/(1 - 0.34) = 0.27$ in the U.K. when the rate of Corporation Tax is 52 per cent and the standard rate of personal tax is 34 per cent. The term T^* is discussed in Chapters 18 and 19.

APPENDIX 8.2 EXAMPLE: PROJECT β VALUES AND REQUIRED RATES OF RETURN

The following provides the necessary divisional and project data to calculate project's risk and required rate of return using the method described in the chapter.

Divisional data		
β-value	=	1.0
Debt to market value of equity ratio	=	0.15
Operational gearing	=	1.2
Expected change in divisional sales revenue with a 10 per cent change in industry revenue	=	10 per cent
Project data		
Expected change in project sales revenue with a 10 per cent change in industry revenue	=	7 per cent
Net cash flow per period		100
Fixed expense per period		30
Interest rate		10 per cent

Analysis

1. First we need to find the ungeared systematic risk of the division employing the adjustment given in Appendix 8.1:

   Ungeared divisional β value $= \beta/(1 + D(1 - T^*))$
   $$= 1.0/(1 + 0.15(1 - 0.27))$$
   $$= 0.90.$$

2. Having estimated the ungeared β value for the division, we can now obtain a table of risk premiums for project risk classes within the division.

Multiplying the risk premiums in Figure 8.3 by 0.90 we obtain the risk premiums for the division, given in Table 8.A1.

Table 8.A1. Divisional risk premiums: β values and risk premiums when the Class B beta coefficient equals 0.90

Class		Risk Premium (per cent)
A	0.30	2.25
B	0.90	6.75
C	1.50	11.25
D	2.10	15.75

3. Now that we have estimated divisional risk premiums, we must estimate the risk class for our project. First we require an estimate of the revenue sensitivity factor:

Revenue sensitivity factor $f_1 = 7/10 = 0.7$.

4. The impact of the revenue sensitivity factor on the project's risk will depend upon the project's fixed and variable cash expense structure. The project's operational gearing ratio is determined from net cash flow and fixed expense per period as follows:

$G = (100A_{N,R} + 30A_{N,R})/100A_{N,R} = (100 + 30))/100 = 1.3$.

On the other hand, the division's operational gearing ratio is already known to be

$G_D = 1.2$.

The project's operational gearing factor f_2 is defined as the ratio between the project and divisional operational gearing ratios:

$f_2 = G/G_D = 1.3/1.2 = 1.08$.

5. The project risk factor is defined as the product of the project's revenue sensitivity factor and its operational gearing factor:

$F = f_1 \times f_2$
$= 0.7 \times 1.08 = 0.76$.

6. Referring to Table 8.4, we find that the risk class is 'B' for the project. The risk premium for Class B projects in this division was estimated in step 2 above to be 6.75 per cent. Therefore, the risk adjusted discount

rate is

$$R = (1 - 0.34)\ 10 + 6.75$$
$$= 13.3 \text{ per cent after tax.}$$

APPENDIX 8.3. OPERATIONAL GEARING

Operational gearing is defined as the percentage change in operating income that results from a percentage change in units sold. In present-value terms, the definition becomes the percentage change in Present Value resulting from a percentage change in the Present Value of units sold:

$$G = \frac{\Delta V}{V} \bigg/ \frac{\Delta Q}{Q},$$

where V is the Present Value of the project and Q is the Present Value of the units sold. Note that in terms of fixed and variable costs, the value of V is,

$$V = Q(p - v) - F.$$

where Q is the Present Value of the units sold, p is the price per unit, v is the variable expense per unit, and F is the Present Value of fixed expense. Thus since

$$\frac{\Delta V}{\Delta Q} = (p - v)$$

$$G = \frac{Q}{V}\ (p - v).$$

Therefore

$$G = \frac{V + F}{V}.$$

REVIEW QUESTIONS

1. Why will a single discount rate reflecting average risk for the company not yield correct capital investment decisions on average when used to analyse all projects?

2. What are the chief methods by which risk has traditionally been taken into consideration in the analysis of capital investment analysis?

3. How can the systematic risk of companies be used to estimate required rates of return for divisions within companies?

4. What are some of the principal factors determining the systematic risk of a capital project?

5. How can the required rate of return for a project be related to the required rate of return for a division?

6. What influence should the term structure of interest rates have on the discount rates of individual capital projects?

EXERCISES

1. A firm is considering three projects A, B, and C, which have β values of 0.5, 1, and 1.5 and expected returns of 10, 12.5, and 14 per cent, respectively. Given a risk-free rate of interest equal to 5 per cent, illustrate graphically the above situation. Show how the firm would accept or reject each project on the basis of

   (a) a Test Discount Rate,
   (b) estimated capital market required rates of return.

   What are the implications of using a Test Discount Rate? Does the use of a Test Discount Rate ever permit Net Present Value maximization What will happen if the firm persistently accepts only type C investments?

2. Crunch Company operates in an industry where $\beta = 1$ and the market value ratio of debt to equity is, on average, 0.18. The industry average operational gearing ratio is estimated to be equal to 2.0. The Company is considering a project for which the revenue sensitivity is known to be 0.4 and the operational gearing ratio is estimated to be equal to 1.6.

   Given a Corporation Tax rate of 52 per cent, a personal Income Tax rate of 34 per cent, and a rate of interest of 12 per cent, what would be the risk class for the project? What would be the required rate of return for the project?

3. Financial staff of the DEF Company are analysing systematic risk of a capital project with the following characteristics:

Expected change in project sales with a 10 per cent change in industry sales	12 per cent
Net cash flow per 100 units of sales	£250
Fixed expense per 100 units of sales (at expected level of sales)	£ 50

   The project will operate in an industry which has a β value of 1.0, a market-value debt-to-equity ratio of 0.16 and an operational gearing of 1.1.

   (a) Determine the revenue sensitivity factor.
   (b) Determine the operational gearing factor.
   (c) Determine the project risk factor and the risk class of the project.

4. The credit manager of the Dash Company is considering a trade credit application from a new customer, the Flyby Co. Flyby's purchases are likely to fluctuate twice as much as those of the average Dash customer. Acceptance of this account will mean an incremental increase in Stocks and Debtors (at marginal cost) of £100 000 of which half is Debtors. Dash is operating well under capacity and so is eager to have the new account. Variable cost per unit sold represents only 20 per cent of the price and fixed expense represents 30 per cent on existing volume. The operational gearing of Dash is 2.0—the same as that of the industry. The average company's (market value) debt-to-equity ratio now equals 0.3. The industry β value equals 1.2. Assuming that Corporation Tax is 52 per cent and Standard Rate of personal tax is 34 per cent, show that the appropriate value of β to apply to this account is 0.985, i.e. show

   $$0.985 = f_1 \times f_2 \times \text{ungeared industry } \beta.$$

9

DIVISIONAL FORECASTS AND PERFORMANCE MEASUREMENT

The company requires an effective means of measuring how efficiently corporate assets have been managed while distinguishing between changes in performance due to management efficiency and those arising out of unexpected general economic and industry conditions. We examine traditional financial performance measurement tools such as Return on Investment and discuss the advantages and disadvantages. We show how this method of financial control can be improved and used more effectively as a diagnostic tool. However, we conclude that in order to distinguish between management performance and the effects of economic change, one must introduce a direct and more comprehensive review of management efficiency.

ROLE OF FORECASTING

Forecasting plays an essential role in large companies: first, as a determinant of planning and strategy; second, as a basis for the evaluation of capital investment; and third, as a criterion for managerial incentive and performance measurement.

Broad macroeconomic and industry forecasts are used to identify those areas in which the company may plan an expansion or contraction of activities. Alternative investment strategies are assessed along two dimensions representing:

(a) the degree in which the strategy serves to fill an expected scarcity in the economy or industry;
(b) the degree in which the company will be able to obtain and to maintain a competitive advantage.

Companies should recognize that the expectation of profit in any activity requires either a condition of scarcity or a comparative competitive advantage in some market segment.

Strategies and plans developed in this way may then provide a framework for the allocation of capital to divisions. Divisions operating in

135

those activities for which market forecasts are most favourable receive the highest priority in the provision of capital for investment. Conversely, forecasts for a division may result in closure or sale of part or all of the assets. In this way, forecasting provides the basis of long run expansion or contraction and for the creation of new divisions through investment or by means of takeovers and mergers.

Divisional forecasting also provides a context within which the cash flow forecasts for individual capital project proposals may be evaluated. Forecasting requires a variety of assumptions about the scenarios of developing economic events which may unfold in the course of time. These assumptions should be developed carefully through extensive research and consultation, making use of all the avenues of intelligence gathering at the disposal of management. The assumptions then provide the foundations on which both divisional and capital project cash flow forecasts may be built.

MONITORING OF DIVISIONAL PERFORMANCE

Once capital has been committed to a division, group management have a responsibility to monitor the performance of divisional investment. Monitoring serves three vital functions:

(a) Monitoring provides feedback on general economic and industry matters which have been used as the basis of original forecasts and strategic decisions.
(b) Revised forecasts may influence future capital allocation and expansion and disinvestment plans.
(c) Monitoring has behavioral implications for operating managers who wish to be seen to have managed the resources at their disposal as efficiently as possible.

Although financial monitoring may reveal symptoms which may be indicative of good or poor management, financial data alone cannot measure management performance in a changing economic environment. Divisional performance measurement is primarily the measurement of the performance of assets not of management.

MEASURING CASH FLOW OR REPORTED EARNINGS

Much of the company's accounting system is designed to report earnings to shareholders. Such a reporting system is based on a desire to inform as well as to conform to certain statutory requirements which may or may not contribute usefully to the flow of information. Often unadjusted earnings may present a picture which is not consistent with the short-term realities of actual cash flows.

Reported earnings on an annual or semi-annual basis are based on an accrual system whereby profits may be reported before the cash is received, or alternatively cash received may be allocated only in part to the period of receipt. Such 'smoothing' adjustments have been a large part of the accountant's trade. However, such methods are not only used in the earnings reports to shareholders, but are part of the management accounts which may influence investment decisions. Management trying to monitor a project's performance against the cash flow estimates may find the use of reported earnings in place of cash flow confusing.

In Table 9.1, we have set out a project's cash flows after taxes. The net Present Value is 24.15 discounted at a risk adjusted rate of return for the project of 15 per cent.

In Table 9.2, we present the project's earnings as they might appear when reported to shareholders.

In the second row of Table 9.2, we have depreciation as a non-cash charge. This number is supposed to represent the cost of using the asset for the year. The basis of allocating depreciation is often on a straight-line basis. (Since depreciation is, of course, only an accounting entry and is not a cash flow, it will not appear in a cash flow statement.) We now have a 'Profits Before Tax' figure.

However, we cannot simply compute the tax charge by subtracting 50 per cent from the Profits Before Tax. The tax authorities are not interested in the depreciation figures computed by the company's accountants. They will take gross profits of the firm and subtract the capital allowance in order to obtain taxable profits in year 0. Either this allowance may be carried forward or it may be set against profits arising from other parts of the business. We shall assume that it is absorbed by other profits. Thus there is a tax credit to this project of £50 because that is the amount of tax

Table 9.1. Project's after-tax cash flows

	0	1	2	3	4	5	6
				Year			
				(£)			
et cash flow		33.4	33.4	33.4	33.4	33.4	
orporation Tax (at 50 per cent)			−16.7	−16.7	−16.7	−16.7	−16.7
apital cost	−100.0						
ısh grant		− 20.0					
ıx effect of initial allowance (100 per cent)		50					
	−100	103.4	16.7	16.7	16.7	16.7	−16.7

Table 9.2. Reported earnings for the project before and after tax

	0	1	2	Year 3	4	5
				(£)		
Gross profit	–	33.4	33.4	33.4	33.4	33.4
Depreciation[1]	–	−16.0	−16.0	−16.0	−16.0	−16.0
Profit before tax	–	17.4	17.4	17.4	17.4	17.4
Tax (+ signifies tax credit)	+50.0	−16.7	−16.7	−16.7	−16.7	−16.7
Profits after tax	50.0	0.7	0.7	0.7	0.7	0.7

1. Accounting depreciation

Cost of asset	£100.0
Cash grant	£ 20.0
Net cost	£ 80.0
Annual depreciation charge	£ 16.0

2. Cash grant credited directly to the balance sheet.

saved by the initial allowance of £100. In all subsequent years, tax is levied on the gross profit. The project looks much less profitable under these circumstances. Indeed, if management uses past reported earnings as a guide to the performance of a project or division, then they may be seriously misled. Confusion can arise when divisional management who use discounted cash flow methods to make investment decisions are subsequently evaluated by measurement on a reported earnings basis.

The previous example is a somewhat simplistic one. After all, we have assumed that the division consists of only one project. However, divisions consist of bundles of projects, each one having started on a different day. Our analysis is affected in two ways. First, if investment is an on-going process, the differences in trend between reported earnings and cash flows may not be so large as illustrated above. Second, it may be difficult to obtain exact cash flow estimates on a project basis. The accounting system of the firm is based to a significant extent upon the accrual system and other accounting conventions that are oriented to profit reporting on an annual basis. As a result, the firm will only be able to obtain approximations to cash flow, and frequently for groups of projects rather than for single projects.

While performance monitoring should not necessarily be limited to a period of just a year, it need not extend over the whole life of the project or group of projects. Performance should be measured over some planning horizon that is suitable for the particular product line and forecasting environment.

Lerner and Rappaport (1968) have shown—with the aid of a linear programming model—some of the implications of selecting groups of projects, taking into account their expected impact on accounting earnings within a planning horizon. In their model, Lerner and Rappaport maximized the Net Present Value of selected combinations of projects subject to a minimum constraint that the resulting expected annual earnings growth for the company be maintained up to a planning horizon. They found that when accounting earnings flows as well as cash flows influence the investment decision, the chosen portfolio of projects has a lower total Net Present Value than would have been the case had the projects been chosen solely on the basis of discounted cash flow.

Whether one believes that such a model represents appropriate behaviour for managers depends upon how one thinks the capital market values companies. What does the market weigh more heavily, the maximization of Present Value or the stability of accounting earnings? As discussed earlier, risk-adjusted discount rates already reflect non-diversifiable risk. Earnings stability constraints should be unnecessary. Recent evidence to be discussed in Chapters 10 and 11 suggests that the market uses earnings reports as a source of information about future cash flows and that the market effects of short-term changes in earnings are temporary. Thus, too much emphasis by management on attaining short-term earnings targets could actually be detrimental to the market value of the firm.

Earnings are usually reported only annually (or semi-annually), and too often company reports fail to convey how funds have been earned or spent. Obscure reports make the task of analysts more difficult when they try to unravel what has happened to the company. Paucity of relevant information conveys uncertainty to the market and adds to the perceived riskiness of investment in the company's securities. If current earnings fall because of a heavy investment programme, the facts should be explained. Management should communicate with the market and shareholders whenever there are significant developments affecting earnings and cash flows which might otherwise lead to uncertainty.

MEASURING ASSET VALUES

The performance of a division is often measured in terms of a rate of return on capital employed. Why should management wish to know the rate of return earned by each of its divisions? Management may wish to have an indication as to whether further capital investment in a division is likely to be worthwhile considering the risks involved in the investment. Companies often use a single cut-off rate for capital investments within a division. Should management be considering contraction or liquidation of part or all of a division, they will wish to compare the rate of return being earned and likely to be earned on existing assets with the return available in the capital market from funds arising from the sale of assets.

Establishing required rates of return for a division or for an individual asset is only one part of the problem. To make profitability comparisons one must know the value of the assets. Issues concerning the measurement of the value of assets can be very confusing as the debate on 'inflation accounting' has shown. The Sandilands Committee of Enquiry was set up in part as a response to these valuation problems (*Report of the Committee of Enquiry into Inflation Accounting*, 1976).

In many company balance sheets the most frequently used estimate of value is based upon historical costs. However, now there is a concern that balance sheet values no longer reflect the underlying economic value of the assets. As a consequence, taxation and possibly even management decision-making is based on erroneous accounting information. Sandilands sensibly suggested three alternative ways of estimating asset values:

(a) market value,
(b) written-down replacement cost,
(c) economic value.

Where an asset's market value is available, the Sandilands Committee recommended that this value should be incorporated into the accounts.

If the market value is unavailable, the asset's economic value (Present Value) or its written-down replacement cost was advised as being appropriate. The economic value could be determined by forecasting the cash flows of an asset (or group of assets) and discounting them at the appropriate risk-adjusted rate of return. However, when the asset's life and the cash flows are highly uncertain, management may be very wary of making such forecasts even though the data requirements are exactly the same as that required for any capital investment appraisal.

ACCOUNTING RETURN ON HISTORIC BOOK VALUE OF ASSETS

Many companies compute the Return on Investment (ROI) for a single project, a division, or even the whole company. What do these figures mean, and what can they be used for? Referring to Table 9.2 and computing the ROI for the project, the profits after tax are quite clear, £50 and £0.70 for years 0 and 1, respectively. If we use historical cost adjusted for depreciation, the ROI would be 50 per cent initially and 1 per cent in the first year, as illustrated in Table 9.3. The ROI for year 0 is high, but is not representative of the rate of return for the project over its life. Since investment in plant machinery and buildings in the U.K. attracts large initial capital allowances, estimates for ROI may vary from one year to another for a particular division.

Table 9.3. Computation of accounting Return of Investment

End of year	0	1
Cost of asset at beginning of the year	100	80
Cash grant	20	–
Net cost	80	80
Annual depreciation charge		16
Written-down value of the asset	80	64
Profits after tax	50	0.70
ROI = Profits after tax ÷ Written-down value of the asset	62.5 per cent	1.1 per cent

Some companies defer the capital allowances over the life of the project for the purpose of this calculation. In effect, they compute a notional tax based on profits net of depreciation. Although this measure produces a smoother trend for the ROI, it does obscure the effect of the investment incentives embodied in the capital allowance.

A reducing ROI may reflect the pattern of cash flows of the project and not necessarily a deteriorating performance. This reality cannot be overcome by smoothing earnings in order to produce a single ROI forecast or target. Of course, if the investment programme is continuous, the pattern of cash flows will be much less uneven than those shown in Table 9.3. However, investment is usually lumpy and highly correlated with the trade cycle. Consequently, a constant ROI target calculated in this way may prove overly simplistic.

As the written-down value of the assets employed in the denominator of ROI is reduced with depreciation, the value of the ROI ratio will tend to increase. When ROI is computed in this way, operating management frequently pursuade themselves of the 'advantage' of operating obsolete machinery beyond its economic life in order to inflate the measured return on depreciated 'investment' for the division. For this reason, the ROI is often based during the life of the asset on a mean book value, usually one-half the historic cost. Although such a valuation will have little to do with economic value, it does minimize excessive inflation of measured ROI as a result of the diminution of the written-down value of the asset over its remaining life.

ACCOUNTING RETURN ON WRITTEN-DOWN REPLACEMENT VALUE OF ASSETS

Another problem arises with the estimation of asset value as part of the ROI calculation. Producing a high ROI is easy in an inflationary period if the historic cost of the asset is being used. Rather than replace obsolete assets with new assets at a higher cost due to inflation, management may be tempted to operate existing assets beyond their economic lives.

An alternative is to use the replacement cost of assets in the measure of capital employed in the denominator of ROI. Obtaining such an estimate requires the current price of the same or a similar asset. If a written-down value is to be used, one can depreciate the replacement value of the existing asset in the same manner as would otherwise be done with the historic value. The use of the written-down replacement value of assets employed has much the same disadvantage as the use of written-down historic value in the denominator of ROI. The ROI measure will become artificially inflated as the written-down replacement value approaches zero. Again one may consider using some constant proportion (usually one half) of replacement value as the measure of capital employed. Some distortion may still result since the above adjustments may not approximate economic depreciation very well.

Should the market for replacement become inactive, a replacement cost figure may be useless. For example, the replacement cost of oil tankers could not have been used in valuing a tanker in 1977 since few people were buying new tankers during that period. Tanker rates were so low that it was unprofitable to replace such assets. This phenomenon was confirmed by the large difference between the market value of an existing tanker and the written-down cost of replacement with a newly constructed one. The oil tanker example serves to illustrate the fact that assets may have to be revalued when economic conditions deteriorate.

The purposes of different methods of valuation are important for management to understand. Management should know whether the profitability of the division could be improved by a sale of assets; therefore they must know the present value of the asset in present use. Management will also wish to know the value of the asset in alternative uses. If there is a ready market for an asset, a value can be obtained easily. If the market value is higher than the (present) value in the existing use, then a sale should be considered. Conventional methods of valuation have a useful role in performance diagnosis. However, when specific action appears to be required, such as the closure or sale of an asset, a more systematic analysis of the economic value of the asset in current use in comparison to alternative uses or resale is required.

RETURN ON INVESTMENT

...ures of accounting rate of return suffer from much the same ...ngs. The accounting profit in the numerator of ROI is often too ...y arbitrary accrual conventions to represent an accurate picture ...c profit'. Similarly, the denominator will not ordinarily reflect

Table 9.4. Comparison of true ROI and accounting ROI

		Period		
	0	1	2	3
Net cash flows	−1000	475	475	475
Present Value at 20 per cent	1000	725	396	−
Change in Present Value		−275	−329	−396
Economic income		200	146	79
True ROI		0.20	0.20	0.20
Book value				
(straight-line depreciation)	1000	667	333	0
Accounting profit		141	141	141
Accounting ROI		0.141	0.21	0.42

the remaining economic value of assets employed. When both the numerator and denominator of a fraction contain distortions, the resulting value cannot be very reliable. The answer, ultimately, must be the use of cash flow return net of *economic depreciation* on the remaining economic value of assets employed.

Economic depreciation of an asset during a period is defined as the loss of Present Value of the asset during that period. Table 9.4 contains the forecast cash flows generated by an asset during its economic life. Also shown is the Present Value of the remaining cash flows subsequent to each period. Note the way in which Present Value declines more and more rapidly as the end of the asset's life is approached, even though the cash flows are constant. The first differences in the Present Value is the economic depreciation as shown. Subtracting the economic depreciation from the cash flows and dividing by the Present Value in each period, we obtain the return on economic value. This return is a constant and does not change unless the forecast changes!

In Table 9.5, we have another example in which the cash flows are forecast to change. Nevertheless the calculated return on economic value remains constant since the forecast of these changing cash flows does not

Table 9.5. Example of true ROI when cash flow changes are forecasted

		End of period		
	0	1	2	3
Cash flows	1000	−500	−1000	1484
Present Value at 25 per cent	1000	1750	1187	−
Change in Present Value		750	−563	−1187
Economic income		250	437	297
True ROI		0.25	0.25	0.25

change. Here we see an advantage to the use of economic returns. Whereas the accounting measures of ROI will indicate spurious changes in performance when expected cash flow changes occur, the return on economic value will not show a performance variance unless changes occur which were *not* forecast.

DIAGNOSING PERFORMANCE VARIANCES

As we have demonstrated, unless ROI is based on cash flow (adjusted for economic depreciation) divided by the economic value (present value of remaining cash flows) of the assets employed, ROI will change frequently and arbitrarily. These changes reflect the pattern of tax allowances and the effects of arbitrary conventions which may have been used to depreciate the assets employed. Thus conventional measures of ROI incorporate arbitrary variations which may obscure changes resulting from management efforts and from unanticipated changes in the economy and industry.

Ideally, if management is to set ROI targets for a division, they should be based as closely as possible on earnings approximating cash flow adjusted for economic depreciation and assets measured in terms of their remaining economic value in each period. By using forecasts to determine economic value, stable ROI targets can be determined against which performance can be measured more effectively. Variations from target will then reflect only those changes and conditions which had not been forecast. As conditions change forecasts will change and resulting new ROI targets will be required. By updating targets in this way the ROI can be maintained as an effective diagnostic tool.

The level of ROI which constitutes a useful target depends upon the riskiness of the division's activities. In this respect, the ROI concept should be linked to the risk-adjusted required rate of return concept discussed in Chapter 8. However, it should be recognized that although the ROI target must be higher for the more risky divisions, the allowable variation from target must also be wider by virtue of the increased variability of earnings that the greater risk implies.

In measuring performance, the critical issue is how to distinguish between changes that are brought about through alterations in the economy and industry and those that are induced by management efficiency. What is important is that the company recognizes the relationship between cash flow targets and subsequent changes induced by changes in market conditions. One is then able to identify that part of performance variance which is within management's control. To the latter usually requires an audit of the divisions' operating

Let us take a simple example to illustrate the problem. An individual gives £100 000 to an investment manager. He requires the sum to be invested in equities, i.e. in companies whose earnings and dividends streams are risky. The investor is well aware of the risks and the possible gains and losses. At the end of 1 year, the investor finds that the portfolio has provided £5000 in dividends. In addition, the value of the portfolio at the end of the year is £50 000—there are capital losses of £50 000! There is a question to be answered before we decide to fire the manager. What are the losses on other portfolios of similar risk? We find that the Financial Times Index has only fallen 25 per cent. However, we are informed that our portfolio is twice as risky as the Financial Times Index. Thus, our portfolio has performed in a way that is not unexpected given the performance of the market and the risk of our shares.

What lessons are there to be learnt from this simple example? The first is that in measuring performance it may not be adequate merely to know the cash flow or earnings of the year. We should know changes in cash flow that are forecast for future years. How far into the future will depend upon our forecasting ability and what we require the forecasts for. Second, we must know what has happened to the rest of the industry. Have we done better or worse than the industry? If we have performed badly, is this result because we are in a riskier segment of the market place? It is probable that to diagnose the causes of performance differences requires a more serious investigation with the objective of evaluating the systems of the division and its operating procedures, the nature of the fixed assets and their operating efficiency, and the calibre of the management. If this sounds costly and time consuming, then determining the causes of performance changes is inevitably costly and time consuming. An analysis of financial statements is a poor substitute for this task.

This example also illustrates the asset valuation problem. If the firm wishes to calculate the ROI of a project, division, or company, it must use reasonable asset valuations. In the example, the portfolio of shares was worth £50 000 at the end of the first year. If a 15 per cent return is required on the assets, should the returns be calculated on the original cost of the portfolio or on the value of the assets at the end of the year? Clearly, it makes little sense pretending that the assets have retained their original value. Similarly, if the portfolio had doubled in value (to £200 000) by the end of the first year, it would have seemed sensible to recognize this change in value in setting targets for the future and in the evaluation of subsequent performance.

Why should we not recognize these principles when we set targets and evaluate performance for industrial companies? Measurement problems would be our first concern. It is easy for the portfolio manager to establish the value of shares because they are traded daily on a Stock Exchange.

However, the individual assets of a company or its divisions are not usually quoted, and therefore valuations can only be made using the rules of thumb discussed previously. For many assets, market values are unavailable without resorting to expensive negotiating procedures. Present values should be calculated, but that compels management to forecast cash flows. Written-down replacement values may provide a reasonable substitute because they are objective and are also often realistic. However, when written-down replacement value is inadequate, another valuation basis must be found which, as we have seen in Tables 9.4 and 9.5, must approximate economic value to be useful.

CONCLUSIONS

It is important for the company to appreciate the link between investment on the one hand and reporting performance on the other. A company that uses discounted cash flows to appraise an investment and then evaluate the profits of investments using an accrual accounting system may be introducing serious inconsistencies. Similarly, if you evaluate investments on an after-tax cash flow basis but monitor on a pre-tax basis additional inconsistencies arise.

The second issue in the chapter relates to setting targets and measuring performance. Targets should be based on cash flows as far as possible. They may differ from one division to another because of differences in risk. Targets may also differ over time if the underlying cash flows vary. The range of permissible performance variation must also reflect the basis of the forecasts and the underlying risk of the assets. The first question is, 'Has the division outperformed the economy and the industry after adjustment for any risk differences?' A second question, 'Has management performed as well as could be expected under the circumstances?', cannot be answered with financial variables alone: we conclude that such judgements require an efficiency audit.

REFERENCES AND BIBLIOGRAPHY

Bernstein, P. H., 'Advice to Managers: Watch Earnings not the Ticker Tape', *Harvard Business Review*, **51**(2), 68–69, Jan.–Feb. 1973.
Cyriax, G., 'The Theory and Practice of Profit Centres', *Financial Times*, 6th April 1967.
Dearden, J., 'The case against ROI control', *Harvard Business Review*, **47**(3), 124–135, May–June 1969.
Henderson, B. D. and Dearden, J., 'New System for Divisional Control' *Harvard Business Review*, **44**(4), 144–160, Sep.–Oct. 1966.
Lawson, G. H., 'The Rationale of Cash Flow Accounting', *The Investment Analyst*, No. 46, 5–12, Dec. 1976.
Lerner, E. M. and Rappaport, A., 'Limit D.C.F. in Capital Budgeting', *Harvard Business Review*, **46**(5), 133–139, Sep.–Oct. 1968.

Myers, S. C., 'Divisional Performance Measurement', Lecture Notes, London Business School, April 1975.

Report of the Committee of Enquiry into Inflation Accounting (The Sandilands Report), *Cmnd* 6225, H.M.S.O., London, 1976.

Searbey, F. W., 'Return to Return on Investment', *Harvard Business Review*, **53**(2), 113–119, Mar.–Apr. 1975.

Solomons, D. *Divisional Performance: Measurement and Control*, Financial Executives Research Foundation, New York, 1965.

REVIEW QUESTIONS

1. What is the purpose of financial forecasting and of measuring divisional performance?

2. List some of the reasons why cash flows and reported earnings differ. Which one of the following should a firm maximize: (a) cash flows, (b) net present values, (c) short-run earnings per share, (d) long-run earnings per share, (e) net present values subject to an earnings growth constraint?

3. How would you decide whether an asset should be sold or scrapped?

4. Under what circumstances would you expect the present value of an asset within a firm to be less than or greater than the replacement cost?

5. Why do many firms measure the Return on Investment for a division or company? How useful is this measure as an indicator of managerial efficiency?

EXERCISES

1. An asset costs £1000. What is the value of that asset at the end of 4 years using straight-line historic cost depreciation rates of 20 per cent per annum?

   Why might this answer differ from the asset's market (economic) value at the end of that period?

2. An asset costs £500. It is depreciated in the books at a rate of 20 per cent per annum straight line. The asset also attracts a 100 per cent capital allowance on purchase cost.

   If the asset were sold for £350 at the end of 3 years, what would be the tax position at the end of the third year? What would be the gain reported to shareholders?

3. Assume that the forecast cash flows in the previous problem are £700 per annum (after taxes) for 7 years.

   (a) Compute the ROI each year using book depreciation rates.
   (b) Compute the 'true' ROI using present values.

   Assume a required rate of return for the project of 15 per cent.

4. An individual invests £1000 in a unit trust that has a portfolio made up entirely of equities. The equities are concentrated in the mining industries. At the end of the year the portfolio is worth £2000. The Financial Times Index has risen 75 per cent during the same period.

148

(a) How would you measure the portfolio manager's performance? Make any necessary assumptions.
(b) Why is it difficult to measure a portfolio manager over 1 year?
(c) What lessons are in this problem for the manager of an industrial company trying to use ROI to measure divisional performance?

PART IV

VALUATION AND MERGERS

10

DIVIDEND POLICY AND VALUATION OF THE FIRM

Shareholders invest when they expect to receive an adequate return on their capital. This return is received by them in the form of dividends and capital gains on their ordinary shares, thereby providing an important management objective to maintain and increase the market value of the firm. What is the relationship between dividends and capital gains? What are the principles and problems in valuing companies, and how can management maximize the value of the firm?

The problem of company valuation is made difficult by a number of important issues. If there were an efficient and active market for all classes of assets, a market value could be placed on each asset in the company. Even so, the market value of the firm as represented by the value of the equity shares can exceed the total market value of the individual assets. Shareholders may be willing to pay a premium for management's ability to find further profitable projects. Accountants would call this additional value 'goodwill'. With fast growing firms the goodwill element of the share price can be substantial, reflecting investors' confidence in management's ability to find highly profitable projects. Since management may leave or otherwise fail to find the necessary projects, fast growing companies with a significant element of such goodwill in their current market valuation are often considered to be relatively risky.

For some classes of assets there is no active or competitive resale market. A piece of machinery can have a second-hand price that is very different from its economic value. By economic value we mean the expected cash flows associated with the present use of the asset discounted at the appropriate rate reflecting risk and the time value of money. The reasons for this difference in value are mostly due to the cost of physically transferring ownership and the differing abilities of new owners to derive economic benefits from the asset.

The value of the firm will usually reflect the economic value rather than the realizable value of an asset, if the economic value is greater. A problem arises when the realizable value is greater than the economic value of the investment. In this case, the value of the firm to the shareholders depends upon whether the firm intends to retain or to sell the asset. In the

151

152

subsequent analysis, we shall assume initially that there is no goodwill element—and that when the economic value is less than realizable value, the asset is sold.

DEBT AND EQUITY: THE TOTAL VALUE OF THE FIRM

The market value of the firm is equal to the value of all marketable claims on the income of the firm. When the firm's debt and its equity share capital are actively traded on the Stock Exchange, it is an easy matter to determine the market value of the firm. For companies whose securities are not traded, we will require a valuation model based on the market process.

The market value of the firm is the sum of the market value of the debt plus the market value of the equity shares. The value of the debt depends upon prevailing interest rates and its maturity. The debt is classified according to its risk, which is a function of the type of debt instrument, the term and the credit worthiness of the borrower. Since suppliers of debt capital receive nothing more than interest and principal at agreed intervals of time, the price of debt actually observed in the market is easily explained as the Present Value of these two forms of cash flow to the lender, discounted at the current interest rate for that class of debt reflecting a premium for the risk of default. The discount rate may be different for different terms if long-term interest rates reflect expectations of changing short-term rates and uncertainty about future rates of inflation.

VALUATION OF EQUITY

In law, the equity shareholders own the firm, or what remains after all the liabilities have been discharged. The earnings, whether or not they are paid out as dividends, belong to the shareholders. This fact makes the market valuation mechanism for equity less clear than for debt. Debt holders are entitled only to those cash flows which are agreed in the Deeds of Covenant, and they are guaranteed such flows while the firm remains solvent. Ordinary dividends need not be paid to shareholders when the cash requirements of the firm are sufficiently great. Another difference between debt and equity is that the market's discount rate for debt is revealed by the structure of the interest rates prevailing in the market. However, there is no such visible term structure for the equity market, and the rate at which shareholders in aggregate are discounting the benefits they expect from share ownership can only be estimated. How capital market required rates of return, or discount rates, are determined was the subject of another chapter. Let us now resolve the question as to which benefits are discounted by shareholders in the current share value.

THE CASH FLOWS OF THE FIRM

In principle, the company should not invest in assets unless the cash flow returns are greater than alternative returns from investments of the same risk in the capital market. Thus the appropriate measure for valuation purposes should reflect the underlying cash flows during the period plus any unrealized gains or losses accruing on assets. These cash flows are often quite different from the earnings figure published in the firm's accounts. Let us review a simple example. The Profit and Loss Account covering the preceding period for a company is as follows:

	Profit and Loss Account (£)
Sales	10 000
Cost of goods sold	4000
Profits before tax	6000

Now, suppose that at the beginning of the period the firm had purchased an additional piece of equipment for £1000. An accountant would ask what the useful life of the equipment is in order to write off or depreciate the cost over its life. If we assume the life is 10 years, how would the company have reported pre-tax earnings?

	£
Sales	10 000
Cost of goods sold	4000
	6000
Depreciation	100
Profits before tax	5900

Now, what is the tax charge, given a Corporation Tax rate of 50 per cent? The charge is not 50 per cent of £5900. When the company purchased a piece of machinery for £1000, it became entitled to a capital allowance on the cost of the machinery. A capital allowance permits the company to offset a percentage of the capital cost against earnings, before arriving at a suitable profit figure for tax purposes. In this case, the capital allowance is 100 per cent; therefore, taxable profits are £5000 and the tax charge is £2500.

	£
Sales	10 000
Cost of goods sold	4000
	6000
Capital allowance	1000
Taxable profits	5000
Tax @ 50 per cent	2500

The accountant might then report post-tax profits as follows:

	£
Sales	10 000
Cost of goods sold	4 000
	6000
Depreciation	100
	5900
Tax	2500
After-tax profits	3400

One should appreciate that the *cash flow* generated from operations is £3500 after taxes:

	£
Reported profit after taxes	3400
Add depreciation	100
	3500

In addition there has been a capital expenditure of £1000. In valuing the business, we are interested primarily in the underlying funds flows. We are not interested in unadjusted earnings figures that represent book entries; rather we are interested in changes in cash flow or changes in the values of unrealized assets. Both the shareholder and the financial analyst require insights into the different components of cash flows. They also require information concerning realized gains or losses from fixed assets and working capital.

Such cash flows accruing to equity shareholders can be observed at two levels: first, 'free cash flow' net of taxes received by the firm on behalf of the shareholders; and, second, dividends actually received by shareholders.

THE DISCOUNTED FREE CASH FLOW MODEL

Free cash flow represents cash distributable to shareholders. With the Discounted Free Cash Flow Model one can value the equity of the firm by discounting expected cash flows in all future periods. Free cash flow estimates usually are based upon forecasts of future reported earnings. Thus to arrive at a gross cash flow it is necessary to add back depreciation and other non-cash charges. Free cash flow is then found by sub racting planned capital expenditure since reinvested funds will not be paid out as dividends:

	£
Reported earnings after tax	3400
Add back depreciation	100
	3500
Less – capital expenditure	1000
Free cash flow	2500

A more detailed analysis of future free cash flow should be employed by making a distinction between projected earnings on existing assets and returns on new assets. The analyst must

(a) project after-tax earnings on existing assets for the future period;
(b) add back depreciation and other non-cash charges to the earnings' estimates;
(c) subtract replacement expenditure necessary to produce the projected earnings;
(d) subtract planned capital investment in new assets during the future period;
(e) add after-tax cash flows including investment incentives on investments which will have been purchased by the future period;
(f) subtract (add) any expected increases (reductions) in non-cash working capital excluding cash.

The free cash flows described above are funds which are expected to be available for distribution to shareholders. Thus the Discounted Free Cash Flow Model merely calculates the present value of a stream of dividends which (it is expected) will eventually be paid to the shareholders. One must be careful in applying this model to make a distinction for discounting purposes between assets in place, which are relatively certain, and assets which are merely planned or in prospect (see Myers, 1977). Items (d), (e), and (f) will almost certainly require a somewhat higher discount rate than items (a), (b), and (c). Since further investment in the future is optional and thus may be very sensitive to changing macroeconomic prospects, such prospective investment is riskier than cash flows from assets already in existence.

CASH FLOW VERSUS ACCOUNTING EARNINGS IN VALUATION

If such valuation models are a correct description of the way the market values shares, accounting adjustments which affect earnings but which have no implications for underlying cash flows would not change the market value of the firm. One U.S. study by Kaplan and Roll (1972) at the

University of Chicago measured the responsiveness of share prices to significant changes in an accounting convention which altered the level of reported earnings but did not affect tax payments or any other component of the company's cash flow. In the U.S. in 1965, the Institute of Certified Public Accountants changed the accounting rules relating to the method by which investment tax credits were brought into the profit and loss account. Up to that time, the Accounting Principles Board had recommended that the investment credit should be reflected in net income over the productive life of the asset. The new principle suggested that the credit could be taken into the net income account immediately after the asset was purchased. The change implied an improvement in reported earnings but with no consequent improvement in net cash flow. The authors sought to test whether share prices responded to such a change in reporting principles.

In Figure 10.1, we represent Kaplan and Roll's results. They measured the returns or losses relative to the market to shareholders during a period covering the 31 weeks prior to the announcement of reported earnings and the 22 subsequent weeks. Two hundred and seventy five companies made the change. Prior to the announcement, there were small losses, but subsequent to the announcement share prices rose and shareholders made

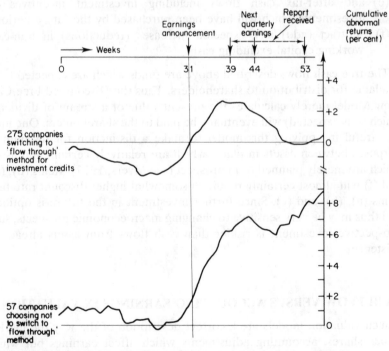

Figure 10.1. Market response to accounting changes which increase reported earnings. (After Kaplan and Roll, 1972.)

small average gains of $3^1/_2$ per cent, approximately. However, 9 weeks after the announcement, these gains began to disappear. The authors of the study suggested that the change to the 'flow through' method boosted reported earnings and for a short time 'fooled' the market (Kaplan and Roll, 1972). By the time the Quarterly Report had been published and digested, the analysts were able to unravel the causes of the earnings' improvement; as a result, the small, temporary gain in market value disappeared. In contrast, the 57 companies (Figure 10.1) which chose not to adopt the more generous reporting principle did well subsequent to the earnings announcement. It is possible they had not felt it necessary to move to the new basis, because they knew their companies were doing relatively well. These results appear to be consistent with models which rely on cash flows rather than reported earnings as the basis on which companies are valued in the capital market.

THE DISCOUNTED DIVIDENDS MODEL

Dividends are the only cash flows actually received by those shareholders who do not sell their shares. The value of a share should therefore equal the discounted present value of the stream of dividends. Thus, if D_t is the dividend expected to be received by *existing* shareholders in time t, the current equity share price P_0 should be given by

$$P_0 = \frac{D_1}{1 + R} + \frac{D_2}{(1 + R)^2} + \frac{D_3}{(1 + R)^3} + \dots, \tag{10.1}$$

where R is the required rate of return or market capitalization rate for this level of risk.

This formula is also appropriate for an investor who expects to sell his shares at some future date. For example, if he expects to sell at the end of the year, the value P_0 is given by the Present Value of the dividend D_1 and of the price P_1 at which the shares are to be sold. However, since the expected value of the future price P_1 is the Present Value of the subsequent dividends, we are left with the same expression as equation (10.1). The Present Value of expected dividends still provides a theoretical basis for the valuation of equity even when shares are to be sold for capital gains.

GROWTH AND THE DISCOUNTED DIVIDENDS MODEL

'Growth stocks' have long been thought to be attractive vehicles for profitable investment. It would be well for us to investigate the implications of growth for the Discounted Dividends Model. If we expect dividends to grow perpetually at the rate g, then the dividend at time t can be related to the current dividend D_0 and compounded growth $(1 + g)^t$.

Thus, the Discounted Dividends Model becomes

$$P_0 = \frac{D_0(1 + g)}{(1 + R)} + \frac{D_0(1 + g)^2}{(1 + R)^2} + \dots \qquad (10.2)$$

If R is greater than g, the sum of this infinite geometric series reduces to

$$P_0 = \frac{D_1}{R-g}, \qquad R > g. \qquad (10.3)$$

This often-used expression provides a deceptively simple means of valuing the equity of a company not quoted on a stock exchange. The required rate of return R and future growth g can often be estimated. Given an estimate of the total dividends to be paid at the end of the next period, one can obtain an estimate of the total value P of the equity shares. However, estimating what would be the market's required rate of return for an unquoted company presents some (though not insurmountable) problems. The calculation of P is particularly sensitive to errors in the difference $R - g$, especially if the difference is small. Thus errors in the estimation of g combined with errors in the estimation of R can make this valuation formula quite unreliable. Indeed, were g to equal R, the value of P would become infinite.

David Durand (1957) discusses the severe limitations of the Dividend Growth Model. No firm can grow forever at a rate exceeding the average growth of the economy without eventually taking over all economic activities of the country—if not the world! If I.B.M. were to be allowed to continue growing at a rate of 18 per cent per annum, its earnings would equal something over 60 per cent of expected total earnings of United States industry in 1995 (projected at a growth rate of 3.6 per cent per annum). There are, of course, political if not competitive limitations on the growth of private companies.

The model has often been used by analysts to place a value on the equity of quoted companies as well as unquoted companies. This practice raises some interesting questions since the market value P of a quoted security is already known. Analysts who use this formula to compute a different value of P than that prevailing in the market presume that they have information concerning D_1, R, and g which is superior to that available to other analysts whose transactions have resulted in the current market value of P.

The model has been put into another form introduced by Gordon (1959) and by Williams (1938):

$$R = \frac{D_1}{P} + g. \qquad (10.4)$$

Thus, for a quoted company where the price P is known and D_1 can usually be estimated, one could estimate the required rate of return R for the company if one could predict g. For stable companies with predictable growth, this expression has proven to be quite useful, for example in determining required rates of return for regulated electric utility companies in the United States. However, the validity of the formula rests on the assumptions inherent in equation (10.3), and one should not deduce that the market's required rate of return *depends* on the dividend growth rate g. The required rate of return on equity of the company depends only on the risk (which may or may not be affected by high growth) associated with investment in the firm's equity and on prevailing interest rates (Chapter 7).

THE PRICE-TO-EARNINGS RATIO

The *price-to-earnings ratio* is widely used by financial analysts in estimating the value of firms. The ratio is simply the current value of the equity divided by the most recent annual earnings figure. If we take equation (10.3) and divide both both sides by the earnings per share, we obtain

$$P_0/E_0 = \frac{D_1/E_0}{R-g} .$$
(10.5)

The price-to-earnings ratio tells us how much investors are willing to pay for £1 of current earnings. In some situations the market will pay £10, in others £20, and so on.

Why are investors prepared to pay more for £1 of earnings of a particular company compared with another? Financial commentators refer to the difference in price-to-earnings ratios as reflecting 'earnings quality'. To be more precise, the difference may be due to varied expectations as to earnings growth or (and) in the required rate of return reflecting the risk of the particular company. From equation (10.5), one can easily see why the price-to-earnings ratio may be misleading. A company that makes temporary losses or very low profits may have a high price-to-earnings ratio. A high ratio in these circumstances can only mean that profits are expected to recover in the future. One could hardly identify such a stock as a growth stock in the usual sense.

GROWTH TO HORIZON MODELS

'Growth situations' almost invariably involve business expansion based upon competitive advantage. A company finds itself in a favourable position with regard to technology, which it can maintain by means of research, patents, and trade secrets. There may be other barriers to entry. Eventually barriers to competition break down, the advantage is lost, and growth rates change. If the firm is successful in maintaining its growth by continually entering new areas where competition is limited, political pressures inevitably enter the picture to limit the economic power of the emerging giant.

Thus, periods of rapid growth cannot be projected indefinitely. It would be more plausible to assume that high projected rates of growth may continue for a time until some horizon, and then alter, for example, to the average growth rate of the economy.

Malkiel's (1963) version of the Dividend Growth Model shows how limited periods of excessive growth can be incorporated. Let us suppose that dividends will grow at a rate g_1 until time-horizon T and thereafter growth falls to rate g_2. The value of the equity would be given by

$$P = \frac{D_0(1 + g_1)^1}{(1 + R)^1} + \frac{D_0(1 + g_1)^2}{(1 + R)^2} + \cdots + \frac{D_0(1 + g_1)^T}{(1 + R)^T}$$
$$+ \frac{D_{T+1}/(R-g_2)}{(1 + R)^T} \tag{10.6}$$

The model can handle rates of growth g_1 in excess of the required rate of return without resulting in an infinite share price. Of course the final growth must be less than R, but this must be the case when g_2 equals the expected average growth for the economy.

FREE CASH FLOW TO THE HORIZON

Malkiel's model (1963) has the severe limitation that future growth is discounted at the same required rate of return as current income. You will recall that, in discussing the Free Cash Flow Model, we said that cash flows associated with prospective investments (i.e. growth) should be discounted at a higher rate than cash flows from existing assets. The reason a higher discount rate is required is that such prospective investments may never take place. Management's future investment decisions will be highly sensitive to macroeconomic developments in the interim period. Thus, in the Free Cash Flow model, we made a distinction between existing assets and growth assets for the purpose of employing different discount rates.

Nevertheless the horizon model contains an important feature which we can obtain by discounting Free Cash Flows up to a planning horizon and by using a horizon value for the firm as a surrogate for cash flow beyond the horizon. Thus, in equation (10.6), Free Cash Flow can be incorporated in place of dividends up to the horizon T. (Growth assumption g_1 will be subsumed in more explicit plans for new investment discounted at a higher rate.) The dividend growth assumption at rate g_2 may still be applied after the horizon in the final term in equation (10.6) representing the discounted horizon value of the firm.

AN ALTERNATIVE VIEW OF GROWTH OPPORTUNITIES

An alternative view of the valuation of a growth company is to regard the share price as equal to the present value of future cash flows from currently planned investment plus some value (previously termed 'goodwill') for the firm's ability to find profitable new projects. Indeed, the shareholder is buying an option on the profits of investments which have not yet been undertaken or even planned. The price of that option is part of the share price. Many financial analysts take this view when valuing private companies for acquisition purposes. Such companies, although relatively small, may be growing rapidly under dynamic management. These analysts will argue that anyone buying a share in the company must pay some price for the ability of management to find future profitable investment opportunities. Evaluating that skill in relation to the profitability of the opportunities is a difficult task. The task is made more difficult by the possibility that management may leave or lose control over a rapidly expanding organization. In any case, the value of potential new projects is normally highly sensitive to uncertain future economic conditions and is therefore associated with high risk. However, it is useful to separate the value of the firm into these two parts in order to see better for what one is paying.

Let us examine an example of an unquoted company active in the retail sector. The company has twenty shops and has grown rapidly under the dynamic management of three people. The owners decide to sell a proportion of the company's equity to a financial institution. How would one go about estimating a value for the company? We are told that the Present Value of the shops currently being managed totals £1.5 million, with after-tax earnings of £200 000. Management points out that they expect to find additional shops in the future and that this expectation must be taken into account in establishing the price. The institution's response is to value the firm at £2 million since other publicly quoted companies in the same industry are valued on a price-to-earnings ratio of ten. The management of the retail company claims that its growth prospects are superior to those of the other more established companies in the sector.

An alternative valuation method would involve adding the Net Present Value of expected cash flows for an estimated number of new shops to be opened in subsequent years to the economic value of existing shops. There are two problems in such an analysis. First, how far into the future can one assume management will be capable and willing to find new shops? Second, is £1 of cash flow from an expected new shop equivalent to £1 of cash flow from a shop that is already constructed and operating?

A rather simple and useful rule of thumb would be to establish the current value of each shop after deducting capital expenditures, etc., and capitalizing adjusted earnings or Free Cash Flow. This analysis provides us with the Present Value of a shop. We must now decide how many new units management will open in the future. We may feel that current management will be able to open five new shops per year for 4 years and subsequently only one thereafter. The latter assumption reflects the average long-run growth of the industry. The Present Value of each current shop is £100 000 and this provides us with some idea of the value of shops once they are in operation. Clearly, for an expected new shop requiring further investment in the future, a purchaser would only pay now a proportion of the Present Value put on an existing shop. Such a proportion constitutes the value of an option on a future asset. The value of the option is a function of when the real asset will be brought into operation and the uncertainty that such an asset will be found and that the earnings will be what is currently projected. Thus, a purchaser might pay as little as perhaps £50 000 for the option on five new shops. A further condition might be that the goodwill or option element should not constitute too large a proportion of the price of the company, for example, less than some fraction of the value of existing assets.

The problem of valuing the earnings of assets which are only a twinkle in the eye of existing management is of real concern to financial analysts: this is the problem of valuing growth in a company. However, there is, as yet, no precise analytical tool available. We can only specify the problem in a form that permits reasoned judgement.

DIVIDEND POLICY

For the purposes of a critical analysis of dividend policy, it will be useful to divide companies into two categories: those which can reinvest cash flow profitably and those which can't.

What do we mean when we say that a company can reinvest its cash flows profitably? We mean that the company enjoys a favourable competitive position with respect to some of its products which allows it to earn economic rents. Through superior technology, patents, scale of production, distribution system, consumer franchise, or other means of obtaining a comparitive competitive advantage in the market, the firm is able to obtain a return in excess of that which would prevail in perfectly competitive product markets and efficient capital markets. Where some element of competition remains, the firm cannot expect to maintain such an advantageous position indefinitely. Thus all projects which can obtain economic rents should be undertaken as quickly as they can be managed effectively. The scale of the investment required could in some cases require capital equalling or exceeding internally generated funds. Under such circumstances, should the firm use any internally generated funds to pay a dividend? Would doing so increase the value of the firm?

Obviously, management should not turn away opportunites to earn economic rents. The required funds could be obtained from a rights issue with some delay and with a flotation cost of perhaps 7 per cent, depending on the size of the issue. Some funds may be obtainable by borrowing and by leasing, but these will be limited by the requirement to maintain a sensible capital structure. Alternatively, some or all the required funds could be obtained by reducing (or at least not increasing) dividends.

The theoretical arguments for not increasing dividends in these circumstances are quite strong. Miller and Modigliani (1961) have shown that in a world without taxes and flotation costs, dividend policy is neutral. A demonstration of their proof is provided in Appendix 10.1. Dividend policy is neutral, they argue, in the sense that shareholders are no worse off if dividends are not paid now providing that the funds can be invested at the shareholders' opportunity cost of funds. The invested funds will provide a larger capital gain or growth in share price than if a dividend had been paid. Taxes, transaction costs, and information aside, the shareholder should be indifferent to receiving income in the form of dividends or in the form of capital gains. Shareholders requiring cash for consumption now can always obtain such cash flows by selling shares and obtaining the resulting capital gains.

However, when we consider the effect of taxes, flotation costs, and transaction costs, dividend policy is no longer neutral: the argument begins to weigh in favour of not paying dividends as long as economic rents are obtainable from new investments. In the United Kingdom, companies enjoy a 100 per cent capital allowance against taxable income for new capital investment. Thus, companies investing at a level equivalent to their annual pre-tax earnings pay no Mainstream Corporation Tax until that day in the future when taxable income exceeds capital allowances (and stock relief, Chapter 5). However, if the firm pays a dividend, it must immediately pay Advanced Corporation Tax on the dividend grossed up at the standard rate of personal tax, currently 34 per cent. The Advanced Corporation Tax (A.C.T.) can be set off against the firm's Mainstream Corporation Tax liability. However, if the latter is zero the firm must still pay A.C.T. and can merely carry forward the credit. The A.C.T. credit is only absorbed when the firm resumes paying Mainstream Corporation Tax. Thus, firms which do not expect to be in a tax-paying position for some years have a strong incentive not to pay a dividend in order to avoid the early payment of Advanced Corporation Tax.

Even if the firm is in a tax-paying position, the payment of dividends may still have the effect of bringing forward tax payments by approximately 6 months since A.C.T. is payable immediately after the quarter in which a dividend is paid while Mainstream Corporation Tax is usually paid nine months after the end of the company's financial year-end. Also, if management declares a dividend and, as a result, has to have a rights issue, they simply provide funds to the shareholder and then ask for the money back again, part of which must be used to pay flotation costs. If there is no rights issue, the shareholder must still pay stockbrokers' commissions and stamp duty if he wishes to reinvest dividends via the Stock Exchange.

Dividends have an information effect on the prices of the firm's securities, which caution one against reducing an existing level of dividend payment. Investors are thought to believe that management is generally loath to reduce a dividend: that the Board recommends a dividend which the Treasurer believes is *sustainable* given a realistic appraisal of future prospects. If investors believe this, then any reduction in the level of dividends would be interpreted as an unfavourable indication of management's view of future prospects. One example in Britain was when Coats Paton suddenly omitted a dividend because management wished to use the funds for profitable investments. There was an immediate drop in the share price, which was followed by a public outcry from Coats Paton's institutional shareholders.

The drop in Coats Paton's share price was not the only matter of concern to their institutional shareholders. Companies which pay a high dividend yield tend to attract a clientele of shareholders consisting of individuals and institutions such as pension funds and universities who pay little or no tax. Such institutions can obtain a refund of Advanced Corporation Tax on their dividends. For this clientele, there are no tax advantages to delayed dividends. On the contrary, if income is required it may be necessary to sell shares to realize capital gains, thus incurring transactions costs. Legal difficulties may also arise in cases where Trustees are entitled to pay out dividends but not capital and thus cannot realize capital gains for beneficiaries.

Consequently, when a company changes its dividend policy, it must obtain a new clientele while the old clientele incurs transactions costs by shifting their investments towards other companies with a more suitable dividend policy. The resulting costs, if expected to be repeated in the future, will be discounted unfavourably in the share price.

Should the firm have a long-established pattern of low dividends and profitable reinvestment, it will have accumulated an appropriate shareholder clientele attracted to this policy. The shareholders will tend to be those in high tax brackets and preferring capital gains to dividends. Capital Gains Tax is currently the lesser of 30 per cent or half the shareholder's marginal tax rate, whichever yields the smaller tax liability on the capital gain. For high tax payers, the argument in favour of a postponement of Advanced Corporation Tax on dividends and the maximization of long-term capital gains on share values at lower rates of tax is a strong one. Conversely, shareholders with marginal tax rates below the standard rate will prefer dividends so that they may reclaim part of the A.C.T. paid by the company.

We have shown that there are strong arguments against companies increasing their dividends while they are in a position of needing available funds for investment in projects earning economic rents. How does the position change for companies which can no longer expect to be in such a favourable competitive position? There should be no doubt that relative to firms in the former position, dividend payout must increase.

When investors recognize that a company is enjoying a phase of profitable growth, they can justify foregoing dividend increases with the expectation of even higher dividends in the future. When the profitable growth phase has passed and management still do not increase dividends, the former justification for such policies no longer exists.

What will management do with the money? Management could accumulate a portfolio of capital market securities, gradually changing the character of the company to that of an investment trust! As investment trusts ordinarily sell at a significant discount on asset values, any moves in this direction are unlikely to be of benefit to existing shareholders. If the company pays tax at a higher rate than current shareholders on investment income, there are further disadvantages to such an option.

Management could also use the funds to take over other companies. However, as we shall see, acquirors normally pay a substantial premium when buying other companies, and sufficient economic advantages from the merger must be expected to justify the premium, otherwise existing shareholders will not benefit. Thus, unless economic rents can be obtained by such uses of funds generated from existing assets, shareholders are likely to expect a higher payout of earnings in the form of dividends.

CONCLUSIONS

In Chapter 2 we found that the opportunities for reinvestment in the capital market imply that expected net cash flows to be generated by capital projects must be discounted to their present worth. We now find that the same process is implied for securities within the capital market itself. Opportunities for reinvestment of interest or dividends from securities imply that these cash flows are discounted in market prices.

Let us suppose that you have been asked by a merger-active company to value a prospective acquisition, which happens to be quoted on the Stock Exchange. Which model would you prefer to use for this purpose—the Malkiel Model? The use of such a model is unnecessary since the present value of the firm's equity is already known: the most recent quoted price on the Stock Exchange multiplied by the number of shares in issue. One of the principle functions of the Stock Exchange is to provide an objective valuation mechanism. Let us not forget to use the market for this purpose. 'But', you say, 'I may disagree with the Stock Exchange quotation'. Either you harbour an angel of prophecy or you have insider information. If not, we can only say that the price is known: you cannot expect to buy the firm for less once your takeover intentions are suspected in the market place. The whole question of mergers is examined in Chapter 12.

166

If the firm is not a quoted company, one can, in principle, determine roughly what the market price would be if the firm had been quoted. At least we can apply the Discounted Cash Flow basis of valuation. If our dividend or Free Cash Flow forecasts are an unbiased estimate of what the market view of expected cash flows from existing and potential new business would be and if our discount rates approximate the market's own discount rate, given the various risks associated with the firm's existing and future assets, we can obtain some estimate of the potential market value of the firm.

As can readily be seen, the value of the firm is very closely related to the value of its constituent capital projects. What is the market value of a capital project? The calculation of this value is the same as that for an unquoted firm. The market value of the capital project is the Present Value of its expected net incremental cash flows exclusive of the capital investment expenditure. From this market value (Present Value) we may subtract the present worth of all investment expenditures to arrive at a 'net market value' (Net Present Value). Thus, when net incremental cash flows for the project are discounted at the market rate for the risk class of the project, the Net Present Value represents an estimate of the net increase in market value of the firm attributable to investment in the capital project. This increase in market value belongs to the equity shareholders, and should be reflected, when it is known or expected, in the total market valuation of the equity. Thus the process of capital investment has as its objective the maximization of the total Present Value or market value of the firm, subject to the many constraints governing the behaviour of responsible management in society.

The proportion of earnings paid out as dividends appear to have relatively little effect on the value of the firm. Earnings not paid out as dividends and reinvested in profitable projects give shareholders a capital gain which compensates them for the loss of dividends. Consequently, firms which can earn economic rents from available projects need not increase dividends if this would result in incurring flotation costs for new capital to finance projects. However, firms which find decreasing opportunities to earn economic rents should pay out cash not required for profitable capital investment so that shareholders can exercise the option either to consume or to seek economic rents elsewhere.

In the following Chapter 11, we look at evidence concerning the efficiency of the capital markets in the determination of the present worth of financial assets.

REFERENCES AND BIBLIOGRAPHY

Durand, D., 'Growth Stocks and the Petersburg Paradox', *Journal of Finance*, **12**, 348–363, Sep. 1957.
Gordon, M. J., 'Dividends, Earnings and Stock Prices', *Review of Economics and Statistics*, **41**, 99–105, May 1959.

Kaplan, R. S. and Roll, R., 'Investor Evaluation of Accounting Information: Some Empirical Evidence', *Journal of Business*, **43**, 225–257, Apr. 1972.

Lintner, J., 'Optimal Dividends and Corporate Growth Under Uncertainty', *Quarterly Journal of Economics*, **88**, 49–95, Feb. 1964.

Malkiel, B. G., 'Equity Yields, Growth and the Structure of Share Prices', *American Economic Review*, **53**, 1004–1031, Dec. 1963.

Miller, M. H. and Modigliani, F., 'Dividend Policy, Growth and the Valuation of Shares', *Journal of Business*, **34**, 411–433, 1961.

Myers, S. C., 'Determinants of Corporate Borrowing', *Journal of Financial Economics*, **5** (2), 147–175, Nov. 1977.

Williams, J. B., *The Theory of Investment Value*, Harvard University Press, 1938.

APPENDIX 10.1. DIVIDEND POLICY AND VALUATION

The proof that dividend policy does not affect valuation involves some simplifying assumptions. The effects of these assumptions on the result will be easily discerned. We assume that the future is known with certainty, that tax effects and transaction costs are unimportant and can be neglected, and that no outside financing is currently planned by the firm.

We will consider two dividend policies as defined by their respective schedules of dividend payments. Under Dividend Policy A the Present Value of the equity is given by,

$$P_A = \frac{D_1}{1 + R} + \frac{D_2}{(1 + R)^2} + \frac{D_3}{(1 + R)^3} + \cdots$$

Under Policy B the first year's dividend D_1 is not paid, but is instead reinvested for one year to earn a return k. Thus the Present Value of equity is given by,

$$P_B = 0 + \frac{D_2 + D_1(1 + k)}{(1 + R)^2} + \frac{D_3}{(1 + R)^3} + \cdots$$

The difference between these two values is:

$$P_B - P_A = \frac{D_1}{1 + R}\left(\frac{(1 + k)}{(1 + R)} - 1\right)$$

Under what conditions would the right-hand side of the above equation be different from zero? When the firm's expected return k on reinvestment is equal to the return R expected by shareholders, the term in the brackets will be equal to zero. In this case there will be no difference between P_B and P_A. The Discounted Free Cash Flow model and the Discounted Dividend model are equivalent if it makes no difference that dividend policy is not designed to pay out all funds available for redistribution.

In imperfect product markets, however, the firm may be able to obtain returns from capital investment in excess of corresponding returns R in the securities markets. This point would argue in favour of the firm withholding dividends if there are floatation costs in raising capital for investment expenditures. When taxes on unearned income exceed taxes on capital gains there would seem to be an argument for paying no dividends at all. (In the U.K., the Corporation Tax system currently in force is designed to neutralize this effect for investors who pay income tax at the standard rate.)

REVIEW QUESTIONS

1. How should the market value of a quoted company be determined?

2. What are the main differences between cash flow and reported earnings for companies?

3. Define Free Cash Flow. When one is employing the Discounted Free Cash Flow Model in valuing a company, which items of Free Cash Flow require the higher discount rate? Why?

4. Under what conditions are the Discounted Dividends Model and the Discounted Free Cash Flow Model equivalent?

5. What problems arise from an assumption of perpetual growth of dividends in valuation models? How can these problems be resolved?

6. What costs are lower when retained earnings are used in place of other sources of capital? In these circumstances, why do most companies continue to pay dividends?

EXERCISES

1. The required rate of return for GHI Ltd as determined by the Capital Asset Pricing Model is 15 per cent. The dividend yield is currently 5 per cent. What expected growth rate in dividends is implied?

2. The JKL Company is expected to continue growing at 3 per cent per year. The company customarily declares an annual dividend equal to 40 per cent of annual earnings. Given a capital market required rate of return for the company of 13 per cent, what would be the value of the company's current price-to-earnings ratio?

3. JKL Company projects the following Free Cash Flows for a company which they wish to purchase. The Free Cash Flows have been projected separately from those expected from existing assets and those expected from new assets:

Year Ending	From existing assets (£)	From new assets (£)
0	100	0
1	80	20
2	60	40
3	40	60
4	20	80
5	0	100

Growth after year 5 is expected to take place at 5 per cent. Dividends in year 6 are expected to be £105. Value the company if the required rate of return on existing assets is 10 per cent and the required rate of return on the anticipated set of growth opportunities is 30 per cent.

4. A company has the following information for the year ending 31st December 1978.

Sales	£20 000
Cost of goods sold	£17 000

During the period, the company purchased fixed assets for £10 000 which will be depreciated over 10 years. There is a capital allowance of 100 per cent for the financial period in which the asset was purchased. The Corporation Tax rate is 50 per cent.

Prepare a Profit and Loss Account, and with the information prepare an analysis of Free Cash Flow for the year.

5. Value an unquoted company which has annual earnings of £100 after taxes. The book value of assets are £500 and depreciation is £100. The current dividend is £50. Capital expenditures were £100 and a 100 per cent capital allowance was taken. Corporation Tax is 52 per cent and personal Income Tax on shareholders is 34 per cent. The industry growth rate is 3 per cent. The risk-free rate of interest is 10 per cent and the company β value is 0.1.

The company has some exceptional expected growth opportunities over the next 3 years and the planned Capital Expenditure Budget for these opportunities is given below.

Year	Capital budget
1	100
2	150
3	100

The above budget excludes capital expenditures for replacement, which are expected to equal book depreciation. The Profitability Index on new opportunities averages a value of 1.33 for this company.

Stating your assumptions, value the company.

11

EFFICIENCY OF THE STOCK MARKET

An efficient capital market is defined as a market in which prices reflect all relevant information. The analysis of the preceding chapter suggests that the market value of the firm should reflect the Present Value of all existing assets plus the Present Value of growth opportunities. It follows that if the stock market is efficient, equity prices will fully reflect the favourable effect of profitable capital investments in fixed assets. Conversely, unwise or unprofitable capital investment decisions would reduce the market value of the firm relative to that of other firms. Managers who neglect shareholder interests in this way thus lay themselves open to the hazards of takeover by more successful firms. The replacement of inefficient management in these circumstances is one way of justifying a takeover.

However, the volatility of stock market prices can give an impression that the market is irrational. In fact, it would be surprising if the market were *not* volatile. The market for long-term Government bonds is volatile, but few would argue that it is irrational. Interest payments and redemption values are known with certainty in this market. However, current bond prices change rapidly with movements in interest rates. The bond market is rational *because* the prices or Present Values of bonds change rapidly with changes in interest rates. By the same token, prices of equities change rapidly in response to changes in the rates at which future dividends are being discounted. Discount rates for equities change in response to alterations in interest rates, risk premiums, and expected cash flows. In a rational stock market, where investors seek returns commensurate with risk, prices will change rapidly in response to changes in risk as well as to changes in interest rates and dividend prospects. The question is, how quickly does the market and individual share prices respond to new information affecting changes in the economic value of the underlying assets of the firm?

The business community still seems largely unaware of the substantial amount of evidence on such questions which has been accumulated by researchers in the past two decades. In this chapter, we will review what we regard to be some of the more pertinent evidence.

PURCHASE AND SALE OF SECURITIES

Equity

An individual who wishes to buy or sell equities must usually complete such a transaction with a jobber through a stockbroker. Jobbers are registered dealers in specific securities usually holding stocks of the securities they deal in. A member of the brokerage firm asks the jobber what price he is quoting for the security in which the customer is interested. The jobber will quote his buying and selling price (unaware of whether the customer wishes to buy or sell).

For I.C.I. the prices quoted on 10th February 1978 were 352 pence and 354 pence. The first was the jobber's buying price and the second was his selling price; the difference is called the spread or the 'turn'. This spread cannot accurately be described as the jobber's profit since the jobber is encouraged by market conditions to hold a number of I.C.I. shares in stock. Since prices change daily and sometimes by large amounts the 'turn' must compensate the jobber for the risk to his capital as well as for the cost of funds. In addition, the jobber requires an adequate salary or income for the job. The size of the 'turn' or spread depends on how risky the security is. Clearly, the more volatile the security, the greater the spread. It is important to realize that the spread is one of the costs to the shareholder of buying shares.

There may be more than one jobber dealing in a security and the stockbroker should shop around just in case there are any differences between two jobbers' quotations. Any differences will be small and will not last very long.

There are additional costs of buying and selling securities. The largest cost comprises the brokerage charge, which will vary depending on the value of the order. However, for a purchase of shares valued at £1000 brokerage fees will be about 2 per cent for purchase. A similar charge will be made on selling unless the sale is made within a limited period of the purchase. In addition the Government exacts a stamp duty of 1 per cent on all buying transactions, whilst small further charges for the registration fee and the contract stamp are made. On a normal buying and selling transaction, the costs will be between 5 and 10 per cent of the value of the transaction. Given these high costs, it should be evident to investors that frequent purchases and sales are unlikely to be profitable.

Once the purchase or sale order has been executed by the broker, a contract note is sent to the customer giving the details of the transaction. The customer does not pay immediately, but awaits the 'settlement day' when all payments are made. The year is divided up into 24 account periods, 20 being of 2 weeks duration and four of 3 weeks duration. Every transaction takes place during an account and payment is made 11 days after the end of the account. Since most accounts end on a Friday, settlement day is usually on a Tuesday. It is of some interest to investors to know that if they buy and sell within the same account they only pay the loss on the transaction or receive the gain on settlement day.

Debt

The costs of purchasing or selling Government or corporate bonds are much lower than for ordinary shares. Government bonds ('gilts') may be purchased directly through a Post Office or through a broker. If the purchase is made through the Post Office, the transactions costs are 10 pence per £100 nominal value, i.e. about 0.1 per cent. The buying and selling prices of gilts are very close, and one need not worry very much about the 'spread' or jobber's 'turn'.

PRIMARY AND SECONDARY SECURITIES MARKETS

A market in securities performs two important functions. The first function (that of a primary market) is to provide both existing quoted companies and new companies with the facility for raising new capital. The second function is to permit holders of existing or outstanding securities to buy and sell, thus facilitating a change of ownership speedily and preferably at low cost. This latter function is usually described as the secondary market.

In Table 11.1, we have reproduced statistics for the market value of British company securities quoted on the London Stock Exchange in March 1971. The total value is in excess of £41 billions. Much of these securities are owned by individuals or their trustees (Table 11.2). The statistics for 1963 are out of date; and, in fact, the proportion owned by individuals has fallen significantly below 40 per cent. Institutions such as the insurance companies and pension funds have substantially increased their shares.

Table 11.1. Analysis of quoted company securities at 31st March 1971

Number of securities	Classification	Market value £ millions
2492	Loan capital (including convertibles)	4 407
1677	Preference capital	565
3074	Ordinary capital	36 936
		41 908

Source: Briston (1975).

Table 11.2. Beneficial owners of U.K. quoted
companies in 1963

	Percentage ownership
Persons, Executors, and Trustees	54.0
Insurance	10.0
Pension Funds	6.4
Investment Trusts	7.4
Unit Trusts	1.3
Banks	1.3
Stock Exchange Firms	1.4
Other financial institutions	2.6
Charities	2.1
Non-financial companies	5.1
Public sector	1.5
Overseas	7.0
	100.0

Source: Briston (1975).

The secondary market functions of the Stock Exchange are often described in critical terms, as though the facility for exchanging ownership hardly contributes to the economy. However, without a secondary market, it is doubtful whether individuals or institutions would subscribe much new capital to companies.

Also, the fact that securities are marketable allows them to be used as collateral for raising fresh capital, e.g. loans. Furthermore, marketability provides a mechanism whereby shareholders can reduce risks by holding a diversified portfolio of securities. The concept of diversification was discussed further in Chapter 7. However, it should be clear that if risk can be reduced by diversification, then the cost of finance to industry will be lower if shareholders can exchange securities and reduce risks as a consequence. In such a market, not only is risk traded but it is also priced. Investing in the North Sea requires greater returns than, let us say, investing in department stores. The market, if it functions properly, will price those risks differently and efficiently.

CONDITIONS CONDUCIVE TO EFFICIENCY IN THE CAPITAL MARKET

A market is defined as efficient if transaction prices fully reflect in an unbiased way all relevant information available to market participants at the time.

The strict assumptions which define perfect markets are not necessary for an efficient capital market. It is only necessary that dealing costs are not too high, that the relevant information is available to a sufficient number of investors and that no individual participant is of sufficient wealth that he can in any sense dominate the market. Such conditions are not very stringent: it should not be too surprising if the evidence indicates that the stock market is efficient.

If securities are priced efficiently, their prices reflect forecasts of expected benefits from owning future cash flows capitalized at appropriate discount rates. Of course, individuals can disagree, and it is this disagreement which results in transactions. The aggregation and resolution of expectations in the transaction process produces an unbiased valuation in an efficient market. Fama (1965) describes such a market as a 'fair game' in which all participants have an equal opportunity for gains. Information emerging subsequent to transactions may prove the market valuation to have been incorrect, and some investors may be seen with hindsight to have experienced unusual gains or losses. However, no individual relying only on foresight can expect exceptional gains (or losses) *on average* if the market is a fair game.

Thus we have the Efficient Markets Hypothesis, which can be subject to various tests. Although a proposition cannot be proved by statistical tests, it can be disproved in the sense that evidence of market behaviour may be inconsistent with either the hypothesis itself or its major implications. Statistical research on this subject is now voluminous and quite sufficient to establish the facts we require. The University of Chicago has a data base containing monthly share prices for all companies listed on the New York and American Stock Exchanges for over 40 years. This data has been distributed to numerous other universities and has been subjected to literally scores of tests by academics and their sponsors on Wall Street. The broad thrust of the results of these tests supports the Efficient Market Hypothesis. Early indications from the new London Stock Exchange data base at the London Business School lead to similar conclusions.

The issue of market efficiency is of such fundamental importance in finance that we should examine the evidence. We can cover only the highlights here. Those who wish to see collections of some of the original research papers are referred to the bibliography at the end of this chapter.

Broadly speaking, the evidence on market efficiency can be divided (Fama, 1965) into three categories of tests:

(a) *Weak-form tests* of the hypothesis that current prices on equities already reflect all information that may be implied in the sequence of past price changes.

(b) *Semi-strong-form tests* of the hypothesis that current equity prices reflect not only the implications of historical price changes but indeed all publicly available knowledge relevant to the valuing of a company's securities.

(c) *Strong-form tests* of the hypothesis that equity prices reflect all relevant information including information available only to company insiders or other privileged groups.

These rough categories classify tests of market efficiency according to the degree and availability of information which may be reflected in share prices. Let us now consider some of the better-known tests in each category.

WEAK-FORM TESTS OF MARKET EFFICIENCY

Weak-form tests of market efficiency concern any information which may be implied in past price changes. If information conveyed by past price changes is not fully reflected in the current price, then a study of past price changes may reveal some useful information for predicting future price changes. If the market is efficient, charting or otherwise analysing past price patterns for the purposes of prediction would be useless since all information which could be gleaned from such analysis would already have been reflected in the current price, which would already reflect any information contained in the price sequence.

Thus share price changes are said to follow a 'random walk' in which all future prices represent a random departure from the current price. These deviations from the current price reflect the influence of *new* information. If changes in share prices follow a random walk implied by the hypothesis of market efficiency, then the expected value of the price of a security at the end of any future period is equal to the current price plus any expected return. No additional information is known which is not already incorporated in the current price. For this reason, *changes* in price would be unrelated to past price changes.

Any relationship or serial correlation between successive price changes can be measured statistically by means of the correlation coefficient. If share prices were to follow a 'trend' and price changes during one period were positively related to price changes in the preceding period, then the measured value of the correlation coefficient would tend to be positive on a scale between 0 and $+1$. If, on the other hand, the market 'over-reacts' and price changes in a period tend to reverse changes in the preceding period, the correlation coefficient would tend to exhibit a value between 0 and -1. Finally, if current prices reflect all available information, the market would exhibit neither trend nor reaction; values of the correlation coefficient would be very nearly equal to zero.

On this basis Kendall (1953) observed that various U.K. economic indices, including shares and commodities, appeared to follow a random series. Fama (1965) reported similar results for New York Stock Exchange prices. In Table 11.3 are given Solnik's evidence for nine countries of average serial correlation for daily, weekly, and monthly returns (log price

Table 11.3. Average serial correlation

Country	Daily returns	Weekly returns	Monthly returns
France	−0.019	−0.049	0.012
Italy	−0.023	0.001	−0.027
U.K.	0.072	−0.055	0.020
Germany	0.078	0.056	0.058
Netherlands	0.031	0.002	−0.011
Belgium	−0.018	−0.088	−0.022
Switzerland	0.012	−0.022	−0.017
Sweden	0.056	0.024	0.140
U.S.A.	0.026	−0.038	0.009

Source: Solnik (1973).

changes adjusted for dividends) (Solnik, 1973). In all cases, the serial correlation coefficients are not sufficiently different from zero to have any economic significance. These results are what the weak form of the Efficient Market Hypothesis would predict, and thus lend support to the view that capital markets in these countries are efficient, at least for the major companies on which these studies are based.

Some analysts have raised the objection that serial correlation tests are insufficiently sophisticated to measure the complex patterns in prices which are supposed to convey the relevant information. In answer to this argument, researchers have proposed the ultimate weak-form test. Those who believe that the stock market is inefficient must demonstrate a trading rule based on historical price patterns which will 'make money'; that is, a set of rules governing the timing of purchases and sales of shares must be shown in exhaustive tests to earn a return after transactions costs superior to a simple buy-and-hold strategy for shares of equivalent risk. One such strategy proposed by Alexander (1961) was shown by Fama and Blume (1966) to be useless. In fact no such strategies have yet been shown to be profitable in relation to the buy-and-hold strategy.

On reflection, the hope that profitable predictions of share price changes could be made on the basis of limited information about past prices was, of course, naive; information from so many other sources relating to the future of the firm are of more fundamental significance. For this reason, many thousands of investment analysts are employed by stockbrokers and their institutional clients to comb through annual accounts and other relevant economic information about the company, the industry and the economy. As a result, information of this nature is likely to be impounded in share prices. It would be a stronger definition of market efficiency to state that all such publicly available information is fully reflected in stock market prices. Thus tests appropriate for measuring market response to other publicly available information have also been formulated.

SEMI-STRONG-FORM TESTS OF MARKET EFFICIENCY

Fama, Fisher, Jensen, and Roll (1969), in their study of stock splits, devised an ingenious method for testing market response to the introduction of publicly available information. Fama *et al.* wished to examine the average behaviour of equity prices of firms preceding and following their announcement of a stock split. Proportional changes in prices were adjusted for capitalization changes and for dividends. These changes were also adjusted for the effect of general market movements around the period of each stock split and for the volatility of each share relative to corresponding price changes for the market index. Adjusted in this way, returns for 940 stock splits between January 1927 and December 1959 were averaged together and cumulated. A plot of these cumulative relative returns in Figure 11.1 showed virtually no average movement at all within the 30 months after the announcement of a stock split. In other words, the public announcement added no new information which was not already reflected in share prices. In the 30 months prior to the stock split, the cumulative relative returns rose rapidly and decisively in the months prior to the announcement.

There is no theoretical reason why share prices should respond favourably in anticipation of a stock split unless the stock split is considered to be corroboration of other evidence that the prospects of the firm are improving. Other corroborating evidence would be a dividend increase, and dividend increases often coincide with stock splits. Fama *et al* divided their sample into those companies which increased their dividends and those which did not and reran the tests. As illustrated in Figure 11.1, those firms which did not increase their dividends suffered a loss in valuation in the 10 months following the stock split announcement, and those firms which had increased their dividends as expected experienced very little additional gain.

Similar tests were devised for measuring share price movements around the date of the announcement of takeover or merger between two companies. Since acquirors usually have to pay a substantial premium over market value to shareholders in the acquiree in order to induce them to sell their shares, one might expect an efficient market to anticipate this windfall. Halpern (1973) and Mandelker (1974) in the U.S.A. found that the market began to anticipate the benefits of mergers up to 8 months on average before the merger. In the U.K., Franks, Broyles, and Hecht (1977) found that market prices began to anticipate mergers at least 3 months before the merger announcement date on average. These results are discussed in more depth in another chapter on mergers.

178

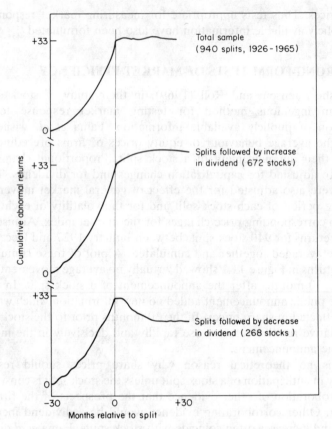

Figure 11.1. Stock splits. (After Fama *et al.*, 1969.)

Because a takeover may be viewed as a capital investment, these results are of particular significance. Evidence indicates that the stock market rapidly reflects the economic benefits of mergers in valuations of securities even before the merger is announced publicly. We would expect a similar market response to extend to other forms of capital investment affecting the economic value of the firm.

A notable exception to the pattern of results reported in most such research is the study by Latané and Jones (1977) concerning the market's response to Standardized Unexpected Earnings (SUE). Latané and Jones compared actual quarterly earnings for U.S. companies with forecasted earnings, using as their forecasting model a least squares extrapolation of earnings in the preceding 20 quarters. Differences between forecasted and actual earnings were standardized to obtain SUE, and all 975 of the New York Stock Exchange companies in their sample were ranked on the basis of the value of SUE in each quarter. Latané and Jones found significant rank correlations between returns on buying and holding the securities and their SUE values. The surprising result was that these correlations persisted after earnings were reported. They show that during a 14 quarter period starting in 1971, one still could have obtained returns averaging over 7 per cent before transactions costs and taxes by buying the top 20 SUE companies and selling short the bottom 20 SUE companies beginning as late as 5 months after the accounting quarter and holding for 3 months.

One should recognize that these results apply mostly to outliers rather than to the great bulk of companies in the sample. The data collection and computing time required to implement an investment programme based on Latané and Jones' study is very great, and thus these results would be of interest only to the large institutional investor. If the market is efficient, institutions will begin to employ the information implicit in SUE and thus eliminate abnormal returns in excess of transactions costs and information handling costs.

STRONG-FORM TESTS OF MARKET EFFICIENCY

That the market discounts publicly available information is not a new or very strange notion. However, the relatively long periods of time before public announcements of important information begin on average to be anticipated command respect. The hoards of professional analysts employed by the stockbrokers, insurance companies, unit trusts, and banks, who have come to dominate the market, are evidently doing their job. Between them they somehow anticipate likely future developments of economic significance to the firm. The resultant buying and selling behaviour of portfolio managers and other investors results in share prices discounting the future in a manner which appears consistent with valuation models and the efficient markets hypothesis.

The efficiency of professional analysis and portfolio management in this respect raises some interesting questions. Surely some professional portfolio managers are more skillful than the general public. Investment in unit trusts must therefore be more profitable than picking shares at random or managing one's own portfolio. The portfolio manager has many advantages which would qualify him as something of an 'insider'. Besides his professionalism, he has many sources of information not generally available to the public, and he has the resources to have this information analysed adequately.

Of course the portfolio manager operates in the market in competition with many other professionals with similar resources. The interesting question is: can professional managers expect to outperform the general market index in a market which has already been demonstrated to exhibit weak-form and semi-strong-form efficiency? Can the private investor hope

180

to improve his investment performance by buying units in unit trusts or mutual funds with a 'good track record'?

Jensen (1968) measured the risk-adjusted performance of 115 mutual funds in the period 1955–64 in comparison to a general market index of equities on the one hand and risk-free Government securities on the other. Mutual funds are the U.S. equivalent of British unit trusts. Each shareholding or unit in such a fund represents a proportion of the underlying assets, consisting of cash and a professionally managed portfolio of securities. The fund agrees to buy back units when required at a price representing a proportion of the current market value of the underlying cash and securities.

Jensen's main findings are summarized in Figure 11.2. The horizontal axis represents a measure of risk. The vertical axis measures monthly (log)

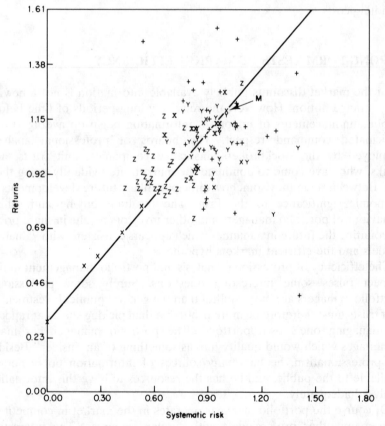

Figure 11.2. Jensen's evidence of mutual fund performance. Scatter diagram of risk and (gross) return for 115 open-ended mutual funds in the period 1955–64. (After Jensen, 1968.) Returns are given as log(Terminal wealth ratio—Gross of expenses)

returns gross of expenses. The diagonal line represents a naive investment strategy of holding various combinations of a risk-free government security (at the intercept) and a holding of a portfolio of all securities in the market at point M. The points represent the returns and associated risk from investment in each of 115 mutual funds. As may be seen, many funds performed relatively badly in comparison to the line. The number of funds performing significantly above the line was not more than would have been expected by the operation of chance.

The average mutual fund given its level of risk did not perform as well as could have been attained by any investor through holding appropriate combinations of government securities and a market portfolio typified by the market index. Any relative advantages of professionalism appear to have been dissipated in management expenses and transaction costs.

Jensen also found that mutual funds selected on the basis of an excellent track record at any point in time did not perform significantly differently from average subsequently.

Nevertheless, one might expect that financial analysts and their respective firms should obtain returns by finding companies and industries which are innovating and expecting increased furture earnings. Speculators can expect to obtain an adequate reward in an efficient market. It is at best a moot point whether speculators are able to make *abnormally* large risk-adjusted returns after transactions costs and taxes.

All this may be a little disappointing to those who had hoped to make their fortune eventually in the stock market without actually soiling their hands in industry. To be sure, *some* insiders must be profiting from advantages not available even to the professionals. An excellent example of an insider is the New York Stock Exchange specialist. The specialist (similar in function to the London Stock Exchange jobber) conducts a market in the shares of various companies on the floor of the Exchange. He does this by buying and selling shares in the companies for which he is the specialist and pays no transaction costs. In this role, he has access to information about various kinds of buying and selling orders which he may execute on behalf of brokers. These orders get first priority before any transactions made on the specialist's own behalf. Osborne and Niederhoffer (1966) have found that the New York Stock Exchange specialists earn a positive return on 82 per cent of their transactions. However, most investors, who pay transactions costs and who do not have access to such privileged information, do not find much comfort in such evidence.

CONCLUSIONS

We have reported only selected highlights of the vast research which has emerged in the last two decades concerning market efficiency. The results have evidenced a substantial consistency: little evidence has emerged that could cast any serious doubt that the capital markets are competitive. In fact, evidence has highlighted the ability of the market to alter valuations of shares relative to other shares before public announcements of the relevant information.

Although some individuals with inside information may gain an advantage from this knowledge, there appears to be no recognizable group other than the market makers on the floor of the exchange who profit in any systematic way from such information. Although Latané and Jones' study (1977) does suggest that prices may not always respond quickly to new information, it remains to be seen whether anybody can profit systematically from such instances.

The evidence supports the assertion that the major capital markets of the world are at least reasonably efficient. As an efficient market, the stock market provides a valuation mechanism discounting forecasts of expected cash flows in the corporate sector. An unbiased capital market valuation mechanism helps to ensure that companies can be financed which engage in investment activities that are profitable in relation to the market's current required rate of return or discount rate. Individual firms which are profitable in this sense should not normally face capital rationing. Finally, management which communicates timely and reliable information to the market about significant company developments may be confident that equity prices will reflect and usually anticipate the economic (cash flow) benefits of its activities.

REFERENCES AND BIBLIOGRAPHY

Alexander, S. S., 'Price Movements in Speculative Markets: Trends or Random Walks', *Industrial Management Review*, **2**, 7–26, May 1961.

Brealey, R. A., *An Introduction to Risk and Return from Common Stocks*, M.I.T. Press, Cambridge, Mass., 1969.

Brealey, R. A., *Security Prices in a Competitive Market: More about Risk and Return from Common Stock*, M.I.T. Press, Cambridge, Mass., 1971.

Briston, R. J., *The Stock Exchange and Investment Analysis*, 3rd ed., George Allen & Unwin, London, 1975.

Cootner, P. H. (Ed.), *The Random Character of Stock Market Prices*, M.I.T. Press, Cambridge, Mass., 1964.

Fama, E. F., 'The Behaviour of Stock Market Prices', *Journal of Business*, **38**, 34–105, 1965.

Fama, E. F. and Blume, M. E., 'Filter Rules and Stock Market Trading', *Journal of Business*, **39**, 226–241, Jan. 1966.

Fama, E. F., Fisher, L., Jensen, M. C., and Roll, R., 'The Adjustment of Stock Prices to New Information', *International Economic Review*, **10**, 1–21, Feb. 1969.

Franks, J. R., Broyles, J. E., and Hecht, M., 'An Industry Study of Mergers in the United Kingdom', *Journal of Finance*, **32**, 1513–1525, Dec. 1977.

Halpern, P. J., 'Empirical Estimates of the Amount and Distribution of Gains to Companies in Mergers', *Journal of Business*, **46**, 554–575, Oct. 1973.

Jensen, M. C., 'The Performance of Mutual Funds in the Period 1945–64', *Journal of Finance*, **23**, 389–416, May 1968.

Kendall, M. G., 'The Analysis of Economic Time Series. Part 1', *Journal of the Royal Statistical Society*, **116**, 11–25, 1953.

Latané, H. and Jones, C. 'Standardised Unexpected Earnings—A Progress Report", *Journal of Finance*, **32**, 1457–1465, Dec. 1977.

Mains, N. E. 'Risk, the Pricing of Capital Assets, and the Evaluation of Investment Performance: Comment', *Journal of Business*, **50**, 371–384, 1977.

Mandelker, G., 'Risk and Return: The Case of Merging Firms', *Journal of Financial Economics*, **1**, 303–335, Dec. 1974.

Osborne, V. and Niederhoffer, V., 'Market Making and Reversal on the Stock Exchange', *American Statistical Association Journal*, **61**, 897–916, Dec. 1966.

Solnik, B. H., 'Note on the Validity of the Random Walk for European Stock Prices', *Journal of Finance*, **28** 1151–1159, Dec. 1973.

REVIEW QUESTIONS

1. (a) What is the Efficient Markets Hypothesis? Under what set of conditions would you expect a securities' market to be efficient?

   (b) Does the available evidence support the contention that the U.K. and U.S. Stock Markets are efficient? Briefly describe two of the tests that have been carried out.

2. If the London Stock Exchange is efficient, what are some of the implications for the Finance Director of a quoted U.K. company?

3. 'Investing on the Stock Exchange is like playing roulette?' In what ways are these two activities similar and dissimilar?

4. Describe the primary and secondary market functions of the Stock Market. How important is the secondary market function for (a) the investor, (b) the allocation of scarce resources, (c) the cost of funds for the firm.

5. Why is the 'efficiency' of the Stock Market fundamental to maximizing net present value as a corporate decision rule?

12

ACQUISITIONS AND MERGERS

In this chapter we examine the evidence relating to the profitability of acquisitions and mergers in the U.K. and the U.S.A. We provide evidence showing that, on average, acquisitions and mergers have benefited the shareholders of the acquired companies and have provided an adequate return to the acquirers. We then describe a framework for valuing a publicly quoted company for acquisition purposes and examine possible profits from a strategy of purchasing shares prior to acquisition. We also point out some errors in the more traditional approaches to valuing companies.

PROFITABILITY OF PAST MERGERS

According to Newbould (1970), half of the managers involved in a survey of companies concluded that their acquisitions had been failures. On the basis of the survey's responses, he felt that mergers generally were not profitable. This result is consistent with a widely held view that acquisitions are expensive and often do not perform as expected. The problem with surveys of this type is that they are difficult to interpret because a manager may be measuring success against a plethora of non-financial as well as financial objectives.

Other authors have tried to isolate the financial consequences of a merger. Mandelker (1974) examined 252 mergers in the United States and estimated the resulting changes in shareholders' returns (dividends plus capital gains). He computed the incremental returns or losses for companies involved in mergers by subtracting from the returns of each company that portion estimated to be attributable to movements in the market rather than to the merger. He computed incremental returns or losses over a period of 40 months prior to the merger and cumulated them. As may be seen in Figure 12.1, Mandelker found that small losses were made by the acquired companies' shareholders during the period between 40 months and 30 months prior to the merger announcement. Subsequently, up to 8 months prior to acquisition, the share prices of the companies moved with the market. At the end of that period, the share

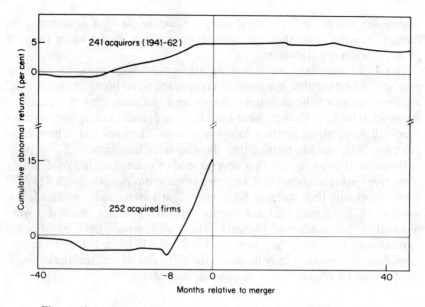

Figure 12.1. Acquisitions in the U.S.A. (After Mandelker, 1974.)

price started to move up relative to the market, and there were abnormal gains of about 18 per cent up to the announcement date (month 0). Similarly, the acquirors also improved prior to the merger, but by a smaller margin of 3¹/₂ per cent. However, this last result is not significant in statistical terms.

Well, what can we say? There must be net gains to mergers simply because one set of shareholders have gained substantially and the other set have either gained or, at least, not lost. 'Not lost' suggests that the acquirers have obtained the risk-adjusted rate of return on the capital outlay for the acquisition, since Mandelker removed market movements and adjusted for any differences in risk between the acquisition and the market.

In the U.K., Franks, Broyles, and Hecht (1977), using a similar method to Mandelker (1974), estimated the gains to shareholders arising from 71 mergers in the Breweries and Distilleries Industry over the period 1955–72. Again, substantial net gains to merging were found for a majority of companies. The acquirees obtained gains of up to 26 per cent over a period of 3 months prior to the announcement of the merger, and acquirers gained about 2¹/₂ per cent on their own market value.

There are, however, some differences between the two sets of results. The U.K. results suggest that most mergers were anticipated less than 3 months prior to the announcement date compared with 8 months prior to merging in the United States. Franks *et al.* obtained similar results to

Mandelker when they employed merger dates in place of announcement dates. They maintain that the announcement date is the more relevant point of reference, however.

The U.K. acquirees were making abnormal losses prior to merging, perhaps indicating that the weaker companies were being acquired. The abnormal gains of the acquirers disappeared subsequent to the takeover. All in all, it looks as though there have been net gains to merging; but most if not all those gains accrued to the acquirees' shareholders. There is no evidence from market returns that the acquirers lost money.

However it must be said that several studies measuring the profitability of mergers using accounting data arrive at different results. Singh's (1975) study concludes that mergers have proved at best neutral, while Meeks' work (1977) suggests that accounting returns on assets employed were reduced in his sample of mergers. These differences may be of some significance; however, they may also reflect differences in the samples employed, or they may only illustrate the difficulty of measuring economic phenomena by conventional accounting numbers.

SOURCES OF MERGER BENEFITS

The most obvious source of merger benefits is an improvement in the operations of the acquired company; that is, the acquirer decides that either he can run the existing operations at a higher level of profitability than the acquiree's management or he is able to improve the growth prospects of the company. There are, of course, a number of problems in trying to estimate the related benefits. The acquirer is usually not sure that the market does not already expect the existing management to obtain the same results. Second, it is important to know why the expected merger benefits have not already been realized. Do they require the unique managerial talents of the acquirer?

Myers (1977) has suggested that one should distinguish between improvements in existing operations and increases in growth opportunities. One cannot assume that future investment opportunities have the same risk as investments that already exist; consequently, a higher discount rate should be used for the forecasting of cash flows associated with such opportunities.

There are, of course, many other reasons for an acquisition. A company may wish to defend its market share, increase its hold on the pricing structure of the industry, or simply prevent an outsider from achieving a toehold in the industry. However these reasons should ultimately be justified in a financial context.

There are plenty of spurious reasons given for merging. For example, a company is rich in cash and the acquirer is in need of such liquidity. This reason is particularly difficult to justify, for who would wish to pay more than £1 for £1 of cash? The acquirer usually has the alternative of going into the market and raising cash through a rights issue.

Another reason given to justify a merger is that the securities of the acquiree are 'undervalued'. This proposition is a particularly dangerous one. If the management believes that they can identify companies or industries which are undervalued, then they should buy shares in a wide variety of such companies. One does not have to acquire and manage other companies merely to take advantage of any undervaluation.

Alternatively, the acquirer may believe that its own shares are overvalued and thus may wish to use 'cheap paper' for an acquisition. If this belief is based on insider information, there are serious ethical problems in not disclosing them to potential new shareholders. If, on the other hand, the presumed overvaluation reflects the acquirer's belief that the whole market is overvalued, then the acquisition will probably be overvalued as well. Such reasons for merging only have some substance if they are based on insider information. The costs of takeover (excluding the bid premium) in the U.S.A. have been estimated by Smiley (1976) at 16 per cent of the acquisition price on average, including managerial time. This cost is high and it is unlikely to be justified solely by insider information, unless it is of an exceptional kind such as a very promising new technology.

MERGERS AND FINANCIAL SYNERGY

There are three additional reasons often advanced to justify an acquisition on the basis of the capital structure of the two merging firms:

(a) unused debt capacity;
(b) reduced risk of bankruptcy as a result of diversification;
(c) lower costs of raising finance.

It has frequently been suggested that if a firm does not utilize its own borrowing capacity, the likelihood of a takeover increases. In Chapters 14 and 15 we shall warn the reader not to overestimate the advantages of debt financing. We show that the advantages of debt lie primarily (and possibly only) in the tax advantages. More specifically, it is claimed that since interest payments are deductible for tax purposes and dividend payments are *not* an allowable expense, some advantage might exist for debt financing. We show in Chapter 14 that the tax advantage to corporate debt is estimated to be at the most 27 per cent, expressed as a percentage of the value of the debt. Given that the firm has an average debt-to-equity ratio of 20 per cent, the value of the firm is increased by 5.4 per cent at most as a result of debt finance.

Suppose a firm has zero borrowings, is it attractive for another firm to acquire it because of the available debt capacity? There are two reasons

188

why it may not be an attractive proposition. The advantage of 5.4 per cent is small and can hardly justify the legal expenses of a merger, let alone the bid premium that must be paid to the acquirees' shareholders in order to gain control. Second, if a firm is undergeared, then other firms or financial intermediaries should buy the shares of the undergeared firm and borrow in order to gain the tax advantage. In fact, such purchases of shares should drive up the price of undergeared companies until their share prices reflect all the unused tax benefits. The important point is that either the share price of the ungeared firm reflects all the tax benefits of the optimum debt-to-equity ratio or other firms need only buy the shares and borrow. It may be unnecessary to mount a full scale bid in order to obtain the tax benefits.

The second reason frequently mentioned to justify a merger is the reduced risk of bankruptcy that results from the co-insurance of the debt of the two companies. What do we mean by the co-insurance of debt? If a firm A defaults, this means that the value of its liabilities is more than the value of the assets. Now if the earnings of another firm B are not perfectly positively correlated with A's earnings, the deficit from A might be met from a surplus of B's assets over its liabilities. In effect, increasing diversification of the firm produces a lower risk of bankruptcy because when one part of the firm does badly, another might do well or less badly.

The benefits of such diversification depend upon the costs of bankruptcy. Such costs include legal and administrative costs of reorganization and liquidation. We know such costs exist, and if the co-insurance effect reduces the risk of bankruptcy and therefore the number of bankruptcies, then the consequent costs will be lower as a result of mergers. However, expected bankruptcy costs have been estimated to be small relative to the value of the firm; and, as a consequence, one should not rely on a reduction in expected bankruptcy costs to justify a significant bid premium. It must also be remembered that co-insurance of debt can take place without mergers, that is by mutual credit insurance.

How are any benefits of the co-insurance of debts distributed? Here we must recognize that existing debtholders may benefit at the expense of shareholders. If a merger reduces the risk of default to existing debtholders, they must benefit. A gain for existing debtholders implies a loss for shareholders. Thus shareholders can lose as a consequence of the co-insurance effect if they cannot call in the existing debt and reissue new debt at a lower interest rate. On the other hand, *new* debtholders will charge less interest as a consequence of the lower bankruptcy risk. In that sense the new debt is correctly priced and therefore there are no wealth transfers.

The other supposed financial advantage of merging concerns the flotation cost of raising new money. By pooling their sources of funds, one or both firms may reduce their costs. This proposition appears to have some substance since we know that the costs of raising a new issue of equity or debt on the stock market can be high, for example, around $7^1/_2$ per cent for an equity issue of £2 million. However, such an advantage could only justify the payment of a large premium for an acquisition which was small and required very large funds for expansion. The message is clear—financial synergy should play a minor role in the justification of most mergers. An exception to this rule may be small companies with substantial growth opportunities being foregone due to insufficient access to the capital markets. In some such cases a merger may offer an attractive alternative to the delays and costs involved in a public flotation of capital.

VALUATION OF A QUOTED ACQUISITION

In previous chapters we have shown that in a competitive stock market the price of a security reflects the underlying worth of the assets plus the Present Value of expected growth opportunities. If we can accept this proposition, then the maximum price that should be paid for a company is its existing market value plus the Present Value of any benefits that may accrue from merging which have not already been anticipated by the market. The maximum premium that can be paid above the current market price is limited by the value of the unanticipated merger benefits if the merger is to be profitable to the acquirer. The valuation of the premium is easier and provides a more rigorous exercise than attempting to value the entire company.

There are some difficulties attached to the valuation of the premium. The current market price might already reflect part of the benefits of this particular merger or of another merger. The evidence reviewed earlier strongly suggests that the market anticipates a merger prior to its announcement. Thus, if the share price of the acquiree rises more than the market (or falls less than the market) after adjusting for risk, the current market price may reflect some of the bid prospects.

An easy method of computing the price *'ex* bid prospects' is to subtract out any abnormal returns over the period when there may have been a rumour circulating about the possibility of a merger. This computation is accomplished by calculating the returns that would have been obtained if the security had moved with the market by means of the market model described in Chapter 7. Roughly speaking, this means that if the market has risen by, for example, 5 per cent over the 3 months prior to the merger announcement and the security is twice as risky as the market, then we would have expected the security to rise by 10 per cent. If the actual increase were 15 per cent, then we would say that there were abnormal returns of 5 per cent. We could assume that the abnormal returns of 5 per cent were related to the merger and subtract these returns from the current share price to obtain the value of the company *'ex* bid prospects'. Let us examine an example.

190

Table 12.1. Estimate of abnormal gains from share price movements

	Dates relative to announcement date		
	−6 months	−3 months	0 months
Financial Times Index	500	512	525
Expected price of acquisition (pence)	80	84	88
Price of potential acquisition (pence)	80	88	97
Abnormal return (pence)	0	4	9

Risk, β, of acquisition = 2.0.

A company is about to announce a bid for another company. The price of the company (Table 12.1) is currently 97 pence. The management have estimated the Present Value of the merger benefits at 25 pence. What is the maximum price the acquiror should pay? If the market expects the bid, and the share price reflects part of the premium to be paid, this must be taken into account in deciding the maximum bid terms. Over the 6 months prior to the announcement date, the share price of the acquisition has risen 20 per cent (after adjustment for changes in the total number of shares), while the market has risen 5 per cent. We would have expected the security to rise more than the market because the estimate of its β value (risk index) is 2.0. In fact, we would expect the security to rise twice as fast as the market, or 10 per cent. The difference between what we would expect, given the movements in the market, and the actual returns constitutes the abnormal gain. Thus, the security has risen by 17 pence against the 8 pence we would have expected; the abnormal gain is, consequently, 9 pence. Thus, the merger cannot be expected to be profitable for the acquiror's shareholders unless the bid price is lower than 113 pence $(97 + (25 - 9))$; that is, the bid price must not exceed the current price plus the difference between the expected merger benefits per share and the past abnormal return per share reflecting the anticipation of the merger.

Of course such abnormal returns may reflect circumstances other than bid rumours; for example, unexpectedly good earnings results. Thus, judgement must be exercised in adjusting market prices to their *ex* bid prospect values.

THE FINANCING OF MERGERS

Acquisitions frequently constitute major capital investments; that is, they can be large in proportion to the acquirer's share capital. For tax reasons as well as for others, the method of financing receives close attention by the firm and its financial advisers. A great variety of financial instruments are used, including convertibles, warrants, and preference shares. As a result, there is a temptation to associate the cost of an acquisition with the specific form of financing.

For example, if an acquisition were all-equity financed, one might suppose that the cost of the acquisition would only reflect that form of financing. This view is difficult to justify and is dangerous in analytical terms. For example, what would we do with a 'run of the mill' capital project? We would initially obtain the present value of the cash flow stream assuming all-equity financing. We would then add the present value of the tax advantages to debt financing, given management's estimates of the project's debt capacity. The mechanics of this procedure are examined in Chapter 14 and apply equally to acquisitions.

We do not wish to imply that the financing package is irrelevant to the acquired company's shareholders. For tax and transaction cost reasons, shareholders might prefer an equity exchange rather than cash. If they received cash, the shareholders would have to pay capital gains taxes and presumably would reinvest in other securities. Similarly, fixed-interest securities might also be unacceptable if they alter the balance of the acquiree's shareholders' portfolios. Since portfolio rebalancing results in transactions costs, the financial package can influence the bid price that is acceptable to the acquirees' shareholders and can ultimately affect the cost of the acquisition. Although the financing package will not significantly affect the present value of the acquisition to the acquiring company, it can affect the value of the bid to the acquired company's shareholders after taxes and transaction costs.

Another consideration is that many shareholders require income and may wish that the income received in the past be maintained after the merger. Although shares can always be sold in order to maintain a level of income, transaction costs and legal limitations on the realization of capital (e.g. for some charities) may make this alternative unattractive.

TRADITIONAL METHODS OF ACQUISITION VALUATION

In the past there has been a great deal of confusion regarding acquisition valuation. In this section, we shall review the more familiar methods and then compare them with the approach suggested in the first part of this chapter. Initially, let us confine ourselves to quoted companies.

The most familiar valuation method is based on an analysis of the earnings per share of the acquirer with and without the acquisition. In Table 12.2 we show the financial details of two companies; company A is the acquirer, and Z is the potential acquisition. In Table 12.3 we have shown the earnings and the earnings per share expected by the market for each company. We assume that A purchases Z on the basis of two shares of A (valued at £5) for every three shares of Z held (valued at £3.90). Thus A

Table 12.2. Financial data

	Company A	Company Z
Current earnings after tax (£m)	1.0	2.41
Number of shares outstanding	10 million	18.5 million
Earnings per share (£)	0.10	0.13
Market price per share (£)	2.50	1.30
Price-to-earnings ratio	25	10
Expected annual growth rate in earnings in the absence of a merger (per cent)	15	0

is paying a bid premium of 28 per cent. If we now calculate the earnings per share of the combined company (AZ) over a period of years and compare them with the earnings per share of A, what do we find?

Initially the combined EPS exceeds the EPS of A alone by an amount totalling 5.3 pence. Is this good news? The answer is, 'Not necessarily', and for two reasons. First, the growth expectations for AZ are lower than for A alone. The effect of growth differences can be seen by following the EPS forecasts. In the fifth year, the EPS of A is expected to be 20.1 pence and that of AZ only 19.8 pence. In the sixth year, the EPS of A is expected to be almost 2 pence greater than that of AZ.

This example suggests that focusing attention on current earnings per share is misleading. Shares are valued for their growth opportunities. Putting it another way, why are shareholders prepared to pay only 13 times the EPS of company Z but 25 times the EPS of company A? It can only be because A's earnings are in some sense more valuable. We have already provided one reason, that of future growth prospects. Another possibility could be that the earnings of A are less risky compared with those of Z. Risk will be perceived in terms of the variability of *future* earnings.

Weston (1966) has suggested that the incremental loss or gain in EPS of the combined company compared with the acquirer on his own should be discounted at an appropriate rate. If the present value of the earnings addition is greater than the present value of earnings dilution, then the acquisition at that price might be considered acceptable. There are a number of objections to this analysis (Franks, Miles, and Bagwell, 1974), and we shall describe a few of them here. First, empirical evidence suggests that shareholders are more directly interested in cash flows rather than reported earnings. Second, the value of a quoted company is measured by the price traded on the Stock Exchange. If the company's analysts are going to try to value the combined company, they are in danger of using different forecasts from those used by other analysts in the market.

Table 12.3. Earnings of A and Z before and after the merger

				Years			
	0	1	2	3	4	5	6
(a) Earnings (£m)							
A @ 15 per cent	1.0	1.15	1.32	1.52	1.75	2.01	2.31
Z @ 0 per cent	2.41	2.41	2.41	2.41	2.41	2.41	2.41
AZ	3.41	3.56	3.73	3.93	4.16	4.42	4.72
(b) Earnings per share (pence)							
A @ 15 per cent	10	11.5	13.2	15.2	17.5	20.1	23.1
Z @ 0 per cent	13	13	13	13	13	13	13
AZ	15.3	16.0	16.7	17.6	18.7	19.8	21.2

Number of shares outstanding: A, pre-merger, 10 million; Z, pre-merger, 18.5 million; AZ, 22.3 million.

Weston's analysis does not separate out the value of the company without the bid prospects from the value of the merger benefits. The important question in valuing a quoted company is, what value to place on the acquirer's ability to extract benefits from the acquisition which are not already impounded in the present market price?

VALUATION OF UNQUOTED COMPANIES

The previous discussion has concentrated on the valuation of quoted companies for acquisition purposes. Valuing unquoted companies is an even more difficult task. One must value the company as it stands and then value the merger benefits. The former can only be accomplished in a very rough and ready manner. One might simply look at existing assets, obtain their resale value, and deduct any liabilities outstanding. Two problems arise with this approach. One may encounter much difficulty in obtaining the market value of the assets. Second, the existing management may feel there are growth opportunities which add significantly to the value of existing assets. In order to overcome this problem, some analysts look at publicly quoted companies in the same industry and use the price-to-earnings multiple established for such companies to value the earnings of the unquoted company. Thus, if the earnings of the latter were £250 000 after tax in the current year, and comparable quoted companies were valued on a price-to-earnings ratio of ten, it could be said that the value of the unquoted company was £2.5 million.

This is all very well if the other companies are really comparable in terms of growth prospects and risk. Very often unquoted companies are smaller and have different growth prospects and possibly different risks. These problems were further discussed in Chapter 10 where it was suggested that a valuation could be obtained by discounting expected free cash flows of the acquiree. It is important to realize that growth prospects (i.e. earnings from *future* investments) are much less certain than the earnings from existing assets of the company. Either the acquirer must apply a much higher discount rate to the cash flows of the growth opportunities or devise a method of relating the acquisition price to the actual profits that flow from future investment opportunities.

Payments for goodwill or growth expectations frequently prove a sticking point in valuing and negotiating a merger with a private company. The problems are evident, since the company's prosperity is often heavily dependent on the existing owner. For this reason, the valuation of the company is frequently related to actual profits subsequent to takeover on the basis of a deferred payments plan. In addition, warranties will be obtained to ensure that stock, debtors, and fixed assets prove to be worth that which is stated in the merger documents.

PRE-MERGER PURCHASE OF THE ACQUIREE'S SHARES

In a highly competitive stock market, we would expect security prices to reflect all available public information. If a company is being mismanaged and is liable to be taken over, one should expect that the market has anticipated the acquisition and the consequent benefits. However, Franks (1978) has pointed out that, if the acquirer's estimates of the merger benefits are greater than the market's estimates, the acquirer may be in possession of superior and valuable information since he may be the only one in the market who knows whether and when he intends to make a bid. The market's premium prior to any announcement will be based upon the mere probability of a bid and a rather uncertain expectation of the resulting benefits. Clearly, if the market is doubtful of the intentions of possible acquirers or underestimates the size of the merger benefits, an intending acquirer may be in a unique position to know if the security is underpriced.

This underpricing will provide an incentive to the acquirer to buy shares in the acquisition prior to the merger announcement. In fact, if the gains from such pre-merger purchases of shares are large enough, the acquirer may consider whether he should postpone the acquisition while accumulating shares. However, the extent of such delays must represent a compromise reflecting a balance between the gains from additional pre-merger purchases of shares and losses of merger benefits due to postponement. The study also suggests that those acquirers with large pre-merger interests in acquirees paid similar bid premiums on average to those who did not accumulate such interests prior to the announcement of a merger. The evidence lends support to certain disclosure principles outlined below, which have been incorporated in the Takeover Code.

THE CITY PANEL ON TAKEOVERS AND MERGERS

The Takeover Code provides a set of principles that must guide the actions of management and financial advisers of both the acquirer and acquiree. The code is administered by the Panel on Takeovers and Mergers, and, although its decisions are not legally binding, they are backed up by sanctions from the Stock Exchange Council. Fourteen principles govern the code and are designed to regulate the conduct of the principals in a bid situation. Specific objectives include:

> fair treatment of acquiree's shareholders,
> adequate disclosure,
> reasonable timetable and procedure,
> no unilateral frustration of a bid by the board of
>   directors of the acquiree.

196

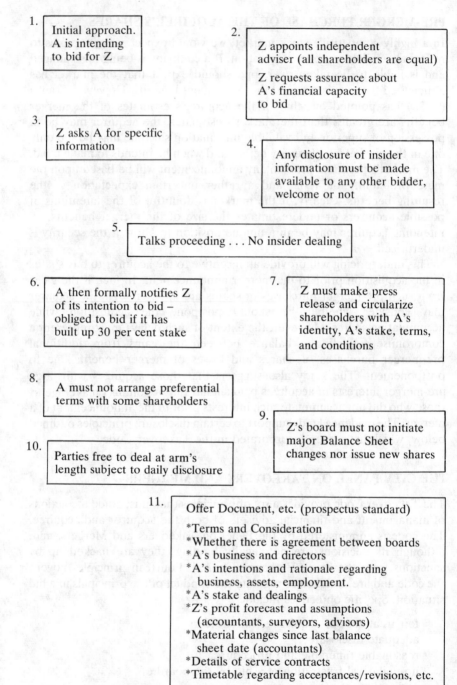

1. Initial approach. A is intending to bid for Z

2. Z appoints independent adviser (all shareholders are equal)

   Z requests assurance about A's financial capacity to bid

3. Z asks A for specific information

4. Any disclosure of insider information must be made available to any other bidder, welcome or not

5. Talks proceeding . . . No insider dealing

6. A then formally notifies Z of its intention to bid – obliged to bid if it has built up 30 per cent stake

7. Z must make press release and circularize shareholders with A's identity, A's stake, terms, and conditions

8. A must not arrange preferential terms with some shareholders

9. Z's board must not initiate major Balance Sheet changes nor issue new shares

10. Parties free to deal at arm's length subject to daily disclosure

11. Offer Document, etc. (prospectus standard)

    *Terms and Consideration
    *Whether there is agreement between boards
    *A's business and directors
    *A's intentions and rationale regarding business, assets, employment.
    *A's stake and dealings
    *Z's profit forecast and assumptions (accountants, surveyors, advisors)
    *Material changes since last balance sheet date (accountants)
    *Details of service contracts
    *Timetable regarding acceptances/revisions, etc.

Figure 12.2. Outline of steps in a bid according to the Takeover Code. (After Warman, 1978.)

In addition, certain rules govern the disclosure of pre-merger interests. A potential acquirer who owns 5 per cent of the prospective acquisition must make a public disclosure of its stake. If the company owns 15 per cent and wishes to make an offer for the remaining share capital, the offer must be made at the highest price paid for any of the purchased shares during the last 12 months. A stake in excess of 30 per cent or more of another quoted company compels the owner to make a bid for the remaining share capital.

Interested parties who are connected with the prospective bidder, eg. his financial advisers and directors' families, must be included within these specified shareholdings. An outline of the appropriate steps in a bid situation is given in Figure 12.2.

THE MONOPOLIES COMMISSION

The Office of Fair Trading may advise the Minister responsible that a particular merger should be referred to the Monopolies Commission. Acquisitions involving gross assets in excess of £5 million or those which may create a potential monopoly are included. Only 44 mergers have been referred so far, but the threat of referral has frequently prevented an acquisition being completed or even initiated. In addition, some mergers have only been permitted after assurances have been given by the companies involved. The Commission may prevent a merger not only on the grounds of monopoly creation but also because the commercial logic has not been justified, or because the merger would lead to unacceptable social costs, such as redundancies in a region of high unemployment.

The main power of the Commission is in the referral itself since this implies a delay in the merger and an almost certain need to renegotiate the terms, assuming that the merger is permitted.

CONCLUSIONS

For the purpose of acquisition, quoted companies can be valued with the aid of current market prices adjusted for abnormal gains reflecting the anticipation of a takeover. To this adjusted value is added the Present Value of expected benefits resulting from the merger. The acquisition can be expected to be profitable to the acquirer if the bid is less than this sum.

Benefits of the merger could arise from an improvement in management obtainable only through merging. Little or no benefits may be obtainable by taking advantage of unused debt capacity. Very frequently an acquirer adopts an aquisition strategy to defend its market share and to increase its hold on the pricing structure of the industry. However, the Office of Fair Trading may ask that such mergers be referred to the Monopolies Commission.

198

Unquoted companies are more difficult to value. Valuations are frequently based on price-to-earnings ratios of similar quoted companies. The price-to-earnings ratio has severe limitations as will by now be obvious. Such methods may overvalue smaller unquoted companies with limited growth prospects unless the quoted companies are really comparable. A more reliable value to use would be the Present Value of expected Free Cash Flow as the most that can be paid if the merger is to have a better than even chance of being profitable.

Mergers can be financed by a variety of securities and by cash. In practice the combination of securities used should be designed to minimize taxes and transactions costs including portfolio rebalancing costs to shareholders.

REFERENCES AND BIBLIOGRAPHY

Appleyard, A. R. and Yarrow, G. K., 'The Relationship Between Take-over Activity and Share Valuation', *Journal of Finance*, **30**, 1239–1250, Dec. 1975.
Dimson, E. and Marsh, P., 'An Introduction to Mergers and Acquisitions', unpublished note, London Business School, March 1977.
Firth, M., 'The Information Content of Large Investment Holdings', *Journal of Finance*, **30**, 1265–1281, Dec. 1975.
Franks, J. R., 'Insider Information, and the Efficiency of the Acquisitions Market', *Journal of Banking and Finance*, Sep. 1978.
Franks, J. R., Broyles, J. E., and Hecht, M. J., 'An Industry Study of the Profitability of Mergers in the U.K.', *Journal of Finance*, **32**, 1513–1525, Dec. 1977.
Franks, J. R., Miles, R., and Bagwell, J., 'Critique of Merger Valuation Methods', *Journal of Business Finance and Accounting*, **1**, 35–53, Spring 1974.
Halpern, P. J., 'Empirical Estimates of the Amount of Distribution of Gains to Companies in Mergers', *Journal of Business*, **46**, 554–575, Oct. 1973.
Han Kim, E. and McConnel, J. J. 'Corporate Mergers and the Co-insurance of Corporate Debt', *Journal of Finance*, **32**, 349–363, May 1977.
Ki Way Lee, 'Co-insurance and Conglomerate Mergers', *Journal of Finance*, **32**, 1527–1537, Dec. 1977.
McCahill, K., 'Profitability of Mergers in the U.K.', PhD. Thesis, London Graduate School of Business Studies.
Mandelker, G., 'Risk and Return: The Case of Merging Firms', *Journal of Financial Economics*, **1**, 303–335, Dec. 1974.
Meeks, G., *Disappointing Marriage: A Study of the Gains from Merger*, Occasional Paper 51, Cambridge University Press, London, 1977.
Myers, S., 'Determinants of Corporate Borrowing', *Journal of Financial Economics*, **5** (2), 147–175, Nov. 1977.
Newbould, A., *Management and Merger Activity*, Guthstead Press, Liverpool, 1970.
Review of Monopolies and Mergers Policy: A Consultative Document, Cmnd 7198, H.M.S.O., London, May 1978.
Singh, A., 'Take-overs, Natural Selection and the Theory of the Firm', *The Economic Journal*, 497–515, Sep. 1975.
Smiley, R., 'Tender Offers Transaction Costs and the Theory of the Firm', *The Review of Economics and Statistics*, **58**, Feb. 1976.

199

Stapleton, R. 'The Corporate Merger: A Study in the Theory of Business Finance'. Ph.D. Thesis, Sheffield University, 1971.
Stapleton, R., 'The Acquisition Decision as a Capital Budgeting Problem', Working Paper, New York University, May 1974.
Warman, L., Unpublished paper on mergers and acquisitions. Lloyds Bank International, London, 1978.
Weston, J. F., 'The Determination of Share Exchange Ratios in Mergers', in *The Corporate Merger* (W. W. Alberts and J. Segall, eds), University of Chicago Press, Chicago, 1966.

REVIEW QUESTIONS

1. Why is it frequently so difficult to value a fast growing, unquoted company?

2. 'Acquisitions which constitute diversification can reduce the variability of earnings and therefore benefit managers and shareholders'. Comment critically on this statement.

3. A quoted property company is totally equity financed; as a consequence, a potential acquirer is willing to purchase the company at a premium on its current market value. The acquirer justifies the bid premium on the basis of the tax benefits to borrowing which would become available after purchase. Can such tax benefits justify the bid premium?

4. Discuss the advantages and disadvantages of using the price-to-earnings ratio as an acquisition valuation tool. Differentiate between quoted and unquoted companies.

5. Why are some industries more susceptible to take over activity than others?

6. Company X wishes to acquire company Y. The required rates of return on the equity of the two companies are 12 per cent and 15 per cent, respectively. Which rate would you use to calculate the present value of any merger benefits which X forecasts? Provide detailed reasoning with your answer.

EXERCISES

1. A merchant bank is about to announce a takeover bid of company X at a price of £1 per ordinary share. The current share price is 90 pence. Over the past 6 months the share price has risen from 50 pence to its current level. The Financial Times Index has risen from 400, 6 months ago, to its current level of 500. Assuming the beta coefficient for the company is 1.25, estimate the bid premium paid by the acquiring firm. What qualifications, if any, would you make to your computations?

2. An acquirer has purchased 10 per cent of a potential acquisition 3 months prior to the launch of a bid. The shares were purchased at a price of 90 pence when the Financial Times Index was 400. At the time of the bid the shares of the acquisition were 110 pence and the Financial Times Index was 440, the bid price was 115 pence and there were 1 million shares outstanding.

   Assuming that the acquiree's beta coefficient equals 1, what is the size of the bid premium? Compute the profit on the pre-merger equity interest.

3. Company A has made a takeover bid for company B, which is a small company engaged in food manufacturing. The offer price is 100 pence in cash for every share in B. Prior to the bid announcement, the market price of B's shares was 90 pence. Company B's management has strongly recommended shareholders to reject this offer on the grounds that the company's shares are worth far more than 100 pence. In particular, they have argued that since B's earnings per share for the past year were 25 pence, A's offer values B on a price-to-earnings ratio of only 4.0. Since the average price-to-earnings ratio for companies engaged in food manufacturing is currently 7.0, B's management argue that their shares must be worth at least 175 pence, and that 200 pence is more realistic when the company's growth opportunities are taken into account. Company B's shareholders seem convinced, and since B's shares currently stand at 115 pence in the market, there seems little chance of A's bid succeeding.

Company A is considering whether to make an increased offer, and if so, at what price. As an adviser to company A, you have been asked to write a brief report explaining the principles of acquisition valuation and how A should establish the maximum bid price.

PART V

FINANCIAL PLANNING

13

FINANCIAL PLANNING AND FORECASTING

Effective financial planning is not only in the interests of management and employees, whose jobs may be at stake in the event of bankruptcy, but also to shareholders, banks, and others who finance the company. In this chapter we explain why financial planning is important, we discuss the principal tools of financial planning, and show how the structure of costs can affect the variability of cash flow. We then discuss the difficulties inherent in financial forecasts, which may be affected by a multiplicity of possible future events. We show how the assumptions underlying forecasts can be organized with the aid of a probability tree and how the analysis of alternative possible futures can be simplified with the aid of scenario building. We then discuss the considerations entering into planning for contingencies which may arise from possible developments in the industry and the economy.

IMPORTANCE OF FINANCIAL PLANNING

The basic investment rules discussed in previous chapters were based on value maximization principles. One such principle states that if a project's expected cash flows produce a positive net present value, the investment opportunity should be accepted. The assumption was that projects can be financed if they are profitable. There are a variety of reasons why this assumption must be qualified. For example, an investment may be profitable, but its acceptance could expose the company to a significant increase in the probability of bankruptcy. There would be significant costs if the company were to go bankrupt. Such costs include not only legal and other fees but the postponement of profitable investment opportunities while the company is being reorganized. Management and employees are usually not diversified. An individual's job usually represents his single most important investment. Indeed, even the possibility of bankruptcy is likely to discourage management from investing in high-risk, albeit profitable, projects.

Financial planning enables the decision maker to appreciate the implications for accepting new investment opportunities on the future cash flows of the firm. Thus, financial planning provides management with some idea of the possible financial risks facing the company. Even if management is more concerned than the shareholders about the financial risk of default, one cannot conclude that management necessarily behaves in a manner contrary to the interests of shareholders. Financial planning enables management to appreciate the financial risks and, if appropriate, insure against them. By sharing the risks with other partners, entering into contracts incorporating escalation clauses, or negotiating long-term finance, the firm may be able to shift or sell some of the risks to other parties. If, by means of the systematic application of foresight in planning, management can forestall unnecessary financial risks associated with a more aggressive investment programme, shareholders can benefit.

Such planning is also important to those interest groups who finance the enterprise. Presenting lenders or shareholders with frequent, unanticipated demands for additional funds can result in unnecessarily high transaction costs.

THE CASH BUDGET AND THE BANK OVERDRAFT

The cash budget is one of the chief tools available to management for determining likely financing requirements in the short to intermediate term. The cash budget is a forecast of cash receipts and cash expenditures for each future period. The choice of periods, for example weeks or months, will depend on the nature and variability of cash flows. Net receipts or expenditures in each period are then used to make cumulative adjustments to the beginning cash balance (or bank overdraft) for the company. Cash balances and bank overdrafts projected in this manner may indicate requirements for additional financing.

Table 13.1 illustrates a simplified example of a monthly schedule of cash receipts based in part on an updated sales forecast and an assumed schedule of payments from credit customers.

The essence of credit sales is the lag between sales and actual receipt of payment. Management is forecasting that 10 per cent of credit sales will be paid with a delay of only 1 month and 90 per cent will be paid with a delay of only 2 months. Thus forecast total collections in a given month represent collections for credit sales in several preceding months and cash sales for that month. Other cash receipts such as dividends from trade investments and sales of fixed assets must also be included. The resulting total cash receipts are then entered on the cash budget in Table 13.2.

Also to be entered in the cash budget in Table 13.2 are total cash payments from Table 13.3. The data in Table 13.3 are based on an operating plan. Purchase of raw materials and subcontracted components in the early months may represent existing commitments based upon an earlier plan. In subsequent months, purchases will reflect current planning and any necessary adjustments to stocks of raw materials and subcontracted components. Wages paid and other operating expenses will

Table 13.1. Projected sales and cash receipts (£'000)

	May	June	July	Aug.	Sept.	Oct.	Nov.	Dec.
Total sales	83	85	88	101	111	103	109	88
Credit sales	74.7	76.5	79.2	90.9	99.9	92.7	98.1	79.2
Collections:								
1 month (10 per cent)		7.5	7.6	7.9	9.1	10.0	9.3	9.8
2 months (90 per cent)			67.2	68.9	71.3	81.8	89.9	83.4
Total collections			74.8	76.8	80.4	91.8	99.2	93.2
Cash sales			8.8	10.1	11.1	10.3	10.9	8.8
Other cash receipts:								
Trade investments			20.0	0	0	0	0	0
Sales of fixed assets			0	0	0	0	40.0	0
Other			1.0	2.0	1.0	1.0	1.0	2.0
Total cash receipts			104.6	88.9	92.5	103.1	151.1	104.0

Table 13.2. Net cash increase/reduction (£'000)

	July	Aug.	Sept.	Oct.	Nov.	Dec.
Total receipts	104.6	88.9	92.5	103.1	151.1	104.0
Total payments	95.0	145.0	105.0	119.0	140.0	90.0
Net cash	9.6	(56.1)	(12.5)	(15.9)	11.1	14.0
Initial cash balance	50	59.6	3.5	(9.0)	(24.9)	(13.8)
Ending cash balance	59.6	3.5	(9.0)	(24.9)	(13.8)	0.2
Maximum overdraft	(20.0)	(20.0)	(20.0)	(20.0)	(20.0)	(20.0)
Excess (shortfall)	79.6	23.5	11.0	(4.9)	6.2	20.2

Table 13.3. Projected expenses (£'000)

	June	July	Aug.	Sept.	Oct.	Nov.	Dec.
Purchases:							
Raw materials	45	45	45	45	50	50	50
Subcontracted components	20	25	25	25	15	15	20
	65	70	70	70	65	65	70
Cash payments for purchases		65	70	70	70	65	65
Wages paid		20	22	22	22	18	18
Other operating expenses		10	13	13	13	7	7
Total operating expenses		95	105	105	105	90	90
Other cash payments:							
Tax					14		
Dividends and interest			40				
Capital expenditures						50	
Total cash payments		95	145	105	119	140	90

also depend upon the operating plan, affecting manpower levels, salary increases, payments for overtime work, etc. Non-operating expenses such as expected payments of taxes, dividends and interest, and capital expenditures should also be included.

The net cash increase or reduction in each period resulting from expected receipts and payments is shown in Table 13.2. For example, at the end of July management expects to have £59 600 in cash when it had an overdraft facility of £20 000. Thus the 'safety margin' or excess is £79 600 as indicated. Note that the excess declines steadily until October when there is an expected shortfall of £4 900.

Cash budgets are generally used for the purposes of short-term financing and cash planning. The forecast may extend to perhaps 18 months into the future on a rolling basis. The frequency with which forecasts are updated depends upon the nature of the business and the speed with which new developments are likely to alter the basis of the forecasts. Normally cash budgets are recomputed no less than once a quarter. In some companies, weekly and even daily forecasts on a computerized basis are required to facilitate money-market operations. For long-term financing the related Funds Flow Projection provides a more convenient planning format.

However, the above procedure often proves to be entirely inadequate as there is nothing in the procedure thus far which can indicate whether the minimum cash balance or maximum overdraft arranged with bankers is sufficient to meet possible deviations from the forecast. It is well worth noting the several points at which uncertainty affects the cash budget, often critically. The sales forecast is usually the least reliable set of data in the budget. Not only may the forecast be inaccurate, but it may incorporate a systematic bias.

A second source of uncertainty is the promptness with which debtors pay their bills. When business conditions are unfavourable for the company, they are likely to be adverse for customers as well. Thus customers (debtors) may be delaying payments at the very time that the cash is most required by the company. Other cash receipts may also have critical effects; for example the projected sales of assets may not happen when expected. Frequently, adjustments to purchases and payments to suppliers cannot be made sufficiently or rapidly enough to neutralize the effects of unanticipated changes in cash receipts. However, if the forecast is not sufficiently conservative, the forecast overdraft requirements are more likely to be exceeded.

THE FUNDS FLOW STATEMENT AND LONG-TERM FINANCING

Long-term financing plans up to 5 years into the future can pave the way for the timely issue of company securities, for example equity, and long-term debt. The provision of long-term finance must reflect major

Table 13.4. A simplified funds flow statement (£'000)

		Year 0 (This year)	Year 1	Year 2	Year 3	Year 4
Profit before tax		95				
Depreciation and non-cash charges to the above		20				
Fixed asset realizations (at market value)		5				
	I	120				
Less						
Stock increase/(decrease)		20				
Debtors increase/(decrease)		10				
Creditors decrease/(increase)		—				
	II	30				
Dividend payments–existing equity		10				
Tax payments		40				
	III	50				
Fixed asset expenditure						
Land and buildings		10				
Plant		10				
Vehicles		—				
Other		—				
	IV	20				
II + III + IV =	V	100				
Net cash accretion/(decrease) I – V =	VI	20				
Net cash movement						
Loans increase/(decrease)		(20)				
New equity issued/(dividends)		—				
Overdraft increase/(decrease)						
Total	VI	(20)				

items such as expected earnings and the acquisition and disposal of fixed assets. For this purpose, projections of sources and applications of funds are employed in the Funds Flow statement.

Table 13.4 illustrates a simplified *funds flow statement*. The problem of uncertainty in the funds flow statement is particularly critical. If profits should turn out to be lower than forecast, the projected requirements for long-term financing will be found to have been inadequate. In this position, the balance of requirements may have to be quickly covered by short-dated debt instruments and bank borrowing. The firm's ability to obtain the needed funds will be determined not only by the profitability of the company but its ability to react to the changed circumstances.

CASH FLOW AND BREAK-EVEN POINTS

As part of the financial planning process it is useful to consider specific components of cash flow, such as revenues and fixed and variable expenses. In this way one can better predict the effects of changes in market conditions on the net cash flows of the firm.

One should be careful to maintain a distinction between those cash flow expenses which are fixed and those which can vary within the span of time under consideration. In particular, one should focus on those expenses which remain unaffected in the short to intermediate term when sales volume declines.

In the presence of high fixed expenses, which today will usually include labour as a major item, the net cash flow from the business will be highly vulnerable to any decline in sales volume below expectations. Thus assessment of those expenses which will remain fixed within the planning horizon is essential when one is planning for possible contingencies.

Figure 13.1 is a *cash flow* break-even chart illustrating the relationship between net cash flow with revenues and fixed and variable expenditure.

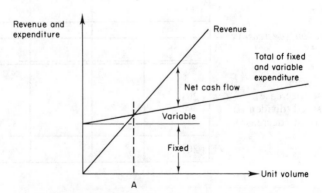

Figure 13.1. Break-even cash flow

Figure 13.1 differs from the usual *profit* break-even chart since we have excluded depreciation, which is not a cash expenditure. Whereas revenue begins at the origin in the figure and rises with a slope equal to the average unit price, total expenditures begin with fixed expenditure and rise with a slope equal to the average expenditure per unit sold.

The net cash flow is generated by the difference between sales revenue and expenditures. In Figure 13.1, net cash flow is represented by the vertical distance between the revenue and total expenditure lines. One can clearly see the 'scissors action' operating on net cash flow when fixed expenditures are high. High fixed expenditure in relation to total expenditure increases the volume of sales (point A) necessary to break even and increases the volatility of net cash flow for a given change in unit volume. Thus fixed expenditure largely determines the vulnerability of the firm to unfortuitous business developments.

If the firm is to remain solvent, management must expect that the firm can operate to the right of the intersection at A in the intermediate to long term. The probability of bankruptcy reflects the likelihood that long-term volume could fall below point A.

Interest payments can become a major item of fixed expenditure. Thus the more the firm borrows the higher the fixed expenditure. Figure 13.2 illustrates what happens to net cash flow when interest charges increase total expenditure. Point A moves to A' on the right, thus diminishing the drop in sales volume which would make net cash flows negative. As a result, increased borrowing increases the probability of bankruptcy should markets deteriorate.

Figures 13.1 and 13.2 illustrate the importance of making a distinction between those expenditures which will remain relatively fixed and those which can change within the planning horizon. As a planning tool, however, the break-even chart is not always useful. More commonly, the structure of fixed and variable expenditure is built into cash budgets and

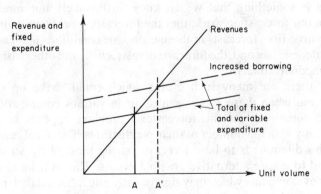

Figure 13.2. Break-even cash flow with increased borrowing

projections of sources and applications of funds. In this way, such cash flow forecasts are made more accurately to reflect the effects of changes in business conditions.

When determining which elements of cash flow will change, one must consider what actions management would take in the relevant circumstances. The important questions to ask are: 'What options are open to the management if trading conditions deteriorate?' and 'What will be the value of the company's assets (and consequently their value in alternative uses) if such conditions arise?'

PROBLEMS OF FINANCIAL FORECASTING

It would be easy to forecast the elements of the cash budget and the projected funds flow statement if one knew what assumptions to make about future developments. All other things being equal, the business would continue in the future as it is in the present; but then there may have been trends, and the trends may continue. . . or they may not, for a variety of reasons. Events intervene: strikes, new competition, even changes in the weather. There are basically two types of uncertain elements in a forecast. First, there are 'averaging' kinds of factors such as growth, trend, and seasonality. Second, there are discrete events which may intervene to alter the average, e.g. Government action and strikes.

Although it may sometimes be reasonable to extrapolate or alter averages and trends on the basis of commercial knowledge and judgement, it is the foreseeable but ignored discrete event which may ruin an otherwise good forecast. 'Tell me what is going to be in the Chancellor's next budget and whether we are going to have an important strike and I can give you a good forecast' is the legitimate retort of the manager who has been asked for a better forecast but has been allowed no formal means of incorporating alternative futures. What the seemingly evasive forecaster is telling us is something that we all know instinctively but rarely make explicit in our forecasting work, that the forecasting problem divides itself into two parts: first, forecasts of those economic conditions upon which the forecasts depend; second, the forecasts of sales, costs, and other cash flows of more immediate concern.

Where there are many such events which could shake up company planning and when these events can occur in various combinations over time, the complexity of the forecaster's problem appears to increase geometrically with the number of such eventualities. The usual resort in the face of this dilemma is to base forecasts on the most likely set of future events and to ignore alternative possible events. The dangers of ignoring possible developments which may significantly affect financial planning are self-evident.

Virtually every forecast must be made conditional on a whole series of possible events and decisions preceding the future period to which each forecast applies. Who is to say which of the many combinations of events which could affect the forecast will actually occur?

The tree diagram is one way of analysing alternative sequences of future events upon which financial forecasts depend. In the following section we illustrate the use of the tree diagram for this purpose.

THE TREE DIAGRAM

Consider the problem of the management of a subsidiary of a soap powder company at 1st October 1971. This subsidiary is a profit centre and is responsible for planning its own cash flow needs and obtains funds from its parent company at market rates. The subsidiary is launching a new product but is still considering the decision to launch regionally or nationally during 1972. The company has decided to introduce the product nationally if the outcome of the market test is sufficiently favourable. If not, the company will take the more conservative strategy of introducing the product regionally. Subsequently, there may be either a favourable or an unfavourable market reception, and at the same time, in this particular case, a strike at the plant may occur. In order to forecast cash flows, management require a clear picture of the combinations of probable events which could affect the forecasts. Fortunately, combinations of uncertain events can be represented quite effectively by a probability tree.

The probability tree in Figure 13.3 may be constructed. Emerging from the first circle or 'node' are two possibilities or 'branches': to introduce regionally or to introduce nationally. Management judges that the outcome of the market test will be sufficiently favourable that they would introduce the product nationally with a probability of only 0.25 or one chance in four. The remaining probability is 0.75 or three chances in four that the outcome of the market test would not be so favourable as to warrant the risks of a national campaign.

In any case, irrespective of whether the company goes national or not with the product, there remains the possibility that within the national or the regional market the market reception may be unfavourable, a chance of one in five or a subjective probability of 0.2. If market reception is favourable (and management assesses this with a probability of 0.8), sales would be vulnerable to the possibility of a strike at the factory.

Management judges the chances of a strike as three out of ten or the subjective probability of 0.3. If the strike takes place, approximately 30 per cent of production will be lost. Thus, in period 2 there are two sets of nodes representing combinations of a favourable and an unfavourable market reception combined with the conditions of a strike or no strike. In this case, management may feel that the subjective probabilities associated with the market reception and with a strike are independent of whether the product

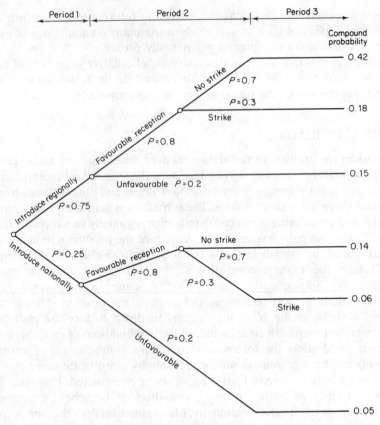

Figure 13.3. Probabililty tree of events explaining forecasts for a new soap powder product launch

is to be launched regionally or nationally. This independence need not hold; and, for example, the probability of a favourable market reception need not be the same on different parts of the tree.

The probability tree provides an analytical framework whereby management can represent those major or significant conditions upon which any well-thought-through forecast must depend. When the knowledgeable manager reveals his various caveats, one must seize upon them as useful information. The manager feels the legitimate need to qualify his forecasts, and the probability tree provides him with a useful opportunity to do so.

DEPENDENT FORECASTS

Given this framework for analysing and predicting those conditions likely to affect forecasts, we may now focus on the second stage in cash flow forecasting. Given any sequence of events which may be encountered by moving along a path from left to right in the tree, a range of possible sales levels associated with and affected by those events may be realized in each period. Starting with the most probable sequence of events, we ask the forecaster, 'Given that we introduce the product regionally and that the product is received favourably and there is no strike, what is the most likely level of sales in each period'? We would also ask for a range of sales for each period: 'What are the highest and lowest sales that can reasonably be anticipated given the same set of assumptions'? If the forecaster introduces important new caveats at this stage, we must adapt the tree accordingly. We then proceed to obtain from him similar forecasts of most likely, 'minimum' and 'maximum' sales along all paths of the tree.

We have described the framework upon which the major caveats of any forecaster can be represented. The probability tree enables him to sort out all the possible combinations of significant events which could affect his forecast and to take them into account in each alternative forecast. Let us now discuss briefly how we use forecasts in this form to generate the implied cash flows within the company and to employ the results for decision making.

CASH FLOW IMPLICATIONS

In the first instance, forecasts of sales and costs are used in major project appraisals, e.g. a discounted cash flow profitability analysis of the new soap powder product launch. If as a result of the discounted cash flow analysis the project is accepted, further forecasts will be required for the project in order to reveal any important possible changes in working capital and longer-term financing requirements which may be expected to occur.

Let us now consider the way in which forecasts of future cash balances are obtained from the sales forecasts conditional on the probability tree. Each possible sequence of sales from period to period has cash flow implications for the company. Given a set of expected sales levels, a cash budget or a sources and uses analysis may be used to project cash balances in every period.

The data required include the initial cash balance, the initial debtor and creditor balances, and existing sales per financial period. The length of each financial period and the number of them to be projected must be defined. Debtor and creditor collection periods must be projected. The relationships between creditors' balances and fixed and variable manufacturing expenses must be defined, and the production lead time for sales must be estimated.

Suppose the above analysis revealed unacceptable levels of financial risk. What course of action can the manager take? There are three possible options available. The first is the simplest and that is to reject the new project, even though it is profitable, because it causes cash flow problems. The second option is to prepare a plan to meet cash flow deficits by new financing (equity or debt), a sale of assets or a termination of certain product lines. The third option is to devise ways of shifting or sharing the risks of the new product with another company. For example, a joint venture could be arranged or large purchasers might be persuaded (at a price) to order and pay for advanced orders. Methods of sharing or redistributing risk are an important way of changing the company's risk profile without rejecting profitable projects. Many managers reject profitable projects because they expose the unit to an unacceptable level of financial risk. This is not the only option open to them and is clearly one that produces a loss for shareholders.

The main disadvantage of such a probability analysis within a decision tree framework is the amount of data required and the specialized skills demanded of the manager. A simpler and less time-consuming process is to develop scenarios of the future, which in essence provide a rough and ready picture of how the company or division will perform under various industry/general economic conditions on appropriately selected branches of the probability tree.

SCENARIOS OF THE FUTURE

A problem with tree diagrams is that frequently there are so many critical uncertain events which should be built into the probability tree that the tree develops too many branches. The number of branches increases geometrically with the number of events one wishes to incorporate. This multiplicity arising from possible combinations of events developing through time is simply a reflection of the realities of business forecasting. Faced with such complexity, must one simply resort to the educated guess?

A better solution would simply be to choose those paths through the tree which are of most interest given the purpose at hand. For example, if one is preparing forecasts for the purpose of arranging finance to meet possible contingencies, one would ask, 'Which plausible sequences of events would cause us to seek the most outside funding?' For each such sequence of events or *scenario*, one must ask what actions will one take now given these possibilities, and how quickly would management respond should such events unfold? Only when such questions have been considered can one be reasonably certain that sufficient funding is available to meet plausible eventualities.

Scenarios can be constructed routinely by the following procedure:

(i) List all future circumstances and significant events for the economy and the industry which could affect the forecast.
(ii) Relist them in order of importance for each future period in the forecast.

(iii) Select a scenario or a sequence of conditions and events relevant to the plan and describe the relationships through time between all relevant variables.

A comprehensive list of economic circumstances which provide the raw material for scenarios can be maintained and updated on a routine basis as an integral part of the planning and forecasting process.

The events to be listed in step (a) above may be classified into several categories. For example:

(a) macroeconomic events and changes,
(b) government intervention,
(c) industry events and changes,
(d) events relating specifically to the company such as strikes,
(e) events affecting the relationships between the company and other firms such as customers, competitors, and suppliers.

How many scenarios should the firm construct? The number depends on how risky the industry is and the level of risk management is prepared to accept. Management which is unwilling to accept any significant probability of default will wish to be most careful in considering all the possible events that may damage the company's cash flow.

SCENARIO BUILDING VERSUS SENSITIVITY ANALYSIS

The use of scenarios in planning differs from sensitivity analysis in that scenarios are defined in terms of plausible sequences of events. A common problem with sensitivity analysis is that the interrelationship between variables is not adequately specified and may even be ignored altogether. Thus there may be no underlying economic rationale to the numbers. For example, in sensitivity analysis one might assume that wage rates will rise 10 per cent in order to measure the effects on cash flows while ignoring the fact that wage forecasts are related to general economic factors such as the rate of inflation, growth prospects, and corporate profits. This is not to say that such variables are not also determined by the strength of particular unions and the attitudes of management. However, to ignore real economic variables that are prime causes of changes in wage rates would constitute an important omission.

The scenario approach eliminates the necessity of analysing every one of the perhaps hundreds of combinations of events which may occur by focusing attention on those chains of possible events which are most potentially relevant to the purpose at hand. The element of judgement is not in any way removed by this procedure—rather judgement is enhanced and comprehensiveness can minimize avoidable oversights. Although it is possible for one to err on the basis of what has been considered, one is more likely to err as a result of what has been overlooked.

PLANNING FOR CONTINGENCIES

Management should forecast the effect of changes in the economy on the revenues of the industry and firm. In addition, estimates of the value of its assets in the existing and alternative uses, given the various scenarios should be made. An example is provided in Table 13.5. This shows how sensitive industry and company forecasts are to changes in Gross Domestic Product (which is in part determined by inflation rates). A deterioration in revenues may necessitate the sale of assets and therefore values of assets in alternative uses should be estimated.

Business adversity can materialize in many forms, each having its own implications for liquidity. The most important circumstances to be considered fall into the three following important contexts:

(a) company business deteriorating in relation to the industry;
(b) industry declining in relation to the economy;
(c) economy deteriorating.

If the company should suffer in relation to the industry, selling of assets to more successful companies in the industry at favourable prices may be possible. However, if the industry is also in decline (but not the economy), the most liquid assets may be those with alternative uses in other industries. If the economy should be deteriorating as well, alternative uses for assets may be difficult to find, and some assets could realize little more than scrap value. In the best of circumstances, some fixed assets take a very long time to sell, and the time lag between the emerging need for cash in an unfolding crisis and actual realization of funds from the sale of these assets may become a critical factor.

Thus, the amount of financing which will be required to meet contingencies depends very much on the nature of the contingencies which arise and the company's likely response to them. How quickly can the company change its strategy and operating plans in response to events? What would be the response to unfolding scenarios which could spell adversity, and what would be the cash flow implications of such changed strategies and plans? These are the considerations that translate a

Table 13.5. Relating general economic changes to company financing

Inflation rate (per cent)	Change in Gross Domestic Product (per cent)	Changes in industry demand (per cent)	Net revenues of the company in 1977 (£million million)	Value of fixed assets (£million million)
10	4	8	1	2.0
15	2	4	0.2	1.5
20	0	−2	−0.6	1.0

conservative financial forecast into an appropriate funds flow projection and cash budget for contingency planning purposes.

There are, therefore, five basic steps in the financial planning and forecasting process:

(a) Determine by means of funds flow forecasts and cash budgets the financial requirements implied by corporate strategy and the operating plan. This provides the basic plan but does not provide for contingencies. Hence the following steps are also required.

(b) Identify those alternative scenarios for the economy, the industry and the company which could plausibly affect future plans and increase requirements for funds.

(c) Assess the liquidity position of company assets under adverse scenarios.

(d) Assess the ability of management to interpret and make responses to unfolding events.

(e) Determine by means of funds flow forecasts and cash budgets the financing implications of alternative adverse scenarios.

These five steps enable financial management to determine how much financing is required to meet the requirements of operating management and how much additional financing is required as a precaution against possible adverse developments. Of more fundamental importance is that until these steps are accomplished management cannot know how fundamentally sound the company's financial position is in an uncertain world. How aggressive should a corporate strategy be if the company's financial posture is not likely to be sound in a variety of plausible circumstances? Thus financial management has an important role to play not only in ensuring the provision of funds for operations and contingencies but in making a contribution to the strategic planning process.

CONCLUSIONS

Effective financial planning is one of the best means of minimizing the probability of bankruptcy of the firm with all the resultant costs to employees, creditors, and shareholders. By helping management to foresee circumstances in which the company could find itself in difficulties, financial planning facilitates defensive financing arrangements and the trading or sharing of excessive risks with other partners. Thus by constructing an adequate defensive posture which can make the firm less vulnerable in the event of a deterioration of business conditions in the economy or the industry, management can undertake a more aggressive investment programme than might otherwise have been thought possible. We have shown how alternative sets of assumptions for financial forecasts may be structured and discussed the means by which financial plans are constructed from such forecasts.

REFERENCES AND BIBLIOGRAPHY

Broyles, J. E. and Franks, J. R., 'Financial Planning and Forecasting', *London Business School Journal*, No. 3, Summer 1974.

Donaldson, G., 'New Framework for Corporate Debt Policy', *Harvard Business Review*, **40**, 117–131, Mar.–Apr. 1962.

Feller, W., *An Introduction to Probability Theory and Its Applications*, Wiley, London, 1957, Vol. 1.

Franks, J. R., Bunton, C. J., and Broyles, J. E., 'A Decision Analysis Approach to Cash Flow Management', *Operational Research Quarterly*, **25**, 573–585, 1974.

Hertz, D. B., 'Risk Analysis in Capital Investment', *Harvard Business Review*, **42**, 95, 1964.

Hespos, R. F., and Strassman, P. A., 'Stochastic Decision Trees for the Analysis of Investment Decisions', *Management Science*, **11**, B-244, 1965.

Hillier, F. S., *The Evaluation of Risky Interrelated Projects*, North-Holland, Amsterdam, 1969.

Moore, P. G. and Thomas, H., 'The Rev Counter Decision', *Operations Research Quarterly*, **24**, 337, 1973.

Richmond, S. B., *Operations Research for Management Decisions*, Ronald Press, New York, 1968, pp. 489–491.

Thomas, H., *Decision Theory and the Manager*, Pitman, London, 1972.

REVIEW QUESTIONS

1. Describe the reasons for financial planning. What options are available to the firm if forecasts suggest an unacceptable level of risk?

2. What is the method of preparation of

   (a) The cash budget
   (b) The funds flow forecast?

   Describe the principal uses of these two projections and explain their importance.

3. Is financial planning complementary to or inconsistent with the use of the Capital Asset Pricing Model in project appraisal?

4. 'A company should accept all profitable investment opportunities'. What qualifications would you make to this statement?

5. What importance does the distinction between fixed and variable expenditures have in financial planning?

6. What are the essential elements in a sound financial planning procedure.

14

BANK LENDING AND BORROWING DECISION

The rapidity with which loans can be negotiated and their low transactions costs has made bank borrowing a popular source of new finance. Loans from banks are available in forms ranging from overdrafts to term loans of up to 10 years. In this chapter we discuss the sources of debt finance. We consider the factors that borrowers must take into account and the general criteria used by lenders in making loan decisions. We examine the data required for lending and discuss methods used by lenders for controlling outstanding loans. In this connection, we look at some accounting ratios used in loan covenants and we discuss the considerations which determine the interest rates charged by lenders.

SOURCES OF FIXED-INTEREST FINANCE

In Table 14.1 we show the various sources of finance for industrial and commercial companies in the years 1974–76. It can be seen that bank borrowing played a major role as a source of new finance in 1974. Bank borrowing comprised over 80 per cent of all external finance and 30 per cent approximately when internal sources of funds were included. In 1975 and 1976 the amount declined (and in one year is negative, signifying loan repayments) as the level of growth and investment in the economy fell.

Bank borrowing has proved a popular source of new finance because of the rapidity with which loans can be negotiated and because of low transaction costs. In Table 14.2, we see that the cost of arranging an issue of equity for a new or currently publicly quoted company ranges from 2.6 per cent to 7.6 per cent. To float an issue of loan stock in the same amount costs between 2.8 per cent and 5.7 per cent. Bank borrowing on overdraft is usually free of transaction costs, while medium- to long-term loans are usually arranged at a commitment fee of 1 per cent or less.

Money can be borrowed from banks on overdraft or on a longer-term basis for up to 10 years. The interest rate is usually variable and changes with the Clearing Banks' Base Rate. The rates quoted are between 2 per cent and 5 per cent above the Base Rate, depending primarily on the

222

Table 14.1. Industrial and commercial companies sources of cash flow

	1974	1975	1976
		(£'000 million)	
A. Internal cash flow	8.6	9.1	11.7
B. External cash flow			
1. Investment Grant	0.4	0.4	0.4
2. Stock Exchange issues:			
Equity	—	1.0	0.8
Loans	—	0.1	—
3. Other loans and			
mortgages	0.1	0.5	0.6
Bank borrowing (net)	4.4	(1.8)	0.7
Total external cash flow	4.9	0.2	2.5
Total cash flow	13.5	9.3	14.2

Source: Evidence to the Committee to Review the Functioning of Financial Institutions, The Stock Exchange, 14th February 1977.

company's financial risk. In July 1977, when the Base Rate was 8½ per cent, most borrowers were paying between 10 per cent and 13½ per cent.

There are other institutions which grant loans, including insurance companies, Export Credits Guarantee Department (E.C.G.D.) and the I.C.F.C.. Such institutions usually provide longer-term loans to industrial and commercial companies. Finally, there are the leasing companies which finance the purchase of specific types of fixed assets. Such leases may be based upon either variable or fixed interest rates and may run for up to 15 years. Most of the important leasing companies are subsidiaries of banks.

Table 14.2. Comparison of typical costs of issuing equity of £2 million

	New Issues Prospectus or Offer for Sale	Further Issues	
		Placing	Rights
Cost as percentage of proceeds of issue (per cent)	7.6	2.6	4.0

Source: The Stock Exchange.

FACTORS A BORROWER SHOULD CONSIDER

The borrower must be able to appreciate the lending relationship from the bank's as well as from his own point of view in order to obtain the best possible terms. Consequently, we will first list some factors which are important to the borrower and then consider criteria important to lenders:

(a) How competitive is the interest rate offered by the bank?
(b) Is the loan of sufficient term to match the period of the company's requirements? If the company has long-term assets, it may prefer to finance them with either equity or long-term debt. The company must take into account the possibility of Government restrictions on borrowing or on specific categories of borrowers. Short-term loans or overdrafts are especially vulnerable in such restrictive conditions.
(c) Has the borrower determined in advance his ability to repay if business conditions deteriorate?
(d) Has the borrower developed a continuing close relationship with a bank which would tend to preclude the bank peremptorily recalling a loan should the business deteriorate?

Answers to some of these questions require financial analysis, some of which will also be required by the lender. The borrower should determine:

(a) How far could profits (and cash flows) fall in a downturn?
(b) How fast could current assets, e.g. debtors, be made liquid to ensure payment of loan interest and principal?
(c) How far and how fast can fixed expenditures be reduced in order to make the company profitable at a reduced level of operation?
(d) How quickly could fixed assets be sold in an emergency? The important factors to note are the marketability of the assets and the variability of the secondhand values.

Answers to these questions will help management to determine how much they can safely borrow, or at least to develop a plan for meeting interest and repayments if business conditions deteriorate.

GENERAL CRITERIA FOR LOAN DECISIONS

The following are seven key considerations in the lending decision from the bank's point of view:

(a) What is the character of the borrower? Is he likely to be really concerned by a default and will he give up-to-date information on a deteriorating financial situation? This is the so-called 'moral hazard' problem.

(b) Is the loan profitable? Does the interest rate charged provide an adequate return given the customer's risk of default and the costs of managing the loan?

(c) Is there adequate security for the loan?

(d) If the loan is secured on the profits of the enterprise, how profitable is the business? How risky is the business and how could management cope in a downturn?

(e) How capable is the bank of monitoring the progress of the business especially if there is a deterioration? Are special skills required for monitoring such a business and what are the costs?

(f) If the business got into trouble, how quickly could assets be sold and how variable are the second-hand values of the assets?

(g) What clauses or covenants should be put into the loan agreement to limit management's ability to change the business? What accounting ratios would predict financial distress and allow the bank an option to withdraw the loan?

One might simply say that the prime problem for the lender is the probability of default: the chance that a borrower will be unable or will refuse to pay the interest charges on the loan or indeed fail to meet the loan repayment. However, this description of the banker's problem is far too simple. The banker will wish to know how he can limit his losses if the borrower's position deteriorates. The ability to limit his losses depends on how quickly the business may deteriorate and on the banker's ability to monitor changes in the customer's financial position. In the extreme case, if the bank could monitor the borrower's performance instantaneously and call the loan at any time, then the risk of the loan would be nil because the bank could always recall the loan before the value of the business became less than the outstanding value of the loan. Paradoxically, under these circumstances the bank might be willing to lend at a relatively low rate of interest to a risky company. For many reasons, continuous monitoring is not usually feasible. The costs of such monitoring would be prohibitive both in terms of data requirements and time. This is one reason why banks favour marketable securities as collateral for a loan. The value of the collateral is easily and cheaply assessed and avoids the need for expensive monitoring of other assets represented in the business of the borrower.

Alternatively, if the customer monitored his own financial position frequently, he could inform the bank when the value of the business was declining to a critical point close to the value of the loan. Two problems arise here. First, the customer's own financial monitoring system may not be adequate for this purpose. Second, as the business deteriorates and as the owner's equity approaches zero, he has little incentive to inform the bank while there is hope for recovery.

ROLE OF TANGIBLE ASSETS IN THE LENDING DECISION

Since a lower rate of interest is usually charged for lending which is secured on a tangible asset than on unsecured borrowing, the bank must consider the existence and nature of the second-hand market for the asset. The value of an asset which is usable only within the owner's plant or factory will depend only on expected future cash flows; these may decline at any time. The minimum value will be the scrap value net of transaction costs. Assets useful to other companies and which have an active secondary market tend to provide a more stable value as collateral. If an airline's profits deteriorate, the value of the aircraft may remain relatively stable unless the experience is shared generally in the industry. Both lender and borrower must ask what would happen to the value of the security if the earnings of the company fall. If the asset is specific to the company or to the industry, the asset's value is more likely to decline with a drop in expected cash flow.

Only if there are alternative uses for the assets is some protection afforded from a decline in cash flows. Clearly, the value of office blocks may hold their value even if the firm's profitability declines, since office blocks can easily be sold for alternative uses. However, if the reduction in profitability is due to a general economic recession, then the asset's value in all uses may have declined. The message here is that one takes risks in assuming that the tangible (and even marketable) assets of a company will hold their value when the company's earnings decline.

DATA REQUIRED FOR LENDING

The data required for lending depends upon many features of the borrower's position. If he can offer adequate security, then little more is required. The banker will usually want a margin to spare (e.g. 20 per cent on blue-chip Stock Exchange securities) if the security is risky and its value is liable to fluctuate. The margin is required because the bank does not wish to monitor the value daily or even weekly. The higher the costs of obtaining a valuation for the security, the greater the margin of security (in excess of the loan) is required. The case of marketable securities is of course the simplest to examine. In other cases, a company may wish to borrow for an investment whose value is unique to the company's purpose; the company may wish to invest in plant and equipment to produce a particular product. How should the banker evaluate the company's assets?

A prerequisite will be to establish the profitability of the company and of the investment and to investigate the cash flow forecasts on the assumption that general economic and industry conditions may deteriorate. Thus earnings and cash flow forecasts for a period of years will be required under different sets of assumptions about the economy and the market. The banker should wish to know how the company would react if conditions deteriorate, how expenses would be reduced or, in the last resort, what the value would be in the event of liquidation.

How far into the future should a bank demand forecasts of costs, revenues, and net cash flows? Clearly, the answer will depend upon the operating life of the asset and the length of the loan. The bank will try to ensure that the outstanding loan is always less than the remaining value of the investment, otherwise it will have to impose conditions on how the firm spends any cash flow thrown up by the investment.

Let us now summarize the questions a lender will wish answered after he has verified the honesty of the borrower.

(a) Can the loan be secured by marketable assets whose value can be monitored easily and cheaply?

(b) Does the value of the security provide an adequate margin above the value of the loan to allow for fluctuations in the value of the security?

(c) What are the cash flow forecasts for the specific investment and for the firm as a whole?

(d) How far might those cash flows deteriorate under different sets of assumptions about the future course of the economy and the industry?

(e) What are the alternative uses for the assets and what would be their value under those economic and industry conditions which could lead to a liquidation?

(f) What repayment schedule will keep pace with the declining value of those assets which may be regarded as security for the loan?

(g) What covenants are feasible which would provide the bank with an option to recall the loan or, if necessary, liquidate the company?

It is important to appreciate that when a company's financial position deteriorates, there may be a serious conflict of interest between banker and borrower. In the extreme case, if the owners' equity is zero, then the owners are merely playing with the bank's money: they have nothing to lose and everything to gain from taking risks. Even if investments were expected to be unprofitable, it would be (unethically) in the owners' interests to play the roulette wheel. This is the moral hazard problem of which banks are keenly aware. When the business is deteriorating and the owners' equity has disappeared, the lender may face the double problem of deteriorating security and an owner whose own interests and prudence are similarly diminished.

CONTROL OF OUTSTANDING LOANS

How does a lending officer control an outstanding loan? There are a wide variety of means: most of them can be explained by common sense; others are based on reasons obscured by time and tradition.

Three important elements of such control are;

(a) Management's scope for increasing the risk of the loan may be restricted by the terms of the loan.

(b) Information is provided by the company so that the bank will become aware of any financial difficulties at an early stage.

(c) In the event of financial difficulty, the bank will want to be able to exercise an option to recall the loan.

These elements are evidenced in the commonest forms of control described below.

The first and simplest control is the requirement to pay interest and make repayments at regular intervals of time. If the lender's cash flow deteriorates very heavily, he may be unable to meet such charges. Default on these payments is often the first sign of trouble received by the banker and is frequently a very effective indicator of financial distress. Of course this signal may be too late since a negative cash flow may reflect a situation where the business is already making losses and when its value has fallen to less than that of the outstanding loan.

The interest and repayment terms not only give some assurance that there is a positive net cash flow, but provides an option to recall the loan should the firm fail to meet the charges. The effectiveness of the provision should not be underestimated where firms have comparatively high borrowings. If there were no repayment provisions until the end of the term of the loan, and interest charges were carried forward to the same date, the bank would be unable to recall the loan during the intervening period, irrespective of the financial state of the company. However, such provisions may not be adequate if the business is deteriorating very quickly. Also, firms often borrow elsewhere in order to pay the bank and prevent recall of the loan.

The bank may therefore wish to impose further conditions in the loan agreement that will prevent the risk of the loan being increased and will provide information on a deteriorating loan. Such conditions incorporated formally or informally into a loan agreement are called *covenants*. There are two kinds of convenant, one which limits management's scope for using company funds to change the financial and business risk of the company, and the other for establishing trigger mechanisms which are supposed to operate when a company's financial position deteriorates.

The first limits management's ability to borrow, to purchase or sell fixed assets, to pay dividends, or to acquire companies, etc. This type of clause is inserted to prevent a company significantly changing the risk of the loan. Otherwise it would be easy for the company to negotiate a loan at a low interest rate based on low-risk business, and then to acquire higher-risk assets; clearly the original interest rate quoted may no longer be appropriate.

The second type of covenant prescribes various accounting ratios that the company must satisfy at all times. If the ratio requirements are breached, the bank has an option either to renegotiate terms or to call in the loan. In another section, we shall describe some of these solvency ratios and review their effectiveness in predicting bankruptcy or financial distress.

TRADITIONAL DEBT RATIOS

The most widely used ratio is the *debt-to-equity ratio*, based usually upon the book (accounting) values of assets and liabilities in the balance sheet. One merely computes the amount of debt (usually the nominal value in the balance sheet) and divides it by the net worth or shareholders' equity. Net worth is the difference between the total assets and total liabilities of a company.

Balance sheet as at 31st December 1973

Bank overdraft	75	Fixed assets	100
Net worth	75	Current assets	50
	150		150

In the above balance sheet, the debt-to-equity ratio is 1 : 1 or 100 per cent. An alternative would be to compute the *debt-to-debt plus equity ratio*, 50 per cent in this example.

The criticisms of such ratios are easy to make. Debt ratios are crude tools in the sense that they do not relate the amount of debt to the current and expected earning power of the company. Thus, such ratios cannot relate the ability to pay interest (and perhaps principal) with the debt outstanding. Ratios represent a point-in-time approach and an historic one at that. The balance sheet is made up on one day of the year and is usually published many months subsequent to that date. The ratio ignores seasonal trends and, in a changing economic environment, may be out of date.

Finally, the ratio is usually computed on book values rather than market values. Some would argue that the shareholders' wealth is determined by share price, which may differ considerably from book values. Very often, book values of assets are not altered in line with their market values or with their economic value (present value of expected future cash flows). As Myers (1977) suggests, even if we revalued all the assets in the company using market values or economic values where appropriate, this might give a total value less than the market value as it would exclude profitable growth opportunities. The shares of small, fast-growing companies sell at a price that may be far above the present value of the existing investments because investors are willing to pay a premium for management's ability to find further profitable investment opportunities. A lender may not wish to lend on the basis of possible future investment opportunities; he may merely lend a proportion of the value of the firm's current investment.

Use of the market value of the equity is appealing because it avoids valuation problems. However, the possibility that the market price of equity may capitalize future investment opportunities may explain why banks prefer to use book values. Also the problem remains of valuing assets which do not have an open-market price. Notwithstanding criticisms, the debt-to-equity ratio is easy to compute; and, for industry comparisons, it is widely used. The ratio is used in two ways: first, as a rule of thumb to determine the amount to be lent to a company. Second, as a measure of the financial risk of the firm. It is for the latter reason that the ratio is used in loan agreements. We shall review subsequently evidence concerning the validity of these ratios.

The second ratio, *interest cover*, is used to reflect the company's ability to pay interest charges out of current reported earnings:

$$\text{Interest cover} = \frac{\text{Earnings before interest and taxes}}{\text{Interest charges}}$$

A generally accepted convention for a manufacturing company is that a ratio of four and above is acceptable. However, the suitability of a value for the ratio depends on the industrial sector and its risk class.

Inevitably, these ratios are only rough guides. The limitations are easy to see. Whereas the ratio is based on reported earnings, the firm's ability to repay its interest charges are determined by its expected cash flows not on reported operating profits.

Defining the 'right' cover or ratio value is difficult since, to be truly covered, interest must be related to both current and future expected cash flows and the associated risk. Indeed, in a particular period, cover may be permitted to be less than one (interest charges would be carried forward) providing future cash flow will compensate for past deficits. When cash flows are expected to vary, lenders may be willing to accept that the cover will be low (even less than one) in some years and high in others.

Finally, interest cover, by definition, does not include the repayment of the principal. There are conflicting arguments over the importance of this point. Clearly, if a company is expected to be profitable in perpetuity, the debt may simply be refinanced. However, a lender may take the view that his loan is secured specifically on the *current* investment portfolio of the firm. The returns on those investments must not only pay interest on capital but must repay the loan itself. Only when new investments are proposed will the bank consider refinancing. Lenders who take this view prefer to use a ratio that reflects interest and annual repayments:

Interest and annual repayment ratio =

$$\frac{\text{Earnings before interest and taxes}}{\text{Interest} + \text{Annual repayment } [1/(1-T)]}$$

where T = Corporation Tax rate.

This ratio informs us how many times interest charges and annual repayments of principal are covered by current earnings before interest and taxes (EBIT). Since loan repayments are not tax deductible, they are paid out of after-tax profits. Thus, they must be grossed-up to be made consistent with the interest component of this ratio.

A widely accepted convention is that the value of such a ratio should exceed two for a manufacturing company, but once again the timing of earnings in terms of the trade cycle and the specific risk of the industry must be taken into account. Clearly, during a recession, firms in particular industries may be making losses simply because of high fixed costs and the sensitivity of sales to general economic effects. The bank must take a view over the life of the investment rather than estimate cover only for a particular year.

The *interest and annual repayment cover ratio* is based upon earnings rather than cash flow. Capital-intensive industries will probably make substantial depreciation provisions. These provisions reduce reported profits but do not reduce cash flow. In prosperous times, capital expenditures for both replacement and expansion may be greater than the depreciation provision. One would expect capital expenditures to be greater at the top of the trade cycle and less near the bottom. On reflection, one could adjust this ratio, adding back depreciation and subtracting capital expenditures:

Interest and repayment cover =

$$\frac{EBIT + \text{Depreciation} - \text{Capital expenditure}}{\text{Interest} + \text{Repayment} \,[1/(1-T)]}$$

One may then ask, 'Why not adjust this ratio for changes in working capital levels or dividend disbursements?' Once we have made such adjustments, we are simply arriving at a cash-flow-based calculation. Thus we would show the expected surplus or deficit in cash in each period after payment of interest and principal. Even if the repayment of principal were not required until the end of the loan period, a notional annual repayment could be deducted in order to arrive at an interest and repayment cover based on cash flow.

Initially, the cash flow must cover interest and repayments over the life of the loan by a satisfactory margin. We can test for the necessary margin after a fashion through sensitivity analysis: we can construct a number of scenarios and see what happens to net cash flows under different sets of assumptions. Methods of doing this were discussed in Chapter 13. This procedure may help to identify how risky the loan is and, consequently, the interest rates that should be charged. In addition, the procedure suggests the need for properly constructed covenants in the loan agreement that could enable the bank to recall its loan or renegotiate the terms when the company's profits deteriorate. Such covenants can also permit the bank to obtain financial information and to monitor financial performance.

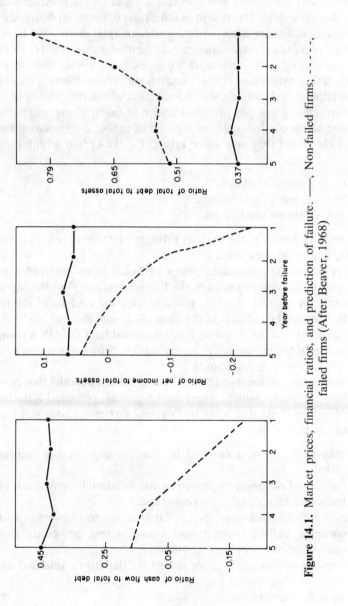

Figure 14.1. Market prices, financial ratios, and prediction of failure. ——, Non-failed firms; ------, failed firms (After Beaver, 1968)

FINANCIAL RATIOS AND PREDICTION OF FAILURE

Companies and lenders use financial ratios to decide the maximum amount of debt that they should carry and as indicators of financial distress. For the latter reason, ratios are incorporated into loan agreements. We have listed a number of reasons why ratios are of limited value. W. H. Beaver, in several pieces of empirical work (e.g. Beaver, 1968), has tested the contention that ratio values reflect underlying events affecting the solvency of the company and can be used as indicators of the probability of failure. He constructed a sample of failed and non-failed firms and tested the predictive powers individually of a group of ratios in forecasting financial distress. He found that only three ratios (Fig. 14.1) had a high predictive power:

(a) Cash flow to total debt,
(b) Net income to total assets,
(c) Total debt to total assets.

However, ratios such as the current ratio, interest cover, etc., proved very poor predictors on their own.

Beaver notes that the share prices of failed firms suffered abnormal losses prior to the deterioration of the financial ratios. Thus the investment community appear to use other, possibly superior sources of information about the financial condition of the firm. Although the use of share prices in loan covenants is not feasible, lenders should take note of a company's share price performance relative to the market before extending a loan, or for monitoring an existing loan.

In a later study, Altman et al. (1977) constructed a model that contained seven financial ratios which, when used together, provided a useful basis for highlighting firms that were in financial distress. The seven variables included the following:

(a) *return on assets*, measured by the earnings before interest and taxes;
(b) *stability of earnings*, measured by the standard (normalized) error of the estimate around a 10-year trend;
(c) *debt service*, measured by the familiar interest coverage ratio, i.e. earnings before interest and taxes/interest payments (included interest imputed in lease payments);
(d) *cumulative profitability*, measured by the firm's retained earnings (balance sheet)/total assets;
(e) *liquidity*, current ratio;
(f) *capitalization*, measured by common equity/total capital (total capital includes preferred stock, long term debt and capitalized leases);
(g) *size*, measured by the firms' total assets.

These seven variables were chosen from a list of 25, and the seven proved the best combination of all when discriminating between a sample of firms that failed and another group of non-failed firms. According to the authors (Altman *et al.*, 1977), banks might rely on such ratios in covenants or in analysing the credit risks of the firm. Thus Altman would claim that, although originally Beaver dismissed many of the above ratios as having poor predictive power individually, used *in combination* they can prove effective.

The problem with such analyses is that, although the device may be helpful in predicting those firms that might get into financial distress, it does not provide sufficient information on how to relate the risk of default to the interest rate that the bank should charge, given a level of default risk. We are left with a 'lend or not to lend' or a 'recall or not to recall' loan decision.

THE DETERMINATION OF LOAN INTEREST RATES

Let us initially assume that a loan is of zero risk to the bank: what interest rate will be charged? The bank will charge an interest rate somewhat above its own borrowing rate for the period of the loan. The margin must be sufficient to compensate the bank for the costs of negotiating and administering the loan plus a profit on the transaction.

The interest rate may differ for loans of different periods because of the interest rate structure; that is, the prevailing term structure of interest rates in the market may reflect higher or lower interest rates for longer-term debt. It will also be important to take account of whether the borrower wishes to fix the interest rate over the period or take out a variable interest rate loan. Since much of a bank's funds are on variable short-term interest rates, the bank will charge a premium if it has to fix interest rates for a term loan. The bank might even refuse to fix the interest rate since it may wish to hold only a limited proportion of its loans in fixed interest business.

If the loan is risky, an additional premium must be charged. The bank has a choice. At one extreme it may monitor the loan to such an extent that the risk of default is negligible. In this case, the costs of monitoring will be reflected in a higher interest rate. Alternatively, it may accept the probability of default and charge a premium that reflects the default risk. In either case, a premium is charged; the bank usually does some monitoring, but not to such an extent that the default risk is zero.

Banks have developed over time a set of risk classes with related interest rates. The greater the risk of a loan the greater will be the costs of monitoring and the higher the probability of default. To the extent that there is a probability of default, the loan represents an equity stake in the company should the bank have to take possession of assets. For these reasons, banks in the U.K. have charged between 2 and 5 per cent above the Base Rate, depending on the risk of the borrower.

Interest rates on corporate bonds may provide some insights concerning the rates charged by banks. Laurence Fisher (1959) published some research that tried to find those variables relating the risk of default to the risk premium incorporated in the prices of quoted bonds. He defined the risk premium on a bond as the incremental rate of return above the rate prevailing on a riskless government security of the same maturity. He suggested that the premium was a function of the risk of default and the marketability of the bond. He further suggested that the risk of default can be explained by the following four variables,

- the variability of the firm's net income over the past nine years (after interest charges and taxes).
- the length of time the firm has operated (without having declared insolvency).
- the ratio of the market value of the equity in the firm to the par value of the firm's debt
- marketability of the bonds represented by the market value of the firm's traded bonds.

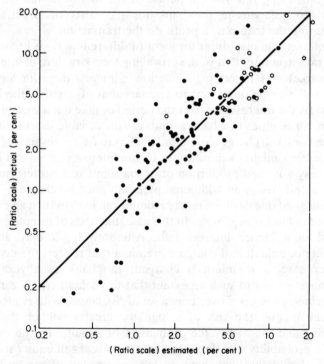

Figure 14.2. Scatter of 31 December 1937 market risk premiums against estimated risk premiums. (After Fisher, 1959.) ● , Firms in regression; ○ , firms not in regression

Using a sample of bonds of between 45 and 89 firms over five periods, he found that these four variables accounted for 75 per cent of the variation in the risk premium between bonds. In Figure 14.2 we show the risk premia implied by Fisher's four variables and the actual risk premia calculated from the market prices of the bonds.

Using the four variables Fisher estimated the risk premia that should have obtained on his sample of bonds. He then estimated risk premia on bonds of varying quality with that actually available on corporate bonds of similar quality. The risk premia, actual compared with those estimated, compare favourably.

Table 14.3. Analysis of industry risk premiums

Industry	Mean (per cent P.A.)	Standard Error of the Mean	Number of Observations
Breweries	0.635	0.05	34
Building	0.936	0.007	13
Chemicals	0.70	0.08	9
Engineering	0.88	0.03	24
Industrial	0.84	0.05	48
Property	0.83	0.04	54

However, there are some qualificiations to Fisher's study. Silvers (1970) has pointed out that Fisher did not incorporate into his estimating procedure the different maturities of the bonds and the different rates that are reflected in the term structure of interest rates. Furthermore, he did not take into account the differences in covenants that might affect the risk premium charged by the lender and may have accounted for some of the differences in rates charged to companies with similar risky earnings' streams. These considerations may not be so important in the United States. However, in the U.K. during the period 1974–1978 a steeply rising yield curve suggests that interest rates may rise significantly as the maturity of the loan lengthens.

In a U.K. study Zinkin and Patel (1978) estimated the risk premiums of company bonds segregated on an industry basis. In Table 14.3 we have reproduced their estimated risk premiums for six industries. It is clear from their analysis that although risks differ considerably within an industry, the differences appear to be insignificant across industries.

Loans by banks are based on a somewhat more complex set of factors made possible by the close relationship which can be developed between a bank and its customers. Nevertheless, bankers are mindful of the same variables which would affect the prices and thus the yields on corporate bonds.

236

CONCLUSIONS

Bank borrowing has been a significant source of company financing particularly during periods of high investment. Bank funds are relatively more accessible with lower transactions costs than other sources of finance. However, much of bank financing is of a short-term nature.

Once satisfied with the character, credit, and capability of management, bankers use a number of further criteria for making the lending decision. A primary question is the value and marketability of the collateral which is offered. The decision also requires further data concerning particularly the likely future cash flows of the company. Sensitivity analyses on cash flow projections are frequently used as an aid to judging the riskiness of the loan. Such analyses will suggest the nature of the covenants which are to be applied and the interest rates which are appropriate.

Once granted, the more risky loans must be monitored, and expected monitoring expenses may account for a large part of the risk premium in the interest charged. The bank often may not know that a borrower is in difficulty until a covenant is breached or until he is in default. If the banker has not already done so, he may require a monthly or more frequent accounting of progress of management towards recovering from the immediate crisis and meeting its obligations to creditors.

REFERENCES AND BIBLIOGRAPHY

Altman, E., 'Corporate Bankruptcy Potential, Stockholder Returns, and Share Valuation', *Journal of Finance*, **24**, 887–900, Dec. 1969.
Altman, E. I., Haldeman, R. G., and Narayanan, P., 'Zeta Analysis: A New Model to Identify Bankruptcy Risk of Corporations', *Journal of Banking and Finance*, **1**, 29–54, 1977.
Beaver, W. H., 'Market Prices, Financial Ratios and the Prediction of Failure', *Journal of Accounting Research*, **6**, 179–192, Autumn 1968.
Donaldson, G., 'New Framework for Corporate Debt Policy', *Harvard Business Review*, **40**, 117–131, Mar.–Apr. 1962.
Donaldson, G., 'Strategy for Financial Emergencies', *Harvard Business Review*, **47**, 71–79, Nov.–Dec. 1969.
Fisher, L., 'Determinants of Risk Premiums on Corporate Bonds', *Journal of Political Economy*, **67**, 217–237, June 1959; also reprinted in *Modern Developments in Investment Finance* (J. Lorie and R. Brearley, eds), Praeger, New York, 1972.
Merton, R. C., 'On the Pricing of Corporate Debt: The Risk Structure of Interest Rates', *Journal of Finance*, **29**, 449–470, May 1974.
Myers, S. C., 'Determinants of Corporate Borrowing', *Journal of Financial Economics*, **5** (2), 147–175, Nov. 1977.
Silvers, J. B., 'An Alternative to the Yield Spread as a Measure of Risk', *Journal of Finance*, **25**, 933–955, 1970.
Zinkin, P. and Patel, H., 'Investigation of Risk Premiums on Corporate Bonds', M.Sc. Thesis, London Business School, June 1978.

REVIEW QUESTIONS

1. What is the role of covenants in a loan agreement?

2. What information should a borrower provide to the bank assuming that the business manufactures television sets and that the business' cash flows constitute the primary security for the loan?

3. Why do banks prefer to make loans secured on property or similar assets?

15

WORKING CAPITAL MANAGEMENT: DEBTORS

It is unusual for industrial and commercial customers to pay cash for goods and services. As a supplier, the choice as to whom one is willing to extend trade credit is a critical factor affecting both the level and the quality of company sales. In this chapter, we consider the implications of Credit Policy for customers, sales, and collections. We also examine the various aspects of credit policy, the costs and benefits of extending credit, the assessment of credit worthiness, the ageing of debtors, and a model of the credit decision.

TRADE CREDIT AND TOTAL ASSETS

Table 15.1 illustrates the relative importance of debtors in the balance sheets of quoted companies in the manufacturing and distribution sectors in the U.K. In the 1960's, Debtors rose from 19.7 per cent of Total Assets to a high of 24.9 per cent in 1970–71. By 1972–73, Debtors had fallen back to 22.3 per cent.

The credit collection period (in days) may be estimated by dividing the value of Debtors by the value of annual credit sales and multiplying by 365 days. For example, quoted companies in manufacturing and distribution reduced their collection periods from 71.4 days to 65.9 days during the 3 years

Table 15.1. The place of debtors in the capital structure of quoted companies

	1960/1*	1970/1*	1972/3*
Number of companies	2241	1308	840
Debtors	3515	8948	7459
Total assets (after deduction of depreciation) (£ million)	17 856	35 895	33 465
Net assets (total assets less current liabilities) (£ million)	13 223	22 454	21 738
Current assets (including investments) (£ million)	9772	20 631	18 695
Debtors to total assets (per cent)	19.7	24.9	22.3
Debtors to net assets (per cent)	26.6	39.9	34.3
Debtors to current assets (per cent)	36.0	43.4	39.9

*Accounting years to 5 April

238

Table 15.2. Credit collection period (in days)

	Manufacturing and Distribution			Manufacturing only		
	Quoted	Non-quoted	Average	Quoted	Non-quoted	Average
1969/70	71.4	83.5	73.3	79.5	96.4	82.1
1970/71	70.9	81.6	72.7	78.7	95.8	81.4
1971/72	65.9	72.9	67.1	71.9	83.3	73.8
Mean sample size	1200	625		820	450	

to 1971–72, as in Table 15.2. Unquoted companies experienced somewhat longer credit collection periods, although the differences may reflect industry variations rather than the size of firms.

CREDIT TERMS

Credit can be extended most liberally with the least cost and risk if the Cost of Goods Sold is small in relation to price, as is the case for some fashion goods. However, it is important that any charges for credit should be related to risk. For example, a furniture shop represents a different credit risk than most of its customers. Thus, if the shop sells furniture on a hire-purchase scheme, it may have to charge a different effective rate of interest than the shop's own bank borrowing rate.

The financing charges for credit to debtors are often built into the price for goods. However, this policy may be seen as unfair and may prove uncompetitive to customers who pay promptly. As a result, some companies charge interest on the balance due on unpaid invoices. The traditional method

Table 15.3 Analysis of credit terms. Distribution of payments

Month	Without discount A	With trade discount* B	Present value factor at 2 per cent per month	Present Value	
				A	B
1	10	38.80*	0.9804	9.804	38.040
2	30	10	0.9612	28.836	9.612
3	30	20	0.9423	28.269	18.846
4	20	20	0.9238	18.476	18.476
5	10	10	0.9057	9.057	9.057
	100	100		94.442	94.031
					94.442
			Present Value of savings		−0.411

*Assumes trade discount of 3 per cent for payment within 30 days.

is, however, to offer a specified discount on goods paid for within a specified period. Table 15.3 illustrates the way in which such credit terms can be analysed. The firm is considering whether it would be worthwhile to offer a discount for early payment. The pre-tax cost of financing debtors for the firm is estimated to be 2 per cent per month. The firm is contemplating the offer of a 3 per cent discount for payment within 30 days. The problem is to predict whether the existing costs of financing debtors can be reduced sufficiently by a change in the pattern of payments to repay the revenues lost as a result of the discount.

The second column shows the average pattern of payments from customers for £100 of sales. Ten per cent is already paid within 1 month. Of the 30 per cent paid in the second month, 20 per cent may pay in the first month if offered the 3 per cent discount. Of the 30 per cent paying in the third month, only 10 per cent are likely to pay early when offered the discount. Customers who pay very late, after 3 months, are thought unlikely to find the discount sufficiently attractive. Thus the pattern of payments is expected to be altered to pattern B in the third column. The figure 38.80 is net of the discount.

Columns 5 and 6 give the present values of each schedule of payments discounted at 2 per cent per month. Since payments pattern B has a smaller present value, the 3 per cent discount does not appear to be financially attractive to the firm. The anticipated speed-up of payments is not expected to reduce financing costs sufficiently to repay lost revenues as a result of customers taking the discount. In theory, the net present value should always be negative since those customers who know that they are poor credit risks have the option to pay late.

A further consideration excluded from the analysis is that many customers paying after the discount period will unscrupulously pay at the discount price. The firm, faced with the possibility of a hostile customer, may not feel it worthwhile to incur the costs in trying to collect the discount. Credit terms are to a major extent dictated by customs and traditions within an industry and this must be a consideration when one contemplates a change in the usual credit arrangements.

A LENDING OR AN INVESTMENT DECISION

The terms of credit are a part of the terms of sale. Since the terms of credit will not be accepted by the customer unless they are favourable to him, the granting of credit can be viewed as a price concession. The greater the credit risk the greater the effective price concession granted.

As in the pricing decision, three questions are paramount:

(a) Will the customer's buying decision be influenced by the terms of credit?

(b) Is the supplier or customer suffering from a shortage of funds: are either in a position of capital rationing?

(c) Is the supplier working at or below capacity?

These questions are important because the answers will determine whether the decision to lend is purely a credit decision or an investment decision. Initially, let us examine the problem from the customer's view. If the customer has adequate funds of his own or has adequate sources of funds so that all profitable opportunities can be taken up, then he can make a strict comparison between trade credit and other kinds of borrowing opportunities. In these circumstances, trade credit may prove attractive because it may bear a lower effective interest rate. Also, the penalties for delaying payment are usually small, and the transaction costs of using trade credit will be less than the costs of setting up new loan accounts.

Why might the interest cost on trade credit be lower than the equivalent bank loan? Simply because the supplier is constantly in touch with industry and firm sources and therefore should have more up-to-date information on the credit risks than the bank. In addition, the supplier often has more leverage or can bring more pressure to bear on a customer who fails to pay his bills. Not only can supplies be cut off, but the supplier may also be able to influence other companies who supply the customer. For these reasons, suppliers may find it possible to offer credit on more favourable terms than are obtainable from banks.

Under different circumstances, the customer may not have access to adequate sources of finance for all profitable projects. Many small businesses do not have the marketable securities or the property which banks prefer as security for loans. The main asset of many customers may be their expected profits or cash flow from selling products. British banks tend not to favour lending solely on the basis of cash flow forecasts. Now a supplier has a choice in this situation. If he does not advance trade credit to the customer, he will not make the sale. If the customer is not forced out of business, he will at least be forced to consider another supplier. In these circumstances, trade credit is an inseparable part of the pricing and selling decision and cannot be considered solely as a lending decision.

For a supplier, extension of trade credit may not be a lending decision if he faces a limited availability of financial resources. Thus, providing trade credit to his customer may exclude other profitable investment opportunities. In these circumstances, trade credit is part of the investment decision for the supplier. Let us now consider trade credit in more detail: first, as a lending decision; second, as an investment decision.

TRADE CREDIT AS A LENDING DECISION

If conditions are such that the refusal of credit would not influence the total volume of sales, then the credit decision may be viewed purely as a lending decision. In this position, three questions arise:

(a) What is the principal and the term of the loan?
(b) Given the creditworthiness of the customer, what effective rate of interest would be required?
(c) Considering the industry's customary terms of trade, how much credit can be extended to a customer given the risk that he may default?

When the credit decision does not affect total sales volume, the incremental investment arising from the extension of credit is the increase in the Debtors account net of discounts for early payment. The effective rate of interest charged to the customer will have to cover the prevailing risk-free rate of interest for the term of the loan plus an additional rate to cover the probability of default and the costs of administration including collection.

Interest charged for credit can be charged explicitly to the customer's account or it may be implicit in the price of goods. More usually, the charge for credit is reflected in the discount for early payment. For example, the terms of the sale may include a discount of 10 per cent for payment within 30 days. If the customer is granted credit, and if he pays after 30 days, he foregoes the discount. Thus the supplier's charge for credit is 10 per cent of the sales price. The expected income from this discount must be sufficient to cover interest on the customer's Debtors account.

However, a number of problems arise in trying to calculate the cost of credit. The first is the exact period of the loan provided by the supplier. If the supplier offers payment terms which demand payment within 30 days, one might get the impression that the credit period is 1 month. However, if the supplier offers a credit limit equivalent to 1 month's sales for as long as the customer continues in business the loan must approach a perpetuity if the customer is expected to stay in business. Therefore, the appropriate interest rate to charge is that which is available on long-term interest-bearing securities of equivalent risk.

Let us consider an example. A customer applies for credit in an industry where it is customary to offer a discount of 2 per cent for payment within 30 days. Let us assume initially that the customer is risk free and will continue making monthly purchases of £1000 at list price indefinitely. How much credit can he be given?

If the customer were to use the credit granted, he would save having to pay £980 immediately for each month's purchases, but will have to pay £20 more later because he will have foregone the discount for cash purchase. Thus the principal of the loan is based on the price net of the discount for cash purchase. The amount of this principal will depend on the number of months' credit granted to the customer. If he is allowed 2 months' credit the principal is £1960.

Since the customer purchases £1000 worth of goods per month, the monthly interest received on the loan is fixed at £20. Although the interest is fixed (by expected sales), the principal depends upon the amount of credit granted to the customer. If the customer takes 2 months' credit, the interest rate is $20/(2 \times 980) = 1.02$ per cent per month. If the customer takes 3 months' credit, the interest is only $20/(3 \times 980) = 0.68$ per cent per month. Thus, increasing the amount of credit which the customer may take, reduces the effective amount of interest received; that is,

$$\text{Interest received} = \frac{\text{Discount} \times \text{Monthly sales}}{\text{Cash value of credit granted}}$$

where the Cash Value of Credit Granted is valued net of the discount for cash purchase. If the customer were really risk-free, the credit decision would consist in choosing that value of credit granted in the above formula which would make the interest received at least equivalent to that obtainable on irredeemable Government securities (War Loan or Consols).

If the customer is risky, however, the above analysis is altered in several ways. First, the customer may default with some probability p in any month. Second, the Credit Department must incur increased administrative costs, including debtor monitoring, collection, and legal expenses. Thus we now have,

$$\text{Interest received} = \frac{\text{Discount} \times \text{Monthly sales}\,(1-p) - \text{Service cost}}{\text{Cash value of credit granted}}$$

where the Service Cost covers the monthly incremental administrative expenses incurred in the Credit Department on average for each such risky credit account which is accepted.

A third consideration involves the amount of credit actually taken by the customer. It may be customary in the trade that 1 months' credit is granted to all credit customers. However, unless the Credit Department is prepared to administer very strict credit controls, some customers will actually take more credit when it suits them to do so. They will simply delay payment for a longer period. In this manner, the customer can reduce the effective rate of interest which he pays. More importantly, he may create credit for himself at any time he may need it should other sources of funds be closed to him.

Thus, the credit decision must reflect also the degree of control which the Credit Department feels is feasible in a changing economic environment. The expected amount of credit actually granted will depend upon the ability of the Credit Department to enforce collections. In cases where little effective control can be exercised in practice, the essence of the decision becomes in each case whether credit should be granted at all. If it is felt that the customer will take more credit than the Credit Department would be willing to grant, then they have the option of refusing to grant credit.

244

The fourth consideration is that trade credit ordinarily represents a risky loan and thus a suitable interest rate must be found which reflects the risk of default of the customer. In a study of 57 long-term U.K. corporate bonds, Zinkin and Patel (1978) estimated that the extra interest paid above comparable Government rates ranged from 1 to 3.4 per cent per annum. For unquoted companies, the risk premium on loan rates would be somewhat higher depending on individual circumstances.

There are a number of qualifications that must be made to the application of risk premiums computed in this manner. First, trade credit is always unsecured, whereas many of the bonds in Zinkin's sample were secured loans. In a liquidation, secured loans are ranked in front of unsecured creditors. This fact suggests that a higher interest rate incorporating a larger risk premium should be sought on trade credit.

A debtor may be wary of not paying his bills to his suppliers because he can be put out of business if his orders are not processed. In addition, the supplier should be among the first to know if the debtor is getting into financial difficulties. We do not wish to minimize the risks taken by suppliers, but merely to point out that the supplier may be in a better position to anticipate bankruptcy than a bank and to obtain the information at a lower cost; as a consequence, he can take action for at least part repayment at an earlier stage. Thus the risk premium actually required may be lower in certain cases according to circumstances.

In summary, the credit decision is a lending decision when the net effect of the decision is merely to change the size of the Debtor account. If the refusal of credit would not result in the loss of business, and if the customer is able to turn to alternative sources of funds, the extending of credit is equivalent to the granting of a loan facility. However, since the implicit interest payment may be hidden in a fixed trade discount (for early payment), the effective interest rate will be determined by the time actually taken by the customer to pay his bills. If the Credit Department feels that they will be unable to enforce prompt payment, they can refuse credit to those customers who they believe are unlikely to pay within the time period necessary to make the effective interest attractive.

There are circumstances, however, in which the credit decision can no longer be considered merely as a loan. In such cases the credit decision can usually be treated as an investment decision.

TRADE CREDIT AS AN INVESTMENT DECISION

Frequently, credit decisions have important effects which extend beyond the Debtor account. For some customers, the use of trade credit is vital for survival. Many companies face a shortage of capital at times, particularly if they are unquoted and have limited access to capital markets. Their assets may not be easily marketable and may provide poor security for bank loans. Such companies, if they have to forego profitable projects due to a lack of funds, are likely to favour those suppliers who are most generous in providing trade credit. Thus credit policy may have an impact on the sales of the supplier as well as on the ability of the customer to operate effectively in conditions where the cost of credit from alternative sources is prohibitively high.

The form of the analysis may change somewhat when the supplier is operating below capacity and the customer does not have a viable alternative source of funds. When the supplier does not expect to be operating at capacity, credit decisions may actually affect the volume of business that he can put through his facilities. If some customers are short of funds, and if there are competing suppliers operating below capacity, then it may be necessary to extend credit in order not to lose sales to competitors. In this position, the credit decision becomes an investment decision whereby an investment in working capital is required to secure the subsequent benefits of cash flow from sales.

If a new customer is accepted, a substantial investment of capital may be required to service the account. This investment may include cash, raw materials, work in progress, and finished goods, as well as an investment in the Debtor balance. More precisely, the lag between the payment of expenses associated with the new business and the receipt of payments for goods and services provided to the customer requires an investment of funds. In return, the supplier must expect a return after taxes commensurate with the riskiness of the resulting net cash flow stream.

Table 15.4 is an example of such a trade credit investment. In order to assess properly the impact of a new class of debtors on the business, one needs to consider all incremental cash flows that can be expected to result. Table 15.4 includes some, but by no means all, the expenses that may be relevant. We show investment in Cash and Stock including raw materials, work-in-progress, and finished goods. We include variable expense, additional sales, and administration, including collection and taxes. Not shown is any charge for incremental capital expenses on plant or machinery

Table 15.4. Cash flow associated with the extension of credit to a new customer

	Month					
	0	1	2	3	4	. . .
Cash and Stock	−200					
Variable expense		−100	−100	−100	−100	. . .
Sales and administration		− 10	− 10	− 10	− 10	. . .
Revenue		120	120	120	120	. . .
Taxes*		− 5	− 5	− 5	− 5	. . .
	−200	5	5	5	5	. . .

*Adjusted for actual lag in payment.

which may be required if new business were to require more capacity. In this case, the decision involves a full capital project appraisal. Also not shown as a separate item are incremental handling and warehousing expenses. Where significant incremental expenditures are required, they should be shown separately in the months in which payments are expected to be made.

When the appropriate monthly discount rate (Appendix 15.1) reflecting the systematic risk of the net incremental cash flows resulting from extending credit to customers has been determined, the cash flows can be discounted to Present Value. A positive Net Present Value would indicate that the incremental business is profitable and that the credit terms assumed in the analysis can be extended. However, one must take care that the analysis reflects an unbiased estimate of the leads and lags associated with supplying the type of product to the appropriate category of customer credit risk and that all the likely incremental working capital and other net expenditures are included.

The advantage of a detailed monthly analysis of this nature is that one often finds that there are classes of customers or credit risks which would be profitable even though less precise and more conventional rules of thumb treating the extension of trade credit as a lending decision would turn the business away.

In order to relieve the company from the job of analysing every new customer in such detail, a risk classification by customer type and product can be instituted. The above monthly cash flow analysis needs to be performed from time to time for each combination of credit class and product.

Because it is not often feasible for Credit Department personnel to make a full investment analysis for individual credit decisions, simple rules-of-thumb are useful as a guide. Earlier in the chapter, we discussed a formula governing the maximum number of months' credit which may be granted when the extension of credit approximated a lending decision. A corresponding rule can be derived when the extension of credit represents an *investment* decision; that is, when the granting of credit will affect sales volume. The formula is

Return received =

$$\frac{\text{Net cash flow } (1 - p) - \text{Service cost} - \text{Stock carrying cost}}{\text{Net investment in working capital}}$$

The Net Cash Flow is that which arises from incremental monthly sales minus cash costs of sales. The term p represents the probability of default in the period. The Service Cost covers monthly incremental administrative costs including monitoring, collection, and legal expenses in the Credit

Department. The Stock Carrying Cost includes such items as storage, handling, insurance, and obsolescence expenses, but excludes costs of finance in this analysis. The Net Investment in Working Capital treats cash, debtors, and stock at marginal cost and is net of creditors. All items should be taken after tax and Stock Relief and should reflect as nearly as possible all the items which would be included in Table 15.4.

The rule is similar to that which we adopted for the lending form of the credit decision, except that the incremental cash benefits and expenses included are more extensive when the granting of credit actually increases (or prevents the loss of) sales. If the after-tax rate of return calculated on this basis exceeds the after-tax risk-adjusted required rate of return for this type of investment, credit can profitably be extended to the customer.

What rate of return is required for such an investment in increased sales? First, we note that an increase in sales revenue involves a degree of systematic risk. Thus a risk premium will be required. How does the risk compare to that of the business or division? If the incremental benefit arising from the marginal increase in sales involves no change in fixed expense, it is very likely that the riskiness of the resulting net revenues will be less than average for the division. The resulting after-tax risk premium should be added to the after-tax risk free rate plus the additional premium for default risk discussed earlier in the chapter.

If the supplier suffers from capital rationing and wishes to compare the credit decision with other investments he may do so with the help of the Profitability Index or the integer programming model discussed in Chapter 4. The value of the index can be obtained by dividing the Return Received in the above formula by the required rate of return. This value can be compared with the index for an alternative project by dividing the Investment into the sum of the Net Present Value and the Investment for the alternative project.

THE CONTROL OF TRADE CREDIT

Trade credit is a useful and flexible source of finance used by most companies. Simply by delaying payment to creditors, companies can increase their liabilities without having to turn to their bankers for further loan financing. The advantages to users of trade credit represent corresponding disadvantages to the providers of trade credit. Thus some form of control is required as a protection against unanticipated financing requirements and associated costs from increases in Debtors.

The Credit Department may base its decision to extend credit to an industrial or commercial customer on information from a variety of sources which include trade references, bank references, credit bureau reports or registers, salesmen's opinions, and published information. Information can be obtained from the company's own sales ledger on the payment habits of an existing customer.

Credit bureau reports or registers include Dun and Bradstreet lists giving financial details and credit ratings on large numbers of companies. Dun and Bradstreet will also prepare special reports on individual companies which may not be included in their lists. Information on companies including Annual Reports and charges on assets can also be obtained at Companies House.

Companies who turn their sales ledgers over to collection agencies known as 'commercial factors' can often obtain information on the payments habits of potential customers from the factor, who may be managing the sales ledgers of a number of other companies already dealing with that customer.

Table 15.5 summarizes 276 responses from U.K. companies to a British Institute of Management survey concerning the sources and effectiveness of information used for checking the creditworthiness of new customers. Most often identified as being effective were credit registers and trade protection associations. Least often identified as being most effective were reports from salesmen.

Table 15.5. Sources of information used for checking creditworthiness of new customers

	Sources used (per cent)	Sources considered to be most effective (per cent)
Banker's reference	69	14
Credit registers	68	27
Trade reference	65	14
Other sources, e.g. reports from salesmen	35	9
Trade protection society/association	29	18
Commercial agencies	21	11
Contact with company concerned	16	9
Other	12	10

Number of companies = 276.

Age classification is a standard procedure used by many companies to spot problems arising within the Debtors account. Table 15.6 illustrates the age classification of debtors based on monthly credit sales. Age classification develops the percentage of sales as yet unpaid for each preceding month. Departure from the normal pattern in these percentages may indicate problems which require a more detailed customer-by-customer analysis of outstanding debtors for one or more months.

Table 15.6. Age classification of debtors based upon monthly sales

Age classi-fication (days)	Month of sale	Monthly credit sales (£'000)	Value of Debtors (£'000)	Monthly Value of Debtors as a percentage of credit sales
1–30	June	400	360	90
31–60	May	600	360	60
61–90	April	600	180	30
91–120	March	400	40	10
121+	Earlier	–	60	–
		2000	1000	

$$\text{Average age of debtors} = \frac{£1.0 \text{ million}}{£2.0 \text{ million}} \times 120 \text{ days} = 60 \text{ days}.$$

Of 287 companies surveyed by the British Institute of Management, 95 per cent operated a standard debt collection procedure. Most companies apply a sequence of collection methods beginning with circular reminders and culminating in court action if required. Table 15.7 summarizes the debt collection procedures used by companies as indicated by the survey.

The method most favoured by companies was found to be telephone reminders from the credit control department. This method involves invaluable personal contact and enables the credit controller to differentiate between companies which normally pay late and those which are becoming a bad credit risk.

Table 15.7. Debt collection procedures used

		Percentage of companies using total sales turnover			
	Total	Up to £1 million	£1 million to £6 million	£6 million to £20 million	Over £20 million
Circular reminders	74	68	74	77	74
Personal reminders	67	50	66	71	72
Telephone by credit section	66	56	59	71	70
Further statements	52	52	44	60	43
Contact by salesman	51	18	47	49	68
Court action	42	18	36	42	53
Account taken to collection agency	41	30	40	50	36
Visited by credit section	21	3	9	17	40
Trade protection association	17	15	17	21	13
Telegram/telex	13	9	5	13	20
Other methods	10	3	16	9	11
Summons	73	50	57	77	80
Number of companies	270	34	58	90	88

250

CONCLUSIONS

In summary, there are several costs to the extension of trade credit. These costs include the cost of financing increased Working Capital, an increase in clerical costs, and the potential costs of bad debts. However, there are benefits to be gained by increasing sales through the use of a more liberal credit policy. The benefits can be made to outweigh the costs if adequate controls are exercised. The amount of credit extended to marginal customers must be strictly limited. The sales ledger must be regularly monitored to ensure that customers do not significantly alter their expected patterns of payment. A systematic reminder system should be operated if only to make the customer aware that he is dealing with an efficient credit department who are likely to apply pressure should credit limits be exceeded.

REFERENCES AND BIBLIOGRAPHY

Baranek, W., *Working Capital Management*, Wadsworth, Belmont, Calif., 1966.
Kim, Y. H. and Atkins, J. C., 'Evaluating Investments in Accounts Receivable', *Journal of Finance*, **33**, 403–412, May 1978.
Levy, F. K., 'An Application of Heuristic Problem Solving to Accounts Receivable Management', *Management Science*, **12** B236–B244, Feb. 1966.
Survey of Credit Management Decisions, British Institute of Management, London, 1974.
Zinkin, P. and Patel, H., 'Investigation of Risk Premiums on Corporate Bonds', M.Sc. Thesis, London Business School, June 1978.

APPENDIX 15.1 MONTHLY DISCOUNT RATES

A monthly analysis is useful for credit analysis since the essence of the Working Capital investment is involved in the leads and lags between monthly payments and receipts. The monthly discount rate can be obtained from the appropriate annual rate R by finding that discount rate r which when compounded for twelve periods will yield the return R:

$$(1 + r)^{12} = 1 + R,$$
$$r = (1 + R)^{1/12} - 1.$$

The appropriate annual risk-adjusted discount rate R which we use to obtain the monthly rate r will depend upon the current risk-free rate plus a premium for the credit risk of default plus a premium for systematic risk.

REVIEW QUESTIONS

1. A furniture shop sells its goods on credit. How should it go about estimating the cost of credit to its customers?

2. Under what circumstances is the decision to provide credit to a customer solely a financing decision?

3. Why is it difficult to define precisely the period of credit implicit in a receivable?

4. Under what circumstances should a firm accept a period of credit and reject a discount for early payment?

5. Under what circumstance is it possible for the provision of trade credit to be profitable to both parties?

EXERCISES

1. Compute the average debtor collection period for a company with debtors outstanding totalling £14 000 and annual sales of £132 000.
   If the maximum credit period granted by the company is 21 days, what might explain the difference in the average collection period? What questions does this raise and what suggestions could you make to management to improve the situation?

2. A company forecasts sales totalling £100 000 for the next quarter on the basis of a 1 per cent discount for payment within 7 days. The maximum credit period is 28 days, although some customers do take longer to pay.
   Assuming a borrowing rate of 15 per cent per annum, should the customer accept the discount for early payment? What difference does it make to your calculations if the customer takes 45 days credit?

3. A firm currently gives 28 days credit for all sales and experiences a repayments schedule listed in column 1 below. Forecast collections are listed in column 2. The company decides to offer 1 per cent discount for payment within 7 days. The company's borrowing rate is 9 per cent per annum and the average borrowing rate of the customers is 12 per cent per annum.

Month	1 Without discount	2 With trade discount
Within 7 days	0	150
1	400	280
2	100	70
3	50	50
4	10	10
5	10	10
Total sales	£570	£570

Is the new credit policy profitable from the company's point of view?

4. A customer X purchases £10 000 of goods from company Y with the usual 2 months' credit period. In addition, Y offers a 10 per cent discount for immediate payment. He is aware that X is a risky customer and considers that there is a 5 per cent probability of default.

252

Is the discount a good idea from the seller's point of view? Assume that X can borrow at 20 per cent per annum and Y can borrow at 10 per cent per annum (which is the risk-free rate of interest). Show your computations.

5. Both the supplier and his customers are very short of funds due to a severe credit squeeze operated by the Government and the banks. In order to attract customers, however, the supplier believes he must offer 1 month's credit rather than the existing terms of cash on delivery.

Existing sales are £10 000 per month and he anticipates an increase in sales to £12 000 per month as a result of the new credit policy. The supplier forecasts that a third of all future sales will be on credit with half of that total on 1 month's credit and the other half on 2 months' credit.

The incremental administrative costs of the new credit policy total £100 per month and the gross margin on all sales is 50 per cent of the sales price. Can you expect the new policy to be profitable?

The reader should note that the company has in the past borrowed funds at 10 per cent, but due to the credit squeeze funds can only be obtained by forgoing profitable projects which all have an internal rate of return of 20 per cent and a required rate of return of 15 per cent. The new credit policy is of a similar risk to these other projects.

16

WORKING CAPITAL MANAGEMENT: STOCK

Investment in stock accounts for between 20 and 40 per cent of total assets for most U.K. companies. Some investment in stock is essential to the smooth functioning of the business. Finished goods stocks smooth the effects of fluctuating sales on production, and raw materials stocks provide insurance against shortages during long and uncertain delivery times from suppliers. An inadquate stock control system will result in the wrong balance of stocks, thereby reducing profitability. Because the costs of carrying stock are very high, the stock control system deserves the attention of financial management.

Although the day-to-day operation of stock control is carried on by specialists, financial management exercise an influence on inventory investment at two key stages. First, inventory reporting and other data processing associated with the stock control system are usually the responsibility of the Management Services Department, reporting to the Controller. Thus the choice, design, and subsequent adaptation of the stock control systems operated throughout the company involve financial staff. The responsibility for an inadequate system must rest ultimately with the Controller. Second, the operation of the system requires periodic monitoring and control. Stock control systems have severe limitations, and the specialists operating them are not always in tune with current top management thinking and strategy. Working capital targets and priorities can change quickly, and the role of stock must be evaluated in the context of developing corporate strategy. If the inventory investment is significant, the Finance Director cannot adequately advise the Board about current and future liquidity unless he is aware of trends in the company's aggregate investment in stock and of its liquidity.

Thus, in this chapter, we will first discuss the major methods by which the broad controls on inventory investment can be exercised by financial management. We will then focus our attention on the kinds of stock control systems which can be installed by financial staff to help inventory managers operate more successfully. Finally, we will consider the problems of operating detailed stock controls within the context of broad policy targets when responsibility is dispersed widely among operating departments with conflicting interests.

PLANNING AND MONITORING STOCK LEVELS

The expected aggregate investment in Stock is a consequence of planned production in relation to the sales forecast. Stock at the end of any period will be determined by initial stocks plus purchasing and production during the period, less sales. Deviations from planned stock will result from deviations by purchasing or by production from plan, deviations of sales from forecast or a combination of the three.

Each identifiable production unit usually requires an operating plan based on existing orders, a sales forecast and planned changes in the inventory investment. Actual production and sales should then be monitored and compared with plans and forecasts so that timely adjustments can be made as market conditions change.

Figure 16.1 is an example of a cumulative Production, Sales, and Inventory chart. This chart provides an effective means of monitoring total stock by profit centre or by product. The solid line is the cumulative forecast. The circled points are cumulative sales to date (through June). The first uncircled point (on the vertical axis) is Finished Stock at the beginning of the year, and subsequent points represent cumulative production. The dashed line represents the cumulative production plan and the vertical distance between the cumulative sales forecast and the cumulative production plan represents the planned levels of finished stock at each point in time.

A similar chart can be used for raw materials. In this case, the circled points would represent usage in production and the solid line the forecast

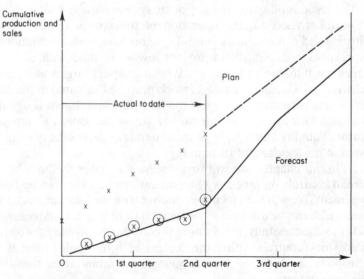

Figure 16.1. Production sales and inventory chart

usage. The points which are not circled and the dashed line would represent cumulative purchases and planned purchases, respectively.

Concentrating as it does on an aggregate view of stocks, such cumulative Production, Sales (or Purchasing), and Inventory charts provide financial management with a very useful visual monitor of trends in requirements for investment in stock.

The charts demonstrate the relationship between stocks, planned production levels, and seasonal changes in sales. This overview helps to counteract the tendency to try maintaining a constant number of weeks' stock in every item, which would require changing production levels unnecessarily with temporary fluctuations in sales activity.

While financial management should take an interest primarily in trends in the total investment in stock, it should also be mindful of their composition. Figure 16.2 illustrates the way in which the composition of stocks are usually related to the total volume of stock usage. Figure 16.2 is a stock turnover profile which emerges as a natural consequence of rates of usage varying for different items of stock. Thus 25 per cent of all items may constitute 60–75 per cent of the total volume. These 'A' category stocks are the most important items, deserving individual attention. The next 25 per cent of items, the 'B' category, may only account for 15–20 per cent of the volume of stock usage, and the 'C' category comprising the remaining 50 per cent of the items may account for as little as 5 per cent of the volume of usage.

Thus possibly 50 per cent of the items will be relatively slow moving and may be held in quantities which are large in comparison to currently anticipated usage. Efforts to reduce stock quickly can be counterproductive

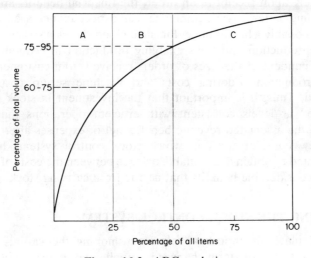

Figure 16.2. ABC analysis

if this means selling off the fast-moving A and B items, leaving an unbalanced inventory consisting of mostly 'C' category items.

COST OF CARRYING STOCKS

The costs of carrying stock are somewhat greater than merely the interest costs of financing inventory. There are at least four items of cost which need to be considered:

(a) *Storage costs, handling, and insurance.* Where there is a surplus of warehouse space with no alternative uses, and when marginal costing is appropriate, only such incremental items as handling and insurance would be included.

(b) *Obsolescence, deterioration, and theft.* The cost arising from these sources are highly dependent on the nature of the item in storage.

(c) *Clerical costs.* Stocks must be recorded and controlled. Costs of operating control systems for additional stocks can be significant.

(d) *Financing costs.* Investment in stocks (as in any other capital investment) is risky and requires the risk-free rate of interest plus a risk premium.

Taking all such costs into account, annual carrying costs for stock can range between 15 and 40 per cent.

Investment in stock can be viewed as a capital project. The problem is to determine the level of investment which maximizes the Net Present Value. Consider, for example, Finished Goods Stock. Carrying Finished Goods enables the company to provide faster service to customers than is possible when goods are made to order. When goods can be shipped and invoiced immediately upon receipt of an order, the financial benefits are obvious. By providing better service, companies can expect an increased volume of sales and possibly a higher price. Finished Goods Stock also acts as a buffer between production and sales enabling production in economical batch sizes independent of the sizes of orders received from customers. By this means production ordering costs and machine set-up costs can be minimized. Thus, it is important that the investment in stock should be maintained at levels consistent with efficient operations that tend to maximize the associated revenue benefits net of expenses after tax.

We now consider ways in which stock control systems have been implemented to obtain a reasonable balance between the costs of stock and the very considerable benefits that accrue from carrying stock.

DESIGNING THE STOCK CONTROL SYSTEM

Inventory plays an important role in cushioning the various stages of production from short-term changes in supply, and reducing delivery lead times to customers. Thus, the inventory system is crucial to the ability of the firm to provide service to customers and to do so efficiently at minimum cost.

Inventories can be categorized as follows:

(a) new materials,
(b) work in progress,
(c) partially processed items including component stocks,
(d) finished goods,
(e) distribution stocks.

Within each of these categories the inventory system often must provide:

(a) inventories in anticipation of seasonal changes in demand;
(b) inventories arising from quantity ordering and batch production;
(c) safety stock serving as a buffer between uncertain demand and supply inventories required;
(d) logistical inventories required to fill the pipeline between stages of production and the distribution system.

The availability of stocks at critical points in the production system can greatly shorten delivery lead times to customers and thus improve the competitive posture of the company while at the same time reducing manufacturing costs. The inventory control system should be designed so as to seek a reasonable if not 'optimum' balance between these advantages and the very considerable costs of carrying stock within the physical limitations of available space.

We shall now examine in more detail the elements required in an effective inventory control system.

ELEMENTS OF A STOCK CONTROL SYSTEM

An inventory control system can be described in terms of the method used to replenish stocks. The method chosen depends on (a) the degree of uncertainty associated with the demands made on stocks and (b) the degree of monitoring which can be justified in each case. There are five basic stock replenishment systems commonly in use.
These are:

(a) re-order level policy,
(b) re-order level policy subject to periodic review,
(c) re-order cycle policy,
(d) (s, S) policy,
(e) Materials requirements planning (MRP).

These various systems are adapted for different degrees of uncertainty of demand and for varying degrees of monitoring.

Re-order level policy

The re-order level policy is adapted to continuous or real-time monitoring of stock where the arrivals of orders follow no predictable pattern. Thus one tends to find variations of the re-order level policy operating in retail and wholesale outlets or in other parts of the system where many customers can make demands on stock.

A forecast of the average rate of sales is required. This policy also requires an estimate of the *lead time* required between the time a replenishment order is placed and the receipt of the goods in stock. For each item in stock, a *re-order level* must be calculated. When stock falls to the re-order level or below, a replenishment order is placed immediately. The re-order level is set high enough so that if sales during the lead time are as forecast, the replenishment stock will arrive before the inventory is entirely exhausted. A margin of safety is provided by the provision of *safety stock* in case sales exceed the forecast during the lead time.

The amount of safety stock required can be determined in terms of the statistical distribution of demand during the lead time. From the mean and variance of lead-time demand there are routine computer methods for determining the probability that a *stockout* will occur before the stocks are replenished. The greater the safety stock the lower the probability of a stockout and the less average waiting time will be required for supply.

Also to be determined is the quantity which should be ordered when replenishment is required. The act of re-ordering requires clerical time; and the opportunity cost of setting up any machinery required to satisfy the order can be costly. If stock were to be ordered in larger quantities, fewer replenishment orders would be required and re-ordering costs would be reduced. However, the size of each batch received in stock influences the size of the resulting *lot-size* inventory which must be held while the batch is being exhausted. The costs of holding stock are particularly high as we have discussed earlier in the chapter. There are formulae (Lewis, 1970) for calculating an *economic order quantity* intended to minimize the sum of re-ordering and stock-holding costs. An example of such formulae is given in Appendix 16.1.

Thus, the re-order level system requires forecasts of the re-ordering lead time, the mean and variance of usage during the lead time, re-ordering and machine set-up costs, and the incremental cost of holding stock for one period. All this information can be derived from the information system.

The re-order level policy suffers from two quite serious drawbacks. First, the usual assumption of random arrivals for orders against stock is inappropriate for a large number of cases, which means that the system does not take advantage of the anticipated timing of demand when replenishment orders are placed. A more serious drawback for many applications is that the re-order level policy requires costly, continuous real-time monitoring of every item of stock.

Re-order level policy subject to periodic review

The re-order cycle policy subject to periodic review is designed to operate without the continuous monitoring required by the policy described above. The periodic review policy operates like the continuous review policy, except that the status of each item of inventory is reviewed only once each period, e.g. each week or month. When stock is found to be below the re-order level, a replenishment order is issued in the same manner and in the same quantity as for the re-order level policy with continuous review.

However, with this system the re-order level must be set higher in order to allow for expected demand during one half of the re-order cycle in addition to the expected demand during the lead time. Also, safety stock must be increased to allow for variance of expected demand over the additional time period.

Although periodic review with the re-order level policy reduces the clerical and data processing costs of operating the inventory control system, there are off-setting holding costs for the additional stock. Formulae are available for determining the optimum re-order cycle time. However, the normal working cycle for control department personnel may not conform easily to a theoretically optimum review period.

Re-order cycle policy

The re-order cycle policy is another periodic review system which provides a more direct control on the stock which is to be carried. In each cycle, a replenishment order is placed for that quantity which would bring the total amount of goods in stock and already on order up to a pre-determined limit. This limit must be sufficient to cover forecast demand for one full cycle period plus the lead time; and an additional amount for safety stock is included to allow for the variability of demand during this total period.

The re-order cycle period is then chosen which minimizes the total of re-ordering costs and average lot-size stock holding cost.

The (s, S) policy

The (s, S) policy is an hybrid between the re-order level policy (with periodic review) and the re-order cycle policy. Under the (s, S) procedure the stock is reviewed periodically but not replenished unless the stock has fallen below the re-order level s. In this respect, the (s, S) policy is exactly like the re-order level policy with periodic review. However, a standard economic order quantity is not used. Instead, the replenishment order is issued for that quantity which makes the total of goods in stock and goods on order equal to the quantity S. In this latter respect, the method operates like a re-order cycle system.

The main difficulty with the (s, S) method is that the calculation of the best combination of s, S, and the review period for minimum total cost is a rather complex mathematical problem. However, a reasonable approach is to make the difference $(S - s)$ equal to the economic order quantity used for the re-order level policy, to make s equal to the safety stock in the re-order level policy with periodic review and to make the review period the same as would operate under the re-order cycle policy.

Material requirements planning

The four policies reviewed earlier all had one assumption in common, that the arrival of individual demands on stock are unpredictable. As demand becomes more predictable, these policies cease to describe the most efficient mode of operation. To take a not uncommon example, suppose that a stock of finished goods is held for one customer who orders the same quantity at the same time virtually every month. No policy would be optimal which did not take advantage of this additional information concerning demand. If a replenishment order equal to the customer's monthly demand were placed just over one lead time prior to the expected receipt of the monthly order, virtually no finished stock need be carried since replenishment would occur almost simultaneously with demand. We know, however, that the resulting machinery set-up costs might be reduced substantially by manufacturing quantities for 2, 3, or more months' requirements. In this case, an inventory must be held equal to the demand being met by the replenishment order *beyond* the first month. The replenishment stock would still be timed to arrive just before receipt of the next monthly customer order. How many months' sales would be included in the replenishment order? Here we have a capital investment decision. We find that re-ordering policy which minimizes the Present Value of the resulting sequence of set-up costs and holding costs.

Thus, we see from the above example that when there are predictable, dependent relationships in the pattern of demand, advantages are to be gained in gearing the ordering policy to take advantage of the additional information. One can also see that operation of such a system requires close attention to the demand characteristics of each such item of stock. Consequently, we are now considering policy refinements applicable mainly to major items amongst those categorized as Class A in Figure 16.2, where the individual attention required might be shown to be justifiable.

To the extent that the firm is manufacturing to a backlog of orders, the demand pattern becomes relatively predictable in the short term. In this situation, the various re-ordering policies discussed earlier are no longer appropriate. Instead, the known demand is used to generate orders for the required parts and materials and components right back through the operating system. The resulting *materials requirements planning* system relies on lists of parts and 'number required' to generate factory requirements from customer orders. These requirements are translated into schedules that take into consideration the need to consolidate demand for common components, existing stock levels, production and procurement lead times, and production batching policy.

Because most manufacturing companies produce to order *and* for stock, they require elements of the material requirements planning and one or more of the stock replenishment policies operating simultaneously. Making the blend of the required systems actually work is an important part of the art of the skilled operations manager.

OPERATING THE INVENTORY CONTROL SYSTEM

Financial management is primarily concerned that the investment in inventory yields the largest possible Net Present Value. This goal cannot be achieved unless management succeeds in superimposing a corporate view on the system of item control. Item stock control formulae are typically suboptimal in the sense that they do not consider the costs of sudden changes in the level of production. Management must judge how quickly production can be changed to meet seasonal or other sources of change in demand and let stocks play their proper role as a buffer between production and short-term changes in demand. Thus production plans are established on the basis of an inventory target and other information underlying the Production Sales and Inventory chart of Figure 16.1.

In the course of time, the combination of starting inventory, sales forecast, and production plan will dictate planned residual changes in inventory. Referring to Figure 16.1, at the end of the second quarter, inventory is planned to reach a maximum and then to fall to a minimum 3 months later.

These planned changes constrain total stock to be different from the target implied by the aggregate of all Economic Order Quantities and Safety Stocks. The stock control system will not operate optimally under these conditions unless replenishment order quantities are scaled up proportionally when the planned total inventory is to be above this theoretical target and scaled down proportionally when the planned total inventory is below this target.

RESPONSIBILITY FOR THE INVESTMENT IN INVENTORY

Stocks are controlled by a variety of departments, each with their own interests in maintaining inventory at a substantial level. Thus it often falls to financial management to ensure that conflicting interests are kept in balance.

Finished Goods Stocks are a necessary ingredient of distribution and good customer service. Thus the Marketing or Sales Department take an active interest in finished goods, often controlling stocks by item for each major customer. Marketing personnel often prefer to err on the side of having too much stock in order to ensure against shortages and to maximize sales.

Finished Goods Stock, providing a buffer between the market and the production process, facilitates long production runs and minimizes short-term redundancy. Thus, production management often plays a critical role in determining the volume of investment in stock. Production management may be less interested in maintaining the balance of items in stock than in keeping operating units and production processes running efficiently. They will often produce an excess of an item which can be produced efficiently in order to keep a particular process going at minimum cost per unit—at the expense of other items which may then fall into short supply. Here again we find an interest in maintaining substantial stocks which may be in excess of what is required.

Raw Materials Stocks are necessary for continuity of operations. Here the responsibility for stock lies with the Purchasing Department. The Purchasing Department is interested in supplying sufficient raw materials item by item and may work to stock-level limits which may be inappropriate in comparison to currently anticipated levels of production.

In manufacturing companies, a Production Planning and Control Department will normally be given the responsibility for the balancing of the interests of the various departments and for the minimization of the financial and other costs of carrying stock. Production Planning and Control Departments usually report to the Director of Production and are frequently located within operating companies of the group. If the Production Control Manager does not report directly (or have a dotted line relationship) to Financial Management, the control exercised by him may not always be consistent with the strategy and policies inherent in the Financial Plan.

SUMMARY AND CONCLUSIONS

Inventories normally comprise a significant proportion of corporate assets and thus require the close attention of financial management. Inventories are one of the more volatile parts of working capital and an accumulating excess of unmarketable stock has led to the bankruptcy of a number of companies. The management of inventories is usually divided amongst a number of departments often outside the direct influence of financial management. Nevertheless, the financial area should have all the necessary information to manage stock readily to hand in the information system and have the ultimate responsibility to see that the aggregate of inventory investment reflects a sound relationship between forecast sales and the costs of production and warehousing. Tools available to financial managers for monitoring aggregates and subaggregates of stock have been discussed

263

and we have given a brief outline of the various item inventory control systems which the Controller should consider adapting to the needs of operating management.

REFERENCES AND BIBLIOGRAPHY

Baily, P., *Successful Stock Control by Manual Systems*, Gower Press, London, 1971.
Brown, R. G., *Decision Rules for Inventory Management*, Holt, Rinehart, and Winston, New York, 1967.
Constable, C. J., and New, C. C., *Operations Management: A Systems Approach through Text and Cases*, John Wiley and Sons, Chichester, 1976.
Lewis, C. D., *Scientific Inventory Control*, Butterworth & Co., London, 1970.
Thomas, A. B. *Stock Control in Manufacturing Industries*, Gower Press, London, 1968.

APPENDIX 16.1. ECONOMIC ORDER QUANTITIES

The *economic order quantity* (EOQ) provides a basis for obtaining reordering quantities used in stock control systems described in the chapter. The purpose of the EOQ is to minimize the sum of ordering costs and holding costs for stock.

Ordering costs

Annual ordering costs equal the number of orders multiplied by the cost D per order (typically administrative and any machinery set-up costs). The estimated number of orders is obtained by dividing the forecast annual usage S by the order quantity Q. Therefore,

Annual ordering cost $= SD/Q$.

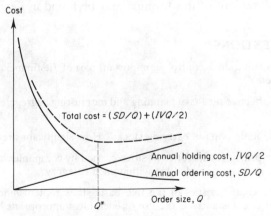

Figure 16.A1. Ordering costs, holding costs, and total costs

264

This cost can be reduced by increasing Q as may be seen by the curved line in Figure 16.A1. However, increasing the order size Q increases the stock and stock holding costs.

Stock holding costs

Receipt of a stock replenishment in the amount Q increases stock initially by Q. This increase diminishes to zero on average when the next replenishment arrives. Thus the *lot-size* inventory due to discrete replenishments of stock averages between Q and zero or $Q/2$. If the cost per unit in stock is V and the annual inventory holding charge is I per unit of value in stock, the cost of carrying lot-size inventory is given by

Stock holding cost $= IVQ/2$.

Thus, stock holding cost increases with the value of Q along the straight line in Figure 16.A1.

Minimum total holding and ordering costs

The objective of EOQ is to minimize the total of holding and ordering costs; that is, to minimize

$$T = (SD/Q) + (IVQ/2).$$

As may be seen in Figure 16.A1, the minimum occurs at the value of Q where the holding and ordering costs are equal. Thus we can solve for the value of Q^* for which these two terms are the same:

$$Q^* = \sqrt{2SD/IV}$$

This result is known as the *economic order quantity* formula referred to in the chapter. Variations of this formula may be found in Lewis (1970).

REVIEW QUESTIONS

1. What factors make stock control an important part of the financial planning and control system?

2. Describe an effective means of planning and monitoring aggregate investment in inventories.

3. What are the main costs of carrying stocks? How significant are they in total?

4. What are the principal categories of stock carried by companies and what types of inventory must be provided for within each category?

5. What are the characteristics of the five basic stock replenishment systems in use? In what circumstances is the use of each most appropriate?

6. Describe some of the problems arising in the operation of stock control systems.

EXERCISES

1. LMN Company are manufacturing Product Line A at the rate of 18 750 units per month. The quarterly sales forecast is given below:

Quarter	Forecast
1	75 000
2	125 000
3	75 000
4	125 000

Aggregate inventory for Product Line A at the beginning of the year was 200 000 units. If the target inventory for the end of the year is equal to 66 667 units, when should normal production be planned to resume? Draw the cumulative Production, Sales, and Stock chart.

2. Identify and label the following on the diagram below: (a) order quantity, (b) re-order level, (c) ordering lead time, (d) safety stock.

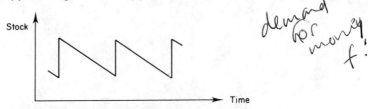

3. For the $S - s$ stock control system, identify S and s on the diagram in Exercise 16.2. How can appropriate values of S and s be estimated?

4. A stock is manufactured only for one industrial customer who orders regularly £1000 worth (at marginal cost) at the end of each month. If the inventory carrying cost is 30 per cent per annum and the re-ordering cost £100, how many months' stock should be made in each batch, and what average amount of stock will be carried?

PART VI

FINANCING

17

LONG-TERM FINANCING

Although most funds employed by established companies are internally generated in the course of their business activities, external sources of finance are an important resource called upon from time to time by nearly all companies. Banks provide the major short-term source of funds, although bank term loans are available for terms of up to 10 years. In this chapter we discuss the sources of long-term financing other than bank borrowing. First, we consider the securities which are issued by companies that give providers of funds certain claims on company profits and, in some circumstances, claims on assets. We discuss both Government and Corporate debt and specific financial instruments such as convertibles, preference shares, warrants, and options. We also outline the methods companies employ in raising new finance. Finally, we discuss the importance of the primary and secondary securities markets in which these securities are bought and sold.

TYPES OF SECURITIES

Government debt

The Government and its various departments issue a variety of fixed (and variable) interest debts to finance public expenditures and to influence the supply of credit. In Table 17.1, we have classified Government bonds according to maturity and the size of the coupon. The *coupon* is the interest rate per £100 of debt. Thus, the debts or bonds which were issued when interest rates were lower than they are today, e.g. Electric $3\frac{1}{2}$ pc ('76–'79), stand at a discount on their nominal value (£100). In each year, interest of £3.50 is paid on each £100 of nominal debt. The fact that the market price of each £100 of debt was £95$\frac{3}{4}$ (10th February 1978), implied that the annual yield (*running yield*) was 3.65 per cent. This annual yield is found by expressing the interest payments per year (£3.50) over the current market price (£95$\frac{3}{4}$). The running yield does not take into account the capital gain that the holder will receive on the bond when it is redeemed by the Government during the period 1976 through to 1979. Government bonds are always redeemed at the nominal price of £100; therefore, a capital gain

Table 17.1. British Government–fixed interest average gross
yields to redemption

		Friday 10th February 1978 (per cent)
Treasury Bills	3 months	$5^{15}/_{16}$
Low coupons	5 years	7.68
	15 years	9.89
	25 years	10.39
Medium coupons	5 years	9.8
	15 years	10.86
	25 years	11.0
High coupons	5	10.37
	10 years	11.78
	15 years	11.87
Irredeemables (undated)		11.48

Source: *The Financial Times*, 11th February 1978.

of £4¼ will be made on redemption. Many analysts calculate a *yield to redemption*, which is the Internal Rate of Return reflecting interest payments *and* capital gain. In our example, the yield to redemption is 6.08 per cent, and it is assumed that the Government will not redeem until the end of the redemption period (i.e. 1979).

Why do we differentiate between Government bonds on the basis of maturity (number of years to run before redemption) and coupon (interest payment)? As can be seen from Table 17.1, the longer the maturity the greater the interest rate demanded by lenders.

The reason the coupon is important is that any capital gains on Government bonds or *gilts* are tax free, providing that the bonds are held for more than 1 year. This provision is important to those investors who are paying high marginal rates of tax. They prefer capital gains (which are tax free) to interest payments which are treated as income and are taxable at the investor's marginal rate. Clearly, relatively low coupon bonds imply much greater capital gains than high coupon bonds. Although low coupon bonds have a lower yield than high coupon bonds (before taxes), the yields after tax in the hands of investors with different tax rates will provide a different pattern of returns.

Bonds of very short maturity (3 months and 6 months) are known as *Treasury Bills* and are issued every week (Friday 1 p.m.) by the Government using the auction method. Bonds with a maturity of less than 5 years are known as *shorts*, 5–15 years are known as *mediums*, and over

15 years (but dated) are known as *longs*. Those bonds which are undated or irredeemable (e.g. Consols) are in a category of their own.

Corporate debt

Companies as well as governments issue debt securities. In the case of the U.K. Government, such debt obligations are free from the risk of default. This fact does not mean that the value of such securities cannot be expected to alter. If a bond is issued at a fixed interest rate of, for example, 10 per cent, any future interest rate change will alter the market value of the bond. However, with corporate debt there may be an additional risk, that of default. This additional risk explains why corporate bonds sell at higher yields compared with Government bonds. The size of the default risk depends upon how risky the underlying assets of the company are and how much debt is outstanding. The greater the risk of the assets of the firm, the higher the probability that at some time in the future the company will be unable to cover interest charges and repayments out of current revenues and reserves. Default may be expected to occur when the value of the company's assets are less than the liabilities. In fact, default may occur prior to this point if the company runs out of cash and is unable to realize its assets sufficiently quickly, i.e. in a liquidity crisis.

A further reason for the interest rate differential between corporate and Government bonds is the lack of marketability of some of the corporate bonds. In an empirical study, Fisher (1959) found that lack of marketability was an important explanatory variable for the size of the risk premium.

The holders of corporate bonds are to some extent protected by appointed trustees and the deeds of the debt contract. Clauses in the deeds will state specific conditions whereby the trustees may require early repayment of the debt or liquidation of the company. If liquidation occurs, the debtholder will obtain the proceeds before any payment is made to the equity holders. Since payments to certain parties—for example employees and the Inland Revenue—will rank in front of the debt-holders, it may be in the interest of the latter not to put the company into liquidation but to agree to changes in the debt contract, for example a postponement or reduction in interest payments.

So far we have treated all corporate debt as being the same. In fact, such debt may be secured on specific assets of the company or may be unsecured. A debt secured on specific assets is called a *debenture* and ranks in front of unsecured debt (called *Loan Stock*) in terms of entitlement to interest and repayment in liquidation. Debentures may also be ranked in preferential order, and if one debenture is ranked behind another, it is said to be *subordinated*. Clearly, it is of the utmost importance in writing the debt contract to state where the particular bond stands in case of liquidation. Such facts will influence the interest rate charged by lenders.

272

Equity

The capital owned by the shareholders of a company is known as the equity or *ordinary share capital*. The company may be a private company whose shares will not be traded on any recognized stock exchange or it may be a 'public' company whose shares are traded. Shareholders of quoted (traded) companies receive their income in two forms—cash dividends and capital gains. Since many companies have invested their funds in risky assets, the earnings are uncertain and fluctuate over time. The risk inherent in the earnings stream of such assets is reflected in fluctuations in dividend payments and share prices.

In Table 17.2, we have extracted from *The Financial Times* the published financial statistics for the Boots Company. Such information is provided each day subsequent to trading on the Stock Exchange for over 1000 companies. The dividend yield is simply the dividend per share (in pence) as a percentage of that day's share price. The reader will notice that the dividend yield is given gross, i.e. before shareholder's taxes have been deducted at the standard rate of 34 per cent. In the 'dividend net' column, the amount of the dividend (pence) per share is given after deduction of shareholders' taxes at the standard rate of tax. The cover ratio shows that the net dividend is covered 4.9 times by earnings of the current year. Another way of looking at the cover ratio is to say that only about 17 per cent of current earnings were distributed in the form of a dividend. The earnings that are retained are reinvested in order to maintain or increase future dividends.

The final column tells us the *price-to-earnings* (per share) *ratio* of the company. This ratio is computed by dividing the market price by the Earnings Per Share (after taxes) and gives the number of years it will take current Earnings Per Share to accumulate to the current share price. In the case of Boots, the price-to-earnings ratio indicates that it will take 15.4 years for the EPS at current levels to accumulate to the price of the share. The reciprocal of the price-to-earnings ratio is the *earnings yield* and for Boots this is 6.49 per cent (1/15.4). Why would a shareholder pay 204 pence in order to obtain an earnings yield of only 6.49 per cent and a dividend yield of 2.0 per cent? Clearly, earnings and dividends are expected to grow as a result of the reinvestment of earnings in profitable new projects. The

Table 17.2. Share prices and financial statistics*

High	Low	Stock	Price (pence)	+ or −	Dividend Net	Cover	Yield Gross (per cent)	P/E
244	115	Boots	204	. . . .	2.72	4.9	2.0	15.4

*Source: *The Financial Times*, 10th February 1978.

growth in earnings and dividends is expected to ensure a higher yield in the future which will result in a higher internal rate of return than is obtainable on bonds.

Convertible bonds

Convertible bonds give the holder the right to receive a fixed rate of interest until either the bond is redeemed or the holder converts the bond into ordinary shares at a specified price. A specific period of time during which this option to convert can be exercised is usually specified.

In Table 17.3, we have reproduced statistics on three convertible bonds which were outstanding in 1978. Let us examine the convertible of Alcan Aluminium. The security provided a return of 9 per cent per annum on each £100 of stock. If the convertible is held to maturity, it will be redeemed during the period 1989–94 (depending on the level of interest rates ruling at the time) at a price of £100. However, the holder also has the option to convert into ordinary shares at any time during the period 1976–78. The number of shares he will obtain for each £100 of convertible stock will be specified in the deeds of the security. Clearly, whether holders of convertible bonds will choose to convert will depend on the subsequent prices of the ordinary shares.

Two points about Alcan's convertible may puzzle the reader. The flat or running yield of the stock appears very low when compared with the yield on Government securities. Second, the redemption yield is even lower than the running yield. The conversion terms (not given in the table) supply the answer to the first question. The option to convert is an option of some value that increases as the ordinary shares increase in price. Since the price of the convertible includes the value of this option, the running yield is correspondingly reduced in relation to bonds which do not have the option to convert. The values of options are discussed later in the chapter.

The answer to the second point concerning the low redemption yield should be more easily perceived since the market price of the convertible is

Table 17.3. U.K. convertible stocks

	Current price (pence)	Terms	Conversion dates	Flat yield (per cent)	Redemption yield (per cent)
Alcan Aluminium, 9pc Cv 89–94	142.50	100.0	1976–78	6.4	4.3
British Land, 12pc Cv 2002	132.00	333.3	1980–97	9.4	9.1
Grand Metropolitan, 10pc Cv 91–96	113.50	120.2	1973–78	9.1	8.7

Source: *The Financial Times*, 11th February 1978. for 10th February prices.

£142.50 compared with the price on redemption of £100. Clearly, if the convertible were held to maturity, a capital loss would occur based on the current market price; the yield to redemption includes this capital loss.

Preference shares

This form of equity usually provides the holder with a fixed interest return, expressed as a percentage of the nominal value of the shares. Such dividend payments are discretionary but must be paid if (and only if) a dividend is made to the ordinary shareholders. In addition, in a liquidation the preferred shareholders obtain repayment of their original capital prior to the ordinary shareholders. Although the company has discretion to omit the preferred dividends as long as no dividends are paid to the ordinary shareholders, the articles of some preference share contracts state that dividend arrears must be paid off prior to the resumption of other payments to shareholders. Finally, such preference shares are usually not redeemable unless the company is in liquidation or an offer is made as a result of a take-over or because of a change in tax legislation.

One of the disadvantages of preference shares is that interest payments are not tax deductible, as is the interest on debt capital. Because preference shares offer greater security than ordinary shares, they offer a lower return; however, they will provide a higher after-tax return than the corporate debt of the same firm. Thus we are dealing with another financial instrument with different risk-return characteristics—making for a more complete market.

Options

An option provides the holder with an opportunity to buy (or sell) an asset sometime in the future at a price fixed at the time the option is purchased. On the London Stock Exchange, investors can buy (as at February 1978) 3-month and 6-month options in the ordinary shares of a variety of companies. There are principally two types of options, *puts* and *calls*. A purchase of a 3-month call option (Table 17.4) in I.C.I. cost 23 pence. The option entitled the holder to purchase one share in I.C.I. at a fixed price of 354 pence in the next 3 months. If the option were not exercised, the holder would only lose the cost of the option, that is 23 pence. Similarly, if the investor bought a 3-month *put* option in I.C.I., he would have the opportunity of *selling* one I.C.I. share at a fixed price anytime during the next 3 months. Clearly, he would only exercise the option if the price fell below 354 pence. If the option is exercised, the holder must, in addition, pay the transaction costs of buying the shares.

In Table 17.4, we have listed the cost of one option for a number of

Table 17.4. Three-month option rates as at 10th February 1978

	Cost of 1* option (pence)	Price of* ordinary share (pence)	Option price as a percentage of ordinary share price (per cent)
Beecham	38	635	6
Bowater	16	169	9
Cadbury's	5	54	9
E.M.I.	18	174	10
Grand Metropolitan	9	99	9
I.C.I.	23	354	5
Shell	28	506	6
Charterhall	$3\frac{1}{2}$	$25\frac{1}{2}$	14
Rio Tinto Zinc	16	171	9

*Source: *The Financial Times*, 11th February 1978.

securities quoted on the Stock Exchange. The price of the option as a percentage of the price of the ordinary shares is also given. Three-month options cost between 6 and 14 per cent of the price of the ordinary shares. Why are there such differences? The answer is simply risk; the more risky the underlying ordinary share the more costly (or valuable) is the option. If the underlying ordinary share were riskless (i.e. the income of the company was not subject to unexpected variations), how much would an investor pay for an option? The answer is zero because the price is not expected to change in the future. The value of an option is primarily a function of the risk of the underlying security and, of course, the period to maturity of the option itself.

Clearly, the longer the maturity, the more valuable the option. Even if the underlying stock were very risky, an option to buy a share for 1 minute would not be very valuable since the price of the ordinary shares change relatively little in a short period of time. The third variable that determines the cost (or value) of an option is the interest rate; the higher the interest rate, the higher the cost of an option. The reason for this relationship is that an option provides the holder with a form of gearing. Suppose the option price for I.C.I. is 23 pence and the underlying ordinary share is 354 pence. The value of the option rises or falls 1 pence for every 1 pence change in the price of the ordinary shares. Put simply, the holder spends 331 pence *less* in capital terms by buying the option, thus an option provides a substitute for borrowing. The higher the interest rate the greater the interest saving by purchasing the option. In Appendix 17.1 we examine Black and Scholes' (1973) option valuation model and compare the actual value of a London option with Black and Scholes' valuation.

The question is, 'Why take out an option at all?' Some readers might think options provide a rather interesting gamble. After all, I buy an option in I.C.I. for 23 pence, and if I.C.I. goes from 354 to 400 pence I recover the cost of my option plus a 100 percent profit. Of course, if the security falls in price from 354 pence, I could lose entirely the cost of the option. If one is prepared to take great risks (compared with a purchase of the ordinary shares) then one may *expect* (but may not necessarily receive) great returns.

However, there are more serious reasons why options provide investors with an important financial instrument. For example, if an individual who owns a portfolio of shares dies, it is possible that tax will be assessed on the value of the shares, let us say, 2 days after death. It is also possible that the shares cannot be sold for 3 months because of legal impediments. We can protect the heirs of the estate against the risk of loss—simply by buying a sufficient number of 3-month put options so that any fall in price will bring an equivalent gain via the investment in puts matching any losses incurred on the portfolio. If the option is not required for 3 months, but possibly only for 1 month and the option is a traded option, one could buy a 1-month option (a 3-month option with only 1 month to expiration). Thus options offer a convenient means of adjusting portfolio risk to meet temporary circumstances without buying or selling securities in the portfolio and incurring unnecessary transactions costs. In April 1978, a traded options market opened in London in a limited number of securities. A market in traded options is already firmly established in Chicago and New York.

Warrants

A warrant is similar to a call option in so far as it permits the holder to purchase a specified number of ordinary shares (per warrant) at a fixed price during a specified period. There are about 40 warrants currently traded on the London Stock Exchange and many were issued during mergers to the shareholders of the acquired companies. Warrants have been issued by companies such as Grand Metropolitan Hotels and National Westminster Bank.

SOURCES OF FINANCE FOR COMPANIES

Most funds employed by companies are generated internally by ongoing operations, but a substantial proportion of capital requirements are obtained from the various institutions of the London Capital Market, known as 'the City'. A list of the different kinds of institutions is provided in Table 17.5.

Institutions	Over-drafts	Term lending loan capital	Other financial services*	Equity finance†	Size of company	Sums available
Banks	✓	✓	✓	–	All	All
Merchant Banks (including Clearing Banks' subsidiaries)	–	✓	✓	✓	Most	Min. £50 000
Finance Houses	–	✓	✓	–	All	All
Specialist bodies‡	–	✓	✓	✓	Small	Min £50 000
I.C.F.C.	–	✓	✓	✓	Small to medium	£50 000–£1m+
F.F.I.	–	✓	–	–	Medium to large	£1m–£25m
E.C.I.	–	✓	✓	✓	Turnover £10m–£100m	£½m–£5m
N.E.B.	–	–	✓	✓	Most	£50 000+
Insurance companies and Pension funds	–	–	–	✓	Most	Min. £¼m
Stock Exchange	–	–	–	✓	Min. market value £½m–£¾m	Min. £1m

*Includes leasing, hire purchase
†Includes development capital, venture capital, assistance with flotations.
‡Includes Charterhouse, Moracrest, N.R.D.C.
Source: Committee to Review the Functioning of Financial Institutions, *Evidence on the Financing of Industry and Trade*, Vol. 1: Treasury and D.T.F., H.M.S.O., London, 1977.

Internally generated funds (profits after tax plus depreciation minus dividends), accounted for between 50 and 78 per cent of funds employed by public companies in the United Kingdom over the past 20 years. The balance, between 22 and 50 per cent, was found externally. The largest source of external funding was bank borrowing, accounting for between 1 and 16 per cent, followed by the issue of ordinary share capital, providing between 1 and 9 per cent of total funds. The balance of funds came from the issue of preference shares, loan stock, and convertible debentures. Funds were also realized from private loans other than bank loans and from mortgages secured on property.

The U.K. public are the ultimate source of most of the external funding of U.K. companies, although some finance comes from abroad. As private investors, the public invest directly in the stock market through purchase of corporate securities including ordinary equity shares and loan stock. Increasingly, however, most private investment is taking place indirectly through financial intermediaries. Various forms of saving provide a steady flow of funds to insurance companies, pension funds, investment trusts, and unit trusts which invest either directly or through the stock market in industrial companies or through such new institutions as Equity Capital for Industry and Finance for Industry. These latter two institutions were established largely through Government pressures to make financing easier to obtain by companies representing higher than normal risks.

As private investors and owner operators, the public also purchase shares directly from firms not quoted on the Stock Exchange. As taxpayers, they participate in investments made by the Government through the National Enterprise Board and the Department of Industry. The National Enterprise Board provide equity or loan finance for selected companies at near commercial rates. They are also agents for Department of Industry rescue schemes for ailing companies. The Department of Industry can provide equity or loan finance under the Industry Act of 1972 on non-commercial terms if necessary. A small number of firms regarded as worthy or essential by the Government may find help from these two agencies as a last resort.

Finally, as bank depositors the public provide the funds when Clearing Banks lend directly to industrial companies. These loans are mainly short-term with a small but growing proportion of medium-term lending up to 7 or 8 years. The Clearing Banks also participate with the institutional investors in Finance for Industry, which provides mainly medium and long-term finance, including equity for small firms through the I.C.F.C.

An important role is also played by the Merchant Banks, who assist small companies with long-term loans—often tied to options to purchase equity—and who participate in the underwriting of issues of equities and loan stock by large companies.

METHODS OF RAISING NEW FINANCE

Existing quoted companies

The usual method for an existing company to raise new long-term equity finance is through a rights issue. This method constitutes an offer to sell existing holders of the company's securities a certain number of new shares as a proportion of their existing holding. Thus an issue of '1 for every 2 held' means that one new share is offered for every two shares already held by the existing holder. At what price should the new shares be offered? Clearly, they must be offered at a price equal to or below that prevailing in the market, otherwise shareholders would prefer to purchase shares in the open market.

Now if the offer of new shares were to be made on, let us say, a Monday morning at 10 a.m. and the offer could close at 10.05 a.m., the price of the new shares need be only a small amount lower than the prevailing market price to attract bidders. There would also be an additional incentive to buyers, since there is no brokerage commission on such purchases. Of course, it is not possible to close the offer within 5 minutes of opening it. Documents accompanying the offer of new shares must be posted to shareholders and their advisers, and time must be given to permit them to make up their minds. At least a week must elapse before investors are compelled to make up their minds whether to purchase the rights. Within that week, the market price of the shares may fall as a result of general economic and industry news or company information. If the ordinary shares fall below the price on the new shares, the issue will fail. The company has two choices: it may set the price on the new shares so far below the prevailing share price that there is only a very small probability of failure; alternatively, it may ask institutions to underwrite the issue. Underwriting guarantees that if the issue is not taken up by existing shareholders, the institutions will purchase that proportion of shares left over.

Let us take a simple example. A company has one million shares outstanding with a current market price of £1 each. The Directors decide that £225 000 additional funds are required to finance a new investment programme and that the money should be raised via a rights issue. The terms are three new shares for every ten currently outstanding with a price for the new shares fixed at 75 pence. The shareholders are given 10 days to consider the offer. A number of questions arise. Does it matter to the existing shareholders at what price the new shares are set? For example, the company could have raised the same amount of money by offering three new shares for every five held with a price of 37½ pence. Shareholders would be no worse or better off since their share of profits and dividends remains unchanged irrespective of the price of the new shares. Shareholders, of course, need not take up their rights to new shares; they can sell them in the market to other investors. Until the closing date of the offer, rights to the new shares are freely traded. Well, at what price will the company's shares trade after the rights issue has been computed and at what price will the rights trade prior to payment of the 75 pence subscription?

It should be easy to calculate the price after the rights issue:

$$
\begin{array}{llll}
1 & \text{million shares at £1 each} & = & £1\text{m,} \\
0.3 & \text{million shares at £0.75 each} & = & £0.225\text{m,} \\
\hline
1.3 & \text{million} & & £1.225\text{m}
\end{array}
$$

$$\text{Price} = £1.225/1.3 = 0.9423.$$

If shareholders are not to be worse off, the new shares must trade at 94.23 pence. Then, prior to the subscription (at 75 pence), the rights will trade at 19.23 pence (94.23 − 75). Thus, if shareholders do not wish to take up the offer of new shares, they may sell the privilege to other parties at this price.

The price of new shares offered via a rights issue is of some relevance to the institution underwriting the issue. The underwriter's commission is usually a percentage of the total value of the issue; and should the issue fail, the underwriters are compelled to take up the remainder of the issue. Thus underwriters generally prefer that the subscription price for the new shares be set sufficiently low relative to the market so that the issue will almost certainly not fail to be fully subscribed.

In the above example, we have assumed that the announcement of the rights issue will have no overall impact on the value of the company. However, such an announcement may change investors' expectations as to earnings and dividends. For example, if it is thought that the funds will be invested in profitable new projects, this might be thought of as good news, and the value will improve. In contrast, the rights issue may be the result of a deterioration in current cash flow and an inability to finance the business with internally generated funds. In this position, the value might decline. However, in recent research Marsh (1977) has found that, on average, the total value of a company's equity does *not* decline after the announcement of a rights issue. Indeed there is some evidence of a rise in price before and after such an announcement, suggesting that the new issues tend to reflect good rather than bad news.

Another method by which a company can raise capital is through a *placing*. This method permits the company to approach institutions or major shareholders and sell new equity or debt to them directly. The cost of raising new finance through this method is comparatively small compared with a rights issue, which involves a mailing to all shareholders and splitting the issue into numerous parcels of stock some of which may be very small. However, the Stock Exchange does not like to see new equity raised in this way because existing shareholders are deprived of the right to subscribe. Since the new shares will usually be placed at some discount on the prevailing market price, new shareholders may enjoy an advantage at the expense of existing shareholders.

The placing method is frequently used for raising debt finance, and the Stock Exchange sees no conflict of interest when this particular method of raising finance is used.

New issues for unquoted companies

Before private companies can obtain access to funds via the Stock Exchange, they must obtain a quotation. In order to obtain such a quotation, the company's directors must satisfy the Council of the Stock Exchange that the company is suitable for quotation. Suitability involves assurances on the way accounts are prepared, the notes relating to the profits and assets, and a profits record that demonstrates that the company is not a 'one day wonder'. The costs of 'going public' are substantial and they are difficult to justify below a company valuation of £2 millions (equivalent to profits of approximately £500 000 pre-tax per annum). In addition, it may take more than a year to fulfil the legal requirements before the flotation of the company's shares is finally made.

Other cheaper methods are available for obtaining a market in a company's shares. Certain brokers will make a market in a particular company's securities, or a company's shares can be traded on the Stock Exchange under Rule 163(2) without going through all the costs and formalities of a new issue. Some 800 companies have had their shares traded in this way during the past 5 years.

Although, in dealing under Rule 163(2), the quality of the transactions is controlled by Stock Exchange regulations, the quality of the securities traded is not. The Stock Exchange obliges the broker to obtain the best possible deal for his client. On the other hand, there is no formal relationship between the Exchange and an unlisted company. It is up to the broker to make sure that the company whose shares he decides to trade or promote give out sufficient and accurate information. *The Financial Times*, in an article in June 1978, set out the essential features of trading under this Rule:

(a) The broker, acting as an agent, will normally find both buyer and seller and negotiate the deal through a jobber. Alternatively, the broker may notify a jobber of his interest and the jobber may satisfy it himself or try to find a seller or buyer through another broker.

(b) Provided normal registration procedures are available, transactions can take place entirely independently of the company and without reference to it.

(c) A broker has to get permission to carry out each transaction from the Stock Exchange. This does not cause delay and no action is required on the part of the investor.

(d) All contract notes for transactions in unlisted shares carry the statement that they are not listed on any stock exchange. Nevertheless contracts are subject to the rules and regulations of the Stock Exchange.

(e) A stockbroker will charge normal commission, but no charges are levied on companies by the Stock Exchange.

IMPORTANCE OF THE STOCK MARKET

The stock market functions primarily as a secondary market. Although new issues and rights issues are floated, most stock exchange activity represents purchases and sales of previously issued shares. Table 17.6 illustrates the relative importance of various sources and uses of capital funds of industrial and commercial companies in the U.K. during the period 1970–74, while Table 17.7 indicates the amount and type of capital raised. The former table makes it clear that the major sources of capital have been undistributed income and bank borrowing, while the major uses of funds have been capital investment and also, in recent years, replacement of stocks at higher prices (stock appreciation) due to inflation.

Such figures have been used in support of the argument that the stock market has become increasingly irrelevant, and that management can pursue policies independently of shareholder interests. However, since

Table 17.6. Sources and uses of capital funds of industrial and commercial companies

	1970	1971	1972	1973	1973 – January	1974 September
Sources						
Undistributed income	3052	3429	4563	6634	4505	5016
Bank borrowing	1126	732	2988	4504	2696	3676
U.K. capital issues by listed companies	193	367	606	149	127	−10
Other sources	1601	1886	1474	2668	1807	1672
Total	5972	6414	9631	13 955	9129	10 348
Uses						
Fixed capital formation	3378	3468	3818	4859	3435	4226
Increase in value of stocks: physical increase	425	−77	−195	475	288	472
stock appreciation	907	852	1105	2516	1700	3887
Bank deposits	121	919	2039	2429	1635	−86
Other	1141	1252	2864	3676	2071	1849
Total	5972	6414	9631	13 955	9129	10 348

Source: *Midland Bank Review*, February 1975.

Table 17.7. Amount and type of new capital raised

	Debt			Equity		
Year	Convertible (£ million)	Other (£ million)	Total (£ million)	Preference (£ million)	Ordinary (£ million)	Total (£ million)
1967	29.7	313.8	343.5	5.7	72.6	421.9
1968	128.3	181.3	309.5	3.1	363.7	676.4
1969	231.7	165.7	397.4		195.0	592.4
1970	101.3	211.6	312.9	17.2	51.9	382.0
1971	96.7	273.4	370.1	12.8	310.4	693.3

Source: Midland Bank statistics.

1974, the increasing trend in rights issues, which has totalled nearly £1000 million per annum since the beginning of 1975, reflects a growing awareness of the stock market as a source funds when, for example, the borrowing capacity of the firm has been reached and a larger equity base is required.

However, if a company's share price falls because management pursues policies contrary to the interests of shareholders, new issues of equity become more difficult. Furthermore, if the share price is allowed to fall below par value, rights issues are not permitted at all. Thus, in a business downturn, when earnings evaporate and debt financing may be difficult to obtain, a management which has failed to maintain the stock market valuation of their company may find they have no source of loan capital available to them which has not become prohibitively expensive.

It is clear that for established companies the stock market represents a potential source of cash and a means of increasing the equity base for borrowing purposes. What is often not sufficiently appreciated is the role of the secondary market in providing a convenient means of valuing the firm. Bankers and other lenders are well aware of the stock market as an indicator of the expected future cash flows within the company. There is also some evidence that companies which are taken over tend to be amongst those whose prices have performed badly relative to other shares of similar risk. The acquirers, on the other hand, tend to be among those companies whose shares are performing relatively well prior to the acquisition. In law the shareholders own the firm; management which follows policies in disregard of shareholder interest may be inviting a takeover.

We may conclude that, although established companies do turn to the stock market for equity funds, the primary importance of the market lies in its functions as a secondary market. The stock market provides a rapid and cheap means of exchanging ownership in a company, allowing shareholders to exchange and to diversify their risks, and functions as an objective valuation mechanism which may serve as a guide both to management and to providers of funds. Without an objective valuation mechanism and the

284

means of easily diversifying risks, such funds would not only be difficult to raise but would be more costly to companies.

CONCLUSIONS

The capital market provides numerous ways in which companies can obtain long-term financing. Companies can borrow by means of term loans of up to 10 years from banks or they can sell bonds or convertible debentures on the market for a longer term. Debt instruments require the payment of interest and repayment of principal according to a pre-set schedule. Default can be very serious. Debt usually involves various covenants which limit the company's freedom of action in order to protect the debt holder.

Most of the remaining capital is called 'equity', consisting largely of earnings retained by management for reinvestment in the firm. The equity belongs to the equity shareholders whose individual claims on assets are proportional to the number of shares held. If retained earnings plus borrowing are not foreseen to be adequate, then more equity shares may be sold to the existing shareholders via a rights issue or to institutions via a placing.

The stock market provides the means of selling equity and debt securities. Most trading in the market represents exchange between investors of securities already issued. Although most of this activity does not provide funds directly to companies, this secondary market activity is quite essential. If investors were unable to obtain current quotations in an active market, they would be highly uncertain as to the value of ordinary capital as is usually the case now with unquoted companies. They would also find it exceedingly difficult to construct well-diversified portfolios or to change the composition of existing portfolios without the means of an active Stock Exchange. The resulting risks for shareholders would have a cost which would have to be borne by companies if investors were to be induced to invest in such adverse circumstances.

REFERENCES AND BIBLIOGRAPHY

Black, F. and Scholes, M., 'The Pricing of Options and Corporate Liabilities', *Journal of Political Economy*, **81**, 637–654, May–Jun. 1973.
Brealey, R. and Schaefer, S. M., 'Term Structure and Uncertain Inflation', *Journal of Finance*, **32**, 277–290, May 1977.
Briston, R. J., *The Stock Exchange and Investment Analysis*, 2nd ed., Unwin University Books, London, 1973.
Carlton, W. T. and Cooper, I. A., 'Estimation and Uses of the Term Structure of Interest Rates', *Journal of Finance*, **31**, 1067–1083, Sep. 1976.
Dimson, E., 'A Description of the U.K. New Issue Market', Revised Note, London Business School, May 1977.
Dimson, E., 'Instant Option Valuation', *Financial Analysts Journal*, **33**, 62–69, May–Jun. 1977.

Dimson, E., 'Option Valuation Nomograms', *Financial Analysts Journal*, **33**, 71–75, Nov.–Dec. 1977).

Fisher, L., 'Determinants of Risk Premium on Corporate Bonds', *The Journal of Political Economy*, **LXVII** (3), June 1959.

Hodges, S. D. and Schaefer, S. M. 'A Model for Bond Portfolio Improvement', *Journal of Financial and Quantitative Analysis*, **12**, 243–260, June. 1977.

Marsh, P. R., 'An Analysis of Equity Rights Issues on the London Stock Exchange', Unpublished doctoral dissertation, London Business School, 1977.

Merrett, A. J., Howe, M., and Newbould, G. A., *Equity Issues on the London Stock Exchange*, Longmans, London, 1967.

Schaefer, S. M., 'The Problem with Redemption Yields', *Financial Analysts Journal*, **33**, 59–67, Jul.–Aug. 1977.

Sharpe, W., *Investments*, Prentice-Hall, Englewood Cliffs, N.J., 1977.

APPENDIX 17.1. BLACK AND SCHOLES' OPTION VALUATION MODEL

Black and Scholes (1973) have developed an options valuation formula that is widely used by professionals on the Chicago Board Options Exchange. The following description of the model is taken from Sharpe's book *Investments* (Sharpe, 1977).

Black and Scholes' important assumptions include the following:

no taxes,
no transaction costs,
no dividends prior to expiration of the option,
the underlying stock's continuously compounded return is assumed to
follow a normal distribution with a constant variance.

The current value of an option is given by

$$P_0 = P_s N(d_1) - \frac{E}{e^{rt}} N(d_2),$$

where

$$d_1 = \frac{\ln(P_s/E) + (r + \frac{1}{2}\sigma^2)t}{\sigma\sqrt{t}},$$

$$d_2 = \frac{\ln(P_s/E) + (r - \frac{1}{2}\sigma^2)t}{\sigma\sqrt{t}},$$

and where P_0 = the current value of the option, P_s = the current price of the stock, E = the exercise price of the option, e = 2.718 28, t = the time remaining before expiration (in years), r = the continuously compounded riskless rate of return, σ = the standard deviation of the continuously compounded annual rate of return on the stock, $\ln(P_s/E)$ = the natural logarithm of (P_s/E), $N(d)$ = the probability that a deviation less than d will occur in a normal distribution with a mean of zero and a standard deviation equal to one.

The formula can be modified for a dividend paying stock.

Example

Boots
Today's share price   225 p,
Exercise price   226 p,
Price of broker's 3-month call option   17 p,

$\sigma = 0.4, \quad r = 0.05 \quad t = 0.25, \quad e = 2.718\ 28.$

Using Black and Scholes' formula,

$$d_1 = \frac{\ln(225/226) + (0.05 + \frac{1}{2}(0.35)^2)0.25}{0.35\sqrt{0.25}}$$

$$= 0.13359,$$

$$d_2 = \frac{\ln(225/226) + (0.05 - \frac{1}{2}(0.35)^2)0.25}{0.35\sqrt{0.25}}$$

$$= -0.04141.$$

Corresponding values for $N(d)$ are

d	$N(d)$
0.13359	0.5531
−0.04141	0.4834

Thus the theoretical price of the option is

$$P_o = P_s N(d_1) - \frac{E}{e^{rt}} N(d_2)$$

$$= 225 \times 0.553 - \frac{226}{e^{0.05 \times 0.25}} \times 0.483$$

$$= 16.6 \text{ pence.}$$

Thus, we can now compare the Black and Scholes' price of 16.6 pence with the price of 17 pence quoted by the broker. Apparent discrepancies should narrow when these options begin trading on the new Options Exchange. However, such differences can also arise when the market's perception of the future riskiness of the underlying share differs from the standard deviation used in the formula (usually obtained from historical data).

REVIEW QUESTIONS

1. Why does a convertible debenture provide a lower interest yield compared with an ordinary debenture of the same company?

2. 'The theory of option pricing may have relevance to many areas of financial analysis'. Give an outline of this theory and examine areas of finance to which you consider option theory is applicable.

3. Why should a company be worth more quoted than unquoted?

4. Why do corporate bonds have a higher yield than Government bonds? What accounts for the differences in yields among corporate bonds.

EXERCISES

1. What is the net present value of a bond traded in a competitive market?

2. A 5-year bond with a nominal value of £100 is issued at £95. The bond carries a coupon of 5 per cent and is redeemable at par.

   (a) Compute the running yield on the bond.
   (b) Compute the yield to redemption. Ignore taxes.
   (c) If the bond is a gilt-edged security, under what circumstances is the capital gain tax free?

3. The ordinary shares of Beecham's are currently standing at 635 pence. A 3-month call option in the security costs 38 pence and the exercise price is 640 pence. The 3-month Treasury Bill rate is 12 per cent and the standard deviation of Beecham's ordinary shares over the past 4 years is 50 per cent.

   (a) What is the value of the option using Black and Scholes' option valuation model?
   (b) What possible reasons could justify any differences between the true price of the option and the price that has been estimated?

   You will require tables for the cumulative normal probability distribution.

18

COST OF DEBT AND CAPITAL STRUCTURE

In the previous chapters we considered projects and companies without paying any attention to their financing—as if they were entirely equity financed. We are now going to examine the differences that debt financing makes. In the first part of this chapter, we consider the risks and benefits relating to the use of debt finance in the firm and estimate the benefits arising from the tax deductibility of interest payments under both the U.S. and U.K. Corporation Tax systems. Finally, we show the relationship between debt financing and the returns expected by shareholders.

The subject is important for a number of reasons. If there is an advantage to company borrowing, management can increase the value of the firm by issuing debt. Similarly, the advantage of borrowing will increase the present value of a project if the project increases the borrowing capacity of the firm. Thus, in order to estimate a project's net present value one must incorporate the advantages of debt financing. Finally, if debt is in some way cheaper than equity, borrowing (or the lack of it) may affect the firm's price competitiveness in the market place.

THE RISK OF DEBT FINANCE—PRE-TAX

We wish to illustrate the way in which debt financing increases the variability of earnings, thus making equity shareholdings more risky. This point is important since, if shareholders are risk averse, they will require a higher rate of return on their equity in compensation for the increased risk of debt financing. Thus the total cost of debt includes not only the explicit cost of interest payments, but also an *implicit* cost of debt reflected in a change in the cost of equity. Let us examine the following example.

A company with assets totalling £100 is wholly equity financed and is expected to produce annual Net Operating Income (NOI) of £10 in perpetuity. There are 100 shares outstanding with a market value of £100: the earnings per share (EPS) are £0.10. If the firm were to be half-financed by debt carrying interest at 5 per cent the firm would then have only 50 shares of equity valued at £50 and debt worth £50. The Net Operating Income would be the same at £10, but what would be the implications of the debt for earnings per share?

Table 18.1. The effect of changes in NOI on EPS under different financing mixes

Net Operating Income (£)	Interest charges (£)	Net Income (£)	EPS with debt financing (£)	EPS With all equity financing (£)
0	2.5	− 2.5	−0.05	0
5	2.5	2.5	0.05	0.05
10	2.5	7.5	0.15	0.10
15	2.5	12.5	0.25	0.15

The first result of substituting debt for equity would be that Net Income would drop from £10 to £7.50 as a result of the £2.50 interest payment; EPS would, however, rise to £0.15 because of the smaller number of shares. There are additional effects if the Net Operating Income changes. Table 18.1 summarizes the results of changes in NOI for the EPS of the firm with and without the 50 per cent debt in the capital structure.

The figures in Table 18.1 should suggest to the reader that debt financing adds to the risk of the firm since debt financing increases the amplitude or volatility of EPS changes. The range for EPS with debt financing is 30 pence (–0.05 to 0.25) compared with 15 pence (0 to 0.15) under all equity financing. Interest payments are like any other fixed cost, unresponsive to changes in revenue. The relationship between NOI and EPS under different financing methods is illustrated in Figure 18.1.

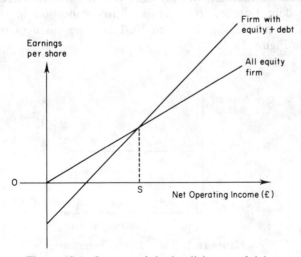

Figure 18.1. Sources of the implicit cost of debt

Not only does debt make EPS more volatile, but there is a level of NOI below which EPS are actually lower than they would have been without debt. This lower level of EPS reflects the effect of interest payments on Net Income. In Table 18.1, the critical level of Net Operating Income is seen to be £5. At this level of NOI, the earnings per share are the same with or without debt financing. Below this level of NOI, the EPS are lower with 50 per cent debt in the capital structure. This critical level of NOI is also observed in Figure 18.1, where the two lines in the figure intersect. Thus debt is a sword that can cut two ways, reducing earnings per share if Net Operating Income falls below the critical level while increasing the volatility of earnings.

In compensation for the increased risk caused by debt financing, shareholders will require some additional return per unit (£) of equity. Thus the cost of debt is not simply the interest rate but also includes the consequent increase in shareholders' required rate of return on equity. This additional cost derives from the increased volatility of earnings, and is the hidden or implicit cost of debt finance. The question arises as to the size of the risk premium required by shareholders to compensate them for the risk due to debt. Two extreme positions have been taken in response to this question, the Net Operating Income approach and the Net Income approach. We shall examine the implications of these two approaches initially on a before-tax basis.

NET OPERATING INCOME APPROACH

The Net Operating Income approach simply states that the hidden or implicit cost of debt is always sufficient to ensure that there is no net advantage of debt financing on a pre-tax basis. Thus the firm does not gain or lose by debt finance, irrespective of its proportion in the capital structure. This relationship between NOI and the value of the firm is illustrated in Figure 18.2.

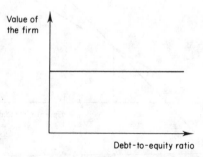

Figure 18.2. The Net Operating Income

The value of the firm may always be found by capitalizing the company's NOI. Thus, treating the Net Operating Income, X, as a perpetual stream (i.e. assuming no growth prospects and that NOI is equal to Free Cash Flow),

$$V = X/R,$$

where
V is the value of the firm, X is the Net Operating Income, and R is the required rate of return on the company's equity (assuming all equity financing). The value of a perpetual stream of cash flows is found by dividing the annual cash flow by the required rate of return.

The value of the firm in our example is simply £100:

$$V = 10/0.1 = 100.$$

If the Net Operating Income approach is correct, the substitution of £50 of debt to the capital structure will not change the total value of the firm if there are no taxes. The market value of the debt plus the market value of the resulting equity will still total £100. This approach implies that the remaining value for the equity will be £50.

A value of £100 for the firm implies a change of discount rate for the equity portion of the cash flow stream. The total value of £100 was obtained by discounting the Net Operating Income (without debt) at 10 per cent. However, we have now split this income into two parts: interest payments and the earnings accruing to shareholders. The interest payments are discounted at the rate of interest of 5 per cent payable on the debt to obtain a Present Value of £50. Unless we increase the discount rate for the earnings accruing to the shareholders, the total Present Value of the two parts will be greater than the £100 value for the whole.

Continuing with our example, we see that the earnings available to shareholders are the Net Operating Income (NOI) minus interest (iD). This difference is to be discounted at some higher rate R^*:

$$S = \frac{NOI - iD}{R^*}.$$

Since, under the Net Operating Income approach, we already know that the equity S is worth £50, we can solve for R^*:

$$50 = \frac{10 - 0.05 \times 50}{R^*},$$

$$R^* = 0.15.$$

Consequently, we can see that introducing debt (which has the lower discount rate) increases the discount rate on the equity, and this increase is the hidden or 'implicit cost' of debt; in this example, an additional 5 per cent. This change in the cost of equity must take place if the market value of the firm is to remain unaltered with changes in capital structure.

Since debt holders have a prior claim on income and assets before shareholders, debt holders have less risk and require a lower rate of return. As debt is increased in the capital structure and pre-empts more of the cash flow (without taking a proportionate share of the risk), the shareholders retain virtually all of the risk while giving up cash flow to holders of debt securities. The risk per unit of equity becomes greater as a result. Naturally, the shareholders will require a higher rate of return or discount rate for the relative increase in risk.

The Net Operating Income approach holds that when putting a value on equity, the market (in a world without taxes) will increase the discount rate just sufficiently to keep the market value of the firm (value of debt plus equity) constant with increasing debt. There can be, therefore, no net advantage to using debt in the capital structure.

This result should not be too surprising to those who believe that the capital markets are reasonably competitive. If two products are selling at different prices in a competitive market, the market must perceive differences in quality or usefulness. The principal distinction between equity and debt is risk. If lenders charge less for debt than for equity, then debt is less risky for them. The risk does not disappear: it is left with the equity shareholders. Thus, if lending is less risky for lenders, it must be more risky for borrowers in relation to their equity stake. This risk has a price in the capital market and borrowers (or their equity shareholders) bear the additional cost. The risk per pound of equity investment is increased as a consequence of the introduction of debt into the capital structure. The reader should always distrust any analyst who purports to show that one product is cheaper than another even though everyone in the market is aware of the relative advantages of each.

THE NET INCOME APPROACH

The Net Income approach, on the other hand, simply assumes that the only cost to debt finance is the interest rate and that there are no hidden or implicit costs. Thus the value of the firm is expected to increase with changes in the debt-to-equity ratio under this alternative approach. The relationship is illustrated in Figure 18.3.

The value of the firm is still the total of the market value of the debt and the market value of the equity. However, the discount rate of 10 per cent for the earnings accruing to shareholders does not change with increases in Debt under this approach. Since that portion of the Net Operating Income which is paid out as interest is discounted at the lower interest rate, 5 per cent, and the remaining portion is discounted at the unchanged rate of 10 per cent, the result is a higher total market value of the firm. Thus, the Net

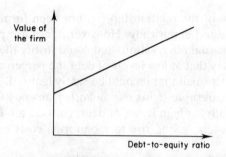

Figure 18.3. The Net Income
approach

Income approach, in contrast to the Net Operating Income approach, implies that Shareholders do not require a higher return or discount rate when the risk of the earnings stream is increased by debt. As a result debt is always cheaper than equity under this approach.

TRADITIONAL APPROACH

The Net Income approach appears to many academics and practitioners to be inconsistent with the evidence of a relationship between risk and required rates of return in the capital markets. As a result, an intermediate position was developed, often called 'the traditional view'. This approach suggests that at very low levels of the debt-to-equity ratio, the only cost of debt is the interest cost—i.e. the Net Income approach holds. However, with significant amounts of debt, equity holders start to perceive the risks and require an added premium. At some point, and the point is not disclosed, the premium required by shareholders equals the incremental advantage or benefits of debt finance, and beyond that point there is a net disadvantage to debt financing. This relationship is illustrated in Figure 18.4.

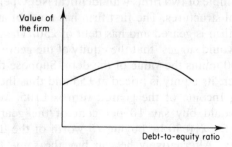

Figure 18.4. The traditional view

294

The exact form of the relationship has not been formulated rigorously nor has it been tested empirically. However, there are plenty of reasons, substantiated by casual observation, that could justify the traditional view. First, one might say that at low levels of debt the perceived increase in risk for a company is so small that it could be safely ignored. Second, that with increasing debt, bankruptcy costs rise and offset any possible advantages to debt finance. Finally, at high levels of debt, bankers are forced to monitor the firm more closely, giving rise to monitoring costs reflected in higher interest rates.

Let us examine the first point briefly. The proposition suggests that at low levels of debt, analysts will not perceive the greater risk of the firm. Indeed, the risk of bankruptcy may not even be altered at all by small amounts of debt finance. However, even if the risk of bankruptcy is unaltered, the variability of earnings will most certainly be increased as a result of the addition to fixed costs. If you look at the bond markets, you will notice how companies' bonds are carefully graded according to risk. Differences in risk are reflected in interest rates. The question arises whether financial analysts are so inconsistent or sleepy as to ignore changes in the variability of earnings and to provide a free gift to shareholders at the expense of debt holders.

The other points relating to bankruptcy costs and transaction costs will be discussed in another section in the chapter.

MODIGLIANI AND MILLER

In 1958, Modigliani and Miller (M–M) wrote an important article which provided an ingenious and rigorous basis for the Net Operating Income approach. They suggested that, aside from the question of tax, the debt-to-equity mix did not change the value of the firm. They reasoned that in a competitive capital market the shareholder would 'arbitrage' until the Net Operating Incomes of all firms in the same risk class would fetch the same price in the market, regardless of financing arrangements made by individual firms.

Consider the example of two firms with identical Net Operating Incomes but different capital structures. The first firm has no debt and is priced at £100. The second firm is geared and has debt of £50. The Net Operating Income approach would suggest that the equity of the geared firm must be worth £50, i.e. £100 minus the value of the debt. Suppose that the geared firm is priced higher: its equity is priced at £55 and thus the total value of the Net Operating Income of the geared firm is £105. What would an investor do? He could buy say 10 per cent of the geared firm's Net Operating Income for £10.50 by buying £5 worth of the debt and £5.50 worth of the equity. Alternatively he can buy the same Net Operating

Income for less by holding only £10 worth of the ungeared firm's equity. Clearly he will prefer to buy the ungeared firm's equity as long as the total value of the geared firm remains above the value of the ungeared firm. In general investors will arbitrage by buying 'cheap' and selling 'dear' until identical Net Operating Incomes are priced identically in the market regardless of the gearing of individual firms. A proof using this arbitrage argument is supplied in Appendix 18.1.

Another way of looking at this valuation problem is from the point of view of the investor who can engage in 'homemade gearing', that is an investor who can borrow and buy shares either on his own or through a financial intermediary. M–M argued that if the market were to value a company's income stream at a higher rate merely because of the company's gearing, investors would sell the shares of the geared firm, gear up themselves by borrowing and buy the shares of a cheaper ungeared firm with the same Net Operating Income. Investors, M–M argued, will not pay a premium for debt financing by the company unless such a financing mix confers an advantage that cannot be obtained by the investor himself or by his financial intermediary.

A simple if rather eccentric example, is the story of the Rolls Royce and the banana. A Rolls Royce was being sold with a banana inside on the front seat—the price was £10 000. An intelligent purchaser wondered if he could buy the car and a banana separately for less than £10 000. Finding the price of the car and banana to total £9000, he decided to arbitrage, by buying cars and putting bananas inside them for resale until prices fell and he ceased to make profits. The lesson is that the value of an asset or company is determined by the operating cash flows. By simply packaging those cash flows in a different way, i.e. by redistributing risk between equity and debt holders, you cannot improve the operating cash flows or the value of the asset.

Similarly, we argued in a previous chapter that management could not increase the value of the firm simply by the device of diversification. Although diversification does reduce shareholder's risk, that benefit can be obtained by shareholders holding a diversified portfolio of securities, thus rendering corporate diversification valueless to shareholders. Similarly, if any advantage of debt finance can be obtained by the shareholder or his agent, then the firm could not increase its share price or market value by mere borrowing. It is only when taxes enter the picture that we find rational grounds for a net advantage to corporate borrowing.

Modigliani and Miller (1958) made a number of important assumptions, including the following:

(a) the shareholder can borrow on the same terms as companies,
(b) there are no taxes,
(c) there is no bankruptcy risk (or bankruptcy costs),

(d) the capital market is highly competitive,
(e) short selling is permitted.

Many academics and practitioners have strongly objected to these assumptions. For example, they claim that individuals cannot borrow on the same terms as companies and such individuals often do not have the security of limited liability. However, a convincing counter-argument is that investors who are unable or unwilling to indulge in home-made leverage can invest through financial intermediaries, such as Investment Trusts, which can obtain debt finance on the same terms as operating companies. It is also important to realize that individuals frequently pay higher interest rates than those paid by companies because they usually represent higher risk. If individuals were charged high rates that did not reflect the costs and risks of lending, then competition would gradually reduce or eradicate the differences.

THE EFFECT OF TAXES

The introduction of taxes and the tax deductibility of interest payments changes the attitudes of proponents of all three views towards debt financing. For brevity, we shall examine the implications of taxes on the NOI Approach and the Modigliani–Miller proposition only.

Modigliani and Miller proved that, under their assumptions, the value of the firm was invariant with changes in capital structure on a pre-tax basis. In an article in 1963, they agreed that if interest on debt were deductible for tax purposes and if the tax deduction could not be obtained by shareholders, then an advantage is conferred on debt financing by the firm (Modigliani and Miller, 1963). For example, if the firm borrows £100 and pays interest at the rate of 10 per cent, the interest charges of £10 per annum are tax deductible. Thus, even if the cost of debt is equal to the cost of equity pre-tax, debt is cheaper post-tax by 5 per cent assuming the corporate tax rate is 50 per cent. How does this advantage affect the value of the company? Let us assume that a company expects annual earnings X in perpetuity (where X is after tax but before interest) and pays interest on riskless debt at a rate i and that the debt is perpetual. The effective corporate tax rate is let us say T^* and the amount of debt borrowed is D. The value of the company is simply

$$V = X/R + T^*D.$$

The right-hand side of this equation represents the present value of the annual net operating income plus the present value of the annual tax benefit attributable to debt. We can compute the tax advantage to debt by simply multiplying the value of the debt by the effective corporate tax rate advantage T^*.

The formula can only be expressed in these terms if the life of the company and of the debt are infinite. If a company's assets in the U.S. were valued at $1 million and it was decided to substitute debt for half the equity, what would be the increase in the value of the firm? The increase in value would be $250 000 with a Corporate Tax rate of 50 per cent. Thus, the worth of the firm, assuming the cash flows and debt are a perpetuity, could change from $1 million to $1.25 million with debt financing. If the life of the company and of the debt were finite, the tax benefit would have to be computed each year and discounted to the present. The reader may wish to review (in Appendix 18.2) the derivation of the term T^*D. In the U.S., T^* is shown to equal the Corporation Tax rate. However, under the U.K. imputation tax system, T^* is more complex. One implication (in either country) is that the advantage to debt improves with increases in the debt-to-equity ratio. As a consequence, management would be encouraged to increase debt to 99.9 per cent of the firm's capital structure! Although management would not care to take this course of action because of the risk and consequent costs of bankruptcy, the fact is that most banks would also not permit such high levels of gearing.

It is too simple to put such limitations on debt capacity down to financial conservatism. Part of the answer may be based on the costs of monitoring and controlling loans. As a company's debt-to-equity ratio increases, so does the financial risk and moral hazard. The lender is forced to monitor the progress of the borrower requiring more information and more-sophisticated lending officers to do the analysis. The consequent

Table 18.2. U.K. tax system: net tax advantage to corporate borrowing

	Corporate borrowing	Personal borrowing
Net Operating Income	100	100
Interest charges	−20	–
Earnings before tax	80	100
Corporation Tax at 52 per cent	−41.6	−52
Dividends	38.4	48
Interest charges to shareholders	–	−20
Tax saving on interest at 34 per cent		+6.8
	38.4	34.8

Net advantage = 38.4 − 34.8 = 3.6.*

---

*This advantage could have been computed more directly from the formula in the text: $(0.52 - 0.34) \times 20 = 3.6$

costs and legal problems may force banks to limit the company's borrowing to manageable levels. The effect of such costs is to produce the downward sloping curve attributed to the traditionalists in Figure 18.4.

Let us now compute the tax advantage of debt under the U.K. Corporation Tax system. In the example in Table 18.2, we compare the tax paid by the U.K. shareholder when he borrows and alternatively when the company borrows. The U.K. now operates an imputation system in which the firm acts in part as an agent for the revenue authorities in collecting shareholders' taxes. The effect of the system is partially to eliminate the double taxation of earnings and dividends. The Corporation Tax rate T is deemed to include a shareholders' tax at the standard rate 0.34. Thus, since T is greater than 0.34, it pays the firm rather than the shareholder to deduct interest. The reader can verify from Example 2 that the undiscounted rate T' of tax saving on corporate interest payments in the U.K. is given by

$$T' = T - \tau$$
$$= 0.52 - 0.34$$
$$= 0.18.$$

If interest payments I are £20, the net saving of taxes for one period in the U.K. example is

$$T'I = 0.18 \times £20$$
$$= £3.60.$$

This is the magnitude of the advantage in a single period from corporate borrowing for shareholders whose tax bracket we may assume to be approximated by the standard rate. When such advantages are discounted at the after (shareholders') tax interest rate, we find that the Present Value of this advantage increases to $T^* = 27$ per cent for a project with constant and perpetual cash flows. We derive this result in Appendix 18.2.

Assuming a project with constant and perpetual cash flows and a debt capacity of 25 per cent, the tax advantage to borrowing would increase the present value of the project by 6.75 per cent (0.25×27 per cent) compared with all-equity financing. The effect of debt financing on projects will be examined in greater detail in the subsequent chapter.

It may be argued that in the U.K. many individuals are unable to deduct interest on borrowings for tax purposes. If this is so, it may be desirable for them to buy the securities of firms who have substantial borrowings or to invest their funds in financial institutions which can borrow on their behalf. The creation of financial intermediaries such as Investment Trusts which can borrow and purchase shares, may also play an important role in capturing this tax advantage for shareholders. In addition, such institutions also provide means of reducing taxes for individuals who would otherwise pay above the standard rate.

Thus the tax advantage to corporate borrowing in the Modigliani–Miller formula is different for the U.K. compared with the U.S. The difference is due to the fact that all personal taxes are paid on dividends in the U.S. *in addition* to corporate taxes. This means that tax benefits from debt that derive from corporate taxes cannot be replicated by the shareholder through home-made borrowing. In contrast, in the U.K., part of the Corporate Tax rate represents a payment of personal taxes by the company on behalf of the shareholder. The tax advantage from debt that derives from the personal tax rate can be replicated in part by the shareholder through home-made borrowing. Only that part of the tax benefit which cannot be replicated represents the net advantage to a company's shareholders when the company borrows.

INTEREST RATES, TAXES, AND ASSET PRICES

If the tax advantages to borrowing which we have illustrated exist, then the demand for debt will reflect these advantages and influence interest rates. Miller (1976) has recently argued that previous analyses, which did not consider the effect of taxes on market equilibrium, may have exaggerated the tax benefits of borrowing. If there are tax benefits to borrowing, and, as a consequence, debt is cheaper than equity, how would the financial manager react? He should continue borrowing rather than using equity to finance new investment. Increased borrowing would raise the level of interest rates and offset the tax advantage to debt. This process would continue until the cost of borrowing at the margin is equal to the cost of equity. Thus at the margin there can be no net advantage to corporate borrowing.

Let us review the current situation (i.e. as in 1978) in the United Kingdom to illustrate Miller's point. Interest charges are tax deductible for companies and for some individuals who have outstanding loans or mortgages. If the Government withdrew the tax subsidy on interest payments, what would be the result? Most people instinctively would say that interest rates must fall, otherwise debt would become far less attractive as a result. If interest rates did not fall immediately, individuals and companies would unwind their borrowings until lenders were compelled to lower their interest rates. Thus Miller's proposition suggests that at least part *if not all* of the subsidy on debt is lost in higher interest rates to borrowers. Those lenders who do not pay taxes gain the most since the higher interest rates provide abnormal returns to them as a result of their special tax status.

Miller (1976) argues that the actual behaviour of corporate debt-to-equity ratios supports his view. Since the 1920's, tax rates have increased dramatically, yet the debt to equity ratio of the average company has moved from 20 per cent to only around 25 per cent. Miller's arguments are based on simple economic propositions. If debt is cheaper than equity, people will borrow more until borrowing rates rise to equate the cost. It does seem that the tax advantages to debt can easily be overstated.

Even if we suppose that there is some tax benefit to corporate borrowing, this benefit still may not increase the value of the firm to the degree indicated in the previous analysis. Let us suppose that product markets are competitive and suppliers are earning no more than the required rate of return for business risk. What will happen when the Government introduces a new tax subsidy for those firms? The resulting initial increase in profitability would largely disappear as competition forces prices down to a level where suppliers earn just sufficient to justify the capital employed. The tax benefits would eventually end up in the hands of consumers rather than shareholders, and thus the value of the firm would return to the pre-subsidy value.

Nevertheless, firms *should* borrow under these conditions. Those firms which did not borrow would find themselves at a competitive disadvantage. Firms which do not borrow sufficiently in relation to competitors will not obtain their full market value if there is some tax advantage to debt. However, the average value of the firm and its competitors would not be enhanced by the tax subsidy under competitive conditions.

The truth probably lies somewhere in between. Interest rates may not adjust sufficiently to completely eliminate the after-tax advantage of debt financing in comparison to equity. The remaining advantage of debt financing to the value of the firm would also not be completely eliminated in imperfectly competitive product markets. However, the remaining advantage could be much smaller than indicated in Table 18.2. A conservative financial analyst might wish to ignore the supposed benefits from debt financing.

BORROWING WITHOUT TAX BENEFITS

The reader of business history may be puzzled by the fact that individuals and companies borrowed prior to the introduction of tax deductibility of interest charges. Putting it another way, would companies still borrow if the Government withdrew the tax advantages to both corporate and personal borrowing? The answer is clearly, 'Yes'. There are three reasons for borrowing in a world without tax benefits. The first and most obvious is one relating to transaction costs. It is frequently cheaper to raise debt finance from a bank than to make a rights issue through the financial markets. Such transaction costs are especially high when the proposed investment is of a short duration. For example, British Petroleum financed a large part of the Forties Field investment with debt finance partly because the capital cost was expected to be repaid within 2 years from the production and sale of the oil. It would have been expensive for B.P. to raise a rights issue and then return the capital to shareholders after 2 or 3 years. The taxes and transaction costs of raising money and subsequently returning it to shareholders would have been unnecessarily high.

A second reason relates primarily to small businesses where the owner has limited capital and wishes to expand. Bank finance may be the only source of finance that is available, enabling the owner to expand without losing control. Finally, the owner or manager may wish to increase the expected returns of the business by using fixed interest capital. If you like, the owner/manager is able to redistribute risk by altering the business' capital structure. The owner/manager may prefer such an alternative when his expectations of returns are different from those of other investors. For example, if he is more optimistic about expected returns compared with outside shareholders, then debt financing may be preferred to selling new equity cheaply. In a world without taxes, some would wish to lend and others would wish to borrow to satisfy different risk preferences and differences in forecasts of future events.

GEARING AND THE COMPANY'S REQUIRED RATE OF RETURN

Some explanation has already been given as to why shareholders would demand a greater rate of return on the equity with an increasing proportion of gearing in the capital structure. The greater volatility of earnings implies that a company's β value increases with higher levels of debt in the capital structure. The implications of the resulting increase in β are illustrated in Figure 18.5. The vertical axis represents the returns for the security subtracting out the risk-free rate of interest, while the horizontal axis represents the corresponding risk premium on the market index. Let us assume that the security j was initially ungeared and that its β value is equal to one. Now if we incorporate debt into the capital structure, the risk or volatility of the earnings will increase; and, consequently, the value of β will rise. For the purpose of obtaining a discount rate for an investment project, it may be necessary to obtain a β value for the company that does

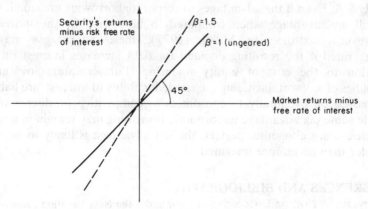

Figure 18.5. Debt and the company's β value

302

not reflect the debt financing element. Therefore, we require a formula relating the value of the β value to the level of debt in the capital structure. If a company is totally ungeared then the beta coefficient obtained by comparing past returns of the market will be the appropriate ungeared β. However, if the company is geared at all, the β value obtained from analysing past share price movements must be adjusted. For this purpose, we can use Rubinstein's equation, given in Chapter 7 (Rubinstein, 1973).

INFLATION AND BORROWING

There is a widespread belief that borrowing is profitable when prices are rising because one is repaying the loan in 'cheaper' pounds. One should understand that, if interest rates reflect expectations about the rate of inflation, then borrowing does not confer an automatic gain or loss on the borrower. If the borrowing is at fixed interest rates and inflation exceeds the rate expected when the loan was taken out, the borrower will gain (because interest rates rise above the loan rate). However, if inflation falls below expectations, the borrower will lose. The mere act of borrowing would not confer an immediate financial advantage. If this proposition were true, everybody would borrow until the prospective advantage disappeared.

CONCLUSION

There appears to be tax advantages to corporate borrowing. Whereas companies can deduct interest payments from their taxable profits, they cannot do so for dividend payments. This apparent net advantage to corporate borrowing is reduced somewhat to the extent that investors can find ways of obtaining such benefits for themselves through 'home-made gearing'. The precise effects of home-made gearing depend on the tax system, and we have noted differences in this regard between the U.K. and the U.S.A. Even if the advantages to corporate borrowing are small, there is still an advantage when compared to borrowing by the individual. However, according to Miller (1977), these advantages may be exaggerated if the resulting demand for debt increases interest rates in relation to the cost of equity financing. Furthermore, Government subsidies of any sort, including the tax deductibility of interest, are liable to be passed on eventually to consumers in competitive product markets. While some tax advantage to corporate borrowing may remain in markets which are not altogether perfect, the net advantage is likely to be much smaller than heretofore imagined.

REFERENCES AND BIBLIOGRAPHY
Brealey, R., 'A Note on Dividends and Debt under the New Taxation', *Journal of Business Finance*, **5**, 66–68, 1973.

Hamada, R. S., 'The Effect of the Firm's Capital Structure on the Systematic Risk of Common Stocks', *Journal of Finance*, **27**, 435–452, May 1972.

Levy, H. and Sarnat, M., *Investment Portfolio Analysis,* John Wiley and Sons, Chichester, 1972.

Miller, M. H., 'Debt and Taxes', Presidential Address at the Annual Meeting of the American Finance Association, *Journal of Finance* **32**, 261–275, May 1977.

Modigliani, F. and Miller, M. H., 'The Cost of Capital, Corporation Finance and the Theory of Investment', *American Economic Review*, **48**, 261–277, Jun. 1958.

Modigliani, F. and Miller, M. H., 'Corporate Income Taxes and the Cost of Capital: A Correction', *American Economic Review*, **53**, 433–443 Jun. 1963.

Modigliani, F. and Miller, M. H., 'Reply to Heins and Sprenkle' *American Economic Review*, **54**, 592–595, Sep. 1969.

Rubinstein, M., 'Mean Variance Synthesis of Corporate Financial Theory', *Journal of Finance*, **28**, 167–181, Mar. 1973.

Stapleton, R. C., 'Taxes, The Cost of Capital and the Theory of Investment', *The Economic Journal*, **82**, 1273–1292, Dec. 1972.

APPENDIX 18.1

Prove that Debt does not change the value of the firm in the absence of tax.

Modigliani and Miller's arbitrage proof was contained in a reply to Heins and Sprenkle (Modigliani and Miller, 1969):

S = value of equity,
D = value of debt,
$V_u \equiv S_u$ value of the unlevered firm,
$V_L \equiv S_L + D_L$ value of the levered firm,
X = stream of operating earnings generated by each firm,
α = fraction of the shares held in the firm,
i = interest rate.

Let us assume that the individual holds a fraction α of the shares in the unlevered firm. He obtains a return αX for a total investment of αS_u. Thus,

$$\alpha S_u \equiv \alpha V_u.$$

However, an identical return of αX can also be obtained for a total investment of αV_L by the following means:

	Investment required	Returns produced
1. Buy a fraction α of shares in unlevered firm	$\alpha S_u \equiv \alpha V_u$	αX
or		
1. Buy a fraction α of shares in levered firm	$\alpha S_L = \alpha(V_L - D_L)$	$\alpha(X - iD_L)$
and		
2. Buy a fraction α of bonds in the levered "firm"	αD_L	$\alpha i D_L$
	αV_L	αX

Thus, if $V_L > V_u$, the investor would not wish to hold shares in the levered firm since he would be obtaining exactly the same return αX by investing αV_u in the unlevered firm, which is a smaller investment by the amount of $\alpha(V_L - V_u)$.

Similar arbitrage arguments hold true for $V_u > V_L$.

APPENDIX 18.2

We show that the Present Value of net tax savings from corporate borrowing is equal to T^*D, where T^* is the Present Value of the net tax rate advantage to corporate borrowing expressed as a rate of tax, $T^* = T'/(1 - \tau)$ for the U.K.;

T' is the rate of tax saving (by the company) on interest net of investors' taxes at the standard rate τ, $T' = T - \tau$;

T is the Corporation Tax rate; D is the value of debt in the capital structure; and i is the interest rate of interest paid.

Proof:

$$T^*D = \sum_{t}^{\infty} \frac{T'iD}{\{1 + i(1 - \tau)\}^t}$$

$$= T'iD \sum_{t=1}^{\infty} \frac{1}{\{1 + i(1 - \tau)\}^t}$$

$$= T'iD \left\{ \frac{1}{i(1 - \tau)} \right\}$$

$$= T^*D,$$

where

$$T^* = \frac{T'}{(1 - \tau)}.$$

The result assumes that the taxes paid on income from shares is *exactly* equal to the taxes paid on income from bonds. If the latter is greater than the former, the advantage to corporate leverage decreases.

Example: for the U.K., if $T = 0.52$ and $\tau = 0.34$ we have,

$$T^* = T'/(1 - \tau)$$
$$= (0.52 - 0.34)/(1 - 0.34)$$
$$T^* = 0.2727$$

REVIEW QUESTIONS

1. A company chairman wishes to finance an investment programme with debt capital. He is told that the earnings per share with debt financing is higher

compared with all equity financing. What qualifications should accompany such an Earnings Per Share analysis?

2. What are the tax advantages to debt for the company? Is the size of these advantages exactly the same for the shareholder? If there were no tax advantages to corporate borrowing, would individuals still borrow?

3. Describe in detail the arbitrage conditions that Modigliani and Miller use to prove that the cost of debt is the same as the cost of equity on a pre-tax basis?

4. How does the size of the tax benefits of debt financing affect a project's value?

5. Is it possible that a project can be unprofitable (have negative net present value) with all equity financing but be profitable with both debt and equity financing?

6. How does the presence of bankruptcy costs affect the amount of debt a company will wish to borrow?

EXERCISES

1. The perpetual operating stream of an ungeared company is valued at £1000. Interest payments are tax deductible, the pre-tax rate of interest is 10 per cent and Corporation Tax is 40 per cent. Assuming the firm could be financed half by debt (perpetual) and half by equity, what would be the value of the perpetual net operating stream? Ignore any personal taxes. How would your answer be affected if the net operating stream was not perpetual?

2. What would the tax advantage to corporate borrowing be in the U.K. if the standard rate of income tax was reduced to 25 per cent and corporation tax was maintained at 52 per cent?

19

DEBT FINANCING AND PROJECT VALUATION

If there are tax advantages to corporate borrowing, a capital project which increases the asset base and borrowing capacity of the firm secures a tax advantage, which should be reflected in the Present Value of the project. What is the most accurate way to reflect the tax advantage of borrowing in a project's profitability? Should the discount rate be adjusted to reflect a project's borrowing capacity or should the tax advantage be quantified as a cash flow?

In this chapter, we consider the relationship between two methods of incorporating the tax advantages of debt into the project decision: the Weighted Average Cost of Capital and Myers' Adjusted Present Value method.

TAX BENEFITS AND THE PROJECT APPRAISAL DECISION

Should the financing decision affect the investment decision? This is a common question. In one sense the answer is, 'No'! Merely financing one project with a block of debt and the next project with all equity does not mean that the cost of finance for the first project should reflect all debt financing and, for the second, all equity financing. The financing decision for a single project should not affect the investment decision. It is in this sense of timing that the investment and financing decision of the firm should be separated. However, this argument does not imply that there are no advantages to a particular source of finance. In the last chapter, we concluded that there was some advantage to debt which mainly derived from taxation. Given that there are tax benefits to debt, should they affect the investment decision and, if so, how should they be incorporated into the project evaluation?

The answer to this question must depend upon how easy it is for the firm to acquire tax benefits without actually investing in new assets. For example, if many firms quoted on the Stock Exchange were undergeared (i.e. had unused debt capacity), it should be possible for one company to buy the shares of undergeared companies, and by borrowing on the ungeared securities thereby obtain the tax advantage. However, we would have expected other companies and financial intermediaries (e.g.

Investment Trusts) to have secured the tax advantages already and, therefore, market prices of companies will reflect the tax benefits of debt capacity, irrespective of whether that debt capacity has been utilized by the firm itself. This process should ensure that the only significant way for the firm to obtain additional tax benefits is by investing in new physical assets. As a result, the new tax benefits created by a project's financing should be incorporated into the investment decision.

There are other sources of financing benefits which should be included in a project evaluation. For example, in some instances the Government may be providing debt finance at a favourable interest rate below market rates. Lease finance can also provide benefits when the company is not in a tax-paying position. For these reasons we shall review the methods available for incorporating such benefits from financing into the investment decision.

THE WEIGHTED AVERAGE COST OF CAPITAL

A traditional approach to the choice of discount rates is to establish the cost of equity and debt to the firm and combine the two to obtain a 'Weighted Average Cost of Capital' (WACC) which reflects the relative proportions of debt and equity in the capital structure. We have already shown, however, that the discount rate for a capital project depends on the risk associated with the specific project and not on the average required rate of return for the firm as a whole.

Nevertheless, the concept of the Weighted Average Cost of Capital might still be considered to have some relevance if required rates of return on debt and equity used for this purpose are the same as that required for the specific project, and if the weights for the debt and equity are based on the additional borrowing power imparted to the firm by the project.

The form of the WACC (R^*) for a project (or firm) is given by the following formula:

$$R^* = \frac{\text{Cost of debt}}{\text{after tax}} \left(\frac{\text{Debt}}{\begin{array}{c}\text{Present Value}\\\text{of project}\end{array}} \right) + \frac{\text{Cost of}}{\text{equity}} \left(\frac{\text{Equity}}{\begin{array}{c}\text{Present Value}\\\text{of project}\end{array}} \right)$$

$$= (1 - T^*)\, i\, \frac{D}{V} + k\, \frac{S}{V}, \tag{19.1}$$

where T^* is the Present Value of net tax rate advantage to corporate borrowing, i is the pre-tax interest rate, D/V is the weight representing the borrowing capacity of the project expressed as a proportion of the Present Value of the project (without debt), $S/V = 1 - D/V$ is the remaining weight, and k is the cost of geared-up equity after tax reflecting the extra volatility or risk due to the debt financing.

The first term on the right-hand side of equation (19.1) is the after-tax cost of debt, weighted by the borrowing capacity of the project as a proportion of the present value of the project. The second term applies the remaining weight to the geared-up cost of equity for the project. This latter cost reflects the systematic business risk of the project augmented by the gearing effect of debt.

It remains for us to determine the geared-up cost k of the shareholders' equity stake in the project. Since borrowing on the project's assets increases the risks of the project in relation to the shareholders' remaining equity stake, the shareholders will require compensation for the additional risk. This implicit cost of debt increases the shareholders' required rate of return R (given the underlying systematic risk of the project). The resulting geared-up cost of equity for the project we have called k. The appropriate formula which would be used for k given the U.K. tax system is derived in Appendix 19.1.

The difficulty with applying these formulae to most capital projects arises from the nature of the underlying assumptions. They are that:

(a) the project is expected to generate a constant and perpetual stream of cash flows;
(b) the project is expected to make a constant and permanent contribution to the firm's debt capacity.

The cash flow profiles of many capital projects are inconsistent with the latter two assumptions. For example, it should be obvious that if a project's life is not infinite, the Present Value of the project declines as the end of the project's life approaches. Consequently, the amount of debt that the project can support and the corresponding (discounted) tax benefits must also decline with the remaining life. The WACC assumes that the amount of debt that the project can support and the related tax benefits are constant throughout the life of the project; and, therefore, the Weighted Average Cost of Capital approach overstates the impact of the tax advantage of debt on the Present Value of the project.

ADJUSTED PRESENT VALUE METHOD

In view of the crude assumptions required in the application of the Weighted Average Cost of Capital concept, it would be desirable to have a solution which would reflect the tax advantages of debt with more precision. Myers (1974) has suggested that it would be more appropriate to discount separately the cash flows attributable to the estimated tax benefits from borrowing. The operating cash flows would then be discounted at the required rate of return for the project assuming all-equity financing. The

Present Value of the tax benefits would then be added to the Present Value of the operating cash flows. This Adjusted Present Value approach explicitly recognizes:

(a) that projects have different debt capacities and therefore have different tax benefits;
(b) that tax benefits are a function of the life of the specific project (the weighted average cost of capital formulation assumed perpetuities);
(c) that debt capacity and therefore tax benefits are not constant throughout the project's life, because the present value of the project declines as the remaining life of the project diminishes. Furthermore, the cash flows of a project are usually not constant.

Table 19.1 illustrates the way in which tax benefits of borrowing can be derived from the operating cash flow stream of a project. These benefits depend on the change in the borrowing capacity of the project with time. At a discount rate of 15 per cent the initial Present Value of the project is £1000. Assuming that the project can support borrowing of 50 per cent of asset value, the initial debt would be £500 as indicated in the third row of the table. However, at the end of the first period there are only four remaining operating cash flows and the Present Value will have fallen to

Table 19.1. Estimation of the Present Value of a project's tax benefits from 50 per cent debt financing

	0	1	2	3	4
			Period		
Operating cash flows after taxes		350	350	350	350
Present Value* at 15 per cent of remaining cash flows	1000	799	569	304	0
Borrowing at $D/V = 0.50$	500	400	284	152	0
Interest at 7 per cent		35.00	28.00	19.88	10.64
Net tax benefit at 18 per cent[†]		6.30	5.04	3.58	1.92
Present Value at 4.62 per cent (7 per cent $(1 - 0.34)$)		6.02	4.60	3.13	1.60

Total Present Value of tax benefits = 15.35

*The Present Value of remaining cash flows is obtained by discounting the net operating cash flows at a rate that would be required under all-equity financing.
[†]Net tax benefit in each period is the difference between rates of tax being paid by the company and by shareholders applicable to interest payments. These benefits should be lagged if the company pays taxes after the period when tax liabilities are incurred.

£799. As a result, the project at that stage would support borrowing of only £400. Similarly, the borrowing capacity of the project is seen to continue to decline until it becomes zero at the end of the project's life.

Having determined the amount of borrowing capacity in each period of the project's life, we can now calculate the interest payments and the resulting net tax savings. In row 4 of Table 19.1, we see that initial borrowing of £500 at the end of period 0 requires an interest payment of £35 at 7 per cent at the end of period 1. In subsequent periods, interest payments decline as a result of reduced borrowing. What are the tax benefits? You should recall from the previous chapter that the net tax benefit in each period to company borrowing in the U.K. is the difference between the corporate tax rate and the investor's (or his financial intermediary's) tax rate. Currently, this difference is $(0.52 - 0.34) = 0.18$. Thus the tax benefit is shown in the fifth row as 18 per cent of the interest paid in row four. These net benefits are then discounted at the borrowing rate after shareholders' taxes. The borrowing rate of 7 per cent adjusted for shareholders' taxes at the standard rate of personal taxation (currently 34 per cent) would be 4.62 per cent. The benefits discounted at 4.62 per cent to Present Value at the end of period 0 total only £15.35. The Present Value of the project should thus be increased by £15.35 to reflect the tax benefits made available by the additional borrowing capacity attributable to the project.

The Present Value of the tax benefits in the example of Table 19.1 amounted to only a 1.5 per cent adjustment to the initial Present Value of £1000 for the project! We have this result in spite of the optimistic assumption that the project can support debt up to 50 per cent of its Present Value at each point in time. In fact the proportion of debt to total assets for most U.K. companies is closer to only 20 per cent. Thus our example may overstate the Present Value of tax benefits to borrowing on the project for the average company.

We should also note that we discounted the tax benefits at the borrowing rate (adjusted for shareholders' taxes) because we assumed that the expected tax benefits are certain. However, the tax benefits depend on the future borrowing capacity of the project, which depends in turn on the Present Value of future cash flows. Since the Present Value is subject to systematic risk, which would require a higher discount rate this assumption also incorporates a favourable bias in the analysis. Furthermore, the tax benefits are themselves uncertain since the earnings of the company might not be sufficient to cover interest payments. In this case the full tax benefits of the tax deductibility of debt could not be realized. The expected tax benefit from borrowing must be reduced by the expectation of possible negative net earnings; and, as a consequence, the discount rate should be increased to reflect the riskiness of earnings. In fact, the discount rate for the tax benefits must be greater than the interest rate on the debt since the probability of having insufficient profits to absorb the tax benefits is greater than the probability of default (Wrightsman, 1977). Thus discounting the full tax benefits at the after-tax borrowing rate results in an overstatement of the Present Value of tax benefits from borrowing on the project. Nevertheless, the adjustment to the Present Value of the project for the tax benefit to borrowing is very small indeed.

COMPARISON BETWEEN THE TWO METHODS

To what extent does the Weighted Average Cost of Capital method exaggerate the tax advantages to corporate borrowing made possible by the project? Let us make the same assumptions as employed previously concerning borrowing capacity and tax rates. Using the Modigliani–Miller formula for the geared up cost of equity, we will require a value for T^*, the present value of the net tax rate advantage to corporate borrowing treated as a perpetuity. In the last chapter we estimated T^* to be equal to 0.27 assuming a perpetual stream of tax savings. Assuming a debt-to-equity ratio $D/S = 1$ we can now use the Modigliani–Miller formula of equation (19.A4) in Appendix 19.1 to calculate the geared-up cost of equity,

$$k = R + (R - i)(1 - T^*)D/S$$
$$= 0.15 + (0.15 - 0.07)(1 - 0.27) \times 1.$$
$$= 0.21.$$

Due to gearing, the cost of equity has moved up from 15 to 21 per cent. Now that we have a value for k we can calculate the Weighted Average Cost of Capital (R^*) using equation (19.1) referred to previously,

$$R^* = (1 - T^*) i \frac{D}{V} + k \frac{S}{V}$$

$$= [(1 - 0.27) \times 0.07 \times 0.5] + [0.21 \times 0.5]$$

$$= 0.13.$$

Thus we have a Weighted Average Cost of Capital of 13 per cent, which reflects the explicit cost of debt (interest payments adjusted for tax) and the geared-up cost of equity assuming an ungeared cost of equity of 15 per cent and interest at 7 per cent. The WACC would, of course, be different for projects of different risk since the cost of equity for a project depends upon the project's systematic risk as discussed in Chapter 8. Conventional use of the WACC would be to discount the after-tax cash flows in row 1 of Table 19.1 by 13 per cent. This calculation would yield a Present Value of 1041.06. The net advantage conferred by borrowing on the project of

1041.06 − 1000 = £41.06 according to the WACC method is nearly three times the £15.35 obtained by the Myers' method.

The Weighted Average Cost of Capital obviously exaggerates the importance of tax benefits to corporate borrowing for projects of finite life, and the error can be very large in comparison with the more exact Present Value adjustment found directly with Myers' Adjusted Present Value method. This bias arises from the fact that the WACC formula treats the Present Value of the tax advantage to borrowing as a constant, whereas the tax benefit actually declines year-by-year with the Present Value of remaining cash flows as the end of the project's life is approached.

Table 19.2 shows some estimates by Myers (1974) of the error in the indicated Present Value from using the Weighted Average Cost of Capital formula instead of the Adjusted Present Value method. Results are presented for a variety of required rates of return on equity and a number of debt ratios. The calculation is based on the U.S. tax system, where the value of $T^* = 0.5$ instead of $T^* = 0.27$ which would be the case for the U.K., under the same set of assumptions. Errors from the use of the Weighted Average Cost of Capital method range from £4 up to £79 for an investment of £1000. While these errors are not large, they involve a consistent positive bias and could result in investment in activities which are not profitable.

Several factors conspire to minimize the tax advantage on borrowing traceable to an individual project. First, debt capacity as a proportion of the Present Value is not large, usually 20 per cent of the Present Value. Second, the borrowing made possible by the project cannot extend beyond the life of the project. Third, the Present Value of the remaining cash flows in the project frequently declines rapidly with time thus reducing the potential amount of borrowing. Fourth, the net tax rate advantage to corporate borrowing is considerably less than the Corporation Tax rate in the U.K. since there are institutional means by which the shareholder can

Table 19.2. Error in indicated NPV from using cost of capital formula to evaluate a ten-period project requiring a £1000 investment*†

Cost of capital for all-equity financing	Target debt ratio		
	0.2	0.4	0.6
0.08	4	8	12
0.12	14	29	47
0.20	22	48	79

*Source: Myers (1974).
†*Assumptions*: Risk free rate is assumed as $i = 0.07$; net tax rate advantage to corporate borrowing, $T^* = 0.5$; project's expected cash flows £150 per period from $t = 1$ to $t = 10$.

obtain this advantage for himself. Fifth, the greatly diminished tax benefits to borrowing with time must be discounted to Present Value. Sixth, as we explained in the previous chapter, competitive pressures on interest rates would tend to reduce any tax advantage to debt in relation to equity. The tax advantages to debt would encourage increased borrowing, thereby raising interest rates and, consequently, offsetting the tax advantages in part, at least.

Finally, we have assumed in our calculations an optimum capital struc-structure for the project. This optimum corresponds to that level of debt that would have been obtained if the project were funded separately by the company. However, the fact that there is an optimum capital structure implies that the cost of borrowing rises with the amount of debt financing. This rise can be explained by the risks and costs of bankruptcy. Thus, at the margin, the costs of bankruptcy must equal the tax benefits of debt. In effect, this means that the tax benefits computed in the previous example have been overestimated and should be revised downwards for expected bankruptcy costs.

For all these reasons, the importance of the tax advantage to borrowing made possible by investment in an individual project, if not insignificant, can easily be exaggerated.

The Myers' APV method is a useful way of separating the financing and investment decisions. Although the tax benefits may be small, this method may be used to solve a variety of problems. If a government provides debt finance below the market rate, the difference constitutes an advantage that can be valued using Myers' method. Finally, the bank lending decision provides an opportunity for demonstrating the usefulness of Myers' approach.

ADJUSTED PRESENT VALUE AND BANK LENDING

The principles underlying the Adjusted Present Value method shed light on the lending behaviour of banks. The term of a loan cannot extend beyond the life of the asset on which the loan is secured if there is no remaining asset value at the end of the project's life. Furthermore, the schedule of repayment of principal is required at a rate which will ensure that the unpaid principal declines with the value of the asset. In principle, the repayments schedule should be made proportional to the decline in Present Value of the project over time. In practice the repayment schedule on most loans only approximates such a schedule. A large margin for error in the debt to initial asset value ratio is required since banks usually do not wish to monitor project performance frequently or in excessive detail.

INTEREST CHARGES AND PROJECT VALUATION

In the previous analysis, we have not explicitly included interest charges in the project evaluation exercise, except in so far as to compute the tax advantages of debt. In fact, the discounting process reflects the cost of financing the project. The reason a project's cash flows are discounted is that money has an opportunity cost expressed in the form of an interest rate (and a risk premium). Consequently, if we were to deduct dividends or interest payments from a project's cash flows, we would be double counting. The difference in cost between debt and equity financed projects derives from the net tax advantage. In effect, Myers' Adjusted Present Value approach initially assumes projects are *all-equity* financed. The second step estimates the additional benefits of debt and applies this tax benefit to the project's cash flows. The Present Value of the tax benefit is added to the initial estimate of the Present Value of the cash flows assuming all-equity financing.

LEASING AND THE INVESTMENT DECISION

Throughout the chapter, we have assumed that the firm is in a tax-paying position and is therefore in a position to acquire any of the tax benefits arising from capital allowances as well as from debt financing. The reader might infer that if the company is in a non-tax-paying position, those tax benefits are forgone and should therefore be excluded from the project evaluation. This conclusion is not necessarily valid if there are other means of capturing the tax benefits. For example, leasing is a common method of financing an investment when the firm is not paying taxes. Leasing, as Chapter 20 will describe, permits one company (the lessor) to buy equipment and borrow in order to capture the tax benefits. The asset is then leased to a non-tax paying company. The lessor passes over a proportion of the tax benefits in the form of reduced lease payments. The value or net present value of the asset must include the value (or NPV) of the lease, reflecting the tax benefits of debt and capital allowances which have been passed through to the firm in the form of lower lease payments. Thus the financing decision can affect the Net Present Value of a project if tax benefits not otherwise available are obtainable by means of leasing. While the tax benefits arising from capital allowances may be substantial, the benefits traceable to debt financing will still be small as we have shown whether or not lease financing is employed. As we shall see when we take a closer look at leasing, lease financing merely displaces debt and does not increase the borrowing capacity of the firm.

CONCLUSIONS

The tax advantage of borrowing arising from the asset base provided by a capital project may be worth estimating, particularly for projects with long lives. There are two approaches which have been suggested for reflecting this tax advantage in capital project appraisal. The more traditional approach involves using a 'Weighted Average Cost of Capital'. This approach involves two dangers. First, the approach often confuses managers about the difference between the cost of capital to the firm as a whole and the required rate of return for a particular project. Second, the Weighted Average Cost of Capital concept involves assumptions about the level and duration of cash flows which are usually inappropriate for individual capital projects and can lead to significant errors.

The second approach, the Adjusted Present Value method, is more accurate since the tax benefits from borrowing are discounted separately. Thus it becomes unnecessary to adopt the artificial assumptions required to construct a weighted average cost of capital. Using this approach, we found that the adjustment required to the Present Value of projects arising from the tax advantages of borrowing for U.K. companies is quite small and may be negligible for short-lived projects. Management often impute exaggerated benefits to debt financing. We have shown methods by which such benefits can be put into better perspective.

REFERENCES AND BIBLIOGRAPHY

Clark, T., *Leasing*, McGraw-Hill, Maidenhead, 1978.

Fawthrop R. A. and Terry, B., 'The Evaluation of an-Integrated Investment and Lease-finance Decision', *Journal of Business Finance and Accounting*, **3**, 79–111, 1976.

King, M. A., 'Taxation and the Cost of Capital', *Review of Economic Studies*, **41**, 21–35 Jan. 1974.

Modigliani, F. and Miller, M. H., 'The Cost of Capital, Corporation Finance and the Theory of Investment', *American Economic Review*, **48**, 261–297, Jun. 1958.

Modigliani, F. and Miller, M. H., 'Corporate Income Taxes and the Cost of Capital: A Correction', *American Economic Review*, **53**, 433–442, Jun. 1963.

Myers, S. C., 'Interactions of Corporate Financing and Investment Decisions—Implications for Capital Budgeting', *Journal of Finance*, **29**, 1–25, Mar. 1974.

Scott, J. H., 'A Theory of Optimal Capital Structure', *The Bell Journal of Economics and Management Science*, **7**, 33–54, Spring 1976.

Stapleton, R. C. and Burke, C. M., 'Taxes, the Cost of Capital and the Theory of Investment: A Generalisation to the Imputation System of Dividend Taxation. *Economic Journal*, **85**, 888–890, Dec. 1975.

Van Horne, J. C., *Financial Management and Policy*, 4th ed., Prentice Hall, Englewood Cliffs, N.J., 1977.

Warner, G., 'Bankruptcy Costs: Some Evidence', *Journal of Finance*, **3**, 337–348, May 1977.

Wrightsman, D., 'Tax Shield Valuation and the Capital Structure Decision', *Journal of Finance*, **32**, 371–388, May 1977.

APPENDIX 19.1

Modigliani and Miller (1958) have shown that the Present Value V of the firm when there is corporate borrowing is given by,

$$V = E/R + T^*D, \tag{19.A1}$$

where E/R is the Present Value of perpetual cash flow stream E discounted at ungeared required rate R, and T^*D is the Present Value of the net tax advantage of debt D.

Modigliani and Miller derive an alternative formulation of the Weighted Average Cost of Capital by noting that

$$V = E/R^* \tag{19.A2}$$

where E is the perpetual cash flow stream, and R^* is the Weighted Average Cost of Capital.

Solving the above two equations simultaneously, they obtain

$$R^* = R(1 - T^*D/V), \tag{19.A3}$$

which relates the Weighted Average Cost of Capital R^* to the ungeared cost R of equity given the risk class of the firm.

We can now solve for the geared-up cost of equity k by substituting equation (19.A3) in equation (19.1) in the text, obtaining

$$k = R + (R - i)(1 - T^*)D/S. \tag{19.A4}$$

REVIEW QUESTIONS

1. Why cannot the Weighted Average Cost of Capital be used as a hurdle rate for all new projects?

2. Describe in detail the Adjusted Present Value method for valuing a project partially financed by debt.

EXERCISES

1. A project's operating cashflows are £250 per annum for 5 years for a capital outlay of £500. The ungeared required rate of return for the project is 15 per cent after taxes, and the firm's borrowing rate is 7 per cent before taxes.

   (a) Calculate the Adjusted Present Value for the project.
   (b) What is the percentage of the Present Value of the tax benefits as a proportion of (i) the Present Value of the project and (ii) the Net Present Value of the project?

   Assume that Corporation Tax is 52 per cent and that the standard rate of Income Tax is 34 per cent. The project can be financed by debt up to 25 per cent of its Present Value.

2. If Miller is correct and that there are no tax benefits to shareholders from corporate borrowing, how would your answer to Exercise 19.1 be altered?

3. A firm's capital structure consists of 40 per cent debt and 60 per cent equity. The interest rate on the debt is 10 per cent pre-tax and the (observed) β value is 1.25 (See appendix 8.A1). Given that the return on the market is estimated at $7\frac{1}{2}$ per cent after taxes, what is the value of the Weighted Average Cost of Capital? Make any necessary assumptions about personal tax rates.

4. The Government agrees to lend £1 000 000 to a company for 5 years at a fixed rate of 8 per cent per annum for a *specific* project. The capital cost of the project is £2 000 000 and the market rate of interest for a similar loan is 12 per cent per annum. The after-tax operating cash flows are £600 000 for each of the five years.

(a) Assuming that Corporation Tax is 52 per cent, and that the standard rate of personal taxes is 34 per cent, what is the value of the project?

(b) What is the value of the tax advantage to debt?

(c) What is the value of the Government's interest rate subsidy?

20

LEASING

The value of outstanding leased assets in the U.K. has risen from an estimated £56 millions in 1965 to more than £1980 millions in 1976. Leased assets account for approximately 7 per cent of total capital expenditures. The greater proportion was transacted by the 40 or more companies that are members of the Equipment Leasing Association. The majority of lessors fall into one of the following five categories:

(a) Subsidiaries of the Clearing Banks (e.g. Lloyds Bank),
(b) Merchant Banks (e.g. Brandts),
(c) Finance Houses (e.g. Mercantile Credit),
(d) Other financial institutions (e.g. I.C.F.C.),
(e) U.S. leasing companies (e.g. Citicorp Leasing).

In value terms, much of the leasing finance is provided for the purchase of ships, aircraft, and computers. Since the traffic in such products is often international, specialized cross-border leasing has also increased. Companies engaged in this international activity include the Orion Bank, Hill Samuel, and Citicorp. With European leasing running at more than £4.0 billion, the subject deserves a more analytical approach than it has received in the past in the U.K.

This chapter provides a review of the main issues in the decision to buy or to lease assets and two analytical methods are compared.

ISSUES IN LEASING

Numerous claims have been made about lease financing and, before we discuss an analytical approach, we should examine some of the more obvious conceptual problems.

We shall consider financial leases, where the lessee agrees to make a series of payments to the lessor for the use of the asset throughout its operating life. All other leases can be classified as operating leases where the contract is expected to terminate prior to the end of the asset's life.

One of the most important advantages attributed to leasing is that the firm is permitted to acquire the use of the asset without recourse to its own funds. This claim is imprecise and even misleading since lease payments are payable to the lessor for the price of the equipment plus interest on capital. The lessee is in an analogous position to an individual who purchases a house with a mortgage provided by a Building Society or an Insurance Company and repays the lender by regular instalments. Each instalment consists of part repayment of the loan and interest on the balance outstanding. In addition, since a lease, like a mortgage, requires a deposit or some form of advance payment, the lessee often contributes to the initial cost of the equipment.

It is unlikely that the lessor would advance a loan for the whole cost of the asset unless the borrower had other assets or equity to support the loan. Even if the lessor finances 100 per cent of the cost of the asset, all-debt financing is not implied because equity in the firm is required to support the loan. The covenants in the lease agreement will often require a minimum level of equity and liquid assets to be maintained in the business. The lease contract is therefore similar to any other secured loan or debenture agreement.

It should be clear that leasing is a form of debt financing which provides for the effective acquisition of the asset. However, some managers believe that because future lease payments are not included as a liability in the balance sheet, investors and lenders do not include the liability as part of the debt burden of the company.

Of course, intelligent bankers require information on any contractual commitments entered into by the company. Likewise, the investor is interested in both the risk and expected returns of the company. Even if the lease does not appear in the balance sheet, the financial analyst will estimate all the fixed costs of the business which contribute to the sensitivity of the company's earnings to changes in revenues. Recent legislation and policy papers by the Institute of Chartered Accountants now require disclosure of important financial leases in the notes to the company accounts.

Another advantage perceived by lessees is that clauses in lease agreements are thought to be less restrictive than corresponding covenants for debenture agreements. This assertion may have been a reasonable one during the early years of leasing, but not so today. What then are the advantages of financial leases? As our subsequent analysis will show, such advantages, where they exist, derive mainly from the special tax position of the lessor or lessee.

Recently the British Institute of Management (B.I.M) carried out a survey which sought information on the advantages of financial leases. The results from 185 respondent industrial companies are summarized below.

We have already discussed most of these points and concluded that they do not generally provide an advantage over other sources of finance. The fourth 'advantage' can be particularly misleading. Most lessors will not

Possible advantage	Percentage of managers affirming (per cent)
1. Provides a source of funds. Does not utilize existing working capital.	76
2. Usually permits 100 per cent financing. The full cost of the asset can normally be borrowed and is secured only on that asset.	37
3. Constitutes an undisclosed source of finance. Leasing effectively increases the gearing of the company because there is no disclosure in the Balance Sheet.	29
4. Reduces capital involvement because the lease can be terminated prematurely if operating losses are incurred	21

permit cancellation or, if they do, appropriate penalties are provided. One should appreciate that if lessors provide concessions, they will exact a suitable charge, otherwise they will not be in business for very long.

Does all this mean that the company has little to negotiate about in concluding a lease agreement? In fact there are some important points to watch out for before signing a lease agreement:

(a) A company should always invite a quotation from several lessors since rates do vary significantly between one lessor and another.
(b) It is useful to negotiate a lease just before the financial year-end of the lessor. After the year-end there will be a 12-month additional delay before the lessor can obtain the tax benefit of the capital allowance.
(c) The rates of interest charged often encompass companies of varying risk. Thus, it may be useful to ensure that the lessor fully appreciates the credit rating of the company prior to settling on the effective interest rate. If the lessee is put into the wrong risk bracket he will be charged an incorrect interest rate.
(d) All companies that engage in leasing should examine the gains or losses from a comparison with purchase.
(e) The major source of gains to leasing are due to taxes. If the user of the equipment is in a temporary (or permanent) non-tax paying position, then he may find it profitable to lease equipment rather than purchase it outright.

ANALYSIS OF THE LEASING DECISION: IMPORTANCE OF THE DISCOUNT RATE

Many managers who have tried to evaluate a lease have wondered how leasing could be quite as advantageous as it first appears. They adopted a 'sensible' discounted cash flow approach to the lease versus buy decision. Leasing was analysed as though it were a capital budgeting decision, and the rate that was used to discount the cash flows was the one required for the investment decision. In fact the decision to lease is primarily a *financing decision*: leasing is equivalent to borrowing and purchase. In the analysis of a lease one wishes to estimate the interest rate the lessor is charging and compare that cost with the lessee's marginal borrowing rate. The lessee who employs a discount rate higher than the marginal borrowing rate may inadvertantly increase the apparent attraction of the leasing alternative. Let us illustrate this point with a simple example.

A company has the opportunity to purchase an asset for £1000. If the company buys the asset, a 100 per cent initial tax allowance is available. The alternative is to lease the equipment for its operating life. Let us assume that the lease consists of five payments of £230 per annum where the first is required in advance and all payments are tax deductible. The company's tax rate is 50 per cent. The lessee's marginal borrowing rate is 10 per cent before tax, and an after-tax discount rate of 15 per cent is used for all risky investment projects.

Table 20.1 shows how the use of a high discount rate reduces the cost of the lease and makes leasing appear relatively more attractive than purchasing. The net present value of £422, discounted at 15 per cent, would be attractive compared to the £500 purchase cost net of tax benefits accruing from the capital allowances. However, since the correct discount rate is nearer 5 per cent, implying a net present value of £522, an incorrect decision would have been made.

The choice of discount rate is clearly very important. Since the alternative to leasing is usually purchase and debt financing, the appropriate rate of discount is usually close to the company's marginal borrowing rate after taxes. Let us now look at the analysis of the lease more closely.

Table 20.1. The discount rate and the value of the lease

Year	Lease payments	Tax relief*	Net cost
0	230	115	115
1	230	115	115
2	230	115	115
3	230	115	115
4	230	115	115

Net Present Value discounted at 15 per cent £442
Net Present Value discounted at 5 per cent £522

*Tax Rate = 50%. Lag in tax payments ignored.

THE MYERS, DILL, AND BAUTISTA METHOD

An approach that is appealing for its rigour and simplicity has been suggested by Myers, Dill, and Bautista (1976). We shall show how the method can be used by applying it to the example in Table 20.1. In a later section, we shall show why the method is correct.

The cost of leasing compared with purchase is initially more easily seen through the eyes of the lessor. The cost of the equipment is simply the purchase cost (£1000) less the tax benefits (£500) arising from the capital allowances. For simplicity, we assume those capital allowances are immediately absorbed by the taxable profits arising from the lessor's other operations and that taxes are paid without any delay. Computing the value of the lease is just as simple; it is merely the present value of the lease payments discounted at the after-tax interest rate that would be appropriate for a secured loan of specific duration for the particular lessee (user) of the equipment. The present value of the stream of lease payments to the lessor is £522.80, thus there is a net gain to leasing (V_0) of + £22.80:

$$V_o = -1000 + 500 + 115 + \frac{115}{(1 + .05)} + \frac{115}{(1 + .05)^2} + \frac{115}{(1 + .05)^3}$$

$$+ \frac{115}{(1 + .05)^4} = +£22.80.$$

Thus, since the present value of the stream of lease payments (£522.80) is greater than the after-tax cost of the equipment (£500), it is profitable for the lessor to lease.

Is it profitable for the lessee or user to lease rather than purchase the equipment outright? We simply subtract the present value of the lease payments from the purchase cost as before, but the signs are reversed. The present value of the lease payments is greater than the purchase cost by −£22.80 and therefore purchasing is preferred on purely a cost-benefit comparison:

$$V_o = +1000 - 500 - 115 - \frac{115}{(1 + .05)} - \frac{115}{(1 + .05)^2} - \frac{115}{(1 + .05)^3}$$

$$- \frac{115}{(1 + .05)^4} = -£22.80.$$

DIFFERENCES IN TAXES

If tax rates are different, the Inland Revenue provides the gain or absorbs the loss. If the lessee's tax rate is zero, and all other assumptions remain the same, we can compute the value of the lease to the lessee by taking into account the loss of tax advantages and using the pre-tax discount rate:

$$V_0 = +1000 - 230 - \frac{230}{(1+.10)} - \frac{230}{(1+.10)^2} - \frac{230}{(1+.10)^3} - \frac{230}{(1+.10)^4}$$

Compare these calculations with those previous, when the lessee was in a taxpaying position. The tax benefits from the capital allowances (£500) do not appear since the lessee does not have any taxable profits against which to offset them. Similarly, the gross lease payments are discounted since, although they are wholly tax deductible, taxable profits are simply not available. Finally, the discount rate reflects the pre-tax interest cost of debt for the same reason: interest charges are tax deductible but taxable profits are not available.

The value of the lease increases to £40.93 on the basis of these assumptions. It should be clear that while the firm is in a non-tax-paying position the tax benefits arising from the interest charges and the capital allowances cannot be obtained. The critical assumption here is that leasing provides the *only* means of taking advantage of the unused tax benefits.

The value of the lease to the lessor is still positive at £22.80. However, the lessee is also finding it profitable to lease. The fairy godmother is the Inland Revenue, whose taxable revenues are reduced by the net benefits to leasing. Of course, it may be argued that leasing permits companies who wish to invest to obtain investment incentives which the Government intended to provide for the very purpose of encouraging the new investment.

It is important to appreciate that any lag in tax payments may have a significant effect on the value of the lease and the final decision. If the lag in tax simply relates to the timing of the capital allowances and the payment of Corporation Tax, an adjustment to the pattern of cash flows is easily made. However, if the tax savings on interest charges are obtained subsequent to the interest payment, the discount rate should reflect this. In Appendix 20.1 a method of reflecting delays in the payment of taxes is given. In addition, the frequency of the lease payments may have a significant effect on the lease's value. For example, if an annual lease payment of £230 (£115 after taxes) was paid instead in two semi-annual instalments, the value of the above lease to the lessee would change from –£22.80 to –£16.48 (we have, of course, used semi-annual discount rates).

LESSEE IN A TEMPORARY NON-TAX-PAYING PERIOD

However, a company may only be temporarily in a non-tax-paying position. Franks and Hodges (1978) have clarified the treatment of this problem. Let us assume that the company is not paying taxes because of a lack of profits, and sufficient profits to absorb all unused allowances are not fore-

Table 20.2. Present value of the lease to the lessee when tax benefits are carried forward to year 2

Year	Payments	Tax benefits Gained	Lost		Net payments
		Leasing	Capital allowance	Interest	payments
0	−230				−230
1	−230				−230
2	−230	+345	−500	−TI	−385 − TI
3	−230	+115		*	−115
4	−230	+115		*	−115

Thus:

$$V_0 = +1000 - 230 - \frac{230}{(1 + 0.10)} - \frac{(385 + TI)}{(1 + 0.10)^2} - \frac{115}{(1 + 0.10)^2(1 + 0.05)}$$

$$- \frac{115}{(1 + 0.10)^2(1 + 0.05)^2}$$

$$= 1000 - 934 - \frac{TI}{(1 + 0.10)^2}$$

$$= 66 - \frac{TI}{(1 + 0.10)^2}$$

The value of I is 136.7 (see Appendix 20.2); Therefore,

$$V_0 = 66 - \frac{T136.7}{(1 + 0.10)^2} = 66 - \frac{0.5 \times 136.7}{(1 + 0.10)^2} = 9.5.$$

*Tax benefits lost on interest are subsumed in after-tax discount rate in tax-paying periods.

cast until year two. The schedule of net payments using the previous example is set out in Table 20.2.

Note that the tax benefits for years 0 and 1 are carried forward to year 2 in columns 3, 4, and 5. Note also that the net payments for the tax-paying period, years 3 and 4, are discounted at two different rates: at the pre-tax rate until year 2, the first tax-paying period, and at the after-tax rate for the remaining tax-paying periods.

The reason that the pre-tax interest rate is used until year 2 is that the tax benefits on interest are foregone until year 2, when they are treated explicitly in the term *TI*. Subsequent to year 2, the tax benefits on interest are being reflected *implicity* in the lower, post-tax discount rate (instead of explicitly as a cash flow). The term *TI* is the tax rate advantage *T* multiplied by the cumulative interest charges incurred during periods 1 and 2 on the value of the lease.

The calculation of the net value V_0 of the lease is a straightforward problem in discounted cash flow, except for the fact that the cumulative interest I on the equivalent loan is unknown initially. The reason that I is unknown initially is that the tax benefit TI plays a role in determining the value of the lease. However, the value of I can be determined by the method given in Appendix 20.2.

Table 20.3. Value of the Anaconda lease with different tax-paying commencement dates*

Tax-paying commencement period (years)	Value of the lease to the lessee ($ million)
0	− 3.03
1	− 2.67
2	− 1.93
3	− .90
4	.38
5	1.85
6	5.70
7	13.07
8	23.64
9	27.97
10	31.17
.	.
.	.
.	.
15	35.56
.	.
.	.
.	.
20	30.31
.	.
.	.
∞	25.17

*After Franks *et al.* (1978).
Value of the lease to the lessor is $3.03 million.
Notes

1. Tax savings arising from depreciation and lease payments can be carried forward a maximum of 5 years. The investment tax credit can be carried forward a maximum of 7 years.
2. Tax rate advantage is 50 per cent.
3. Present value of salvage value is $0.847 million.
4. Asset cost is $110.7 million.
5. Tax depreciation shield assumes an 11-year depreciable life and a 5 per cent book salvage value, A double declining balance method was used for the first 2 years, in the third year, a switch was made to sum-of-the-years' digits.
6. Discount rate is 8.926 per cent pre-tax (compounded semi-annually).

In this position, one finds that leasing the asset is more profitable than purchase. The longer the non-tax-paying period, the greater the value of the lease. The change in the value of the lease depends not only upon the expected tax-paying date, but also upon the pattern of capital allowances obtained under purchase compared with those prevailing under the leasing alternative.

In Table 20.3, we have reproduced the results of a series of calculations (Franks *et al.*, 1978) for a lease purchased by the Anaconda Company in the United States. The purchase cost of the asset was $110 millions and the company was in a non-tax paying position for many years as a result of the expropriation of its assets in Chile. The value of the lease to the lessee (Anaconda) increases significantly as the tax-paying commencement date is pushed further out in time. For the lease to be profitable compared with purchase, Anaconda would have had to be in a non-tax-paying position for at least 4 years. The value of the lease reaches a peak of $35.56 millions (about a third of the cost of the asset) in year 15 and then declines. This decline may seem puzzling, but is simply due to the changing present value (with time) of the capital allowance obtained under purchase netted with the tax deductions from the lease payments.

In Appendix 20.3, we review another method of lease valuation which is commonly used by analysts. We show how such a method can be adapted only under certain circumstances to provide the precise solution to the lease versus borrow problem.

RESIDUAL VALUES

In most U.K. lease agreements, there is a clause which stipulates that a specified proportion of the proceeds from the sale of the asset will accrue to the lessee at the end of the lease. The proportion typically ranges from 85 to 95 per cent. Assuming that the amount taken by the lessor represents the transactions cost of selling the asset, the proceeds on sale are the same under purchase or lease. Thus, in the previous analysis we have been able to ignore residual values only because they are common to both the decision to lease or purchase. Clearly, if tax laws forced the company to lease for a secondary period at a specified rental, a residual value must be estimated. A useful approximation to the real value of the asset at the end of the primary period is the current second-hand value of identical or similar equipment of an age corresponding to the term of the lease. This real value must be inflated at the expected rate of inflation over the term of the lease in order to obtain the expected nominal residual value. Thus we would suggest using the current price of a two-year old car (inflated by the expected rate of inflation) as a proxy for the residual value two years hence of a new car purchased today. 'When valuing the lease one discounts the estimated residual value at a nominal, risk-adjusted discount rate. A risk premium based on the volatility of second-hand values would already reflect not only the risks of possible technological change but also of changes in substitutes.

CHOICE OF LEASE PAYMENTS' SCHEDULE

In the previous analysis, the schedule of lease payments was arbitrarily taken as being a constant annual amount. However, given the assumption that the lessee is in a non-tax-paying position, it may be that the best lease payments' schedule should not be based on a constant annual sum. In fact, Franks and Hodges (1978) have shown that it will pay the lessee to postpone lease payments to the end of the lease period. We can illustrate the importance of the lease payments' schedule by considering our previous example. In that example, the lessor received annual lease payments of £230 and the cost of the asset was £500 net of the tax benefits of the capital allowances (£500). Let us now fix one lease payment of £1270.93 (£635.46 net of tax) to be paid to the lessor at the end of the fourth year instead of a series of five payments of £230. The value of the lease to the lessor is still +£22.80:

$$V_0 = -1000 + 500 + \frac{(1270.93 \times 0.5)}{(1 + 0.05)^4} = +£22.80.$$

However, the value of the lease to the lessee is no longer £41.87

$$V_0 = +1000 - \frac{1270.93}{(1.10)^4}$$
$$= 1000 - 868.06$$
$$= £131.94.$$

Thus the gain from leasing to the lessee has been increased from £41.87 to £131.94 by simply moving the lease payments to the end of the lease period. It may be that the lessor will demand a higher interest rate since the lease payments would be riskier. Also, the lessor may object that it is a most unusual repayment schedule. However, the example is set out to illustrate a point: that the profits from leasing can be increased by postponing the lease payments as far as possible into the future. It is important to appreciate that the gains from leasing can never exceed the tax benefits foregone via direct purchase, as a result of a temporary or a permanent non-tax-paying position.

We have described why the postponement of lease payments is profitable when one party to the lease agreement is in a non-tax-paying position. It should be obvious that in this position a longer lease will provide the lessee with greater tax benefits than a shorter lease.

BASIS OF THE MYERS, DILL, AND BAUTISTA METHOD

The Myers, Dill, and Bautista (MDB) method (Myers *et al.*, 1976) looks simple, and it is. however, because so many approaches to lease valuation have been suggested, one should try to see why the method is correct. In Table 20.4, we show how the MDB method is based upon a comparison of leasing and purchase financed by borrowing. In all future years, the cash flows of leasing are made equivalent to purchase by constructing an appropriate and unique interest and repayments schedule. The unique value of the loan that is implicit in the lease is £407.80. The value of the loan must be equal to the sum of the implied repayments (of principal) in years one through four. The value of the loan must be found simultaneously with the value of the lease, as we describe below. The cash flows for leasing (plus borrowing) dominate those for purchase by £22.80 in the initial year. This provides the value of the lease to the lessee (−£22.80) which we have found directly by use of the formula described previously.

Purchase cost of the asset	−1000
100 per cent capital allowance × 50 per cent tax rate	+ 500
Net cost of the asset	+ 500
− Net lease payment (period 0)	− 115
+ Value of the lease	+ 22.80
Loan in period 0	£407.80

It is important for the reader to understand how the discounted net value of the lease (£22.80) affects the size of the loan. Furthermore, the value of the loan is critical to estimating the value of the lease since the former determines the pattern of interest payments and consequent tax benefits. Finally, the interest charges estimated for the lease must reflect the value, term, and repayments schedule of the loan which is implicit in the lease. One of the advantages of Table 20.4 is that both the lender and borrower are able to see the explicit loan repayments' schedule and can, therefore, determine an appropriate interest rate. In our example, the implied repayments are similar from one year to another; however, this need not necessarily be the case for all leases.

LEASING AND THE INVESTMENT DECISION

Leasing may be viewed as a financing decision *contingent* on the investment decision. As with contingent projects the analysis must answer

Table 20.4. A comparison of leasing with purchase financed by borrowing

	Period				
	0	1	2	3	4
Leasing: cash flow					
Lease payments	− 230.0	−230.0	−230.0	−230.0	−230.0
+ Tax savings	115.0	115.0	115.0	115.0	115.0
Net cash flow	− 115.0	−115.0	−115.0	−115.0	−115.0
Purchase cash flows					
Purchase costs	−1000.0				
+ Tax saving on					
Capital allowance	500.0	0.0	0.0	0.0	0.0
− Loan repayment	407.8	− 94.6	− 99.3	−104.3	−109.5
− Interest on loan	0.0	− 40.8	− 31.3	− 21.4	− 11.0
+ Interest tax					
savings	0.0	20.4	15.7	10.7	5.5
Net cash flow	− 92.2	−115.0	−115.0	−115.0	−115.0
Loan account					
Previous balance	0.0	407.8	313.2	213.8	109.5
− Repayment	407.8	− 94.6	− 99.3	−104.3	−109.5
New balance	407.8	313.2	213.8	109.5	0.0
Advantage (disadvantage) to leasing					
Difference in cash					
flows	− 22.8				

two questions:

(a) Is leasing profitable for the project?
(b) Is the project profitable when financed by the lease?

A lease contract should not be signed unless the answer to both questions is, 'yes'; that is, the net present value of the lease must be positive and the sum of the net present value of the project as an investment (without the lease) and the net present value of the lease must be positive. Clearly some projects for non-tax-paying companies will appear unprofitable until combined with lease-financing or other means of taking advantage of capital allowances.

A second point must also be made that if a company is in a non-tax-paying position because of unused capital allowances or unused tax losses, then it is in the company's interests to obtain the tax advantages as quickly as possible. A number of alternatives may be available. The company may be able to buy profitable companies in a similar business, sell tax-loss companies, or enter into a lease agreement. Thus, there may be more than one scheme available to obtain the benefits of unused allowances; leasing is only one of those schemes. Leasing should be compared with other methods of obtaining relief on unused capital allowances.

Finally, in our analysis we have assumed that the tax-paying date is known and that the proposed lease does not affect the forecast tax-paying date. This assumption will often be incorrect and one should examine the sensitivity of the results to this assumption.

CONCLUSIONS

The main advantage of financial leases is their ability to bring forward the tax advantages from investment that otherwise would not be available by purchasing the equipment directly. The size of the advantage depends critically on the future profits of the firm and the predicted tax-paying position. Furthermore, we have shown that the value of the lease can be increased by altering the schedule of lease payments or even by timing the commencement of the lease with the accounting year-end of the lessor.

It is interesting to speculate on how the profits from leasing are divided between lessor and lessee. This division will vary from one year to another, and will be determined by the supply of finance (resulting from taxable profits) available to leasing companies, the demand for leased assets from companies in temporary or permanent non-tax-paying positions, and the negotiating skills of individual lessees.

REFERENCES AND BIBLIOGRAPHY

Bower, R. S., 'Issues in Lease Financing', *Financial Management*, **2**, 25–33, Winter 1973.
Clark, T., *Leasing*, McGraw-Hill, Maidenhead, 1978.
Fawthrop, R. A. and Terry, B., 'The Evaluation of an Integrated Investment and Lease-finance Decision', *Journal of Business Finance and Accounting*, **3**, 79–111, 1976.
Franks, J. R. and Hodges, S. D., 'Valuation of Financial Lease Contracts: A Note', *Journal of Finance*, **33**, 657–669, May 1978.
Gordon, M. J., 'A General Solution to the Lease or Buy Decision: A Pedagogical Note', *Journal of Finance*, **39**, 245–250, Mar. 1974.
Hodges, S. D., 'Analysis of the Lease or Buy Decision', Teaching Note, London Business School, Feb. 1978.
Johnson, R. W. and Lewellen, G., 'Analysis of the Lease or Buy Decision', *Journal of Finance*, **27**, 815–824, Sep. 1972.
Miller, M. H. and Upton, C. W., 'Leasing, Buying and the Cost of Capital Services', *Journal of Finance*, **31**, 761–786, Jun. 1976.
Myers, S. C., Dill, D. A., and Bautista, A. J., 'Valuation of Financial Lease Contracts', *Journal of Finance*, **31**, 799–819, Jun. 1976.
Schall, L. D., 'The Lease-or-Buy and Asset Acquisition Decisions', *Journal of Finance*, **29**, 1203–1204, Sep. 1974.
Vancil, R. F., 'Lease or Borrow — New Method of Analysis', *Harvard Business Review*, **39**, 122–136, Sep. 1961.

APPENDIX 20.1 THE EFFECT OF LAGS IN TAX PAYMENTS ON AFTER-TAX DISCOUNT RATES

Frequently, cash flows are paid or received which are deductible for tax purposes. For example, a lease payment is made by a lessee which is deductible for tax purposes. If the tax rate is 50 per cent, the tax advantage is worth £115 for a lease payment totalling £230 and the net cost of the lease payment is only £115. However, this explanation is simplistic in one sense. The tax benefit applying to the lease payment may not be received simultaneously when the lease payment is made. This time lag between the cash outflow (the lease payment) and the tax benefit (the cash inflow) can easily be incorporated into a project appraisal or into a lease evaluation. It is simple to discount the payment and the tax benefit when they actually occur. Tax benefits usually occur when the company pays taxes. In the U.K., a portion of such taxes are paid at the end of the quarter in which dividends are paid and the balance approximately 9 months after the accounting year-end of the company. Providing that the analyst is aware of the details of tax payments, cash flows can be incorporated and discounted appropriately.

However, Hodges (1978) has correctly pointed out that a similar time lag is present for the payment (or receipt) of interest and the receipt of the benefit or tax deduction on interest charges. If a company is using a discount rate that reflects the cost of debt after taxes, then the time lag between the interest payment and the tax payment should be reflected in the discount rate. In our analysis so far, the after-tax discount rate is represented by the following simple equation:

$$r^* = r(1 - T),$$

where r is the before-tax interest rate, T is the tax rate, and r^* is the after-tax interest rate. However, this equation assumes the tax payment is made simultaneously with the interest payment. Usually, there is a lag, and in the U.K. this lag could be as long as 21 months since an accounting year is 12 months and the bulk of taxes are paid 9 months after the end of the accounting year.

For a lag in tax payment of n periods, the after-tax interest rate r^* is given by:

$$r^* = r \left(1 - \frac{T}{(1 + r^*)^n} \right)$$

where r is the pre-tax interest rate and T is the rate of Corporation Tax. The difficulty here is solving for r^* when n is not equal to one. For one period the solution was shown by Hodges (1978) to be

$$r^* = \tfrac{1}{2}\left(-1 + r + \sqrt{(1 + r)^2 - 4Tr}\right).$$

For example, if the pre-tax interest rate (*r*) equals 10 per cent, the after-tax discount rate *r** will be 5.245 per cent (compared with 5 per cent) with a lag in the tax subsidy on interest of 1 year. When *n* is greater than one, a method of successive approximations may be required to obtain *r**.

Clearly, if there is more than one time lag there may be more than one after-tax discount rate (*r**). Furthermore, the effect of the lags will change in the leasing case where one party is in a *temporary* non-tax-paying position.

APPENDIX 20.2 DETERMINATION OF THE VALUE OF TAX BENEFITS *TI*

Franks and Hodges (1978) suggest the following solution to the problem of determining *I*. Let year *N* be the *first* tax-paying period. Determine the cash flows of an equivalent loan as follows:

(a) Discount to period *N* any *subsequent* net payments using the *post-tax* cost of borrowing and combine the result with the period *N* net payments. This establishes the payments pattern of an equivalent loan repayable at the end of period *N*.
(b) Find the total interest charges *I* which would have been paid on the loan. The total interest paid on a loan is equal to the difference between the total undiscounted payments subsequent to period 0 and the total of these payments discounted at the pre-tax borrowing rate. By this means we obtain an initial estimate of the value of *I*. It is only an approximation because we have assumed the term *TI* (tax rate × interest charges carried forward) is equal to zero.
(c) Adjust the value of *I* found in (b) for the initial assumption that *TI* was equal to zero.

Applying these steps to the example of Table 20.2, we find that:

(a) Combining the discounted net payments subsequent to period *N* (i.e. beyond period 2) with period *N* (period 2) payments, we obtain £598.80:

$$598.80 = 385 + \frac{115}{(1 + 0.05)} + \frac{115}{(1 + 0.05)^2}.$$

Thus the payments stream can be summarized as being £230 in period 1 and £598.80 in period 2.
(b) The total interest payments on the value of the lease payments (i.e. equivalent to a loan) through period 2 is the difference between the

undiscounted and the discounted payments:

$$\text{Undiscounted payments} \quad \text{Discounted payments}$$

$$I = (230 + 598.8) - \frac{230}{1 + 0.10} + \frac{598.8}{(1 + 0.10)^2}$$

$$= £124.80.$$

This value of I is only an approximation because the corresponding tax benefits on these accumulated interest charges actually increase the value of the lease to the lessee. If the reader has had enough he may use this value of I (£124.80) in his calculations. If the exact figure is wanted, go on reading.

(c) This initial estimate of I must be adjusted. The adjustment factor is 1.095 (computed below) and I equals £136.70 (124.80 × 1.095).

Calculation of Adjustment Factor F

$$F = 1/ \left(1 - T \left(1 - \frac{1}{(1 + i)^N}\right)\right),$$

where T is the net tax (rate) advantage to borrowing, N is the first tax paying period, and i is the pre-tax interest rate.

This adjustment factor has the effect of finding exactly in only one step the result of an iterative trial and error solution.

Example in Table 20.2

$$F = 1/\left(1 - 0.5\right)\left(1 - \frac{1}{(1 + 0.10)^2}\right)$$
$$= 1.095;$$
$$I = F \times 124.8$$
$$= £136.70.$$

APPENDIX 20.3 BORROWING OPPORTUNITY RATE METHOD (VANCIL)

Since many analysts use another more complex but less precise approach it might be useful to compare the methods. We shall examine the Borrowing Opportunity Rate method originally proposed by Vancil (1961). We have incorporated a number of changes in that method, reflecting current thinking on risk, and we have provided further exposition on the measurement of the debt implicit in the lease.

The basic assumption in this approach is that leasing is equivalent to purchase with 100 per cent debt financing; that is, leasing displaces debt on a pound-for-pound basis. We shall relax this assumption later. Vancil suggests that the lease payments should be discounted by the pre-tax borrowing rate and that the tax benefits should be discounted by an after-tax rate to obtain the net present value of the lease. The net present value of the lease can then be compared with the after-tax cost of purchase.

However, two problems arise. The lease payments consist of the repayment of the loan and interest on the outstanding balance. In addition the lessee obtains tax benefits on the total lease payments (interest plus principal). Since we have not included interest charges in the evaluation of the purchase cost of the asset, we must exclude the interest charges from the lease payments. Similarly, we must establish the value of the lease in order to measure the debt capacity and the consequent tax advantage. Thus a two-stage analysis is required in the Vancil method.

Initially, we discount the lease payments by the pre-tax interest rate; in effect subtracting out the interest charge. Now all that remains is to compute the tax benefits so that they may be deducted from the present value cost of the lease. However, we must estimate the tax benefit not on the total lease payments, but rather only on the repayment portion, that is the tax benefit on the lease repayment net of the imputed interest charges.

Let us use our previous example to demonstrate the method. The gross cost of purchase is £1000 and the initial allowance of 100 per cent is worth £500 assuming a tax rate of 50 per cent. If the tax advantage were received over more than one period, we would discount it at a relatively low rate, reflecting the low risk of the tax allowances. For simplicity, assume it is the company's borrowing rate (10 per cent pre-tax or 5 per cent after taxes). What is the cost of the lease? Let us compute the net present value of the gross lease payments. To do this we discount the lease payments at the gross marginal borrowing rate of 10 per cent in Table 20.A1.

We should subtract the present value of the tax benefits from the present value of the lease payments, but only after excluding the estimated interest charges. In order to estimate the interest charges we must assume a debt

Table 20.A1. The present value of the lease discounted at the pre-tax borrowing rate

Year	Lease payment	Present value discounted at 10 per cent
0	230	230
1	230	209.09
2	230	190.08
3	230	172.80
4	230	157.09
Total Present Value		959.06

repayment schedule. This schedule is analogous to the one adopted by the building society lending money for the purchase of a house. The repayments consist of principal plus interest charges. As each repayment is made, the outstanding balance of the loan is reduced. Vancil does not state how the precise loan schedule is to be estimated, but we shall assume the repayments are constant from year to year; therefore, the repayment of principal increases with time and the interest portion declines with time. (This is not necessarily the precise loan schedule implicit in the lease.)

We shall assume that the lessee borrows an amount equivalent to the value of the lease, which is approximately £959, and repays the loan in five equal annual instalments (the first is made in advance) with an interest rate of 10 per cent. What equal annual instalments would repay the interest and the loan over 4 years? We can solve for the annual instalment using the following expression, where X is equal to the annual payments:

$$X = \frac{\text{Loan}}{\text{Annuity factor for 4 years at 10 per cent}}$$

In our example, the loan is only £729 because £230 is paid immediately. Therefore,

$$X = 729/3.17$$
$$= £230 \text{ (after rounding to nearest whole number).}$$

The interest payments are computed for each period on the outstanding balance of the loan (Table 20.A2).

We can now compute the tax benefits on the loan repayment portion of the lease payments. We discount the tax benefits at a rate that reflects the risk of such inflows, approximated by the pre-tax borrowing rate.

Since the present value of the lease payments is £959, the net cost of the lease is £558.48 after the deduction of the tax benefits (959.06 − 400.58 = 558.48). The result is larger than the cost of purchase, totalling £500, and therefore, the company should purchase.

Table 20.A2. Estimation of interest charges subsumed in the lease payments

Year	Outstanding loan*	Interest portion	Annual payments	Repayment portion
0	729			
1	571.9	72.9	230	157.1
2	399.09	57.19	230	172.81
3	208.999	39.909	230	190.091
4	0	20.8999	230	209.1

*Rounding error

Table 20.A3. The present value of the tax benefits excluding the imputed interest charges

Year	Lease payments	Imputed interest charge	Lease payment – imputed interest charge	Tax benefits at 50 per cent	Present value discounted at 10 per cent
0	230	0	230	115.0	115.00
1	230	72.9	157.1	78.5	71.36
2	230	57.2	172.8	86.4	71.4
3	230	39.9	190.1	95.1	71.45
4	230	20.9	209.1	104.5	71.37
					400.58

Using the Vancil method, the value of the lease to the lessee is −£58.48 (558.48 − 500). In the Myers *et al.* method, we computed a value for the lease of −£22.80, assuming both parties pay taxes. The difference is due to the arbitrary way in which the debt repayment schedule was computed in the Vancil method. If we had computed the exact repayments schedule the answer would have been identical to the Myers *et al.* method. Thus, if we had computed the value of the lease to the lessor using Myers' simple formula, we would have found that the initial loan granted by the lessor to the lessee totalled £407.80, calculated as follows:

Purchase cost of the asset	−1000
100 per cent capital allowance × 50 per cent tax rate	+ 500
Initial lease payment	+ 230
Tax on initial lease payment	− 115
Profit on the lease (V_0)	− 22.8
	−£407.80

It is important to appreciate that the net profit (in present value terms, V_0) is part of the initial loan to the lessee.

Table 20.A4.

Year	Outstanding Loan	Interest portion	Annual payments	Repayment portion
0	407.8			
1	313.2	40.78	135.39	94.61
2	213.8	31.32	130.66	99.34
3	109.5	21.38	125.69	104.31
4	0*	10.95	120.47	109.52

*Rounding error

Table 20.A5. The present value of the tax benefits excluding the imputed interest charges

Year	Lease payments	Imputed interest charge	Lease payment – imputed interest charge	Tax benefits at 50 per cent	Present value discounted at 10 per cent
0	230	0	230	115	115
1	230	40.78	189.22	94.61	86.01
2	230	31.32	198.68	99.34	82.10
3	230	21.38	208.62	104.31	78.37
4	230	10.95	219.05	109.53	74.81
					436.28

We can now calculate the interest charges implicit in the lease payments schedule. Already, in Table 20.4 (page 329) we have calculated the annual repayments schedule, and we may now insert them directly into the column headed 'Annual payment', in Table 20.A4. It is important to note that Vancil recommended a constant (and thus *arbitrary*) repayments schedule.

We can now recompute the present value of the tax benefits as shown in Table 20.A5. The present value of the lease payments is now £522.78 (959.06 − 436.28) compared with the purchase cost of £500 giving a profit to the lessee of £22.78. This is the same as computed earlier under the Myer's method.

What we have tried to show here is that Vancil's method can be used correctly to compare lease versus purchase if, and only if, the exact repayment schedule implicit in the lease used. There are two qualifications. First, in order to find the exact repayment schedule we must use Myers' simple formula. If we are to do this, why use Vancil's method at all? Second, it is difficult to see how Vancil's method would be adapted to *temporary* non-tax-paying periods.

REVIEW QUESTIONS

1. What differences are there between a financial lease and a secured loan? Can a company borrow more, at a given interest rate, using lease finance compared with debt finance?

2. Why has lease financing grown so rapidly during the last decade?

3. Discuss the differences between a fixed and variable rate lease. How would you go about evaluating a variable rate lease?

4. What effect does a rising rate of interest have on the incentive to lease?

EXERCISES

1. A company X (a charity) is in a non-tax-paying position in perpetuity and wishes to purchase an item of equipment totalling £1000. A 100 per cent allowance is normally provided on such equipment. The company is able to borrow at 15 per cent at fixed rates for up to 10 years.

    A lessor offers to lease the equipment for 10 years to the company for an annual rental of £140, payable in advance. The lessor pays Corporation Tax at a rate of 50 per cent with a 12-month lag. In addition, it is able to borrow money from a parent company (a bank) at 12 per cent gross (6 per cent net of taxes) fixed over 10 years.

    (a) Should X lease or buy the equipment?
    (b) How much money is the lessor making from the lease?
    (c) What suggestions could you make in order to increase the profits from leasing to both parties?

2. What difference would it make to your answer in Exercise 20.1(a) if the lessee was in a temporary non-tax-paying position for (i) 1 year, (ii) 2 years.

3. The SBP Company requires a new articulated lorry. They can either buy the lorry for £31 000 or they can lease it for £7212 per annum on a 5-year lease.

    (a) Using both Vancil's and Myers' method of analysis determine which of the two choices is cheapest for SBP. Assume that SBP can borrow at a fixed rate of 10 per cent for the period of the lease and that their tax rate is 50 per cent. The first lease payment is made in advance and the residual value of the lorry is zero at the end of 5 years.
    (b) How would you estimate the residual value of the lorry and incorporate the estimate into the cash flows of leasing and purchase?
    (c) Would you expect the SBP company to be able to lease equipment at a lower cost compared with purchase? Support your answer with appropriate argument.

Appendix A

Future Value Tables

Appendix A. Future value of £1.00

n/i*	1.0	1.5	2.0	2.5	3.0
1	1.01000	1.01500	1.02000	1.02500	1.03000
2	1.02010	1.03022	1.04040	1.05062	1.06090
3	1.03030	1.04568	1.06121	1.07689	1.09273
4	1.04060	1.06136	1.08243	1.10381	1.12551
5	1.05101	1.07728	1.10408	1.13141	1.15927
6	1.06152	1.09344	1.12616	1.15969	1.19405
7	1.07214	1.10984	1.14869	1.18869	1.22987
8	1.08286	1.12649	1.17166	1.21840	1.26677
9	1.09369	1.14339	1.19509	1.24886	1.30477
10	1.10462	1.16054	1.21899	1.28008	1.34392
11	1.11567	1.17795	1.24337	1.31209	1.38423
12	1.12682	1.19562	1.26824	1.34489	1.42576
13	1.13809	1.21355	1.29361	1.37851	1.46853
14	1.14947	1.23176	1.31948	1.41297	1.51259
15	1.16097	1.25023	1.34587	1.44830	1.55797
16	1.17258	1.26899	1.37279	1.48451	1.60471
17	1.18430	1.28802	1.40024	1.52162	1.65285
18	1.19615	1.30734	1.42825	1.55966	1.70243
19	1.20811	1.32695	1.45681	1.59865	1.75351
20	1.22019	1.34685	1.48595	1.63862	1.80611

*n = number of time periods; i = rate of interest in per cent.

n/i	3.5	4.0	4.5	5.0	5.5
1	1.03500	1.04000	1.04500	1.05000	1.05500
2	1.07122	1.08160	1.09202	1.10250	1.11302
3	1.10872	1.12486	1.14117	1.15762	1.17424
4	1.14752	1.16986	1.19252	1.21551	1.23882
5	1.18769	1.21665	1.24618	1.27628	1.30696
6	1.22926	1.26532	1.30226	1.34010	1.37884
7	1.27228	1.31593	1.36086	1.40410	1.45468
8	1.31681	1.36857	1.42210	1.47746	1.53469
9	1.36290	1.42331	1.48609	1.55133	1.61909
10	1.41060	1.48024	1.55297	1.62889	1.70814
11	1.45997	1.53945	1.62285	1.71034	1.80209
12	1.51107	1.60103	1.69588	1.79588	1.90121
13	1.56396	1.66507	1.77220	1.88565	2.00577
14	1.61869	1.73168	1.85194	1.97993	2.11609
15	1.67535	1.80094	1.93528	2.07893	2.23248
16	1.73399	1.87298	2.02237	2.18287	2.35526
17	1.79468	1.94790	2.11338	2.29202	2.48480
18	1.85749	2.02582	2.20848	2.40662	2.62147
19	1.92250	2.10685	2.30786	2.52695	2.76565
20	1.98979	2.19112	2.41171	2.65330	2.91776

Appendix A (*cont'd*). Future value £1.00

n/i	6.0	6.5	7.0	7.5	8.0
1	1.06000	1.06500	1.07000	1.07500	1.8000
2	1.12360	1.13422	1.14490	1.15562	1.16640
3	1.19102	1.20795	1.22504	1.24230	1.25971
4	1.26248	1.28647	1.31080	1.33547	1.36049
5	1.33823	1.37009	1.40255	1.43563	1.46933
6	1.41852	1.45914	1.50073	1.54330	1.58687
7	1.50363	1.55399	1.60578	1.65905	1.71382
8	1.59385	1.65500	1.71819	1.78348	1.85093
9	1.68948	1.76257	1.83846	1.91724	1.99900
10	1.79085	1.87714	1.96715	2.06103	2.15892
11	1.89830	1.99915	2.10485	2.21561	2.33164
12	2.01220	2.12910	2.25219	2.38178	2.51817
13	2.13283	2.26749	2.40984	2.56041	2.71962
14	2.26090	2.41487	2.57853	2.75244	2.93719
15	2.39656	2.57184	2.75903	2.95888	3.17217
16	2.54035	2.73901	2.95216	3.18079	3.42594
17	2.69277	2.91705	3.15881	3.41935	3.70002
18	2.85434	3.10665	3.37993	3.67580	3.99602
19	3.02560	3.30859	3.61653	3.95149	4.31570
20	3.20713	3.52364	3.86968	4.24785	4.66096

343

n/i	8.5	9.0	9.5	10.0	10.5
1	1.08500	1.09000	1.09500	1.10000	1.10500
2	1.17722	1.18810	1.19902	1.21000	1.22102
3	1.27729	1.29503	1.31293	1.33100	1.34923
4	1.38586	1.41158	1.43766	1.46410	1.49090
5	1.50366	1.53862	1.57424	1.61051	1.64745
6	1.63147	1.67710	1.72379	1.77156	1.82043
7	1.77014	1.82804	1.88755	1.94872	2.01157
8	1.92060	1.99256	2.06687	2.14359	2.22279
9	2.08386	2.17189	2.26322	2.35795	2.45618
10	2.26098	2.36736	2.47823	2.59374	2.71408
11	2.45317	2.58043	2.71366	2.85312	2.99906
12	2.66169	2.81266	2.97146	3.13843	3.31396
13	2.88793	3.06580	3.25374	3.45227	3.66193
14	3.13340	3.34173	3.56285	3.79750	4.04643
15	3.39974	3.64248	3.90132	4.17725	4.47130
16	3.68872	3.97030	4.27195	4.59497	4.94079
17	4.00226	4.32763	4.67778	5.05447	5.45957
18	4.34245	4.71712	5.12217	5.55992	6.03283
19	4.71156	5.14166	5.60878	6.11591	6.66627
20	5.11204	5.60441	6.14161	6.72750	7.36623

Appendix A (*cont'd*). Future value of £1.00

n/i	11.0	11.5	12.0	12.5	13.0
1	1.11000	1.11500	1.12000	1.12500	1.13000
2	1.23210	1.24322	1.25440	1.26562	1.27690
3	1.36763	1.38620	1.40493	1.42383	1.44290
4	1.51807	1.54561	1.57352	1.60181	1.63047
5	1.68506	1.72335	1.76234	1.80203	1.84244
6	1.87041	1.92154	1.97382	2.02729	2.08195
7	2.07616	2.14252	2.21068	2.28070	2.35261
8	2.30454	2.38891	2.47596	2.56578	2.65844
9	2.55804	2.66363	2.77308	2.88651	3.00404
10	2.83942	2.96995	3.10585	3.24732	3.39457
11	3.15176	3.31149	3.47855	3.65324	3.83586
12	3.49845	3.69231	3.89598	4.10989	4.33452
13	3.88328	4.11693	4.36349	4.62363	4.89801
14	4.31044	4.59037	4.88711	5.20158	5.53475
15	4.78459	5.11827	5.47356	5.85178	6.25427
16	5.31089	5.70687	6.13039	6.58325	7.06732
17	5.89509	6.36316	6.86604	7.40615	7.98608
18	6.54355	7.09492	7.68996	8.33192	9.02427
19	7.26334	7.91084	8.61276	9.37341	10.19742
20	8.06321	8.82058	9.64629	10.54509	11.52039

n/i	15.5	15.0	14.5	14.0	13.5
1	1.15500	1.15000	1.14500	1.14000	1.13500
2	1.33402	1.32250	1.31102	1.29960	1.28822
3	1.54080	1.52087	1.50112	1.48154	1.46214
4	1.77962	1.74901	1.71879	1.68896	1.65952
5	2.05546	2.01136	1.96801	1.92541	1.88356
6	2.37406	2.31306	2.25337	2.19497	2.13784
7	2.74204	2.66002	2.58011	2.50227	2.42645
8	3.16706	3.05902	2.95423	2.85259	2.75402
9	3.65795	3.51788	3.38259	3.25195	3.12581
10	4.22493	4.04556	3.87306	3.70722	3.54780
11	4.87980	4.65239	4.43466	4.22623	4.02675
12	5.63617	5.35025	5.07768	4.81790	4.57036
13	6.50977	6.15279	5.81395	5.49241	5.18736
14	7.51879	7.07570	6.65697	6.26135	5.88765
15	8.68420	8.13706	7.62223	7.13794	6.68248
16	10.03025	9.35762	8.72746	8.13725	7.58462
17	11.58494	10.76126	9.99294	9.27646	8.60854
18	13.38060	12.37545	11.44191	10.57517	9.77069
19	15.45459	14.23177	13.10099	12.05569	11.08974
20	17.85005	16.36653	15.00063	13.74348	12.58685

Appendix A (*cont'd*). Future value of £1.00

n/i	16.0	17.0	18.0	19.0	20.0
1	1.16000	1.17000	1.18000	1.19000	1.20000
2	1.34560	1.36890	1.39240	1.41610	1.44000
3	1.56090	1.60161	1.64303	1.68516	1.72800
4	1.81064	1.87389	1.93878	2.00534	2.07360
5	2.10034	2.19245	2.28776	2.38635	2.48832
6	2.43640	2.56516	2.69955	2.83976	2.98598
7	2.82622	3.00124	3.18547	3.37931	3.58318
8	3.27841	3.51145	3.75886	4.02138	4.29982
9	3.80296	4.10840	4.43545	4.78545	5.15978
10	4.41143	4.80683	5.23383	5.69468	6.19173
11	5.11726	5.62399	6.17592	6.77667	7.43008
12	5.93603	6.58007	7.28759	8.06424	8.91610
13	6.88579	7.69868	8.59936	9.59645	10.69932
14	7.98752	9.00745	10.14724	11.41977	12.83918
15	9.26552	10.53872	11.97374	13.58953	15.40701
16	10.74800	12.33030	14.12902	16.17154	18.48842
17	12.46768	14.42645	16.67224	19.24413	22.18610
18	14.46251	16.87895	19.67324	22.90051	26.62332
19	16.77651	19.74837	23.21443	27.25161	31.94798
20	19.46075	23.10559	27.39302	32.42941	38.33758

n/i	21.0	22.0	23.0	24.0	25.0
1	1.21000	1.22000	1.23000	1.24000	1.25000
2	1.46410	1.48840	1.51290	1.53760	1.56250
3	1.77156	1.81585	1.86087	1.90662	1.95312
4	2.14359	2.21533	2.28887	2.36421	2.44141
5	2.59374	2.70271	2.81531	2.93162	3.05176
6	3.13843	3.29730	3.46283	3.63521	3.81470
7	3.79750	4.02271	4.25928	4.50767	4.76837
8	4.59497	4.90771	5.23891	5.58951	5.96046
9	5.55992	5.98740	6.44386	6.93099	7.45058
10	6.72750	7.30436	7.92594	8.59442	9.31322
11	8.14027	8.91165	9.74891	10.65708	11.64153
12	9.84973	10.87221	11.99116	13.21478	14.55191
13	11.91817	13.26410	14.74913	16.38633	18.18989
14	14.42099	16.18220	18.14143	20.31905	22.73736
15	17.44940	19.74228	22.31395	25.19562	28.42170
16	21.11377	24.08558	27.44616	31.24257	35.52712
17	27.54766	29.38441	33.75878	38.74078	44.40890
18	30.91267	35.84857	41.52330	48.03857	55.51113
19	37.40433	43.73575	51.07365	59.56783	69.38891
20	45.25924	53.35716	62.82059	73.86410	86.73613

Appendix A (*cont'd*). Future value of £1.00

n/i	26.0	27.0	28.0	29.0	30.0
1	1.26000	1.27000	1.28000	1.29000	1.30000
2	1.58760	1.61290	1.63840	1.66410	1.69000
3	2.00038	2.04838	2.09715	2.14669	2.19700
4	2.52047	2.60145	2.68435	2.76923	2.85610
5	3.17580	3.30384	3.43597	3.57230	3.71293
6	4.00150	4.19587	4.39805	4.60827	4.82681
7	5.04189	5.32876	5.62950	5.94467	6.27485
8	6.35279	6.76752	7.20576	7.66863	8.15730
9	8.00451	8.59475	9.22337	9.89253	10.60450
10	10.08568	10.91533	11.80591	12.76136	13.78584
11	12.70796	13.86247	15.11157	16.46215	17.92160
12	16.01203	17.60534	19.34280	21.23618	23.29807
13	20.17515	22.35878	24.75679	27.39467	30.28749
14	25.42069	28.39565	31.69125	35.33912	39.37374
15	32.03007	36.06248	40.56480	45.58746	51.18586
16	40.35789	45.79935	51.92294	58.80783	55.54161
17	50.85094	58.16517	66.46136	75.86209	86.50410
18	64.07218	73.86976	85.07053	97.86210	112.45532
19	80.73095	93.81460	108.89028	126.24210	146.19191
20	101.72099	110.14453	139.37955	162.85230	190.04947

n/i	31.0	32.0	33.0	34.0	35.0
1	1.31000	1.32000	1.33000	1.34000	1.35000
2	1.71610	1.74240	1.76890	1.79560	1.82250
3	2.24809	2.29997	2.35264	2.40610	2.46037
4	2.94500	3.03596	3.12091	3.22418	3.32151
5	3.85795	4.00746	4.16158	4.32040	4.48403
6	5.05391	5.28985	5.53490	5.78933	6.05344
7	6.62062	6.98260	7.36142	7.75771	8.17215
8	8.67302	9.21704	9.79068	10.39533	11.03240
9	11.36165	12.16649	13.02161	13.92974	14.89374
10	14.88376	16.05976	17.31874	18.66585	20.10655
11	19.49773	21.19889	23.03392	20.01224	27.14384
12	25.54203	27.98253	30.63511	33.51640	36.64418
13	33.46005	36.93694	40.74470	44.91197	49.46964
14	43.83267	48.75675	54.19045	60.18204	66.78401
15	57.42079	64.35891	72.07329	80.64393	90.15841
16	75.22124	84.95376	95.85748	108.06286	121.71385
17	98.53982	112.13896	127.49044	144.80422	164.31370
18	129.08716	148.02342	169.56228	194.03765	221.82348
19	169.10417	195.39090	225.51782	260.01044	299.46169
20	221.52645	257.91598	299.93869	348.41398	404.27326

350

Appendix A (*cont'd*). Future value of £1.00

n/i	36.0	37.0	38.0	39.0	40.0
1	1.36000	1.37000	1.38000	1.39000	1.40000
2	1.84960	1.87690	1.90440	1.93210	1.96000
3	2.51546	2.57135	2.62807	2.68562	2.74400
4	3.42102	3.52275	3.62674	3.73301	3.84160
5	4.65259	4.82617	5.00490	5.10888	5.37824
6	6.32752	6.61185	6.90676	7.21522	7.52953
7	8.60542	9.05824	9.53133	10.02455	10.54135
8	11.70337	12.40979	13.15323	13.93536	14.75788
9	15.91659	17.00141	18.15146	19.37015	20.66104
10	21.64656	23.29193	25.04901	26.92451	28.92545
11	29.43932	31.90994	34.56754	37.42507	40.49563
12	40.03747	43.71662	47.70334	52.02084	56.69388
13	54.45096	59.89177	65.83060	72.30897	79.37142
14	74.05330	82.05172	90.84623	100.50946	111.11999
15	100.71248	112.41085	125.36779	139.70814	155.56797
16	136.96897	154.00285	173.00754	194.19431	217.79515
17	186.27779	210.98390	238.75039	269.93007	304.91319
18	253.33778	289.04792	329.47552	375.20278	426.87845
19	344.53936	395.99564	454.67620	521.53185	597.62980
20	468.57351	452.51400	627.45312	724.92923	836.68167

Appendix B

Present Value Tables

Appendix B. Present value of £1.00 due at the end of n years*

n	1%	2%	3%	4%	5%
1	0.99010	0.98039	0.97007	0.96154	0.95238
2	0.98030	0.96117	0.94260	0.92456	0.90703
3	0.97059	0.94232	0.91514	0.88900	0.86384
4	0.96098	0.92385	0.88849	0.85480	0.82270
5	0.95147	0.90573	0.86261	0.82193	0.78353
6	0.94204	0.88797	0.83748	0.79031	0.74622
7	0.93272	0.87056	0.81309	0.75992	0.71068
8	0.92348	0.85349	0.78941	0.73069	0.67684
9	0.91434	0.83675	0.76642	0.70259	0.64461
10	0.90529	0.82035	0.74409	0.67556	0.61391
11	0.89632	0.80426	0.72242	0.64958	0.58468
12	0.88745	0.78849	0.70138	0.62460	0.55684
13	0.87866	0.77303	0.68095	0.60057	0.53032
14	0.86996	0.75787	0.66112	0.57747	0.50507
15	0.86135	0.74301	0.64186	0.55526	0.48102
16	0.85282	0.72845	0.62317	0.53391	0.45811
17	0.84438	0.71416	0.60502	0.51337	0.43630
18	0.83602	0.70016	0.58739	0.49363	0.41552
19	0.82774	0.68643	0.57029	0.47464	0.39573
20	0.81954	0.67297	0.55367	0.45639	0.37689
21	0.81143	0.65978	0.53755	0.43883	0.35894
22	0.80340	0.64684	0.52189	0.42195	0.34185
23	0.79544	0.63414	0.50669	0.40573	0.32557
24	0.78757	0.62172	0.49193	0.39012	0.31007
25	0.77977	0.60953	0.47760	0.37512	0.29530

*$PV = £1/(1 + r)^n$.

n	6%	7%	8%	9%	10%
1	0.94340	0.93458	0.92593	0.91743	0.90909
2	0.89000	0.87344	0.85734	0.84168	0.82645
3	0.83962	0.81630	0.79383	0.77218	0.75131
4	0.79209	0.76290	0.73503	0.70843	0.68301
5	0.74726	0.71299	0.68058	0.64993	0.62092
6	0.70496	0.66634	0.63017	0.59627	0.56447
7	0.66506	0.62275	0.58349	0.54703	0.51316
8	0.62741	0.58201	0.54027	0.50187	0.46651
9	0.59190	0.54393	0.50025	0.46043	0.42410
10	0.55839	0.50835	0.46319	0.42241	0.38554
11	0.52679	0.47509	0.42888	0.38753	0.35049
12	0.49697	0.44401	0.39711	0.35553	0.31863
13	0.46884	0.41496	0.36770	0.32618	0.28966
14	0.44230	0.38782	0.34046	0.29925	0.26333
15	0.41726	0.36245	0.31524	0.27454	0.23939
16	0.39365	0.33873	0.29189	0.25187	0.21763
17	0.37136	0.31657	0.27027	0.23107	0.19784
18	0.35034	0.29586	0.25025	0.21199	0.17986
19	0.33051	0.27651	0.23171	0.19449	0.16351
20	0.31180	0.25842	0.21455	0.17843	0.14864
21	0.29415	0.24151	0.19866	0.16370	0.13513
22	0.27750	0.22571	0.18394	0.15018	0.12285
23	0.26180	0.21095	0.17031	0.13778	0.11168
24	0.24698	0.19715	0.15770	0.12640	0.10153
25	0.23300	0.18425	0.14602	0.11597	0.09230

Appendix B (*cont'd*). Present value of £1.00 due at the end of *n* years

n	11%	12%	13%	14%	15%
1	0.90090	0.89286	0.88496	0.87719	0.86957
2	0.81162	0.79719	0.78315	0.76947	0.75614
3	0.73119	0.71178	0.69305	0.67497	0.65752
4	0.65873	0.63552	0.61332	0.59208	0.57175
5	0.59345	0.56743	0.54276	0.51937	0.49718
6	0.53464	0.50663	0.48032	0.45559	0.43233
8	0.48166	0.45235	0.42506	0.39964	0.37594
8	0.43393	0.40388	0.37616	0.35056	0.32690
9	0.39092	0.36061	0.33288	0.30751	0.28426
10	0.35218	0.32197	0.29459	0.26974	0.24718
11	0.31728	0.28748	0.26070	0.23662	0.21494
12	0.28584	0.25667	0.23071	0.20756	0.18691
13	0.25751	0.22917	0.20416	0.18207	0.16253
14	0.23199	0.20462	0.18068	0.15971	0.14133
15	0.20900	0.18270	0.15989	0.14010	0.12289
16	0.18829	0.16312	0.14150	0.12289	0.10686
17	0.16963	0.14564	0.12522	0.10780	0.09393
18	0.15282	0.13004	0.11081	0.09456	0.08080
19	0.13768	0.11611	0.09806	0.08295	0.07026
20	0.12403	0.10367	0.08678	0.07276	0.06110
21	0.11174	0.09256	0.07680	0.06383	0.05313
22	0.10067	0.08264	0.06796	0.05599	0.04620
23	0.09069	0.07379	0.06014	0.04911	0.04017
24	0.08170	0.06588	0.05322	0.04308	0.03493
25	0.07361	0.05882	0.04710	0.03779	0.03038

n	16%	17%	18%	19%	20%
1	0.86207	0.85470	0.84746	0.84034	0.83333
2	0.74316	0.73051	0.71818	0.70616	0.69444
3	0.64066	0.62437	0.60863	0.59342	0.57870
4	0.55229	0.53365	0.51579	0.49867	0.48225
5	0.47611	0.45611	0.43711	0.41905	0.40188
6	0.41044	0.38984	0.37043	0.35214	0.33490
7	0.35383	0.33320	0.31392	0.29592	0.27908
8	0.30503	0.28487	0.26604	0.24867	0.23257
9	0.26295	0.24340	0.22546	0.20897	0.19381
10	0.22668	0.20804	0.19106	0.17560	0.16151
11	0.19542	0.17781	0.16192	0.14756	0.13459
12	0.16846	0.15197	0.13722	0.12400	0.11216
13	0.14523	0.12989	0.11629	0.10420	0.09346
14	0.12520	0.11102	0.09855	0.08757	0.07789
15	0.10793	0.09489	0.08352	0.07359	0.06491
16	0.09304	0.08110	0.07078	0.06184	0.05409
17	0.08021	0.06932	0.05998	0.05196	0.04507
18	0.06914	0.05925	0.05083	0.04367	0.03756
19	0.05961	0.05064	0.04308	0.03669	0.03130
20	0.05139	0.04328	0.03651	0.03084	0.02608
21	0.04430	0.03699	0.03094	0.02591	0.02174
22	0.03819	0.03162	0.02622	0.02178	0.01811
23	0.03292	0.02702	0.02222	0.01830	0.01509
24	0.02838	0.02310	0.01883	0.01538	0.01258
25	0.02447	0.01974	0.01596	0.01292	0.01048

Appendix B (*cont'd*). Present value of £1.00 due at the end of *n* years

n	21%	22%	23%	24%	25%
1	0.82645	0.81967	0.81301	0.80645	0.80000
2	0.68301	0.67186	0.66098	0.65036	0.64000
3	0.56447	0.55071	0.53738	0.52449	0.51200
4	0.46651	0.45140	0.43690	0.42297	0.40960
5	0.38554	0.37000	0.35520	0.34111	0.32768
6	0.31863	0.30328	0.28878	0.27509	0.26214
7	0.26333	0.24859	0.23478	0.22184	0.20972
8	0.21763	0.20376	0.19088	0.17891	0.16777
9	0.17986	0.16702	0.15519	0.14428	0.13422
10	0.14864	0.13690	0.12617	0.11635	0.10737
11	0.12285	0.11221	0.10258	0.09383	0.08590
12	0.10153	0.09198	0.08339	0.07567	0.06872
13	0.08391	0.07539	0.06780	0.06103	0.05498
14	0.06934	0.06180	0.05512	0.04921	0.04398
15	0.05731	0.05065	0.04481	0.03969	0.03518
16	0.04736	0.04152	0.03643	0.03201	0.02815
17	0.03914	0.03403	0.02962	0.02581	0.02252
18	0.03235	0.02789	0.02408	0.02082	0.01801
19	0.02673	0.02286	0.01958	0.01679	0.01441
20	0.02209	0.01874	0.01592	0.01354	0.01153
21	0.01826	0.01536	0.01294	0.01092	0.00922
22	0.01509	0.01259	0.01052	0.00880	0.00738
23	0.01247	0.01032	0.00855	0.00710	0.00590
24	0.01031	0.00846	0.00695	0.00573	0.00472
25	0.00852	0.00693	0.00565	0.00462	0.00378

n	30%	29%	28%	27%	26%
1	0.76923	0.77519	0.78125	0.78740	0.79365
2	0.59172	0.60093	0.61035	0.62000	0.62988
3	0.45517	0.46583	0.47684	0.48819	0.49991
4	0.35013	0.36111	0.37253	0.38440	0.39675
5	0.26933	0.27993	0.29104	0.30268	0.31488
6	0.20718	0.21700	0.22737	0.23833	0.24991
7	0.15937	0.16822	0.17764	0.18766	0.19834
8	0.12259	0.13040	0.13878	0.14776	0.15741
9	0.09430	0.10109	0.10842	0.11635	0.12493
10	0.07254	0.07836	0.08470	0.09161	0.09915
11	0.05580	0.06075	0.06617	0.07214	0.07869
12	0.04292	0.04709	0.05170	0.05680	0.06245
13	0.03302	0.03650	0.04039	0.04472	0.04957
14	0.02540	0.02830	0.03155	0.03522	0.03934
15	0.01954	0.02194	0.02465	0.02773	0.03122
16	0.01503	0.01700	0.01926	0.02183	0.02478
17	0.01156	0.01318	0.01505	0.01719	0.01967
18	0.00889	0.01022	0.01175	0.01354	0.01561
19	0.00684	0.00792	0.00918	0.01066	0.01239
20	0.00526	0.00614	0.00717	0.00839	0.00983
21	0.00405	0.00476	0.00561	0.00661	0.00780
22	0.00311	0.00369	0.00438	0.00520	0.00619
23	0.00239	0.00286	0.00342	0.00410	0.00491
24	0.00184	0.00222	0.00267	0.00323	0.00390
25	0.00152	0.00172	0.00209	0.00254	0.00310

Appendix B (*cont'd*). Present value of £1.00 due at the end of *n* years

n	31%	32%	33%	34%	35%
1	0.76336	0.75758	0.75188	0.74627	0.74074
2	0.58272	0.57392	0.56532	0.55692	0.54870
3	0.44482	0.43479	0.42505	0.41561	0.40644
4	0.33956	0.32939	0.31959	0.31016	0.30107
5	0.25920	0.24953	0.24029	0.23146	0.22301
6	0.19787	0.18904	0.18067	0.17273	0.16520
7	0.15104	0.14321	0.13584	0.12890	0.12237
8	0.11530	0.10849	0.10214	0.09620	0.09064
9	0.08802	0.08219	0.07680	0.07179	0.06714
10	0.06719	0.06227	0.05774	0.05357	0.04973
11	0.05129	0.04717	0.04341	0.03998	0.03684
12	0.03915	0.03574	0.03264	0.02984	0.02729
13	0.02989	0.02707	0.02454	0.02227	0.02021
14	0.02281	0.02051	0.01845	0.01662	0.01497
15	0.01742	0.01554	0.01387	0.01240	0.01109
16	0.01329	0.01177	0.01043	0.00925	0.00822
17	0.01015	0.00892	0.00784	0.00691	0.00609
18	0.00775	0.00676	0.00590	0.00515	0.00451
19	0.00591	0.00512	0.00443	0.00385	0.00334
20	0.00451	0.00388	0.00333	0.00287	0.00247
21	0.00345	0.00294	0.00251	0.00214	0.00183
22	0.00263	0.00223	0.00188	0.00160	0.00136
23	0.00201	0.00169	0.00142	0.00119	0.00101
24	0.00153	0.00128	0.00107	0.00089	0.00074
25	0.00117	0.00097	0.00080	0.00066	0.00055

n	36%	37%	38%	39%	40%
1	0.73529	0.72993	0.72464	0.71942	0.71429
2	0.54066	0.53279	0.52510	0.51757	0.51020
3	0.39754	0.38890	0.38051	0.37235	0.36443
4	0.29231	0.28387	0.27573	0.26788	0.26031
5	0.21493	0.20720	0.19980	0.19272	0.18593
6	0.15804	0.15124	0.14479	0.13865	0.13281
7	0.11621	0.11040	0.10492	0.09975	0.09486
8	0.08545	0.08058	0.07603	0.07176	0.06776
9	0.06283	0.05882	0.05509	0.05163	0.04840
10	0.04620	0.04293	0.03992	0.03714	0.03457
11	0.03397	0.03134	0.02893	0.02672	0.02469
12	0.02498	0.02287	0.02096	0.01922	0.01764
13	0.01837	0.01670	0.01519	0.01383	0.01260
14	0.01350	0.01219	0.01101	0.00995	0.00900
15	0.00993	0.00890	0.00798	0.00716	0.00643
16	0.00730	0.00649	0.00578	0.00515	0.00459
17	0.00537	0.00474	0.00419	0.00370	0.00328
18	0.00395	0.00346	0.00304	0.00267	0.00234
19	0.00290	0.00253	0.00220	0.00192	0.00167
20	0.00213	0.00184	0.00159	0.00138	0.00120
21	0.00157	0.00135	0.00115	0.00099	0.00085
22	0.00115	0.00098	0.00084	0.00071	0.00061
23	0.00085	0.00072	0.00061	0.00051	0.00044
24	0.00062	0.00052	0.00044	0.00037	0.00031
25	0.00046	0.00038	0.00032	0.00027	0.00022

Appendix C

Annuity Tables

Appendix C. Present value of an annuity of £1.00 for n years*

n	1%	2%	3%	4%	5%
1	0.9901	0.9804	0.9709	0.9615	0.9524
2	1.9704	1.9416	1.9135	1.8861	1.8594
3	2.9410	2.8839	2.8286	2.7751	2.7232
4	3.9020	3.8077	3.7171	3.6299	3.5459
5	4.8535	4.7134	4.5797	4.4518	4.3295
6	5.7955	5.6014	5.4172	5.2421	5.0757
7	6.7282	6.4720	6.2302	6.0020	5.7863
8	7.6517	7.3254	7.0196	6.7327	6.4632
9	8.5661	8.1622	7.7861	7.4353	7.1078
10	9.4714	8.9825	8.5302	8.1109	7.7217
11	10.3677	9.7868	9.2526	8.7604	8.3064
12	11.2552	10.5753	9.9539	9.3850	8.8632
13	12.1338	11.3483	10.6349	9.9856	9.3935
14	13.0038	12.1062	11.2960	10.5631	9.8986
15	13.8651	12.8492	11.9379	11.1183	10.3796
16	14.7180	13.5777	12.5610	11.6522	10.8377
17	15.5624	14.2918	13.1660	12.1656	11.2740
18	16.3984	14.9920	13.7534	12.6592	11.6895
19	17.2261	15.6784	14.3237	13.1339	12.0853
20	18.0457	16.3514	14.8774	13.5903	12.4622
21	18.8571	17.0111	15.4149	14.0291	12.8211
22	19.6605	17.6580	15.9368	14.4511	13.1630
23	20.4559	18.2921	16.4435	14.8568	13.4885
24	21.2435	18.9139	16.9355	15.2469	13.7986
25	22.0233	19.5234	17.4131	15.6220	14.0939

* $A_{n,r} = \{1 - 1/(1 + r)^n\}/r$.

n	6%	7%	8%	9%	10%
1	0.9434	0.9346	0.9259	0.9174	0.9091
2	1.8334	1.8080	1.7833	1.7591	1.7355
3	2.6730	2.6243	2.5771	2.5313	2.4868
4	3.4651	3.3872	3.3121	3.2397	3.1699
5	4.2123	4.1002	3.9927	3.8896	3.7908
6	4.9173	4.7665	4.6229	4.4859	4.3553
7	5.5824	5.3893	5.2064	5.0329	4.8684
8	6.2098	5.9713	5.7466	5.5348	5.3349
9	6.8017	6.5152	6.2469	5.9852	5.7590
10	7.3601	7.0236	6.7101	6.4176	6.1446
11	7.8868	7.4987	7.1389	6.8052	6.4951
12	8.3838	7.9427	7.5361	7.1607	6.8137
13	8.8527	8.3576	7.9038	7.4869	7.1034
14	9.2950	8.7454	8.2442	7.7861	7.3667
15	9.7122	9.1079	8.5595	8.0607	7.6061
16	10.1059	9.4466	8.8514	8.3125	7.8237
17	10.4772	9.7632	9.1216	8.5436	8.0215
18	10.8276	10.0591	9.3719	8.7556	8.2014
19	11.1581	10.3356	9.6036	8.9501	8.3649
20	11.4699	10.5940	9.8181	9.1285	8.5136
21	11.7640	10.8355	10.0168	9.2922	8.6487
22	12.0416	11.0612	10.2007	9.4424	8.7715
23	12.3033	11.2722	10.3710	9.5802	8.8832
24	12.5503	11.4693	10.5287	9.7066	8.9847
25	12.7833	11.6536	10.6748	9.8226	9.0770

Appendix C (*cont'd*). Present value of an annuity of £1.00 for *n* years

n	11%	12%	13%	14%	15%
1	0.0009	0.8929	0.8850	0.3772	0.8696
2	1.7125	1.6901	1.6681	1.6467	1.6257
3	2.4437	2.4018	2.3612	2.3216	2.2832
4	3.1024	3.0373	2.9745	2.9137	2.8550
5	3.6959	3.6048	3.5172	3.4331	3.3522
6	4.2305	4.1114	3.9976	3.8887	3.7845
7	4.7122	4.5638	4.4226	4.2883	4.1604
8	5.1461	4.9676	4.7988	4.6389	4.4873
9	5.5370	5.3282	5.1317	4.9464	4.7716
10	5.8892	5.6502	5.4262	5.2161	5.0188
11	6.2065	5.9377	5.6869	5.4527	5.2337
12	6.4924	6.1944	5.9176	5.6603	5.4206
13	6.7499	6.4235	6.1218	5.8424	5.5931
14	6.9819	6.6282	6.3025	6.0021	5.7245
15	7.1909	6.8109	6.4624	6.1422	5.8474
16	7.3792	6.9740	6.6039	6.2651	5.9542
17	7.5488	7.1196	6.7291	6.3729	6.0472
18	7.7016	7.2497	6.8399	6.4674	6.1280
19	7.8393	7.3658	6.9380	6.5504	6.1982
20	7.9633	7.4694	7.0248	6.6231	6.2593
21	8.0751	7.5620	7.1016	6.6870	6.3125
22	8.1757	7.6446	7.1695	6.7429	6.3587
23	8.2664	7.7184	7.2297	6.7921	6.3988
24	8.3481	7.7843	7.2829	6.8351	6.4338
25	8.4217	7.8431	7.3300	6.8729	6.4641

n	16%	17%	18%	19%	20%
1	0.8621	0.8547	0.8475	0.8403	0.8333
2	1.6052	1.5852	1.5656	1.5465	1.5278
3	2.2459	2.2096	2.1743	2.1399	2.1065
4	2.7982	2.7432	2.6901	2.6386	2.5887
5	3.2743	3.1993	3.1272	3.0576	2.9906
6	3.6847	3.5892	3.4976	3.4098	3.3255
7	4.0386	3.9224	3.8115	3.7057	3.6046
8	4.3436	4.2072	4.0776	3.9544	3.8372
9	4.6065	4.4506	4.3030	4.1633	4.0310
10	4.8332	4.6586	4.4941	4.3389	4.1925
11	5.0286	4.8364	4.6560	4.4865	4.3271
12	5.1971	4.9884	4.7932	4.6105	4.4392
13	5.3423	5.1183	4.9095	4.7147	4.5327
14	5.4675	5.2293	5.0081	4.8023	4.6106
15	5.5755	5.3242	5.0916	4.8759	4.6755
16	5.6685	5.4053	5.1624	4.9377	4.7296
17	5.7487	5.4746	5.2223	4.9897	4.7746
18	5.8178	5.5339	5.2732	5.0333	4.8122
19	5.8775	5.5845	5.3162	5.0700	4.8435
20	5.9288	5.6278	5.3527	5.1009	4.8696
21	5.9731	5.6648	5.3837	5.1268	4.8913
22	6.0113	5.6964	5.4099	5.1486	4.9094
23	6.0442	5.7234	5.4321	5.1668	4.9245
24	6.0726	5.7465	5.4509	5.1822	4.9371
25	6.0971	5.7662	5.4669	5.1951	4.9476

Appendix C (*cont'd*). Present value of an annuity of £1.00 for *n* years

n	21%	22%	23%	24%	25%
1	0.8264	0.8197	0.8130	0.8065	0.8000
2	1.5095	1.4915	1.4740	1.4568	1.4400
3	2.0739	2.0422	2.0114	1.9813	1.9520
4	2.5404	2.4936	2.4483	2.4043	2.3616
5	2.9260	2.8636	2.8035	2.7454	2.6893
6	3.2446	3.1669	3.0923	3.0205	2.9514
7	3.5079	3.4155	3.3270	3.2423	3.1611
8	3.7256	3.6193	3.5179	3.4212	3.3289
9	3.9054	3.7863	3.6731	3.5655	3.4631
10	4.0541	3.9232	3.7993	3.6819	3.5705
11	4.1769	4.0354	3.9018	3.7757	3.6564
12	4.2785	4.1274	3.9852	3.8514	3.7251
13	4.3624	4.2028	4.0530	3.9124	3.7801
14	4.4317	4.2646	4.1082	3.9616	3.8241
15	4.4890	4.3152	4.1530	4.0013	3.8593
16	4.5364	4.3567	4.1894	4.0333	3.8874
17	4.5755	4.3908	4.2190	4.0591	3.9099
18	4.6079	4.4187	4.2431	4.0799	3.9279
19	4.6346	4.4415	4.2627	4.0967	3.9424
20	4.6567	4.4603	4.2786	4.1103	3.9539
21	4.6750	4.4756	4.2916	4.1212	3.9631
22	4.6900	4.4882	4.3021	4.1300	3.9705
23	4.7025	4.4985	4.3106	4.1371	3.9764
24	4.7128	4.5070	4.3176	4.1428	3.9811
25	4.7213	4.5139	4.3232	4.1474	3.9849

n	26%	27%	28%	29%	30%
1	0.7937	0.7874	0.7813	0.7752	0.7692
2	1.4235	1.4074	1.3916	1.3761	1.3609
3	1.9234	1.8956	1.8684	1.8420	1.8161
4	2.3202	2.2800	2.2410	2.2031	2.1662
5	2.6351	2.5827	2.5320	2.4830	2.4356
6	2.8850	2.8210	2.7594	2.7000	2.6427
7	3.0833	3.0087	2.9370	2.8682	2.8021
8	3.2407	3.1564	3.0758	2.9986	2.9247
9	3.3657	3.2728	3.1842	3.0997	3.0190
10	3.4648	3.3644	3.2689	3.1781	3.0915
11	3.5435	3.4365	3.3351	3.2388	3.1473
12	3.6060	3.4933	3.3868	3.2859	3.1903
13	3.6555	3.5381	3.4272	3.3224	3.2233
14	3.6949	3.5733	3.4587	3.3507	3.2487
15	3.7261	3.6010	3.4834	3.3726	3.2682
16	3.7509	3.6228	3.5026	3.3896	3.2832
17	3.7705	3.6400	3.5177	3.4028	3.2948
18	3.7861	3.6536	3.5294	3.4130	3.3037
19	3.7985	3.6642	3.5386	3.4210	3.3105
20	3.8083	3.6726	3.5458	3.4271	3.3158
21	3.8161	3.6792	3.5514	3.4319	3.3198
22	3.8223	3.6844	3.5558	3.4356	3.3230
23	3.8273	3.6885	3.5592	3.4384	3.3254
24	3.8312	3.6918	3.5619	3.4406	3.3272
25	3.8342	3.6943	3.5640	3.4423	3.3286

Appendix C (*cont'd*). Present value of an annuity of £1.00 for *n* years

n	31%	32%	33%	35%	35%
1	0.7634	0.7576	0.7519	0.7463	0.7407
2	1.3461	1.3315	1.3172	1.3032	1.2894
3	1.7909	1.7663	1.7423	1.7188	1.6959
4	2.1305	2.0957	2.0618	2.0290	1.9969
5	2.3897	2.3452	2.3021	2.2604	2.2200
6	2.5875	2.5342	2.4828	2.4331	2.3852
7	2.7386	2.6775	2.6187	2.5620	2.5075
8	2.8539	2.7860	2.7208	2.6582	2.5982
9	2.9419	2.8681	2.7976	2.7300	2.6653
10	3.0091	2.9304	2.8553	2.7836	2.7150
11	3.0604	2.9776	2.8987	2.8236	2.7519
12	3.0995	3.0133	2.9314	2.8534	2.7792
13	3.1294	3.0404	2.9559	2.8757	2.7994
14	3.1522	3.0609	2.9744	2.8923	2.8144
15	3.1696	3.0764	2.9883	2.9047	2.8255
16	3.1829	3.0882	2.9987	2.9140	2.8337
17	3.1931	3.0971	3.0065	2.9209	2.8398
18	3.2008	3.1039	3.0124	2.9260	2.8443
19	3.2067	3.1090	3.0169	2.9299	2.8476
20	3.2112	3.1129	3.0202	2.9327	2.8501
21	3.2174	3.1158	3.0227	2.9349	2.8519
22	3.2173	3.1180	3.0246	2.9365	2.8533
23	3.2193	3.1197	3.0260	2.9377	2.8543
24	3.2209	3.1210	3.0271	2.9386	2.8550
25	3.2220	3.1220	3.0279	2.9392	2.8556

n	36%	37%	38%	39%	40%
1	0.7353	0.7299	0.7246	0.7194	0.7143
2	1.2760	1.2627	1.2497	1.2370	1.2245
3	1.6735	1.6516	1.6302	1.6093	1.5889
4	1.9658	1.9355	1.9060	1.8772	1.8492
5	2.1807	2.1427	2.1058	2.0699	1.9352
6	2.3388	2.2936	2.2506	2.2086	2.1680
7	2.4550	2.4043	2.3555	2.3083	2.2628
8	2.5404	2.4849	2.4315	2.3801	2.3306
9	2.6033	2.5437	2.4866	2.4317	2.3790
10	2.6495	2.5867	2.5265	2.4689	2.4136
11	2.6834	2.6180	2.5555	2.4956	2.4383
12	2.7084	2.6409	2.5764	2.5148	2.4559
13	2.7268	2.6576	2.5916	2.5286	2.4685
14	2.7403	2.6698	2.6026	2.5386	2.4775
15	2.7502	2.6787	2.6106	2.5457	2.4839
16	2.7575	2.6852	2.6164	2.5509	2.4885
17	2.7629	2.6899	2.6202	2.5546	2.4918
18	2.7668	2.6934	2.6236	2.5573	2.4941
19	2.7697	2.6959	2.6258	2.5592	2.4958
20	2.7718	2.6977	2.6274	2.5606	2.4970
21	2.7734	2.6991	2.6285	2.5616	2.4979
22	2.7746	2.7000	2.6294	2.5623	2.4985
23	2.7754	2.7008	2.6300	2.5628	2.4989
24	2.7760	2.7013	2.6304	2.5632	2.4992
25	2.7765	2.7017	2.6307	2.5634	2.4994

INDEX

Note: See also detailed summary of book in Contents, pp. ix–xv.

abandonment decision, 89–90
ABC analysis, 255–6
account periods, 171–2
accountants, 13
Accounting Rate of Return, 37–9,
   140–42
accounting ratios, 224, 227–33
acquirees, 185
acquirers, 185
acquisitions, *see* mergers
Adjusted Present Value method,
   308–11, 312–13
administrative expenses, 243
Advanced Corporation Tax, 43,163,164
adversity, 218
age classification, 248–9
Alexander, S. S., 176
alternatives, 80
Altman, E. I., 232
analysis, financial, 14–15
announcement date of merger, 186
annuities, 26–8
annuity factor, 27, 87–8

balancing charge, 35
bank borrowing, 11, 12–13, 221–37
bank lending, 313
bank overdrafts, 204
bank references, 247
bankruptcy, 187, 188, 211, 244
barriers to entry, 52
Base Rate, 221–2, 233
Bautista, A. J., 322, 328
Beaver, W. H., 232
benefits, tax, 306–15, 322, 323
benefits of merger, 186–7, 189

beta coefficient, 104, 301–2
beta risk, *see* systematic risk
biased forecasting, 37, 81
bid premium, 189, 190
bid prospects, 189
Black, F., 108, 109, 275, 285
Blume, M. E., 176
bonds, 172, 234–5, 269–74
   convertible, 273–4
borrowing, 73–5
   from banks, 11, 12–13, 221–37
borrowing capacity, 309–10
Borrowing Opportunity Rate method,
   333–7
borrowing rate, 233
break-even chart, 210–11
British Institute of Management, 248,
   249, 319
brokerage fees, 171
Broyles, J. E., 177, 185
business conditions, 223

calls, 274
capacity, 82
capital allocation, 136
capital allowances, 34, 38, 64–7, 72, 137,
   140
Capital Asset Pricing Model, 107
capital budgets, 58
capital gains, 96, 151
Capital Gains Tax, 70
capital investment decisions, 79–90
Capital Market (*see also* market. . .),
   19–22, 24, 282–4
   efficiency of, 170–82
   London, 276–7

370

Capital Market equilibrium, 108
Capital Market Line, 115, 116
capital market opportunities, 21–2
capital market opportunity cost, 108,109
capital rationing, 54–6, 245
capital structure, 187, 288–305
capitalization, 232
cartels, 52–3
cash balance, 204
cash budget, 204–8
cash flow, analysis, 79–90, 152–5, 230
    measurement of, 136–9
    patterns of, 19
cash flow, free, 154–5, 194
cash flow break-even chart, 210–11
Chicago Board Options Exchange, 285
Chicago University data base, 174
'City', the, 276–7
classification of risk, 117–19, 126
Clearing Banks, 278
clientele of shareholders, 164
co-insurance, 188
collateral, 224
collection period, credit, 238–9
commercial factors, 248
company valuation, see valuation
competition, 81, 300
competitive advantage, 14–15, 135
Compound Factors, 22–4
computer simulations, 118
conflict of interest, 226
Consols, 28, 271
constraints, 57
consumer expenditure, 71, 74
consumption, 74
contingencies, planning for, 216,
    218–19
contingent projects, 57, 84
contraction, 136, 139
Controller, functions of, 10
convertible bonds, 273–4
corporate debt, 271
corporate planning, 80
Corporation Tax, 31, 32, 34–5, 42, 64–7,
    69, 70, 119, 120, 297, 298
    Advanced, 43, 163, 164
    Mainstream, 43–4, 163
correlation, 99, 100, 175–6
cost, of carrying stock, 256
    of credit, 242–3
    of debt, 288–305
    of raising finance, 163, 187, 188–9
cost advantage, 82

cost reduction projects, 84–5
coupon, 269
covenants, 224, 226, 227, 319
credit, cost of, 242–3
credit bureau reports, 247–8
credit collection period, 238–9
credit decision, 240–47
Credit Department, 246, 247
credit limit, 242
credit policy, 238–52
credit terms, 239–41
crises, 120
cumulative profitability, 232
cut-off rate, 116

data base, 174
debenture, 271
debt, 11
    cost of, 288–305
    tax advantages of, 298–9
debt capacity, 187–8, 309
debt collection, 249
debt financing (see also leasing),
    288–317
    effect of taxation on, 296–300
    risk of, 288–96
debt service, 232
debt-to-equity ratio, 227–8
debtors, 238–52
DCF, 39
decision-making process (see also
    financing decision; investment
    decision), 79–90
deeds, 271
default, 12, 224, 233, 243
demand, 82
Department of Industry, 278
depreciation, 38, 137, 138
development areas, 31, 32, 33
Dill, D. A., 322, 328
disclosure, 195, 197, 319
discount, 242
discount period, 240
discount rate, 25–6, 72, 118, 128–9,
    321
Discounted Cash Flow, 39
discounted dividends model, 157–9
discounted free cash flow model,154–5
Discounted Payback, 36
disinvestment, 136
diversification, 98–102, 295
dividend policy, 162–5, 167–8
dividend yield, 272

dividends, 96, 151, 157–60, 177
  growth of, 157–9, 160
divisional performance measurement,
  136–46
divisions of companies, 121–2, 135–6
Dun and Bradstreet, 248
Durand, David, 158

earnings, reported, 137–9
Earnings per Share, 95–6, 191–2, 272,
  288–90
earnings quality, 159
earnings yield, 272
economic depreciation, 143–4
economic life, 85–8
economic order quantity, 258, 263–4
economic rent, 52, 81, 162
Economic Value (see also net economic
  value), 13–14, 140, 170
  return on, 144
efficiency of stock market, 170–82
  semi-strong-form tests, 177–9
  strong-form tests, 179–81
  weak-form tests, 175–7
Efficient Markets Hypothesis, 174
Equipment Leasing Association, 318
equity, 11, 171, 272–3
  valuation of, 152
Equity Finance for Industry, 278
equity prices, 170
equivalent annual cost, 87–8
equivalent annual net cash flow, 88
excess return, 105
expansion, 136
expected return, 21
Export Credits Guarantee Department,
  222

fair game, 174
Fama, E. F., 64, 175, 176, 177
FIFO, 67–8
finance, cost of raising, 163, 187, 188–9
  sources of, 221–2, 276–8
Finance Director, functions of, 8–10
Finance for Industry, 278
financial accountant, 13
financial analysis, 14–15
financial analysts, 179
financial distress, 227, 230–33
financial gearing, 121, 301–2
financial intermediary, 295, 296, 298
financial leases, 318
financial management, functions of, 8–16

financial package, 191
financial planning, 54–6, 58, 203–20
  long-term, 208–10
financial ratios, 230–33
financial risk, 216
financial synergy, 187–9
Financial Times Index, 107
financing decision, 306, 321
financing of mergers, 190–91
finished goods stock, 254, 256, 261–2
first-in first-out, 67–8
Fisher, Irving, 63
Fisher, Laurence, 177, 234, 271
Fisher Effect, 63–4
fixed expenses, 124–5, 210, 211, 223
fixed rates of interest, 74
flotation, 281
  costs of, 163, 187, 188–9
forecasting, 135–6, 208, 212–13, 214–15,
  254
Franks, J. R., 177, 185, 323, 327
free cash flow, 154–5, 194
functions of financial management, 8–16
funds, internally generated, 276, 278
funds flow statement, 209, 210

gearing, financial, 121, 301–2
  operational, 122, 125
gilts, 172, 270
goodwill, 151, 161, 194
Gordon, M. J., 158
Government debt, 269–71
Government intervention, 217
Gross Domestic Product, 72, 73, 218
growth of dividends, 157–9, 160
growth prospects, 186, 189, 194
growth to horizon models, 159–60

Halpern, P. J., 177
Hecht, M., 177, 185
Hodges, S. D., 323, 327, 331
horizon to growth, 160

Ibbotson, R. G., 73
I.C.F.C., 222
imperfect markets, 81
imperfect product markets, 81
implicit cost of debt, 288, 289, 291–2
income, redistribution of, 71
income tax, progressive, 71
inflation, 62–75, 302
inflation accounting, 140
inflationary expectations, 74

Inland Revenue (*see also* taxation), 271, 323
integer programming, 56, 57, 58, 247
interest and annual repayment ratio, 229–30
interest cover, 229
interest rates, 72, 223, 227, 233–5, 242, 299
  fixed, 74
  nominal, 62
  real, 72
  term structure of, 127–8, 234
  variable, 74
Internal Rate of Return, 39–42, 47–52
internally generated funds, 276, 278
international diversification, 101–2
Interval Rate of Return, 25
inventory, 253
inventory system, *see* stock control systems
investment decision, 306–7, 328–30
Investment Trusts, 298

Jensen, M. C., 108, 109, 177, 180
jobbers, 171
Jones, C., 178

Kaplan, R. S., 155–7
Kendall, M. G., 175

last-in-first-out (LIFO), 68
Latané, H., 178
lead time, 258
lease payments schedule, 327–8
leasing, 314, 318–38
  effect of taxation on, 322–30
leasing companies, 222
legal limitations, 191
lending (*see also* borrowing), 221–37
  by banks, 313
lending decisions, criteria for, 223–6
Lerner, E. M., 139
linear programming, 57, 58, 139
Lintner, J., 107
liquidation, 139, 271
liquidation value, 89
liquidity, 36, 68, 219, 232
Loan Stock, 271
loans (*see also* lending), outstanding, 226–7
  variable interest rate, 74
London Business School data base, 174
London Capital Market, 276–7

London Stock Exchange, 172–3, 276, 281–2
  Council, 195
long-term financing plans, 208–10
longs, 271
lot-size inventory, 258

macroeconomic events, 217
Mainstream Corporation Tax, 43–4, 163
maintenance costs, 86
make or buy decision, 84–5
Malkiel, B. G., 160
Malkiel model, 165
management accountants, 13
management expenses, 181
Management Services Department, 253
Mandelker, G., 177, 184, 185
manual for capital expenditure, 10
marginal borrowing rate, 321
market model, 102–5
Market Portfolio, 104, 105–7
market rates of return, 22
market risk, 100
market segments, 82
market share, 82
market value (*see also* valuation), 140, 152, 170, 228–9
marketability, 173, 223, 234, 271
markets, imperfect, 26, 81
  perfect, 81, 173
  primary, 172
  secondary, 172–3, 282–3
Markowitz, H. M., 104
Marsh, P. R., 280
material requirements planning, 260–61
mathematical programming, 56–8
measurement error, 121
mediums, 270
Meeks, G., 186
Merchant Banks, 278
mergers, 136, 165, 177, 184–98
  benefits of, 186–7, 189
  financing of, 190–91
Miller, M. H., 294–6, 299, 315
Modigliani, F., 294–6, 315
money, time value of, 20
monitoring (*see also* performance measurement), 136, 224, 233, 254–6
Monopolies Commission, 197
Mossin, J., 107
multiple Internal Rates of Return, 51
mutual funds, 180–81
mutually exclusive projects, 57, 88–9

374

Myers, S. C., 155, 186, 228, 308, 322, 328

National Enterprise Board, 278
net economic value, 14
Net Income approach, 292–3
Net Operating Income, 288, 289, 290–92, 294–5
Net Present Value, 25–6, 47–53, 96
Net Terminal Value Rule, 24
Net Terminal Wealth, 24
net worth, 11
New York Stock Exchange specialist, 181
Newbould, A., 184
Niederhoffer, V., 181
NOI, see Net Operating Income
nominal rate of interest, 62
nominal required rate of return, 62
nominal terms, 72
non-diversifiable risk, 100, 122–3
non-tax-paying position, 323–6
normal probability distribution, 97
NPV, see Net Present Value

objective function, 56
objectives, financial, 13–15, 50
Office of Fair Trading, 197
operating leases, 318
operating life, 226
operating plan, 254
operational gearing, 122, 125
opportunity cost, 20, 83
   capital market, 108, 109
option, 161, 162, 226, 274–6, 285–6
ordering costs, 256, 263–4
ordinary share, 11–12
ordinary share capital, 272–3
Osborne, V., 181
overdrafts, 12, 204
overvaluation, 187

Patel, H., 235, 244
Payback Period, 36–7
perfect markets, 81, 173
performance measurement, divisional, 136–46
performance variances, 144–6
perpetuities, 28
placing, 280–81
planning, 135
   financial, 54–6, 58, 203–20
plant and machinery purchase, 34

portfolios, 98–102
   managers, 179
preference shares, 274
premium, 233
Present Value, 309
Present Value, Net, 25–6, 47–53, 96
Present Value method, Adjusted, 308–11, 312–13
Present Value of tax benefits, 310
price to earnings ratio, 95–6, 159, 272
primary market, 172
probability, 97–8
probability tree, 213–14
production, 254
Production Control Manager, 262
Production Planning and Control Department, 262
Production, Sales, and Inventory chart, 254–5
profitability, 20–22, 109
   cumulative, 232
profitability comparisons, 47–59
Profitability Index, 53–4, 247
profits, 13
   maximization of, 14
Profits Before Tax, 137, 138
progressive income tax, 71
project risk factor, 123
purchasing, 254
puts, 274

qualitative considerations, 82
quotation, 281
quotations, share, 171
quoted acquisition, 189–90, 191–4
quoted companies, new finance for, 279–81

random walk, 175
ranking procedure, 54
Rappaport, A., 139
raw materials, 254–5, 262
real rate of interest, 72
redemption yield, 273
redistribution of income, 71
Regional Development Grants, 31–2, 33, 42
reinvestment, 19, 20, 22–4
re-order cycle policy, 259
re-order level policy, 258–9
repayment, 226
repayment terms, 223, 227
replacement cost, 142

replacement period, 86–8
reported earnings, 137–9
required rate of return, 72, 140, 290
residual values, 70, 326–7
resources, scarce, 82
Return, Accounting Rate of, 37–9,
140–42
Return, Internal Rate of, 39–42, 47–52
Return, Interval Rate of, 25
return, market rates of, 22
return, nominal required rate of, 62
return on assets, 232
Return on Capital Employed, 37–9,
139–40
return on economic value, 144
Return on Investment, 37–9, 140–44
returns to shareholders, 21–2, 95–6
revenue sensitivity, 123–5
revenues, 210, 211
volatility of, 123
rights issues, 12, 163, 279–80, 283
risk (see also systematic risk), 12, 20–21,
96–134, 216
non-diversifiable, 100, 122–3
unique, 127
risk-averse investors, 105
risk classification, 117–19, 126
risk-free rate of interest, 21, 119, 127
risk of debt finance, 288–96
risk premiums, 119–20, 235, 244, 290
risky securities, 21
Roll, Richard, 108, 155–7, 177
Rubinstein, M., 302
Rule 163(2), 281
running yield, 269

safety stock, 258
sales, 254, 255
Sandilands Committee of Enquiry,
140
scarce resources, 82
scarcity, 135
scenarios, 216–17, 230
Scholes, M., 108, 109, 275, 285
second-hand values, 223, 225, 326–7
secondary market, 172–3, 282–3
securities, risky, 21
types of, 269–76
security, 224
semi-strong-form tests, 174, 177–9
sensitivity analysis, 118
set-up costs, 256
settlement day, 171

shares (see also dividends; equity),
ordinary, 11–12
preference, 274
Sharpe, W. F., 104, 107
shorts, 270
Silvers, J. B., 235
Singh, A., 186
Sinquefield, R. A., 73
size of firm, 232
Smiley, R., 187
Solnik, B. H., 175, 176
sources and applications of funds, 210
spread, 171
stability of earnings, 232
stamp duty, 171
standard deviation, 97, 98
standardized unexpected earnings,
178–9
stock, cost of carrying, 256
stock control systems, 253–65
design, 256–7
Stock Exchange (London), 172–3, 276,
281–2
Council, 195
Stock Exchange (New York), 181
stock gains, taxation on, 65, 67–8
stock holding costs, 264
stock market, efficiency of, 170–82
stock relief, 65, 68–70
stock replenishment systems, 257–61
stock split, 177, 178
strategy, 135
strong-form tests, 175, 179–81
subordinated debenture, 271
sunk cost, 83
supplier, 241
systematic risk, 100, 102–9, 123, 126–7,
247

Takeover Code, 195–7
takeovers (see also mergers), 96, 136,
177, 178
tax advantages, of debt, 298–9
of leasing, 329
tax allowances, 34
tax benefits, 306–15, 322, 323
tax liability, 34
tax payments, lags in, 331–2
taxable profits, 323
taxation (see also Capital Gains Tax;
Corporation Tax; income tax;
Inland Revenue), effect of on debt
financing, 296–300

effect of on leasing, 322–30
  on stock gains, 65, 67–8
TDR, 116, 117
technology, 82, 86
term loan, 12
term structure of interest rates, 127–8,
  233
Test Discount Rate, 116, 117
time value of money, 20
track record, 180, 181
trade credit, 238–52
  control of, 247–50
trade credit investment, 244–7
trade references, 247
transactions, 174
  costs of, 181, 191, 300–301
Treasurer, functions of, 10–11
Treasury Bills, 270
tree diagram, 213–14
trend, 175
True Return on Investment, 142–4
trustees, 11, 271

uncertainty, 72–3, 82, 208, 210
undergeared companies, 188
underpricing, 195
undervaluation, 187
underwriters, 11–12, 279, 280
unique risk, 127
unit trusts, 180–81
unquoted companies, new finance for,
  281–2
  valuation of, 194
utility theory, 98

valuation, 187
  equity, 152
  firm, 95, 151–62
  methods, 142, 145–6
  quoted acquisitions, 189–90, 191–4
  unquoted companies, 194
Vancil, R. F., 333
variable expenses, 210, 211
variable interest rate loans, 74
variance, 98
volatility, 170
  earnings, 290, 301
  revenues, 123

WACC, 116, 307–8, 311–12
warranties, 194
warrants, 276
weak-form tests, 174, 175–7
wealth maximization, 14
Weighted Average Cost of Capital, 116,
  307–8, 311–12
Weston, J. F., 192
Williams, J. B., 158
working capital, 83, 238–65
written-down replacement cost, 140
written-down replacement value, 142
written-down value, 141

yield to redemption, 270

Zinkini, P., 235, 244